New Light on
GEORGE BOOLE

ATRIUM

Dedicated to the memory
of George Boole's sister
MaryAnn Boole

New Light on
GEORGE
BOOLE

Desmond MacHale and Yvonne Cohen

First published in 2018 by Atrium
Atrium is an imprint of Cork University Press
Youngline Industrial Estate
Pouladuff Road, Togher
Cork T12 HT6V, Ireland

British Library Cataloguing in Publication Data
A CIP catalogue record for this book is available from the British Library.

ISBN-978-1-78205-290-6

Typeset by Studio 10 Design
Printed by HussarBooks in Poland

CONTENTS

ACKNOWLEDGEMENTS

MANY PEOPLE AND MANY INSTITUTIONS have assisted us in writing this book. Our first thanks are due to our spouses and families for their support and patience over many years. We thank Anne MacHale and Pat Moynihan for their tolerance; John, Ruth and Sarah Moynihan; Peter, Catherine, Simon, John and Dominic MacHale, Brenda Long, Stephanie Fuller, Magnus Gunnarsson, Becky and Ellie Long-MacHale, and Josef Ruarai MacHale-Gunnarsson. We are especially grateful to Sarah and Peter for their generous assistance and technical expertise. We remember Lionel and Mary Cohen who would have been so proud to see the completion of this project.

Our colleagues at University College Cork have been generous with their help and encouragement too. President Emeritus Michael Murphy was a tower of strength behind our project, as is his successor President Patrick O'Shea. To the Boole Librarian John Fitzgerald, we owe a special debt, for his exceptional support, and for his contribution of a piece on the poetry of Mary Ellen Boole Hinton, in Chapter Thirteen. The staff of the Boole Library have eased our path in every possible way, promptly and courteously. In particular, we would like to thank Crónán O'Doibhlin, Colette McKenna, Emer Twomey, Elaine Harrington and Emma Horgan.

We would also like to express our gratitude to our colleagues Michael Holland, Olivia Frawley, Pat Fitzpatrick, Stephen Bean, Kathy Bunyan, Michel Schelleckans, John Morrison, Joseph Manning, Barry O'Sullivan, Chryss Ngaa, Claus Koestler, Finbarr Holland, Paddy Barry, Brian Twomey, Bernard Hanzon, Michael Mortell, Gareth Thomas, Teresa Buckley, Declan Kennedy, Maria Carroll, Lynn Nolan, J.P. Quinn, Dara O'Shea, Lorna Moloney, Pat Riggs, Neil Buttimer, John A. Murphy, Virginia Teehan, Thomas Tyner, Mark Poland, Joe Scanlon, Donna O'Driscoll and the late Seán Pettit.

We are indebted to the many institutions and organisations for their help in providing materials and giving us permission to reproduce extracts from them. In particular, we wish to thank the Birmingham Library, the Lincolnshire Archives, Boole Library University College Cork, the Archives Department of the National University of Ireland Galway, Bishopstown Public Library Cork, John Mullins, Patricia Looney and Stephen Leach of Cork City Libraries, Peter Beirne and Dolores Meaney of Clare County

Library, Chandra X-ray Center, Ontario Archives, University of Guelph Library, Wellington County Museum and Archives, Ordnance Survey Ireland, the Bishopsgate Institute London and Birr Castle. We gratefully acknowledge the assistance of Dr Rebecca Loader, Senior Archaeologist with the Isle of Wight Archaeology and Historic Environment Service and Sarah Gearty of the Royal Irish Academy.

We are grateful to the extended Boole family for their support and in particular we thank Gerry Kennedy, Marni Rosner and family, Annie Taylor, Nikolaus Boulting and Geoffrey Hinton.

We thank Sally and Eoin Gunn and Brendan Cotter for their help in identifying 'Analore', the location of the Booles' residence in Blackrock. We are grateful to Maria O'Driscoll and Colm Crowley, the current owners of 'Analore', for their hospitality and allowing us to view their beautiful home, even at the most inconvenient of times! Thanks also to Rev. Adrian Wilkinson of St Michael's Church of Ireland in Blackrock for allowing us access to the church and graveyard and for his assistance in researching Church of Ireland figures. Thanks also to Rev. Brigid Spain and Fritz Spengeman of the Unitarian Church in Cork and Dr Raymond Refausse of the RCB Library in Dublin for their assistance.

We extend our thanks to Harry Lande for his assistance in tracing the history of the Boole Window in the Aula Maxima at UCC, and Rachel Clare and Rachel MacGregor of the Birmingham Library for their help with the Hardman Archives.

We wish to sincerely thank the Rollett family for their generous donation of the Rollett papers to the Lincolnshire Archives. We are indebted to Adrian Wilkinson for facilitating our visit to the Lincolnshire Archives and for the assistance and courtesy extended to us during our stay in Lincoln. Thanks also to Rev. Mark Hucknell and Dave Kenyon of Lincoln for their help and encouragement.

Thanks to George 'Daw' Harding for permission to reproduce his poem, 'Leaving Lichfield', in Chapter Thirteen of this book. We extend our gratitude to Tadhg Foley, Professor Emeritus of English at NUIG for his help and support.

We would like to thank Tony and JoAnn Ryan for their enthusiasm for the George Boole project. Tony has published three articles on George Boole from a medical perspective, graciously citing us as co-authors when our contribution to the work was minimal in comparison to his own.

Many people helped us to source and reproduce images which we feel have greatly enhanced our book. These include Eddie Saleh at *Argunners Magazine*, Grainne O'Malley of Birr Castle, Don Bull of the Virtual Corkscrew Museum, Peter Goulding, Chris Kemp, Martin Bowen, Stephen Roberts, Kieran McCarthy, Ian Ellis, Cameron Lazaroff-Puck, Lincoln City Libraries, the Royal Society, Heinz Schmitz, Jude Harley, Renata Vickery of Central Connecticut State University, Maggie Wilson of National Museums Scotland, Tommy Barker of the *Irish Examiner*, Ed O'Riordan, Richard Murphy, Brian McGee of Cork City and County Archives, Gillian O'Leary of the Port of Cork Company, Marina Wild of the Arts Office of NUIG and William Cumming of the National Inventory of Architectural Heritage. Cork City Libraries' website *CorkPastandPresent.ie* was a veritable treasure trove of illustrations for this book.

We express our appreciation to Pat Powell, Conor Harding, Olga Selznova, John Miller, Mary Leland, John Moriarty, Colm Mulcahy, Seán Dineen, Stanley Burris, Donald Knuth, Peter Lynch, Pat McGrath, Gordon and Christina Sharp, Cal Hyland, Micheal Ó Súilleabháin, James Lundon, Aideen Rynne, Luke Gibbons and Jane Stanford.

We are extremely grateful to Alannah Hopkin for her valuable advice on the structure and content of the book. Finally, we wish to thank the team at Cork University Press, especially our editor Maria O'Donovan, Agnes Nagle, Alison Burns, Aonghus Meaney and Mike Collins.

ILLUSTRATIONS

FOREWORD

F EW SELF-EDUCATED SCHOLARS have had the opportunity, and ability, to single-handedly launch a major new direction in any academic subject, much less in one that had been essentially frozen for more than two thousand years. Although George Boole (1815–1864) was duly celebrated in his lifetime for his research in algebra, calculus and probability theory, it was his creation of an algebra of logic in his two books *The Mathematical Analysis of Logic* (1847), and *Laws of Thought* (1854), which brought him enduring fame. These books would lead to the end of the dominance of Aristotle's work in deductive logic.

Boole's algebra of logic was based on the ordinary algebra of polynomials, augmented by the idempotent law $x^2 = x$ for variables. Boole introduced 1 and 0 into logic as canonical names for the universe and the empty class, as well as for true and false in propositional logic. These two numbers have since become the most recognised symbols of the digital age – look at your electric kettle, for example.

His algebra of logic, constructed on the algebra of numbers, was not the easiest approach to develop rigorously and it was not until 1976 that Theodore Hailperin found a justification for a large portion of his work. Boole's algebra had a mystical quality to it, at times involving the use of meaningless expressions in intermediate steps of a derivation. But others such as Peirce, Jevons and Schröder found a replacement algebra, which was not based on numbers and avoided meaningless expressions. Nevertheless, the meaningful conclusions of the main results of Boole's algebra of logic were essentially the same as in the alternative version.

Around 1900 the Harvard philosopher Josiah Royce and his students, strongly influenced by the work of Charles Peirce, gave the name Boolean algebra to this alternative version of Boole's algebra of logic. Boolean algebra remained a topic of interest to just a small group of mathematicians and philosophers until the late 1930s, when Claude Shannon showed it could be used to encode and study switching circuits. With the development of electronic computers during the Second World War, and the creation of transistors shortly afterwards, the importance of Boolean algebra was more widely recognised. In the late 1940s, Howard Aiken, director of the Harvard Computation Laboratory, decided that, for the purpose of cataloguing switching functions used in computer designs, it was best to return to Boole's original numerically based algebra of logic. With the rapid development of electronic computers in the 1950s the subject of Boolean algebra finally went mainstream in mathematics and philosophy departments worldwide.

A coherent picture of the life of Boole, whose work has had such an impact on our modern world, did not appear until more than a century after his death, namely in the biography published in 1985 (2nd edition 2014) by Desmond MacHale of University College Cork. The present book, *New Light on George Boole*, containing further extensive insights and new information about the life of this remarkable scholar, is most welcome.

Stanley Burris
Distinguished Emeritus Professor of Mathematics
University of Waterloo
Canada

August 2018

INTRODUCTION

THIS BOOK is in many ways a complement to *The Life and Work of George Boole: a prelude to the digital age* (Boole Press, Dublin, 1985; reissued by Cork University Press, 2014). George Boole (1815–1864) was a largely self-taught mathematician and logician who has variously been described as the originator of symbolic logic, the founder of pure mathematics, and one of the fathers of computer science. His work on logic in the mid-nineteenth century led to the digital revolution and all of the electronic devices that so affect our lives today are directly based on the Boolean algebra he invented in 1847.

But Boole was many other things besides – a highly accomplished teacher at second and third levels; a skilled researcher and writer of mathematical textbooks that are still in use today; an enthusiastic poet; a social reformer; an ardent religious and philosophical thinker; and a reluctant whistleblower.

In this complementary volume we concentrate on Boole the man, the personality, the generous benefactor, the family man, the moralist, the educator, and above all the social being, as revealed in his correspondence with his close family and his many friends, and in the biographical letters written by those friends and acquaintances after his death.

A fuller, more personal picture of George Boole emerges in this book – that of a loving son and brother; a generous lender and giver of money from his own meagre income to relatives, friends and those down on their luck; a romantic at heart; a lover of nature and the countryside; a musician and music lover; and a lonely exile in Ireland. We examine Boole's views on religion, discipline, social order, health and medicine and his happy transition from bachelorhood to marriage and fatherhood.

We delve more deeply too into Boole's contact with other mathematicians, such as Gregory, Ellis, Hirst and Todhunter. Boole's relationships with the Chartist Thomas Cooper and his former pupil Charles Clarke, who became Speaker of the Legislature of Ontario in Canada, are explored, and there is an epilogue on Boole's tragic and premature death. We present a cornucopia of Booleana, from Hamilton, Darwin and Maxwell, to memorial windows, Leviathan, comets and poetry. Finally, there is a surprising theory on the connections between Boole and Sherlock Holmes' nemesis, Professor James Moriarty.

The 1985 biography of Boole was not the first effort in this direction. In the mid-1960s, Arthur P. Rollett, a Lincolnshire mathematician, began to collect materials for such a work and amassed a large amount of papers and original letters. He died in July 1968, having written the first five chapters of his book. The project was then taken over by his son Dr John Rollett, a physicist, who continued collecting Boolean material but did not add any further chapters. Sadly, he passed away in 2015, and his family generously donated all their Boolean material to the Lincolnshire Archives, so that it is now effectively in the public domain. Having gained access to the Rollett Collection shortly before this book was completed, we have used this material sparingly. Indeed, much of the content had already been covered in the 1985 biography. However, we wish to acknowledge the contribution that A.P. and John Rollett made to the study of the life of George Boole and their industry in collecting such a significant body of material.

The vast proportion of the material in this book is based on the Boole Collection held in the Boole Library Archives at University College Cork. This was bought at auction from Sotheby's in London in 1984 by UCC, but the source of the papers was then unknown. We now believe the collection was originally assembled by MaryAnn Boole, George's only sister, and was inherited by Mary Ellen Hinton, his eldest daughter, and remained stored in a chest in the United States for over a hundred years. A large part of the collection is made up of original handwritten letters exchanged between Boole and his family and friends, and it also contains transcripts of other letters, probably made by Mary Ellen. These letters use the Victorian spellings of many words such as 'honor' and 'labor' and we have not changed these to their modern spellings in order to preserve the integrity of the correspondence. To distinguish between Mary Ann Boole, George Boole's mother, and his sister MaryAnn Boole, we write the mother's name as Mary Ann, with a space between the two words, and the sister's name as MaryAnn as a single word.

Our story begins with Mary Ellen and MaryAnn. The first chapter of this book contains a transcription of a handwritten notebook by Mary Ellen detailing her family history. The second chapter reproduces MaryAnn's biography of Boole based on family history and biographical material which she collected prior to and after her brother's death but which was never previously published. Boole's widow, Mary Everest Boole, also wrote to her husband's friends and colleagues to gather their thoughts after his death in 1864 but never produced a biography of her husband, despite becoming a prolific writer in later life. In contrast, MaryAnn never became a published author and her name never came to light; not even a photograph of her seems to have survived. We dedicate this book to MaryAnn in recognition of her efforts to honour the memory of her beloved brother George.

Chapter 1

BOOLE FAMILY
HISTORY
NOTEBOOK

N THE BOOLE PAPERS in the Boole Library at University College Cork there is a handwritten notebook which appears to have been written by George Boole's eldest daughter, Mary Ellen (Hinton). The notebook details the Boole family history, followed by an account of the life and character of John Boole, George Boole's father. Its significance lies in the fact that George's personality, talents, and maybe even his religious views, were modelled on those of his father and clearly nurtured by him. It also includes some details of the background of George's mother, Mary Ann.

As Mary Ellen was only eight when her father died, it is not possible that George Boole dictated this text – it probably emanated from his sister MaryAnn Boole, but its authenticity is not in doubt. The notebook was clearly a first draft but no second or further version seems to have survived. In places, the handwriting is extremely difficult to decipher, with many crossings out and amendments in what is possibly a different hand, necessitating in some instances educated guesses on the part of the present authors. The text of the notebook is reproduced below.

The Boole Family

Broxholme (about six miles from Lincoln) was the home of the Boole family, which can be traced in the parish registers nearly as far back as the year 1600. Beyond this date nothing is at present known of them. The name is supposed to have been originally Scotch, a corruption of Boyle [Boole or Boyle, Balburnie]. The Booles were yeomen for many generations, renting their own land and tilling it, fathers and sons together with their own hands.

Around the latter part of the eighteenth century, Lord Munson, in common with many other landowners, took up the idea that it was better for the land to be less subdivided (Lord Munson was their landlord and owned much of the land around Broxholme). He therefore amalgamated the small farms which belonged to him into a few larger ones. So, many of the yeomen were reduced to the position of labourers, a fact which seems to have distressed them deeply. But others went into trade – vide John Boole, father of Professor George Boole.

The Booles had been known for many generations as the most reading men of their village. An old chest of books was preserved among them from father to son and was added to as time went on. The collection was dispersed at the death of my grandfather John Boole when his property was sold by auction. Amongst those books were a Unitarian hymn book (with the name John Boole printed on the cover); a copy of the *Pilgrim's Progress* which his sister Mrs Chaloner used to say he had read nine times by the time he was nine years old.[1]

John Boole (George Boole's father)

Born at Broxholme in the year 1777 and died in the year 1848. He inherited from his father a passion for knowledge and a powerful intellect which, however, circumstances prevented him from cultivation to any great extent.

Schooling: Mr Basset was his teacher when he was very young and he was a great favourite with Mr Basset. He could read any chapter in the Bible when five years and had read most of it. He had to pass through a farm yard where geese were kept. A gander ran after him as he went to school, so one day he got a hot potato and threw it down. The gander ate it and went screaming all round the yard. It never ran after him again.

George Boole said his father used to take the children out on fine nights to point them out the stars. John Boole studied mathematics. He always kept a book in the drawer of his shoemaker's bench. He was known as the cleverest man in Lincoln. Thomas Cooper says there was no better-informed man or mathematician in Lincoln in any rank of life.[2]

In those days, it was thought advantageous for a boy to have a trade rather than be a common labourer. He was at the age of fourteen apprentice to a shoemaker at Saxilby in whose service he remained probably for seven years, as that was the usual term. Saxilby is situated in a low-lying valley on the river Witham a few miles from Lincoln. It was a very damp place. The rain used to pour through the roof onto the floor of the workshop where my grandfather worked with the other apprentices. And this to such an extent that the water used to lie in pools on the floor of the room where he and the others used to work and he used to sit with his feet on bricks to keep out of it. It is very probable (my aunt thinks) that it was here her father laid the foundation of the chest infection from which he suffered so severely in after years. Coarse food at Saxilby helped to weaken him. Country people used to live almost entirely on bacon for meat.

The term of his apprenticeship being over, John Boole took employment as a journeyman (which means a paid workman in contradistinction to an apprentice) under a shoemaker in Watling Street, London. (Johnson was the master at Saxilby or London – I don't know which.) During his residence here he was taken by a friend of his, a Mr Lawson to whom he taught mathematics, to see someone (probably another one of the servants) whom this friend knew. His future wife was then lady's maid to Mrs Walmsley, wife of a minor canon of St Paul's, at the same house. John fell in love with her at first sight. He used to record his first impression thus – when I saw her I thought, 'Oh if I could make that angel mine'.

They were married at St Martin in the Fields. He being however still too poor to take himself a wife, they parted at the church door and went their several ways – he to his employer in Watling Street, she to her mistress Mrs Walmsley.

It was owing to the kindness of his brother-in-law Mr Chaloner that my grandfather finally settled in Lincoln. Mr Chaloner represented to him that there was a good opening there.

The couple lived together in lodgings in London for some time before they went to Lincoln. Accordingly, the husband and wife gave up their respective situations and went down together to Lincoln. They were childless for nine years after their marriage and the birth of their eldest child George nearly cost the mother her life. So proud was the father of this fine boy that he insisted on taking people up to see the pair of them before his wife was sufficiently recovered to bear the excitement safely. The result was a relapse which endangered her life and much retarded her recovery.

During the nine years of comparative freedom from expenses and care, my grandfather might have laid the foundation of a thriving business and been, if not rich, at least well-to-do. He was without a rival in the city of Lincoln and intelligence and gentlemanly bearing must have told in his favour. But alas! The ruling passion for science led him aside from the duties he had undertaken. He neglected orders or executed them carelessly, leaving the bulk of his work to his apprentice and was not taking sufficient trouble to see that it was properly done. Then, when other shoemakers set up in the town, he lost customers and had no longer the chance of establishing himself firmly without opposition.

The struggles of Mary Ann [John Boole's wife and George Boole's mother] when her family began growing up around her are pathetic to hear. At one time she was obliged to let lodgings and with four young children she could not keep a servant.

The little girl MaryAnn [George Boole's only sister] remembers once playing on the door step with a neighbour's children and some dispute arose. 'Well', said one of the children, 'everybody knows that your father is a man of no principle at all.' My aunt indignantly denied it. 'I did not know what "no principle" meant but I knew that it did not mean anything good', she said to me. 'I knew it was something bad, so I denied it.' 'He's been in prison – my father says so', added the little girl. MaryAnn immediately ran to ask her mother about it and tell her how angry she was with the little girl for saying such a thing. But her mother told her it was true. He had been in prison – for debt.

My aunt remembers well what a day of rejoicing there was when her father received an appointment as auditor at the [Lincoln Savings] Bank with a small salary. She does not remember the date but knows that it was some time after the birth of all four children. This employment did not oblige him to relinquish his trade and the two were carried on together for many years.

From that day, MaryAnn was the chosen confidante of her mother's troubles and 'it cast a cloud over my young life', she says. They were always in money difficulties and obliged to endure actual hardships and privations while it was in vain that my grandmother and various friends tried to turn the head of the family aside from his beloved but unremunerative scientific pursuits. And here it may be well to see what were the forms in which this passion for knowledge showed itself. John Boole had a considerable knowledge of optics. In after years he lectured on this subject at the Mechanics' Institute, preparing coloured illustrations and diagrams beforehand with great ingenuity. In this he was assisted by his daughter MaryAnn. He studied navigation and attained such proficiency in this subject that he was able to add to his income by taking pupils. It was owing to careful and intelligent training in Mathematics that my father [George Boole] received the first impetus in that direction. Apropos of these lessons there is a long story which I cannot help repeating here. The father had gone out for the afternoon leaving his son a task of Euclid to be learnt by his return. But George, in this instance not so conscientious as usual, played with the apprentices instead. But towards the end of the afternoon, when the time of the father's expected arrival drew near, George ran to the door and saw him and others coming down the street. Immediately he set to work and was quite ready by the time he came in.

Is there not a lesson of nature here? The boy who has genius cannot work so long as the boy who has not, for he has a power of tapping himself so to speak and sending out his vitality suddenly onto one point or thought. Then it is time for him to rest. Woe betide that child if he is forced to write on till a certain hour be come!

Whatever John Boole neglected there was one thing he always did thoroughly and that was teaching George. However irregular he was about the others' lessons and especially his daughter's, he stinted neither time nor care.

Mr Boole had also a genuine mechanical talent both of mind and of hand. He was always inventing and making. Now it was a telescope, now a camera obscura, now a kaleidoscope, now a microscope, now a machine of some kind. He constructed a model of a steam paddle with improved action which touched the water lightly instead of awkwardly, which he sent to the Royal Society (this was before he went to the Mechanics' Institute). But he was poor and unknown – a shoemaker and not even a thriving one. The model, which was made of mahogany on wheels of brass – the wheels dropped in noiselessly and without difficulty – was returned without recognition or encouragement. Shortly afterwards the steam paddle came into general use! It is said that Mr Boole was never the same man again. He was crushed bitterly by the disappointment. He seemed to have worked his life's hope into that small world and it had cost him untold labour. He was a middle-aged man then after its rejection and he never recovered his former energy. It was not many months afterwards before the steam-paddle, reinvented and patented by someone else, came into general use. Steam-paddles had been made before but John Boole made an improvement.

Oh ye men of science!

It is a curious coincidence that George Boole's paper 'On a General Method in Analysis',[3] sent in like manner to the Royal Society, was well-nigh rejected without examination by the council of fifteen fellows. But one of their number rose and contended that just because a man was poor and unknown, that was no reason why his paper should not be fairly treated. Not only did he carry his point at the time, but his paper was finally selected out of a number of others for the gold medal which they awarded now for the first time in nine years.

Oh ye men of science!

Another disappointment in store for my grandfather was in connection with a great eclipse. It had taken him considerable time to construct a telescope with which to view it but when the day came it was a day of clouds and storm. Nothing could be seen of the eclipse and there was not another due for many years nor did my grandfather live to use his instrument.

During father's first school, John Boole made an instrument to observe the transit of Mercury. The instrument threw the image of the sun's disk upon a white sheet and then Mercury was seen as a little black body travelling across.

In 1834 my grandfather was appointed curator to Lincoln Mechanics' Institute. He was the first curator and left when George Boole opened his first school in Lincoln. He said goodbye to the shoe-making for life and probably without a shadow of regret. This new sphere was one in every way calculated to suit him. His time was to be occupied in lecturing, teaching, making out the timetable, arranging specimens, conducting correspondence etc. with of course increased opportunity of intercourse with educated men. Such was the light at least in which he himself regarded his new position. He was to be responsible for the intellectual duties of the institution and to superintend the performance of menial ones. He was taking this view of the matter, the right man in the right place.

He might have had a very happy life then. And as he was not likely to neglect these duties, his family would have been maintained in some fair amount of comfort, although his great chance of making money had been thrown away in early life.

It was very unfortunate for the new curator that no definite agreement was made at starting as to what he was and what he was expected to do. But it is probable that had it not been for the members of the Institute he would have been allowed to settle down quietly and take up naturally the duties that came to hand into his natural position and come gradually to an understanding with that body. The next question is of course who? But because whereas he was a very young man then, and he is an old man now and a well-known man, and also because he has bitterly repented his conduct in the matter over it, I forbear to write his name here. Sufficient to say that he made Mr Boole's position an impossible one. He ordered the new curator about like a servant, expected to be waited on by him and spoke insolently at every fancied neglect of duty. One point of dispute was whether it was Mr Boole's business to tend the fires and carry up the coals. The latter declared it was not and indignantly protested against being called to account for such matters by a man so much his junior, a man as humbly born as himself and far inferior to him in knowledge – though a man who directly has made a mark in the world.

It is easy to understand the issue. When matters get down to a question of exactly how little a man need do, the old loving willing service is over, and lowered Mr Boole's status to that level and finally he was obliged to resign his appointment. That I think must have been a misfortune for the Institute as well as for the curator. It was a great grief to George and indeed to all the family. Trouble and pecuniary troubles were again before them, for then there remained only the appointment at the bank and that was a very small one, considerably less than 100 a year, but how much exactly my aunt does not know.

Then for many years afterwards, George became the mainstay of the family. He was now twenty years old. He had been earning his living partially from the time he was fifteen years old and fully from the time he was sixteen.

For eighteen months before his death Mr Boole never left one room and suffered intensely. He could not sleep without morphia. Sometimes his family in despair gave him the pills before the right time. He was terribly depressed, so much that sometimes his daughter would go down to the school and fetch out George to come and amuse him and talk to him. Sometimes even that would fail, but George cheered him better than anyone. He was the best of sons to both parents. Mr Boole died [1848] before George left Lincoln. He was able to provide every comfort to his father during his illness. That queer old armchair was bought to give him greater comfort.

The old man was dying all Sunday. On Monday morning he left them. His grave is one of the very few in the Cathedral Close at Lincoln. It is a large stone placed lying on the ground. The letters were deeply cut and are every one distinct. To the left side of his grave is that of his wife, buried four or five years later. There is no gravestone over her, but her name is written on her husband's gravestone and the place of her burial indicated thereon.

John Boole's life had failure, greatness, misery and genius.

Mary Ann Joice afterwards Mary Ann Boole (George Boole's mother)

It is very difficult to write this strange story but I will try to do so. Mary Ann Joice was the illegitimate daughter of a clergyman whose surname was Cecil, by his housekeeper. Two places in Berkshire, Abington and Wallingford, were respectively the homes of Mr Cecil and the Joices, Mrs Boole's maternal grandparents with whom she lived during childhood, but my aunt does not remember which place they lived in and in which he lived. I believe they are near together.

Miss Joice went home to be confined. Afterwards she probably went away to service. At least we do know that Mary Ann was entrusted to the care of her maternal grandparents and a happy home they made for her. Floating across the memories of her childhood was a story that in infancy, while in London with her mother, her mother had hidden her in a drawer to protect the baby from its father who came to take it away. Be this as it may, it was with her maternal grandparents that little Mary Ann spent her childhood. It was to them that her memory went back in after years. Mr Joice had a beautiful voice. He was clerk to the parish church. He played the organ and she kept a small sweet-stuff shop.

Mary Ann was exquisitely beautiful in youth and she too had a beautiful voice. She used to sing old ballads to her children which she said she learned from the wandering minstrels. They used to pass through, singing for their livelihood. They wanted a stool to sit on while singing. The little Mary Ann would … [Here the manuscript ends abruptly.]

COMMENTARY ON BOOLE FAMILY HISTORY NOTEBOOK

The origins of the Boole family and name are uncertain, but they may have had Scottish, English or Irish roots – a John de Bole of Lincolnshire was recorded in 1273 in the Hundred Rolls census. The Booles were certainly yeomen farmers who lived off the land for many generations. In the nineteenth century, the Booles progressed into trades such as shoemaking and professions such as schoolteaching, based on their undeniable love of reading, learning, languages, the sciences and mathematics.

The passage of a box of books from generation to generation as described by MaryAnn in the notebook was the equivalent of the family silver, a rather unusual heirloom for a farming family, but it indicates the value they placed on learning. When the books were auctioned along with John Boole's other property it must have broken the family's heart. Indeed, one wonders why such an auction had to take place – perhaps to pay off John Boole's debts. But surely at this stage in 1848 the family, especially George, would have been more financially secure and would not have needed the proceeds from the sale of the books.

John and George Boole obviously valued learning, especially scientific, very highly. They made telescopes with which to view the visible universe, their free laboratory. Significantly, mathematics underpinned their scientific investigations. Parallel to their scientific views ran their religious views: they were devout Christians, well-behaved and sober, admiring the heavens as God's most magnificent creation. The Bible was read both as an aid to reading and learning, and for sincere religious reasons. And yet, their religious views did not entirely conform to the orthodoxy of the day, leaning towards Unitarianism, as did those of Sir Isaac Newton, the greatest scientific hero of Lincolnshire. When one adds to the mix optics, natural philosophy, mechanics, astronomy, geometry, and the calculus, the influence of Newton on the Booles becomes even more striking.

It was a sad reflection of the times in which he lived that a man of John Boole's intellect and ability was denied even a formal secondary education because of a lack of money, a fate that also befell his son George. He was undoubtedly well versed in both the theory and practice of the physical sciences, a frustrated inventor, a builder of scientific instruments, and a good and enthusiastic teacher at the Lincoln Mechanics' Institute. But he was temperamental and easily frustrated, as is evidenced by the incidents of the eclipse and especially the steam paddle and it is not surprising that the trade of shoemaking did not satisfy him or fulfil his scientific longings. It is little wonder therefore that he neglected his trade and fell into severe financial difficulties. His daughter MaryAnn, and presumably George and the other children too, had to endure the jibes of their playmates about their father being 'a man of no principle', and John Boole's incarceration in a debtors' prison must have brought lasting shame and humiliation on his wife and young family.

This incident had a profound effect on George Boole's character. All his life he was extremely conscientious in carrying out his duties to the letter of the law both at his school in Lincoln and at Queen's College Cork, and indeed very intolerant of those he believed were neglecting their obligations.

Figure 1.1: Silhouette of George Boole

Though generous to a fault in giving financial help to relatives and friends and people down on their luck, he was extremely careful with his money and financial accounts and never allowed himself to get into debt. This was an entirely natural reaction to his father's predicament which must have terrified him as a boy.

But George also inherited some aspects of his father's highly strung and non-conformist character. Throughout his career he was involved in several disputes, academic, social and work-related. Undoubtedly, he believed that his attitudes were always based on principle, and that such disputes were the price one had to pay for taking a definite stand on issues. At times, he based his life and behaviour on almost mathematical principles, which when accepted, had to be followed to their logical conclusion.

Boole's relationship with his mother Mary Ann is more difficult to analyse. Clearly, he loved her very deeply, and inherited many of his finer feelings from her – his love of literature, music and poetry, his almost female sensitivity and reverence for beauty, and above all his deep appreciation of and respect for family life. But the stigma of her ancestry, for which of course she was not even remotely responsible, must have troubled him deeply. His sister MaryAnn knew the facts of her mother's birth, and undoubtedly George did too, and he must have dreaded the thought that cruel opponents could taunt him with these facts. Both of his parents had skeletons in the cupboard and he had little or no financial or social resources to fall back upon. All of his life George Boole pursued a strategy of almost painful subservience to authority of all kinds – to superiors, established academics, bishops and clergy, and educational officers, as is evidenced by his terms of address in letters and other documents. His attitude was often cap-in-hand and he was careful never to give his opponents an opportunity to hurt him.

Yet, paradoxically, Boole was possessed of supreme self-confidence at almost all times in academic matters. He thought long and very deeply about most issues, scientific, religious and moral, and acted only after he was convinced he was following the correct course of action. He then pursued his ends without wavering, regardless of the difficulties his decisions caused himself and others, as if strengthened and justified by the power of logic.

But there is a final fact we must face: the revelations in this chapter introduce a new element into the story of George Boole. His maternal grandfather was a Berkshire clergyman, presumably well-educated, and occupies an important position in Boole's ancestry. This must have had a bearing on his talents and abilities.

Many years later his widow, Mary Everest Boole, no doubt informed of his family background by her husband, paid tribute to her mother-in-law in the following words:

> There was another woman, whose name shall be wrapped in silence. She was the 'illegitimate' daughter of a well-to-do man. She refused to accept from her 'honorable' father the insolent patronage which such men offer to those who have inherited their own pride; preferring to face the struggle for life in a world of strangers. She bequeathed, to some who have helped me, a large share of hereditary intellectual power and a determination to base a true morality on solid fact, and not to be satisfied with any imitation constructed of parchments tied together with red tape, smeared over with white paint, and stuffed with corruption.[4]

Chapter 2

LIFE OF GEORGE BOOLE
BY HIS SISTER
MARYANN BOOLE

BACKGROUND

EORGE BOOLE'S ONLY SISTER MaryAnn Boole (1818–1887) admired George almost to the point of worship and spent a great deal of her time attempting to ensure that he received due credit and recognition for his achievements. In her eyes, George could do little wrong, and there is virtually no criticism of him, direct or implied, in her biographical text that follows. Despite her obvious bias her account is invaluable, as it preserved a great deal of information about George and his parents that would otherwise have been lost. She uses facts gleaned from biographical letters written by Boole's friends, acquaintances and colleagues after his death, and relies on family anecdotes and folklore as well.

She did her brother a great service by compiling her memoir of him, expending tremendous energy on the project, with no personal gain to herself. She realised that George truly abhorred publicity and was genuinely more interested in progress and achievement than the trappings of fame. In particular, she knew there was no way that he would agree to having a biography written while he was still living, and probably not even after his death. She carefully kept a great number of the letters he wrote to her, many of which now reside in the Boole Archive at University College Cork. She also quietly asked for and acquired from others the letters they had received from George, and planned and even perhaps began to write a biography of her brother long before his death in 1864. Indeed, in letters as early as 1853 she begged Boole's friends Dr John Bury and Thomas Dyson not to breathe a word to him of her plans.

It is doubtful if MaryAnn ever submitted the material for publication, perhaps fearing conflict with Boole's widow. In her will, she bequeathed her manuscript, letters and all papers relating to her brother to Boole's eldest daughter, Mary Ellen Hinton. It is believed that her biography of her brother lay in a chest in the United States until 1984, when it was bought at auction at Sotheby's in London by University College Cork.

It is clear from their letters that George and MaryAnn loved each other very deeply in a truly brotherly and sisterly way – he was concerned for her health, her income, her welfare, her employment prospects and every other aspect of her life; she in turn was concerned with his health, success and every facet of his welfare. He obtained employment for her in Ireland as governess to the children of William Fitzgerald, Bishop of Cork and afterwards Bishop of Killaloe, where MaryAnn moved with the family. George continued to keep a close and brotherly eye on her in a foreign country.

George was a confirmed bachelor until he was nearly forty and showed little sign of settling down before that time. MaryAnn was financially dependent on him until 1855, and his sudden marriage to the twenty-three-year-old Mary Everest must have come as a tremendous and unwelcome shock to her. There was forever afterwards a tension between the two women, some would say even an antagonism, evidenced by the fact that Mary Everest Boole does not receive even a single mention in the biography that follows. Reciprocally, MaryAnn receives no mention in Mary Everest Boole's account of the life of her husband.[5]

Around the time of George's death, it appears that MaryAnn entertained a suspicion that her sister-in-law was at least in part responsible for her brother's premature death, because of her unorthodox medical beliefs and treatment. But his death seems to have united them somewhat, and in later letters they even addressed each other as 'My dear Sister'.

We present an edited version of what MaryAnn wrote. Her memoir of her brother George Boole is now appearing in print for the first time.

MaryAnn's Biographical Memoir of George Boole

From the record of births in the old family Bible I copy the following entry:

> George Boole, son of John and Mary Ann Boole, born 2 November 1815 at 4 o'clock in the Parish of St Swithin, in the City of Lincoln.

In the same Bible is a long register of births and deaths of our ancestors, extracted from an old black leather Bible, dated 1613, which is still in the possession of another branch of the family. The house my brother first saw the light is No. 34 Silver Street. It was built originally for my father by his friend Mr Charles Curtois, but it was very inconvenient; anyway my father did not occupy it for more than two years. My father was not a native of Lincoln – his family for a long period had resided at Broxholme, a small low-lying village about six miles east of Lincoln. They were of humble origin holding no higher a rank in life than cottagers or small farmers. The mud-walled cottage roofed with thatch which they occupied is still standing, but within the last few years it has undergone considerable alterations and repairs and now wears a comparatively modern aspect.

Here our forefathers for several generations lived and toiled and brought up their families in humble respectability. The few acres of ground which they rented, with the cow and the orchard and garden attached to the house, sufficed for their simple wants, until the grown-up sons and daughters went forth into the world and became in their turn tillers of the soil and heads of families.

My father, John Boole, was born in the year 1777, and was one of a numerous family. His father, considering his position and surroundings, was a remarkable man. He had considerable mental cultivation, though living in a lonely secluded village where books were scarce, it was not easy to ascertain how he acquired it. He loved reading and was a great admirer of Cowley's poetry.[6] He was looked up to by his fellow villagers as a man of superior intellect, and his memory was affectionately cherished by his children. It is recorded that he used to take them out, on starlit nights, to point out to them the planets and constellations, with which he was familiar.

As a child my father was remarkably quick and forward, and several anecdotes have been preserved of his precocity. He had little education, for his parents were not in circumstances to spend much upon his schooling nor indeed in those days was it considered necessary to give much education to a youth who could aim at nothing higher than farm labour or an inferior trade. What regular instruction he had was obtained first from an old woman who kept a small school in the village and afterward from the Rev. Basset, the minister of the parish, who appears to have acted as schoolmaster, and with whom from his quickness and industry my father was always a favourite. Whether he received from that gentleman any assistance on his early mathematical studies I am not able to say, but it is certain that the proficiency he obtained was due almost wholly to his own industry and perseverance. During the years of his apprenticeship and afterwards when working as a journeyman in London and elsewhere he was rarely without a mathematical book which was concealed in the drawer of the seat on which he worked, and referred to at every leisure moment. In this manner he also gained a great deal of general information and became conversant with the history and literature of his country.

In 1791 at the age of fourteen he was apprenticed to a shoemaker at Saxilby near Lincoln. The shoemaker's name was Johnson and he was bound to him for the usual term of seven years. The trade was unfortunately chosen, for its sedentary and merely mechanical nature was unfavourable for the exercise of the inventive powers with which he was highly endowed. As a natural consequence he acquired a deep-rooted dislike of his occupation and unfortunately in after life he permitted this feeling to influence him so far as to neglect the business for the attractions of science, and that too at a time when the wants of a growing family required increased diligence …

… He then went to Lincoln, for the purpose of obtaining better instruction in his business, and there he remained working under different masters until about the age of twenty-four, when he set off to seek his fortune in London. There he obtained work from some of the principal establishments, from which it may be inferred that he possessed considerable skill in his craft. While thus engaged he contrived to pursue his favourite studies with unabated ardour and diligence, occasionally assisting and instructing others. The knowledge thus imparted was in one instance the means of procuring for the recipient, a young man of the same calling as himself, a valuable and permanent situation in the Excise.

My father's qualifications fitted him admirably for the office of a teacher: his method was clear, attractive and so simple as to adapt itself to the humblest capacity; his illustrations were happily chosen; his explanations lucid, and his patience inexhaustible. Of the many who, in after years, availed themselves of his instruction, all would bear testimony to the truth of this. One of his pupils, a Mr Hewson, a surgeon of Lincoln, to whom he gave private lessons, spoke of him as 'a more remarkable man than his son'.

It was in 1806 during this residence in London that he first met with my mother, who was a native of Berkshire, but at that time was residing in London and after a very short acquaintance they were married on 14 September 1806 at St Martin in the Fields. Immediately after the ceremony the newly-married pair separated, he to go back to his rooms and his work and she to her situation. She was then acting as a lady's maid to a Mrs Walmsley, the wife of a minor canon of St Paul's. They lived apart for some weeks, and then took lodgings in London where they remained until their removal to Lincoln. About six months after the marriage he was induced by the representation of friends to return to

Lincoln and commence business on his own account. He soon acquired a thriving trade and had he been content to plod on in patient devotion to his calling he might have become an independent if not a rich man.

It was not until 1815 in the tenth year of her marriage that my mother showed any promise of a family, and the birth of his eldest son George, after all hope of such an event had been abandoned, was a cause of great rejoicing to my father. Indeed, the extravagant demonstration of his joy had well-nigh cost my mother her life, for in the excess of his hospitality on the occasion he would introduce some of her most intimate friends into the sick chamber, to drink the health of his first born, while she was still too weak to bear the excitement, and for days she was seriously ill.

I am not aware that my brother in his infancy was remarkably precocious. He was a strong healthy child and as his faculties developed he showed more than the usual amount of childish curiosity asking innumerable questions about everything he saw and often puzzling his mother either to answer or evade them. He was very observant and while a mere child would at any time leave his sports to listen to the conversation of his father and older friends. At the age of a year and a half he was sent to a dame's school in the neighbourhood conducted by a Mrs Holmes for the sole purpose, it would seem, of being kept out of the way.

Soon after his birth my parents had removed to the house at 49 Silver Street immediately opposite the national school, where they resided for fifteen years and where I and my two other brothers were born. The house, which had been pulled down and rebuilt, was high rented and as it was larger than necessary my mother let off her best rooms to help meet the expenses of an increasing family. In an adjoining house the windows of which look into St Peter's churchyard lived two ladies named Clarke, who a short time before had commenced a sort of preparatory school for children of respectable tradesmen and persons of the middle classes. To their care George was next consigned, and Miss Clarke claimed the honour of being his first teacher. This may have been the case since it is likely that the sole advantage he derived from Mrs Holmes was being kept out of harm's way. Miss Clarke was living when these notes were first penned, an intelligent old lady, and from her I obtained this information. Her recollections of her pupil are very indistinct – she thinks he did not remain with her more than a year, but that he was an amiable child and at that tender age he gave indications of talent.

One day while he was yet in frocks and pinafores he was missed from home. A long and anxious search was made and he was at last found by his mother in the national school opposite surrounded by the beauty and fashion of Lincoln (for it was a public examination of the pupils), spelling hard words and being rewarded for his successful attempts with a shower of small coins. This would be long before he became a pupil of the national school probably while he was still with Miss Clarke. Miss Clarke says that though she was not naturally fond of children she was much attached to him, and was sorry when my father removed him to place him under the care of Mr Gibson, a personal friend who at that time conducted a commercial school in Mint Lane. With Mr Gibson he remained until about his seventh year when he was again removed and sent to the national school which had been but a few years established. The master of the school, Mr John Walter Reeves, with whom my father was on terms of intimacy, had the privilege of taking a certain number of pay scholars to educate on the same system as the free scholars and many of the respectable tradesmen availed themselves of the opportunity, for the means of education were not nearly so great then as at the present day.

A cousin who was considerably his senior says, 'I recollect seeing him only once, as a child about six or seven years old, and he was so intent on receiving some mathematical instruction from his father that he did not turn his head or seem to notice my presence at all.' About this time, he used to spend a good deal of time with an aunt, Mrs Chaloner,[7] a sister of my father, who lived in the town. She was a woman of cultivated mind and a very superior understanding, and from her love of reading had acquired a great deal of general information. She was the mother of a large family and at this time in declining health, but she took great pleasure in the society of her inquisitive little nephew to whose thirst for knowledge she was both able and willing to minister. Many of his Saturday afternoons were thus spent in conversation and argument with the kind aunt who fondly called him her boy. The cousin mentioned above told me that she well remembered him on one of these visits sustaining an argument with her mother on the divinity of Christ, founded on the words 'I and my Father are one', which had stimulated his curiosity.

A favourite science with my father was optics, and as he had great ingenuity and skilful fingers but was too poor to purchase optical instruments, he used to make them – cameras, kaleidoscopes, compound and solar microscopes and even a telescope. We had a sundial of his construction over the door of a summer house in the garden and if I do not err, some of his calculating machines are still in use in two of the libraries and the Savings Bank in Lincoln. George possessed no such mechanical skill and was always rather awkward with his fingers, but he took the liveliest interest in his father's inventions and was taken into council when anything new was projected. I believe he never had any assistance with his mathematics but such as he obtained from his father. After he had reached the limits beyond which this assistance was of no avail, his own indefatigable industry and perseverance supplied the place of his teachers …

… At the end of the 6th book of Leslie's *Geometry* these words were written in pencil by my father: 'GB finished the 6th book November 1st 1826.' This would be the day before he completed his eleventh year. On that very day the Rev. G. Quilter of Canwick[8] chanced to call and my father, proud of his pupil's progress, mentioned the circumstance to him. Mr Quilter was surprised, and perceiving, as he thought, indications of talent of no common order, urged the necessity of an effort to send him to college, but earnestly as my father desired it he never possessed the requisite means.

As soon as he was able to connect words with ideas George became a great reader, eagerly devouring every book that came his way, travels, history, biography, poetry and romances not a few.

There is a pleasant common, the Monk's Leys, now the arboretum, just outside the city to the east, lying on the sunny slope of a hill, where from time immemorial the Lincoln schoolboys have been accustomed to resort on half-holidays for cricket and other active sports. Here, perched on the branch of a favourite tree, he used to spend many of his Saturday afternoons absorbed in the perusal of some book; it was in this spot that he first read Scott's delightful romances. Many years afterwards he used to take his own pupils to play there, and while they were busied in their games he would read or write or meditate. I believe many of his poems were composed there. He possessed, in a remarkable degree, the faculty of retaining, and that apparently without effort, the substance of all he read that was worth preserving, and the vast amount of knowledge thus stored up in his early life was ready for practical application in after years, always in the proper place and at the right time. I once expressed to him my surprise at the extraordinary power of memory that seemed to enable him to avail himself of everything he had ever read. 'This does not result,' he said, 'so much from strength of memory as from the power of arrangement which provides its proper place in the mind for every fact and idea and thus enables me to find at once what I want, just as you would know in a well-ordered set of drawers where to lay your hand in a moment upon any article you required.'

Much of the time thus spent in reading was stolen from his play-hours. I do not ever recollect his ever being much associated with my younger brothers and myself in our various sports and amusements. His image rises before me as a grave thoughtful-looking boy absorbed in some favourite book, seated at the window of the sitting room that opened into the garden where I and my brothers were enjoying a merry game. I have a distinct recollection of his once presiding at the funeral of a tame rabbit which had died under his care and was buried in the little garden at the back of the house. He made a Latin oration over the grave which impressed us younger ones greatly though we had no idea of its meaning. As he had been learning Latin only a short time I suppose it must have been something out of the Delectus.[9] He was however fond of such sports as required considerable physical exertion and would occasionally join heartily in play with boys of his own age – he excelled particularly in running and jumping. Fishing was also a favourite amusement at this time and it was in returning from a fishing excursion that he narrowly escaped drowning. Some alterations had been made in the lock, and the sides of the river between the high bridge and the lock had been walled up but was not there protected by a railing. He had been one afternoon with a school-fellow to Washingborough to fish, and on his way home walked along the southern edge of the river, when partly from his defective eyesight and partly from the darkness of the evening, he did not perceive that one of the large iron rings that are fixed at regular intervals into the stone coping for the purpose of fastening the boats was erect; his foot caught in the ring and he fell into the water. There was no one in sight on that side of the river and the water was low at the time. The boy who was with him and who was a little older than himself could render him little or no assistance; but his cries brought a man from the opposite side, who, throwing himself on the ground and holding out a long pole, succeeded in reaching him just in time, for his strength was almost exhausted, and in thus sustaining him until further assistance was procured and he was drawn out of the lock. The fright and shock to his nervous system made him very ill for a day or two but no more serious effects resulted. He was however much distressed at the loss of a very valuable fishing rod that had been given by a friend, and which after holding it as long as possible he was compelled at length to let go into the water.

It was discovered that his sight was defective. Mr Snow, a medical attendant of the family, coming in one day when George was reading, observed a painful and unnatural straining of the eyes and on examination found that there was very little power of vision in the left eye. To remedy this defect, he advised that the right or strong eye should be bandaged, and the weak one only used, thinking that the faculty might be restored or at least strengthened by exercise. The experiment was tried, but without success, for the health and spirits of the patient suffered so much from the effort to read and the partial abstinence from books that the plan was abandoned and no further means were resorted to.

George was next transferred in his educational career to the care of Mr Thomas Bainbridge, for many years proprietor of a large commercial school in the town ...

... I believe that George was indebted for his earliest instruction in Latin to the kindness of Mr William Brooke of the well-known firm of William Brooke and Sons, Printers. With this gentleman who became a lifelong friend he went through the Delectus, etc. [see Chapter Eight]. Afterwards he was assisted in his classical studies chiefly in Latin and Greek by the Rev. Richard Andrew who for several years occupied my mother's apartments and took a great interest in the young student.[10]

I may here cite an anecdote that belongs to this period and which I have frequently heard from my mother. She had taken advantage of Mr Andrew's temporary absence to visit some friends in the country. She was away from home about a week and on their return was alarmed to find George looking very pale and thin. She questioned him closely on the subject of his health but could get from him no admission that he felt ill. She then with much anxiety mentioned the subject to my father, who said, 'Oh he has only been reading too much.' Upon sifting the matter further, she discovered that availing himself of Mr Andrew's permission to make use of his library during his absence he had literally spent the whole of his time in reading, shutting himself up in the room and leaving it only for the purpose of snatching a hasty meal. Exercise and play had been alike neglected, but my mother's return soon restored things to their ordinary course.

She used to tell another story showing the only instance of anything approaching wrongdoing in her boy. She had put some choice apples that she wished to keep in a sort of cupboard formed out of a disused steam bath which she kept locked. On going sometime after to the cupboard she thought the apples had diminished in number but as no one but herself had access to the place she concluded that she must be mistaken but determined to watch. The next visit left no room for doubt – the apples were certainly diminishing but by what agency she puzzled herself in vain to conjecture. She was becoming seriously uneasy as the idea of false keys, dishonest servants etc. passed before her imagination when suddenly it flashed upon her that at the top of the bath was a round hole to admit air and that upon this hole rested a loose lid which on being raised would give to a skilful thief access to the treasures within. The mystery thus far was solved but great indeed was her surprise when after a searching investigation she discovered that George was the culprit. He did not attempt to conceal or palliate his crime but confessed that the apples being out of reach of his arm he had night after night when he went to bed 'harpooned them' i.e. fished them up from the shelf on which they rested, by means of a stick with a pin stuck in the end, and then generously shared them with his friends.

Among the multifarious subjects which composed George's course of juvenile reading, poetry, of which he was very fond, held a prominent place. In his poetical reading he was probably directed by his father, who possessed excellent taste and was intimately acquainted with the works of many of our finest poets. George had a fine appreciation of the higher kinds of poetry and himself possessed poetical powers of no mean order, which might have won him a name if the more severe charms of science had not proved more attractive to him. He was fond of translation and at various times produced beautiful renderings of Italian, French and German poems. His first introduction to the public was in the capacity of a translator, and it is singular that this first step to Parnassus involved him in a quarrel that attracted towards him the attention his verses would scarcely otherwise have commanded.

When in his fourteenth year he made several translations from the Greek and Latin poets into English verse, which considering his age and the short time he studied the languages were remarkable. One of these, *An Ode to Spring* from Meleager, signed G.B., my father sent to the *Lincoln Herald*, a weekly paper edited by a Mr James Amphlett. It appeared in the

Herald on the 28th of May 1830 with a note by the editor announcing it as the production of a boy of fourteen. A fortnight afterwards in the same paper appeared a letter signed P.W.B. containing a coarse and ungenerous attack upon the youthful poet whom the writer accused of plagiarism stating his own suspicions that the lines were smuggled from some periodical ...[11]

... In the following summer of 1831 when he was in his sixteenth year, George went to Doncaster to enter upon his first situation as classical teacher in a respectable Wesleyan boarding school conducted by a Mr Heigham with whom he remained two years. Mr Dyson of Gainsboro who was also an assistant in this school has kindly supplied me with some particulars of my brother at this period [see Chapter Ten]:

> I can recollect little of this, except that he felt a good deal the first going from home, and that he wrote frequently and affectionately. How thoroughly he enjoyed his vacations and what pains were taken to make them really a recreation and a refreshment! He had deep affections and though rarely demonstrative he was never so happy as when surrounded by his family and a few chosen friends. He mentioned that nobody made such gooseberry pies as his mother, an opinion he retained as long as he lived. Probably as much was due to the keenness of youthful appetite as to the excellence of manufacture.

Perhaps this is the place to speak of my mother of whom there is so little yet so much to be said – so little as to herself, so much as to the mother of her son. She was one of those women who without being talented or witty or accomplished or showy or in any way cultivated are yet universal favourites and within their own circle possessed of considerable influence. Her education was of that limited character that in her school days was considered sufficient for a girl belonging to the middle classes, but she had much natural refinement and a large share of that sound common sense that so often atones for the want of education. She had great vivacity of temperament, a light elastic spirit that met troubles bravely and threw them off easily, a sweet, even temper that was rarely ruffled, and the genuine childlike sympathy that was so strikingly a characteristic in her son. It was these qualities that made her so popular among her friends and acquaintances; if any of them were sick or sorrowful or in need she was immediately sent for and she was always ready with her help and sympathy. She was an affectionate but not a demonstrative mother; on her devolved the early training of her children and her rule over them was of the mildest and gentlest character; she never scolded or lectured, and personal chastisement was a thing almost unknown in the household yet while less restraint was exercised than would be generally advisable, instances of disobedience or childish naughtiness were rare. She strove to the best of her ability to make us love and practise truth and goodness.

Though widely differing from my father in character and disposition, her union with him was on the whole a happy one; her cheerful, practical nature supplemented his more reserved and speculative one and helped him through many a difficulty that his sensitive spirit would have shrunk from. When troubles came, and they came fast enough in our childhood, it was she who looked them steadily in the face and devised the means to overcome them, and early and late she toiled and struggled and economised that she might be able to educate and bring up her family in respectability. Her reverence for her husband was very great; she thought him one of the wisest of men and always regarded George as second to him. 'I suppose,' said a gentleman to her one day when George's fame as a mathematician was established, 'you are proud of your son, Mrs Boole.' 'Yes,' was her reply, 'I believe George is clever, but did you know his father? He was a philosopher.' But she thought there never was such a son as George and she was not far wrong and he used to say his mother had always spoiled him – both possessed a nature that nothing could spoil.

She used to tell how an officious neighbour once persuaded her to whip George for some childish fault when he was very young, and that his grief at the degradation rather than the pain of the punishment was so touching that it made her ill, and she mentally resolved that nothing should ever induce her to repeat the punishment, and she never did. Nobly did her boy repay all the love and tenderness bestowed upon his early years.

Mr Joseph H. Hill of Hull, solicitor, George's chosen friend, was at this time and for many years his chief correspondent. He has placed at my disposal several of George's early letters, extracts from which will serve to show the nature of his occupations, studies, and opinions on various subjects at the time they were written:

Lincoln
December 26 1832

I have concluded my engagement at Doncaster. I shall next reside at Liverpool, direct to me at Mr Marrat's, No. 4 Whitemill Street, Liverpool. My new situation will be in many respects superior to my old one – Mr Marrat is a very clever man and will assist me in my studies as much as possible. I have been studying a work of his in this last half year.[12]

His stay at Liverpool lasted not more than six months. Mr Marrat, who was personally known to my father, was an exceedingly clever man and as kind and ready to help George in his studies as he had anticipated, but he was very unfortunate in his domestic relations, and the advantages derived from his instruction and companionship were more than counterbalanced by the utter discomfort and disorganisation of the household. George heard and saw there what was distasteful to him as it was novel, and while he sincerely pitied his unfortunate friend he felt that he could not remain under his roof without injury. Even on his pure and refined nature the brief familiarity with the spectacle of gross appetites and passions unrestrainedly indulged and domestic duties ill discharged or entirely neglected had had a deteriorating effect. It was agreed by all at home that George was anything but improved by his residence at Liverpool. But a spirit so finely tuned could not long be at discord with itself. There was about him at all times a purity and childlike innocence that at once shrank from and repelled whatever had even a tinge of coarseness or sensuality.

He was more fortunate in his third and last engagement as an assistant teacher to Mr Hall of Waddington, near Lincoln, and as his connection with Waddington was destined to continue

Figure 2.1: Sketch of George Boole (1832)

for several years and to have an important bearing on his future career, I may be allowed to give a brief sketch of the locality.

Southward from Lincoln there extends as far as Grantham an elevated tract of land known as Lincoln Heath now generally recognised as an advanced school of farming but not more than two generations back as uncultivated, wild, pathless and fenceless and crossed with rabbit warrens. The approach to the city across this heath was so beset with difficulties that it was deemed necessary to erect a land lighthouse for the guidance of benighted travellers. This lighthouse was converted in 1810, into a pedestal for the support of a statue of George the Third to commemorate the jubilee of fifty years of his reign, and is still standing under the name of Dunstan Pillar, but the aspect of the surrounding country is entirely changed. Thriving villages, highly cultivated farms, excellent roads, and an abundant population attest the march of progress and an improved system of agriculture. The western border of this heath plateau slopes steeply down to an extensive plain dotted over with villages that stretches away in one uniform dead level to Nottinghamshire. Tradition speaks of this flat as the bed of an ancient sea whose waters washed the base of the cliff or sloping side of the table land.

A line of pleasant villages, The Cliff Row, skirts the western border of the heath, and in the first of these, about five miles from Lincoln, Mr Robert Hall, forty years before, began his career as a schoolmaster. The comparative scarcity of schools of the class at that period and the ability and energy he possessed had made him eminently successful in his vocation. His school was the resort not only of the agricultural youth of the county but also of the sons of the respectable citizens of Lincoln. Mr Hall was a man of great worth and integrity held in universal esteem and endeared to his intimate friends by his many social and domestic virtues. With this good man George was very happy. There was much that was akin in their simple earnest character; each was quick to perceive and appreciate the sterling qualities of the other and, based on mutual esteem, there grew up between them a sincere affection that never knew a check. Mr Hall was accustomed to speak of George as 'my boy' or 'that lad of mine'. He placed unbounded confidence in him, afforded him opportunities of self-improvement, laughed good-humouredly at his peculiarities, for George was always extremely absent-minded and apt to make droll mistakes in his fits of abstraction, and took the warmest interest in his studies.

It was while residing with Mr Hall that George wrote and delivered the lecture on Sir Isaac Newton. The Mechanics' Institute had recently been established in Lincoln and its patron the Earl of Yarborough presented to the members a marble bust of Sir Isaac of the value of £200. It was felt by the committee of the Institute that advantage should be taken of the circumstance and the interest it excited to have a word in season spoken to those who were present at the inauguration festival regarding the lessons to be learned from the life and labours of the Lincolnshire philosopher, and so high was their appreciation of the ability and competency of George Boole that he was urgently requested to deliver an address. To this he gave a reluctant consent having stated as his objection his own youth and the magnitude of the topic.

The lecture was delivered on Feb 5 1835, in the presence of Lord Yarborough and a large audience of the citizens of Lincoln, and excited intense interest. George was a little over nineteen at the time and he stood slight and boyish-looking with a pale countenance but perfectly calm and collected confronting for the first time a large audience of people, and uttering with deep feeling but with perfect simplicity his own pure and beautiful thoughts. He was listened to with breathless attention interrupted only by occasional bursts of applause while the good old nobleman who sat opposite gazed at him in wonder with tears running down his cheeks. The lecture was afterwards printed at the request of the committee, but so long an interval elapsed before it was brought out that the interest its delivery had awakened subsided, and the sale was inconsiderable.

The very high estimate Mr Hall had formed of George's intellectual powers made him earnestly desire for him the advantage of a college education, and George himself at that time much wished it, and from a remark in a subsequent letter of Miss Davis[13] had fully determined upon it; but as his parents were not in a position to furnish the necessary means, either Mr Hall had engaged to provide them, or another friend, a gentleman in good circumstances in Lincoln, who was for some time a private pupil of my father's and who had spoken of sending him to college. Much, however, as George desired this at the time, he used in after years to express his satisfaction that he was prevented from carrying out his wishes, from a conviction that it would have a contracting effect on his mind and that he might have become a 'mere mathematician'. At the same time, he always entertained the belief that not having passed through college stood in the way of his advancement in life, and even when at the zenith of his fame he was more than once urged to apply for appointments that would have been advantageous to him he declined, on the ground that against Cambridge and Oxford men he would have no chance whatsoever of success.

While he was thus leading a life of great happiness and winning golden opinions from all around him, events were occurring at home that led to the rather abrupt termination of his engagement with Mr Hall, and the temporary abandonment of any plans that might have been formed relative to college.

On the establishment of the Mechanics' Institute in Lincoln, my father, who had taken an active part in its formation, accepted the office of curator which was offered to him, and removed with his family to the old monastery of Grey Friars, the lower part of which had been converted into a suite of rooms, library and museum etc. [This was in 1833–4.]

The duties of his office as he interpreted them promised a more congenial occupation than his business, which he gave up on accepting the curatorship. He was to have the general supervision of the establishment, the charge of the museum, the formation and instruction of classes in various subjects, and was occasionally to deliver lectures on popular subjects. For the most important part of his office he was eminently qualified; he loved his work and, thoroughly conversant with its details, he had great power of illustrating his subjects and placing them before his pupils in the clearest and most attractive form, inexhaustible patience, and that experience as a self-taught man that enabled him to anticipate and provide against the difficulties of those who were following in the same track. He was besides heartily interested in the success of the Institute, and desirous to forward it by every means in his power, and he entered upon his office with the ardour of one who feels himself to be the right man in the right place and who looks forward to many years of happy usefulness.

He formed his classes, prepared lectures, constructed philosophical instruments etc. and for some time all went on smoothly. But his connection with the Institute was destined to be of short duration. Among the members composing the committee of the management were three fussy officials and not very scrupulous, who by virtue of their office and the services they had rendered in the formation of the Institute constructed themselves an authority, and assumed the right of controlling and directing, not only the internal policy of the Institute but also the officers attached to it. They regarded my father as their servant and soon made this evident to him. They interfered with his plans, dictated to him his duties and even ordered him to wait upon them and to perform all sorts of menial offices. He was not a man to submit quietly to what he considered an unjust assumption of power and he resented their behaviour and refused to obey them. They then commenced a system of petty tyranny and persecution that never relaxed or ceased until they had succeeded in dislodging him from his situation. He was misrepresented, bullied and hectored and at last so cruelly insulted in the presence of the assembled members that with a broken spirit and failing health, no recourse remained to him but to send in his resignation and begin life afresh, for having disposed of his business he had nothing to rely on except the slender stipend attached to his office as auditor at the Savings Bank. I cannot now recall the details but I well remember my father's distress of mind and the indignant sense of wrong and injustice aroused among the other members of the family.

(Note: It is only justice to one of my father's persecutors who for many years held a very respectable position in Lincoln to add that some time before my father's death he called upon him, acknowledged the unkind part he had taken in this affair and the forgiveness that was so freely accorded.)

It was a most painful chapter in the family life, and would perhaps have been better left in oblivion, but that it seemed necessary to notice it in explanation of George's next step. He had felt deeply the unjust treatment to which his father had been subjected and which he was powerless to prevent, but now that a crisis had been reached he hesitated not a moment to take a decisive step. On this as on all other occasions on which he was called upon to act, having satisfied himself as to what was the right thing to do, he determined to do it, at whatever cost to himself.

He thought only how best he could provide a home for his family, and laying aside all plans and prospects of self-advancement, made his father send in his resignation and resolved at once to open a day school in Lincoln. He was placed in a particularly delicate position with respect to Mr Hall to whose kindness and affection he owed so much. It seemed almost like ingratitude to open within five miles of his a school which might become a formidable rival to the Waddington establishment, while at the same time he was depriving his old friend of services that had become almost indispensable, but conscious of his own integrity and urged by the pressing necessity of his care, he did not shrink from his purpose; he stated the whole matter fairly to Mr Hall and announced his intention of leaving him. Mr Hall was sincerely sorry to lose him but he was too good and too just to allow this to make any difference in his friendship for George; it seemed rather to raise him in his estimation and the most friendly intercourse was maintained between them as long as Mr Hall lived.

(1836–1837) A suitable house having been procured in Free School Lane, Lincoln, the family removed hither and George began his career as schoolmaster. Young as he was, a very high estimate had already been formed of his character and abilities, and soon after its commencement he found himself at the head of a flourishing school in the management of which he was assisted by his father. He devoted himself to his work with the zeal he carried into everything in which he was engaged and in the intervals between teaching found time to prepare manuals for the use of his pupils, to help his father in his various schemes and inventions and to add continually to his own store of knowledge.

This was perhaps one of the happiest periods of his life; he had made a home for his family and was living in their midst, his school was prospering, his occupation agreeable, and he was forming valuable friendships, rising daily in public estimation.

It was at this time that his friendship commenced with the Rev. George Stevens Dickson, perpetual curate of St Swithin's in which parish George lived. He has been spoken of in various obituaries of having afforded George valuable assistance in his mathematical studies; this is a mistake. Dickson himself took up mathematics late in life and was a pupil of George's, not a teacher. George used to complain that though remarkably industrious and persevering, Mr Dickson impeded his own progress because he persisted in following step by step his own roundabout methods of arriving at results to which George or any experienced teacher would have led him by shortcuts.

Mr Dickson was a remarkably fine pianist, a pupil of Cipriani Potter,[14] and discovering George's great love of music, he offered to give him instruction on the piano, but the time necessary to be given to practice and his defective eyesight obliged George to decline the offer which Mr D. afterwards made in favour of a younger brother [Charles], and which was accepted. George's love of music was inherited from both parents. His mother had a very beautiful voice which had not been cultivated, for she lived before the age of pianos and singing for the million and sang as the birds sang from pure gladness of the heart. In the early years of their married life, my father used to accompany her songs on the German flute. Her memory was stored with an inexhaustible fund of songs and ballads, which she learned in her childhood in Berkshire and which were afterwards the delight of her own children. The regular Saturday night washings, over which she always presided, were enlivened and made memorable by these songs of which 'Lord Thomas', 'O Nanny' and some others were special favourites. George learned the flute from his father and played with great sweetness and taste but the blowing was always distressing to him and he did not achieve any great proficiency in it.

He also played a little on the violin at one time, but the piano was his favourite instrument. Some years later he bought one, and having overcome some of the chief mechanical difficulties and made himself acquainted with the laws of harmony he succeeded without any great outlay of time, so as far as to be able to harmonise hymn tunes and simple airs and this modest proficiency was a life-long pleasure to him.

He had a belief that as he advanced in years he would become blind, and he pleased himself with the idea that, like Milton, he could solace his dark and lonely hours with the companionship of sweet sounds. He spent some time in the invention of a new system of musical notation, which was very ingenious but he did not find it of much practical use.

He delighted especially in sacred music and in the Sunday afternoon services at the cathedral. Many who like himself were in the habit of attending these services regularly may recall his image as unconscious of all around him as he stood drinking in with rapt attention the divine strains of Handel, Haydn, and Mozart, his head thrown slightly back, his gaze turned upward, his countenance illuminated with rare spiritual beauty of expression, his whole being absorbed and elevated by the music, which seemed to him a golden link connecting the languages of earth and heaven.

For those who have thus seen him, his beautiful sonnet on music will have a far deeper significance and interest.

Sonnet on Music (George Boole)

Thou who breathe in human souls the might
Of noble impulses unfelt before
Or soothe the bosom into calm delight
With heavenly airs thy sweet and varied store
Or bid the past revive, and from the might
Of years long fled its vanished forms restore
Immortal now and in the golden light
Of love and hope to fade and die no more.
Whether I hear thee at the twilight hour
Stream from beloved lips, or with rapt mood
Stand in the Minster Aisle when arch and tower
Seem shaken with the organ's swelling flood,
How do I bless Thee, Elevating Power!
Thee to the source Divine, Giver of Good!

[*Editor's Note: There follows another poem by George Boole on the same theme of his love of music and the cathedral. It is too long to reproduce here.*]

Mr Dickson always took a warm interest in George's mathematical researches and I think he entered into a sort of partnership with him on the publication of *The Mathematical Analysis of Logic* by which he was to have a share in either the profit or loss of the work. He foresaw that George would attain a high position as an original investigator, and it was he who first suggested to me the importance of preserving some records of a life of no common interest. He lived to see his anticipations realised, his death taking place little more than a year before that of his friend.

It was during this part of his life in Lincoln that George's attention was turned to the study of ethics and biblical criticism, and I think it probable that his researches in this direction were interrupted by the change that unfortunately he was induced to make soon after this date.

In September 1837, his kind friend Mr Hall died, and his family at once made George an offer of the Waddington school. George had reason to believe that Mr Hall had been grooming him as his successor and that had he lived a little longer he would have given up the school to him on such terms as would have tended to make the speculation a successful one. He had realised a fortune and his family were willing to persuade themselves and George that his successor might do the same, but they did not take into account the changes that forty years had effected in educational matters as well as in other things. During that period, commercial schools had multiplied and competition was great. Mr Hall had lost energy as he advanced in years, and during his illness and for some months after, the school had been so grossly neglected that the parents of the boys were prejudiced against it.

George was quite inexperienced in matters of business but he knew that his kind old friend had wished only to benefit him, and his generous unsuspecting nature led him readily to credit the representations of those who were interested in the disposal of the concern, and whom he believed to be equally friendly to him. He acceded to their extravagant demands and bound himself to take the school on a lease of 29 years at a rent of 110 pounds per annum, Mr John Hall, the eldest son of the late owner, pledging himself on the part of the family to ensure 30 boarders to start with. My father, who was of a sanguine temperament and usually the first to see the advantages of any proposed change, was from the beginning opposed to the speculation; he saw in it only risk and danger, and did his utmost to dissuade George from it but without success. He even said that if George had been a few months younger (he was then a little over twenty-one) he would have interposed to prevent it. But the arrangement was finally made and in December 1837 the whole family removed to Waddington.

A considerable number of the Lincoln pupils followed him, and as long as he remained at Waddington he was well supported by his own connection, but the affair from the first was a losing one. The promises of support made by the Halls were not fulfilled, the old connection dwindled away by degrees until after three years of anxious striving he found that to continue his engagement would involve him in utter ruin. He was placed in a most painful position; to abide by the terms of the lease was to lay himself open to legal consequences, or what to him was worse, the charge of dishonourable conduct.

The struggle was terrible, but there was only one course to follow. He deliberated calmly and carefully, decided what was the just and right thing to do, made his proposals, and after a long and unpleasant correspondence prevailed upon the lessers who had signally failed to fulfil their share of the contract, to release him from his engagement on payment of a considerable sum of money.

It was perhaps well that he found himself so soon compelled to throw up the concern. Waddington was a dull place for a man of any cultivation to spend his life in – there was no society, none of the resources of city life, and in spite of its elevated position it was not a healthy locality. Parts of the great plain beneath were frequently flooded by heavy rains and if this was followed by a west wind the miasma engendered by the stagnant water was borne over to the level of the cliff and then typhus fever broke out. Twice during our residence at Waddington it appeared in the school, and though it did not do much mischief it added another to the many anxieties that pressed upon George at this time.

So in 1840 he again removed to Lincoln, this time to the house in Potter Gate at the entrance to the Cathedral Close, which he occupied until his removal to Cork, on his appointment to the professorship of mathematics in the newly established Queen's College in 1849 …

… The first years of his residence in Potter Gate were beset with cares and anxieties. He was striving to pay off the debt contracted by the Waddington engagement for which he had to borrow money, and this debt was further increased by the sum he had agreed to pay to be freed from the concern, and until this object was effected, he never seemed to breathe freely. Then too another obstacle stood too long in the way of his success in his new undertaking. During his residence at Waddington the diocesan school had been established in Lincoln and the clergy of the town and county were exerting their utmost influence on its behalf. It was most disheartening, half year after half year, to find himself only just able to hold his ground while such heavy responsibilities devolved upon him, and at times he was greatly discouraged, but gradually as he became known and appreciated his school filled with pupils, and anxiety as to ways and means was at an end. How much he accomplished in those years of patient waiting, directing, sustaining, helping others, leaving the impress of his own mind upon all with whom he came into contact, and working as few men could work. His brain was never at rest, his pupils absorbed much of his time and thoughts, he loved his boys and devoted himself to their well-being and comfort – what little leisure he could command was given to his own special pursuits. He wrote papers for the *Cambridge Mathematical Journal*, to which, and afterwards to the *Cambridge and Dublin Mathematical Journal*, he was for many years an industrious contributor, as well as to the London and Edinburgh

Philosophical Transactions. His first paper on 'Analytical Transformations' was published in the *Journal* in February 1840[15] ...

... Altogether he contributed to that journal no fewer than twenty-four separate articles, some of them very considerable, and all of them dealing with questions of greater or less difficulty in mathematical analysis.

He was again strongly urged by some of his friends at this period to enter himself at the University of Cambridge, and a correspondence on the subject with Mr Gregory ensued, but again the idea had to be abandoned (see Chapter Eleven).

If he entered Cambridge he must give up his school, the means of support for his parents, who were entirely dependent on him, and he must abandon everything in the shape of original research, which to him would have been impossible. In after years he used to say he was glad he had not gone to Cambridge.

In 1841 a new society was formed in Lincoln entitled the Lincolnshire Topographical Society, of which George became a member, and which he described to Mr Hill as having for its object topography, statistics, local antiquities, in the first instance, and Science and Literature in the second ...

... In December of the same year he writes to the same friend:

I suppose you are aware that I some time ago read a paper before the Topographical Society on the subject of mythology. If you are still curious to see it I will take an opportunity of letting you have it for perusal. This I cannot do at present, because it is usual for papers to remain some time with the secretary of the society in order to be transcribed. I am at present amusing my leisure with the composition of a paper on the subject of light, which, should I complete it to my own satisfaction, I think of following it up by a second on physical astronomy.

I do not know whether either of those papers was read in public; they may have been intended for his boys to whom he was in the habit of giving a weekly lecture, or the last named may have been identical with a paper on the question 'Are the Planets Inhabited?' which he read before the Topographical Society. I believe it was before the same society that he read a paper on the philosophical writings of Bishop Grosseteste, once Bishop of Lincoln, which paper was published in the society's *Transactions*, or in the Archaeological Institute's Lincoln volume.[16] This paper introduced him to the notice of Dr Kaye, the Bishop of Lincoln, a learned and amiable prelate, with whom as long as he remained in Lincoln, George maintained a friendly and pleasant intercourse.

An old pupil residing in America asks many years afterwards:

What has become of the Topographical Society? When I left in 1846 it promised to grow into a very useful institution. Reuben Trotter, another old pupil will remember sketching for Mr Boole several copies of Egyptian and Hindu mythological drawings, illustrative of serpent worship, to be used in a paper prepared for the Topographical Society by our late friend, but I cannot say if it was ever read. He spent some time in its preparation, and we had the benefit of it upon the blackboard when at Waddington. It formed one of the series of Friday afternoon lectures upon all sorts of subjects to which we looked forward in those days with such great pleasure. Friday afternoon was the red letter day of the week – we wrote letters – then listened to the lecture – and then came the carrier's cart from Lincoln with clean clothes, a note from home, and something good as a proof of normal affection. I have looked forward with keen expectation to many things in the world since then, but nothing can equal the longing for the hair-covered little box, studded with brass nails and leather back.

In 1843, he wrote a paper 'On a General Method in Analysis' that gained him the Royal Society's gold medal.[17] It was too long for publication in the *Mathematical Journal* and he hesitated for some time whether he should print it separately at his own cost or send it to the Royal Society on the chance of its being published in their *Transactions*. He consulted his friend Gregory on the subject, who replied:

My advice certainly is that you should endeavour to get your paper printed by the Royal Society, both because you will thereby avoid a considerable expense, and because a paper in the *Philosophical Transactions* is more likely to become known and read rather than one printed separately. If you know any member of the society you may ask him to communicate it, but in the event of your not knowing any such person, I can ask Mr Airy to do so, etc. etc.

This advice was acted upon, the paper was sent, and in January 1844 it was communicated to the Royal Society by S.H. Christie, Esq, one of the secretaries.[18] Very anxiously did George and his father await the result of the venture and so convinced was George of its merits that he exclaimed more than once I should not wonder if it gained the medal, but when months and months passed and no notice was taken of the communication, he began to doubt whether it was accepted, and at last gave up all hope of its acceptance. At length in November of the same year, nine months after it was sent, came the announcement that it was not only accepted, but that the medal was awarded to him. It was the first distinction of the kind that had been conferred by the society in the department of mathematics and consequently a distinguished honour, and great was the excitement when it became known. Crowds of friends and acquaintances and strangers flocked to the house to see the beautiful medal and its silver duplicate, and to congratulate its fortunate possessor who from that time became a man of mark. Several years later, George had to consult Dr Marshall Hall[19] concerning his health, and learned from him that the paper was very near to being rejected. According to the usual rule the council referred the paper to two of the fellows of the Society to report on its merits. One of them reported unfavourably; he could see nothing in it and recommended its rejection. The other thought differently, and stating his opinion that it was above their comprehension advised its being sent to Professor Kelland of Edinburgh.[20] This was done and Professor Kelland on reading it pronounced it one of the most remarkable papers that had appeared before the Society. Dr M. Hall offered to give George the name of the objector, but he promptly declined to hear it. It was afterwards revealed to him incidentally by Professor De Morgan, who remarked that the fellow could not have read the paper or he would not have thus condemned it.

The next four or five years may be reckoned amongst the busiest of a busy life; his school was full, he seldom had fewer than thirty boarders, a good many scholars, and some private pupils, quite enough one would think to occupy the energies of one man, and he never allowed anything to interfere with the performance of his duty to those committed to his care, but laboured incessantly for their intellectual and moral advancement. Yet he did not neglect his duty as a citizen; he furthered by his active help and encouragement every benevolent and philanthropic movement on behalf of his fellow men ...

... A letter to his friend Hill in March 1847 gives some information as to the result of his efforts on behalf of the Mechanics' Institution, in which as long as he remained in Lincoln he continued to take an active interest. He was a member of the committee, he helped to form the library and museum, he gave gratuitous instruction to the members in classics and mathematics and he gave occasional lectures. In September 1846, he writes to Rev. E.R. Larken:

I have been thinking of offering a course of lectures here, at the Mechanics Institution – if the committee would have them on natural philosophy. Moral philosophy I should greatly prefer, but the other seems at present to be most congruous to my position and prospects. What do you think of the likelihood of their being useful?

He was also a trustee of the Female Penitents' Home, in the formation of which he took a deep interest, and vice-president of the Early Closing Association, before the members of which, in 1847, he delivered his lecture 'On the Right Use of Leisure', which was afterwards published at the expense of a member of the association. And yet he found leisure to read extensively on all sorts of subjects and continued to send paper after paper to the *Cambridge Mathematical Journal* and to the Royal Irish Academy. It was during these busy years too that most of his poems were written; he had a fine appreciation of the higher kinds of poetry and in his youth was a great admirer of Mrs Hemans[21] and Byron's *Childe Harold*, portions of which he used to make his boys commit to memory, or copy into manuscript books. Later in life he had a great admiration for Wordsworth, especially *The Excursion* and *Intimations of Immortality*.

He had himself great poetical power and it was an infinite relief to him from his severer studies to pour out his thoughts in poetry, some of which is so beautiful that one cannot help regretting that he did not give more time and attention to this department of literature. He used to give those poems to me as he wrote them to transcribe and preserve them for him, but several were found after his death in his pocket books. He often engaged in poetical correspondence with his intimate friends – sometimes playful and humorous, sometimes serious, but always pure and playful in character. Some of these poetical epistles have been preserved.

His father was wont to remark how very unusual a circumstance it was to find the poetical and musical faculty combined with a mind so profoundly scientific. George himself used to say that of all the things in the world he should most dislike was to be a 'mere mathematician'. He at one time contemplated publishing a volume of his poems …

… But which he never did publish, his mathematical researches absorbing more and more his time and thoughts …

On *The Mathematical Analysis of Logic* [22] … the work did not excite the interest and attention he anticipated, as it was either too novel or too obscure; and he decided that he had put forth his views too hastily and with not sufficient clearness. He himself never wavered for an instant in the estimate he had formed of this or any other of his published works. 'It must ultimately make its way' was his oft repeated remark when at times he could not but feel disappointed of the tardy recognition justice done to him. When years passed away, and his claims were recognised and his name as a mathematician known all through the scientific world, he would sometimes say, rubbing his hands together, while a glow of pleasure lighted up his countenance, 'Yes, I think my fame is established now,' but there was such a childlike simplicity in his manner while speaking thus as showed that fame in itself was the last thing in his thoughts. In truth no man ever worked less for fame as his ultimate object, though he could not be ignorant that he had attained it, or fail to be gratified by its attainment.

He worked with all his might at whatever he found to do, not alone because it was a pleasure to him but because he regarded it as the task assigned to him on earth, which it would have been a breach of duty to leave undone. So great was his love of work and his conviction of the necessity of doing it while he had the power, that he never went from home for a day without taking books and writing materials with him. When he felt that he needed a change from the labours of the school he would go off for a few days to some quiet village in Derbyshire, or to the seaside, and work and walk by turns, thus striving to keep up the balance between mind and body. Very often on returning at eleven or twelve at night from an evening party he would sit down to work for an hour before going to bed. 'It calms me down after the excitement of the evening,' he would say, 'I shall sleep the better for it.'

He possessed in a remarkable degree the power of abstraction that enabled him to write, or to carry on long processes of thought while conversation was going on all around him. If a question or a remark were addressed to him at table while he was thus lost in thought he would start, look in a bewildered manner at the speaker and, connecting with an effort the links of association, arrive gradually at the subject mentioned, but very often it had to be repeated to him. When ribbed on his absence of mind he would laugh good-humouredly and sometimes pretend that he had been falsely accused. There were times however when he was engaged upon some deep subject when the slightest sound in the room where he was writing would distract and annoy him. I have had to cease sewing or retire to another room because he could not bear the click of the needle.

He told me that from boyhood he had had the conviction that Logic could be reduced to a mathematical science, and that he had often made himself ill on the attempt to prove it, but that it was not until 1847 that the true method flashed upon him. When he first began to work at *The Mathematical Analysis of Logic*, his absorption was so extreme it seemed as if his brain was never at rest; by day he moved about like one in a dream, and at night lay awake for hours thinking out what had been before him as a vision all his life and many a time unable to sleep had he risen in the dead of the winter night and, wrapping himself in a cloak, descended to the family sitting room to write down the fast-coming trains of thought that would not be repressed.

Afterwards he invented a little instrument by means of which he was able to write as he lay in bed. In this manner, he used to fill little notebooks with pencilled notes, that in the day were expanded and transferred to his MS writings.

When in 1847 the true light flashed upon him and he entered upon the investigations that resulted in *The Laws of Thought*,[23] he was literally like a man dazzled with excess of light, his restlessness and excitement were extreme, he seemed to be dwelling in a world apart and unconscious of all that was going on around him; his countenance was lighted up with a mingled expression of delight and something like awe, and sleep and appetite deserted him. If he could have communicated his thoughts and feelings to some sympathetic mind it would have been a relief to him, but his father was gone, and there was no one near to whom he could have made himself intelligible.

Of course, his health suffered when his mind was wrought up to this high tension, sometimes the physical disturbance manifested itself in the shape of indigestion or susceptibility to colds. Whatever it might be, he was generally unwilling to attribute it to the right cause; he would debar himself from the use of nourishing food, stimulants etc. and too often have recourse to medicine until at length from sheer exhaustion he was compelled to lay aside his work and so by degrees the balance was restored.

When remonstrated with by his friends on the too ardent devotion to science and on the injury he was inflicting on himself he would say 'Well, when I have finished this paper, I really do intend to lay mathematics aside.' But the rest thus promised was never taken; something more important was sure to grow out of the labour that was to be his last, and all personal considerations were forgotten when the interests of science were in question.

He had an abiding impression that his life would be a short one and this was strengthened by the derangement caused by overwork. Some lines written in pencil in a notebook probably in 1848 and found after his death show how strongly he was at that time impressed with the feeling that he was dying, and a sonnet written in the following spring refers to the same subject. He did not however communicate his suspicions to his friends except when on some special occasion he spoke of his conviction that his life would not be a long one – more than once he expressed this conviction to me. He thought a sudden death by no means to be dreaded but rather the reverse; he considered a lingering illness, and the gradual wasting of the powers of the mind and body, much more painful to think upon. To him such a wearing out would have been a great trial, and he was mercifully spared it.

He thought the attempt to prolong life by medicine, perpetual stimulants and artificial means in the case of a very aged or hopelessly diseased person was wrong and cruel, and that it would be showing more real love and consideration for the sufferer to follow the indication of nature, and let him pass away as quietly and quickly as possible. He even thought that there were cases where incurable disease was accompanied by intense pain in which the faculty would be justified in making use of means to shorten life if at the same time they could lessen the violence of the suffering.

In 1846 he sent in an application, accompanied by testimonials, for a professorship in one of the Queen's Colleges about to be established in Ireland, but it was not until 1849 that he was appointed to Cork, and meantime the suspense and uncertainty were very trying to him and he was prevented from applying for other positions that might have been even more advantageous. His chief reason for wishing to give up the school was that he might command leisure for original research which began to demand more and more of his time and thoughts, and which he felt to be his real life work. In 1847 he went to London as a mathematical examiner to the students in the recently established College of Preceptors, of which he was a member.

It was from no distaste for his vocation that he wished to give up his school; he enjoyed teaching and loved the society of his boys and he used to say that he thought the life of a schoolmaster a singularly agreeable one from the variety and cheerfulness it afforded, but he felt that he could not continue for many years working at such high pressure; either the interests of his school or those of science must suffer from the strain, and science had the stronger claim upon him.

His relation to his pupils resembled more that of a father to his children than of a master to his pupils. He loved children, he understood boys' nature, he took a warm personal interest in them, entered heartily into their plans and pursuits, sympathised in their joys and sorrows, and was never so happy as when he saw them happy, and the boys knew it and gave him their entire love and confidence. He was lenient to the little outbursts of folly or mischief, but maintained strict discipline, and visited severely any manifestation of vice or immorality. To the little boys he showed all the caressing tenderness and affection of a woman and seized every opportunity to praise and encourage their diligence and good conduct. Many a happy smiling little fellow had been brought down to the parlour to have his work inspected, a neatly written copy, a well-spelt exercise book or a sum correctly worked, and to receive there his due need to approval and something more substantial. I remember well the amusement and delight that were created by the first epistle of one of these little ones to his master beginning 'My dear love'.

His birthday, November 2, was a special gala day for the boys, looked forward to with eager anticipation. Everything that could be done to make it a happy day was done; a whole holiday, spent when weather permitted in outdoor games and sports; a dinner on a scale of unwonted magnificence; a bountiful tea to which the day pupils were invited and some young lady friends to assist in the tea-making for so large a party and to contribute to the amusements of the evening.

'I was so happy with my boys,' he used to say in after years, when troubled or annoyed by the bickerings and dissentions in the college; he looked back half regretfully to his life in Lincoln, and in the last year of his life he had almost decided to resign his professorship and again commence a school in England.

On several occasions when he wished to give the boys a treat of a different kind, he would invite his mother into the schoolroom and induce her to relate some of the stories, chiefly from her own experience, that had made such an impression on him as a child. There was one story that had a special interest, connected with one of her ancestors, great-grandmother I think, which she used to tell with considerable detail and great animation. This grandmother was a widow with a rather large family to support for whom she kept a wayside inn in a lonely part of the country, Berkshire I think. One night after all were in bed she was aroused by a party of men knocking at the door, and thinking they were in need of refreshment, she dressed herself and admitted them, but their object was plunder, and so after compelling her to bring forth the best the house afforded in the way of food and drink, and regaling to their hearts' content, they bound and gagged the mother and the children whom they forced to leave their beds, and the servant, and warning them on pain of death not to attempt to free themselves or make the least noise, they proceeded to ransack drawers, cupboards and boxes, taking possession of everything that was portable and of value, including a sum of money that had been put aside for rent, and after spending a considerable time in these performances they departed, leaving the trembling inmates still bound and gagged, and threatening if they attempted to set themselves at liberty or get help by screaming, to return and kill them. So they remained through that miserable night unable to stir, the children terrified and hungry, and it was not until the next day was pretty far advanced that a party of travellers found and liberated them. A hue and cry was raised, and the county was scoured in search of the robbers, but without avail, and the stolen property was never recovered. If the story had ended there it would have been a sore disappointment to the boys' sense of justice, but happily she was able to add that some years after this event several men were hanged for a daring robbery in another part of the county, and before their execution they confessed that they were the men who had robbed the widow in the lonely wayside inn.

While the story was being told it was difficult to decide to which of the parties the recital gave the greatest pleasure – to the boys listening with keen interest, to the old lady seated in their midst with bright eyes and animated countenance, and, evidently, proud of her large and attentive audience, or to her son hearing the oft-told story with new interest and eagerly watching the countenance of the boys to discover the effect on them.

George had a great deal of quiet humour, and a boyish love of fun which often found gratification in the amusing incidents of school life, and which he used to repeat with great zest afterwards. He was in the habit of lecturing to the boys on a Friday afternoon on a variety of subjects: History, the exploits of great men and heroes of antiquity, electricity, astronomy, etc. etc., and these lectures were very popular among his pupils. One afternoon he had been lecturing on chemistry and in illustration of some part of the lecture, had made some carburetted hydrogen gas which was contained in a stoppered bottle. When the lecture was concluded, he told the boys that he was going down to the playground to discharge the gas, but as it had a very offensive smell, he advised them not to follow him. 'I do not forbid your going,' he said, 'but I strongly recommend you to remain here until my return.' He took the bottle down to the playground, 'and,' said he, laughing heartily, 'every boy in the school rushed down to enjoy the smell.'

One morning he was awakened very early by the sound of many voices and footsteps outside his bedroom door, and judging that something unusual had occurred he dressed himself in haste and ran downstairs where a singular sight presented itself. On the grass plot in front of the house and the street all the boys were assembled in their nightshirts, and most of them barefooted, each sitting on a box or a carpet bag. It appeared that an alarm of fire had spread through their bedrooms, and in the panic that ensued they had not waited to dress but each boy had secured what he considered to be his most valuable possession and rushed out of the house waiting and watching for the flames that they expected to burst forth from door and window, and which they were disappointed not to see, for it was only a chimney that had caught fire and it was soon extinguished.

Another story of a different character tickled him greatly and he could never speak of it without laughing. The school became so large that a third assistant was engaged, a very young man, obliging, industrious and amiable, but with some weak points, one of which was an undue regard for personal appearance. He was sedulously cultivating a moustache which at that time was a much less common ornament than it is now. This and other little fopperies attracted the attention and it seems excited the indignations of the boys, though no comments were openly made. One Sunday morning not long after the advent of the unfortunate junior, the master entered the dining room where the boys were assembled waiting to begin breakfast, and glancing round the tables at which they were seated, he saw with amazement that every boy, from the oldest to the youngest, had adorned his upper lip with a moustache. They were very grave and quiet and appeared most innocently unconscious of any wrongdoing, but the whole thing was so absurd that the impulse to laugh was almost irresistible. Controlling himself by a strong effort, the master rebuked them seriously for their unkind and ungentlemanly conduct towards one who was esteemed fit to be their teacher and to whom it was their duty to show respect and then sent them off to their bedrooms to divest themselves of their ornaments. No other punishment was inflicted, the rebuke was sufficient, and that species of practical joking was never repeated.

Music and silent communion with nature were influences that of all others could best soothe and refresh him when over-excited or over-wearied; the last especially was a necessity to him. As a boy his favourite resort on half holidays and summer evenings, whether for play or for reading, was the pleasant fields known as Greetwell, lying to the east of the city, and as long as he remained in Lincoln he found in them ever a new delight. This was especially the case when he was engaged in severe study, the restless energy of his brain communicated itself to his whole body and rendered active exercise an absolute necessity. He was an early riser and began the day by a solitary walk in his favourite fields, and often when more than usually absorbed in intense study, he would repair there again and again through the day. On removing to Ireland, he was at once painfully struck by the absence of field walks, a want which he never ceased to deplore, and which of itself sufficed to make him feel not at home in the country of his adoption. 'I shall never be reconciled,' he used to say, 'to the absence of field walks.' Yet no one was more ready to do full justice to the beautiful scenery of Ireland, and he spoke and wrote enthusiastically of the scenery around Cork and the localities he visited from time to time. His ardent love of nature and his ready perception of the beautiful, under whatever form it presented itself, could not fail to make the wild and grand features of Ireland deeply impressive.

He loved the society of ladies and used to say he could never enjoy parties where ladies were not present, and with ladies almost universally he was a favourite. The awe with which he first commonly inspired them invariably wore away as they discovered how gentle and unpretending and utterly free from pedantry he was, how ready to be interested in their pursuits and pleasures, and to give help and counsel if such were needed, and how entirely in their presence the philosopher was lost in the friend.

He was a steadfast friend, and chose his friends not for their position or attainments but for their moral worth. 'I believe him to be a thoroughly good man' was the verdict most passed on his friends. He was quick to discernment, slow to discover evil or to believe in the shortcomings of others. It was intensely painful to him to have to administer rebuke, to express disapproval, and especially to expose wickedness, but this he never shrank from if he thought duty required it of him.

His friendships were as catholic as his acquirements; he recognised in every man the right to a free exercise of his opinions in matters of religion, and claimed for himself the same freedom of inquiry. He numbered among his most intimate friends at different periods men of the most diverse creeds, Catholics, Unitarians, Methodists, Baptists, Quakers, and though himself a member of the Church of England, and attached to her services, he liked to go occasionally to dissenting places of worship where he could hear the truth preached in simplicity and sincerity. The Rev. John Hannah,[24] a Wesleyan minister, was an especial favourite and when he preached in Lincoln, of which city he was a native, George always went to hear him. While living in Waddington he frequently attended the services at the little Wesleyan and Baptist chapels and always went to the former when a certain local preacher, a shoemaker from a neighbouring village, preached. He was an uneducated man but fond of reading, and he had a flow of simple eloquence that was very attractive to George.

I remember to his being greatly charmed by the preaching of a young woman of the Ranter[25] persuasion at Hornsea afterwards on the Yorkshire coast. From his description of her afterwards, her modesty, her earnestness, and her eloquence, I think she must have borne a close resemblance to Dinah in *Adam Bede*.[26]

This is perhaps the place to speak of his religious views. But I am not prepared to say what he did and did not believe. He made no profession, and rarely talked about religion, yet no one who knew him could fail to be convinced that he was a deeply religious man. He hated cant and hypocrisy and distrusted the sentimental and exciting demonstrations of some of the religious bodies, and he thought the Church of England allowed more latitude to her members than any other church.

It was at one time currently reported that he was a Unitarian and this belief was for a time very prejudicial to his interests; if he was one, it was unknown to his family. His father was a Unitarian and we as children used to accompany him to the little chapel where the body worshipped, but only as children; as we grew up we ceased to do so. I have heard George speak of Unitarians as a highly intellectual body but cold and self-opinionated and priding themselves too much on their morality, yet he was a great admirer of the works of Channing and Martineau, whose books found a place in his library.[27]

He did not like to have religion introduced into common conversation or into novels, but it formed part of his daily life. It was manifested in his ardent love of truth, in his uncompromising rectitude, in his modesty and humility, in his cheerful self-sacrifice when the interests of others required it, in his devotion to duty however painful, in the purity of his spirit that shrank from all that was mean or base in thought, word or deed, in the large loving heart that overflowed in kindness and benefits to all dependent on him, in his ready sympathy with the sorrows and anxieties of others, his tenderness to their faults and weaknesses, and the help rendered to their necessities.

The devotional cast of his mind is evidenced in his poems, many of which were intended for no eye but his own. He was an earnest and loving student of the Scriptures, and knew most of the psalms by heart. He was liberal often beyond his means, and could never resist an appeal for help if he considered the object of it worthy and really in need, but rarely allowed his left hand to know what his right hand did. Besides gifts of money, he lent largely to needy friends and relatives often without expectation of payment. There was one case in which the borrower would return the money at the time fixed, but would ask for it again soon after, and this occurred so often that George became tired. 'I don't think,' he said, 'that I am doing him any real good; I will give him £5 and have done with him.'

One of the men who had been my father's greatest persecutor in the affair of the Mechanics' Institute was, some years after, in very needy circumstances, and George not only gave him a considerable sum of money, but educated and boarded one of his sons for some time free of charge; and although I was the keeper of the cash box and the accounts, I did not know until after he had left Lincoln that he had for some years been allowing £20 yearly to an uncle to whom he was much attached and who from age and infirmity was unable to support himself.[28]

In 1848 his father died. He had been in declining health for a long time, and for more than a year before his death never quitted his bedroom, which however was a very pleasant one, large and light with a cheerful outlook. As long as he was able to do anything, he used to amuse himself by making philosophical toys in which he was adept, but the time soon came when he was almost entirely dependent on others for amusement, and when he was often incapable of being amused. He suffered greatly at times from the chest affection, and in order to enable him to sleep at night his medical attendant administered morphine in small doses. Frequently towards evening when the sedative effect of the medicine had worn off, he was the victim of terrible depression of spirits and when all that my mother and I could do to rouse him was of no avail, I had to fetch George from the schoolroom to try his power of soothing, but even this was sometimes ineffectual, and another small dose of morphia had to be given, which gradually soothed him until the time came for the usual one.

When at length early in the morning of the 12th of December (1848) the summons came that was to free him from his sufferings, it was George who, kneeling by the bedside and holding his father's dying hand, received the last faint pressure that told of recognition, and when all was over he made a solemn promise to be the guardian and protector of those that were left, a promise that he faithfully fulfilled. His love for his father was very great, and he mourned him sincerely, but he restrained his own feelings that he might become his mother's comforter. He devoted himself to her with the utmost tenderness, sat by her, and endeavoured to withdraw her mind from sad thoughts, and when he sent her to bed calmed and cheered by his loving efforts he shut himself up in a darkened room and played solemn music for an hour or two. None but himself knew how much these efforts cost him.

His father had a remarkably beautiful head, in form like the head of Shakespeare, and he had been asked more than once to allow a cast of it to be taken, but he would not submit to it. He lies in the burial ground of St Margaret's – the parish is joined to St Peter's in Eastgate to the south east of the cathedral – and my mother who survived him more than five years, lies beside him. The burial ground is now disused.

Some lines written in 1849 on the anniversary of his father's death, and found soon after his own death in an old pocket book, show how he mourned him and how tenderly he cherished his memory.

Upon one subject, politics, father and son felt little in common. George was not a politician in the strict sense of the word, though always well informed on the current politics of the day. 'Politics is a subject on which I do not generally feel much interest, probably from the situation in which I am placed, and the habits of life to which I have grown accustomed.' And again in 1847 he says, referring to a Liberal meeting:

> There was a meeting of Seely's friends last night in the new market.[29] I went with Mr Brooke, who is a great lover of such things. For a few minutes heard a little of the roar of that wild beast – the people – felt its pressure in my ribs, and came home, leaving Brooke to fill up the measure of his curiosity, and slate his thirst for tumult.

His father, on the contrary, was an ardent politician, a liberal of the liberals, or as some called him, a radical. During the stirring times that preceded and followed the passing of the Reform Bill,[30] party split ran high in Lincoln, where for many years the political and personal interest of the Sibthorps who represented the Conservative interest secured their return to parliament, and the excitement of a contested election operated on all classes.[31]

My father was in the habit of meeting in the evening a little knot of friends of the same politics at the Falstaff Inn which was kept by a personal friend and as he was an excellent reader he was usually selected to read aloud the political articles in the papers while the rest smoked their pipes, drank their glass of beer and gravely discussed the situation. I remember that when we were children our sitting room was adorned by two small black busts of Fox[32] and Sir Francis Burdett.[33] When the latter changed his politics, he was ignominiously expelled by my father from his post of honour on a bracket in the sitting room and placed in the outer office with his face to the wall! [Here the manuscript ends.]

Chapter 3

1849–1855:
HOME AND WORK

THE BOOLE ARCHIVE in University College Cork contains over one hundred and fifty letters written by George Boole to his mother and siblings during the period 1847 to 1854. Most of these letters are addressed to his sister, MaryAnn, with a small number written to his mother, Mary Ann and his brothers, Charles and William. Boole intended that his letters be preserved. In a letter dated 9 January 1850 he wrote:

> I propose to write letters at regular intervals which may be sent to William and Charles, etc. and afterwards preserved as I wish to record my impressions of this country.[34]

His wishes were honoured by MaryAnn, and his correspondence provides an unrivalled view of Boole's early years in Ireland, particularly of his first impressions of Cork and the conditions in which he lived and worked.

George Boole arrived in Cork in late October 1849, as the country was emerging from the ravages of a five-year famine. Boole's first impressions of Cork are recorded in a letter dated 25 October 1849:

> I have at length arrived at the scene of my future labours and have taken what I think will prove comfortable lodgings close by the college. The situation and the prospects around are all that could be desired. The River Lee flows in front of us through a beautiful valley the sides of which are covered with wood in many parts, an unusual sight in Ireland, and with it suburban villas. Cork is, so far as I have yet seen it, a very pleasant and indeed a rather fine city. Like every other large hive of men, it has of course its wretched quarters, abodes of misery and want, but of these I have only heard as yet in Cork. What I have seen presented nothing very repulsive. Neither have I been annoyed by what some so much complain of the importunity of mendicants. The weather is wet and stormy and this may have kept the streets rather freer than they are usually said to be.[35]

Boole was damning in his criticism of Cork in a letter to his brother Charles, written the same week. He remarked that 'I do not like Cork or its climate. The former is dirty, the latter damp and both in extreme.' However, Boole appeared to be warming to his surroundings when he wrote to his mother on 30 October:

I had a delightful walk yesterday afternoon along a road which overlooks the Lee and conducts to, some say, romantic scenery quite equal to the most beautiful parts of Derbyshire and I think on a larger and grander scale.

The house in which I live is surrounded by fields and gardens and the people <u>are clean</u> and really kind as well as attentive. The father is a farmer on a rather large scale and his son who will be a pupil of mine is a most intelligent and amiable youth.[36]

Boole's first lodgings in Cork were with the O'Brien family in Castle White. His landlord was John O'Brien of Castle White House, College Road North.[37] The house was located at the northern edge of the Queen's College Cork campus. He told his mother that the people of the house were clean, kind and honest and that he expected his expenses there to be moderate at £6 per month. He wrote:

Provisions here are very cheap – salmon only 4d per lb, fowls etc. very low indeed in price. Mother would be surprised at some of our customs – turkey with beef, roast goose with roasted bacon, cheese invariably accompanied by butter, etc. Excellent apple tarts but not enough of them.[38]

He had a private sitting room, bedroom and dressing room. He adopted his mother's suggestion of airing the bed every day with a hot water bottle in the moist and damp climate of Cork.

Raymond De Vericour, professor of modern languages, and Francis Albani, registrar of QCC, also resided at Castle White. The professors had a public day once a week on which they each invited a friend to dine with them. In a letter to his brother Charles in November 1849, Boole explained:

I should rather say with us for we of this house 'Castle White' have a common table and invite our guests in common. In our private rooms we are monks, in our common hall coenobites.[39] The members of this little fraternal community are

1. Raymond De Vericour, professor of modern languages (prioure of the order)
2. Francis Albani, registrar of Queen's College Cork, logician and metaphysician (subprioure)
3. George Boole, professor of mathematics (lay brother)

I can at least say for this society that it is a very harmonious one and that its objects are perfectly innocent and lawful.[40]

In January 1850, they were joined at Castle White by Mr Shaw, the professor of natural philosophy.

Boole's friendship with Raymond De Vericour predated his time in Cork. Boole told MaryAnn in November 1849 that De Vericour was 'an unbounded favourite in Cork especially with the ladies whom he has won over by his lectures, his graceful manner and fine person'.[41] He found Mr Albani a 'very amiable and clever man', who was educated at Trinity College Dublin (TCD) and afterwards became a barrister. Mr Albani was very well travelled.[42] He had been an unsuccessful candidate for the professorship of logic in QCC.

Boole's landlord, Mr O'Brien lent him a pianoforte for his room. Boole told MaryAnn:

It is only a tinkling affair but it will do. This is pleasant. Nothing really can exceed the kindness and attention of the whole family. I really do not think that there is anything like it to be found in England except in rare instances. The eldest son is a student in the college.[43]

Boole was very pleased with his colleagues and classes in QCC and appeared to be settling in well. He told his mother:

I have now seen most of my associates here and think them very agreeable men, some of them really very likeable. The president and vice president appear extremely amiable, if anything too soft and gentle in character. These are of course first impressions.[44]

He was free to conduct his classes as he pleased and the vice president, Dr Ryall, told him he was to form his own school of mathematics.[45] He felt that his work would be agreeable and would not place too much of a burden upon him. He described his students as 'nice intelligent lads' but found their standard of attainment lower than he had expected. Hence in November he began working on a scheme for the opening of a schoolmasters' class in QCC, as 'the style of mathematical teaching is wretched'.[46] He subsequently wrote to Augustus De Morgan, professor of mathematics at the University of London, asking his advice on the matter as De Morgan had started a similar scheme in London.[47] He told his brother Charles that he was going to inspect some schools run by the Christian Brothers for the education of the poor, but the letters do not contain any subsequent details of those visits.[48]

In December 1849 Boole reported that everything was going on pleasantly and his classes were 'all that could be desired except in numbers'.[49] On the anniversary of their father's death in December 1849, he wrote to MaryAnn expressing his gratitude for the fortunate circumstances in which they found themselves:

> You know of what event this day is the anniversary. We shall all think of it and feel it not the less because of the changes that have taken place since then. Yet we have so very much to be thankful for – our lot is so much happier than that of the greater part of our fellow creatures (how much the greater part!) that we ought to look to the past events of our lives only to trace God's goodness to ourselves and to draw from them lessons of wisdom for the future.[50]

By Christmas 1849, Boole noted that QCC had fifty-eight students, of whom about forty were studying under him. On his return to Lincoln for the Christmas holiday, Boole warned MaryAnn:

> Tell Mother that for her special gratification I shall bring with me my professor's robes. But don't mention this to anyone as I don't want to be teased by people. I only do it because it may give mother pleasure and from what you say I think she would be disappointed if I did not. I do not like the 'scarlet'.[51]

The reference to the 'scarlet' relates to the scarlet robes worn by the Roman Catholic hierarchy. In an earlier letter to MaryAnn Boole he had explained:

> The robes of the science faculty are faced with scarlet. To so sound a Protestant as I am this is a rather uncongenial colour. It is to be worn during examinations and on all state occasions.[52]

On his return to Cork after Christmas, Boole makes the first reference to a book on logic that he was working on. He asked MaryAnn:

> I believe that I brought home with me and left there that portion of a

book of mine on logic which I had before troubled Mr Collins to send me from Lincoln. If Mathew can find it I should wish him to send it to me by post again.[53]

By January 1850, the number of students had grown to eighty-nine, with about sixty of these in Boole's classes. In February 1850, he wrote:

Our college advances rapidly in public esteem. I am told that we are getting a high name for our teaching – so much the better. We shall need all the support we can get, the Methodists of Ireland have I am told just decided on supporting us. The Catholics are divided – the more moderate faction being with us, the firebrands violently against us. The senate of Queen's University is now being appointed, I am told, but I have not heard the names of the members of it.[54]

A few weeks later he shared his optimism for the future with MaryAnn:

I have every reason to think that this will be a viable institution. I am now quite sure that I am more fully discharging my duties to society than I have ever before been doing. If I had but a family around me I should want for nothing. But I feel very thankful for all the good that has befallen to me, both to enjoy and to do.[55]

The viability of QCC was crucial for Boole on a financial as well as an academic front. His family's finances were directly dependent on the success and popularity of the new college, as professors' salaries were supplemented by class fees paid directly by the students in their classes. Boole had been the breadwinner of the family long before his father's death in 1848 and continued to support his mother and MaryAnn after his arrival in Cork. The pressure to run a school, study and provide for his family must have been a strain. The appointment to the professorship in QCC represented an improvement in the fortunes of the whole family and a relief of part of the burden that Boole had carried for many years.

In the Boole Family History Notebook, Mary Ellen Boole wrote of the financial struggles of her grandparents (John and Mary Ann Boole) due to her grandfather's neglect of his business for scientific pursuits, his imprisonment for debt and the effect this had on their family. Throughout his correspondence with MaryAnn, Boole's desire for honesty and fairness in all matters financial is apparent. During his early months in Cork, he was concerned with closing out his affairs in Lincoln. In January 1850 his friend Mr Collins was acting on his behalf and he told MaryAnn:

I wish him to above all act justly and liberally towards any persons with whom he may have to transact business for me. A little loss of money may easily be made up.[56]

MaryAnn had set about opening a school for young ladies in Lincoln in late 1849. Boole told her she was 'perfectly competent to teach arithmetic' and that her school would be distinguished from others in which ladies are taught by masters. However, by early 1850, he appeared concerned for MaryAnn and told her not to trouble herself with too much work. He advised her to give up the school rather than injure her health. MaryAnn's school does not appear to have been successful and Boole wrote in a letter dated 1 February 1850:

You must not make yourself uneasy about the smallness of your opening. You will get pupils in time I doubt not. If you do not, you will still have the satisfaction of thinking that you tried to make yourself useful – the failure will not then rest with you. Perhaps your ultimate sphere will be in Cork and not in Lincoln.[57]

A letter dated 30 March 1850 showed that the financial responsibility for MaryAnn's school ultimately rested with Boole. He wrote:

I suppose the money will be wanted immediately for the rent, etc. I send a cheque for £30 the receipt of which acknowledge immediately. Let me know how you are going on in pecuniary affairs. I should have sent you £25 for your quarters' allowance if I had known that it was necessary.[58]

Charles Boole also appeared to be reliant on George for money. In December 1850, Boole told MaryAnn:

Charles wrote to ask me to lend him some money, which of course I shall be very happy to do, but he wished it to come by a cheque from you, and in a fictitious name lest the clerks at the bank should suppose that he was needy. I wrote to tell him that I thought all this was weakness and begged him to write at once and give explicit directions to you or me what to do. He has not written to me, has he to you? PO order would be the simplest way, but I am afraid to send it without hearing from him again.[59]

Although Boole was careful with money, he appears to have been very generous in assisting friends and acquaintances financially, perhaps hoping to spare other families the trauma of the problems he grew up with. In a letter to his mother dated March 1850 he asked:

Has MaryAnn heard any more about the Atkinsons? I almost wish that she would make the attempt to raise a little money for them. She might also I think find someone who would be able to direct her as to the best mode of settling them in some little business. Unless something of this kind can be done, their prospect I fear is but a dark one.[60]

He followed up with a letter to MaryAnn, instructing her to set the Atkinsons up in the toy business as the capital required was small. He was willing to finance 'all the pecuniary deficiencies'.[61] In a letter dated 16 March, he told her:

You must go on in your good work for the Atkinsons. It is worth the experiment. Nobody will think any the worse of them if it does not succeed and they need not feel any delicacy about accepting aid. Of course the aid is given, not lent. It will not in any case be expected that the money should be returned.[62]

The letters do not reveal how the Atkinsons' business venture fared. Boole's last word on it was in a letter written to MaryAnn on 14 April 1850 when he told her that their contribution should not be less than one sovereign.[63] However, the same letter shows that Boole had also given loans to other families in financial difficulty. He wrote:

I believe that I have lent Mr Bennet £3 but I have not any memorial I think of the times. It will not therefore I fancy be allowed and indeed I scarcely expected to recover it. If it is allowed I should like it to be given or at least a part of it to the widow. I would not have you be pressing about the matter.

After his return to Cork after Christmas 1849, Boole found that his social life with his fellow professors at Castle White was beginning to interfere with his studies. He explained in January 1850:

> Yesterday evening I was at a soirée given to our body at the house of one of the medical professors and met with very many pleasant people. I have found that a little change of this kind does me good and it is pleasant that Mr De Vericour and Mr Shaw can so often accompany me. I do not feel that I am working so steadily as I ought to and I am beginning to doubt whether living in lodgings is so favourable to the progress of one's studies as I had hoped to find it. Still, I do not allow any day to pass without doing something in addition to my college work. I hope however gradually to form habits of more steady application. I don't think it is so much will that is now wanting as a better arrangement of the times of meals. Dining at 5 or later I lose the evening, which has always been a favourite time with me for mental labour.[64]

Boole found that he was working at his own studies but not in a methodical manner. He told MaryAnn:

> I keep working at my papers and get a great deal done but in a somewhat irregular way. I thought a few days ago that I was idle but I do not think upon serious examination that this is the case. I cannot work so many hours as some people but I get more done in a given time when I am engaged.[65]

He was determined to make good use of the extra leisure time he now had:

> I must endeavour to get up early in the morning and make use of the hours which I at present spend in sleep or sloth. Time seems to fleet rapidly by and nothing to be done.[66]

In March 1850, Boole moved to the house of the Misses Knowles in Strawberry Hill, Sunday's Well. This was about one and a half miles further from the college, located on a hill at the northern side of the River Lee. He told MaryAnn:

I did not reply to your letter yesterday because I wished to write to you from my lodgings to which I had removed this morning. You will be surprised at the change. I have contemplated it some time not on account of any dissatisfaction with my old ones or with the family but because I found that I was not getting on with my work – that too much time was taken up visiting and receiving visits, in conversations pleasant but unprofitable and in loitering over a variety of books in my room without steadily pursuing any one subject. I hope to change all this now that I have got out of the fascinations of the Castle White society. My rooms are extremely pleasant and command an almost unrivalled prospect. Before the window of the sitting room stretches a very well-kept orderly garden down the hill. The aspect is southern, in which respect my new lodgings have the advantage over the old ones, which faced the north, the family with which I am lodging consists of three sisters middle aged and apparently very intelligent and respectable, well spoken of by those who know them. The house is very clean and sweet and everything about it betokens care and good economy. These are virtues which do not generally thrive in the soil of Cork.[67]

Boole intended to keep dining with his colleagues at Castle White once or twice per week but only when he felt he had earned this indulgence following hard work. He felt he would accomplish more in Strawberry Hill with less divided attention. He described the location of his new lodgings as 'one of the most enviable little spots in the neighbourhood of Cork'. He felt that nothing could exceed the kindness of his landladies. The lodgings cost fifteen shillings per week, in addition to which Boole paid for coal and candles. However, he would not be charged during the long summer holiday and found this to be a reasonable arrangement.[68]

Hints of loneliness due to separation from his family are discernible in his letters around this time. He chided MaryAnn for allowing a fortnight to elapse without sending him a letter from home.[69] In another letter he urged her to write regularly as every matter concerning her was important to him, saying that 'mere gossip is interesting'.[70] Boole told MaryAnn of his correspondence with his brothers:

I have heard from William and from Charles. William's letter was all about Eliza, quite a pattern letter for an affectionate husband. I am sincerely rejoiced to think that they are so happy.[71]

William and his wife Eliza had a son, Walter John, in March 1850.

Boole's loneliness is also echoed in a letter he wrote to his mother from Strawberry Hill in Cork in March 1850:

> I have just been standing at the window looking over the fair valley below which stretches before me and at the stars which are just beginning to show themselves here and there like little lamps in Heaven and thinking how pleasant it would be if you and MaryAnn were with me to enjoy the scene and enhance its pleasures by sympathy. Ah would you were! But why wish for what cannot be. Enough have we to be thankful for. If there were few around us in Lincoln who seemed to us to be in circumstances so happy as our own how much fewer are there here, how much fewer in the world at large. However much I regret the loss of your society and MaryAnn's, yet I cannot but feel that my position in all essential respects a more desirable one than that which I before occupied. My present duties certainly do not interfere with my health. The freedom from the anxieties of a school, light as to me they comparatively were during the last few years of my residence in Lincoln, is of itself a great means of health and comfort and in addition to all this I meet with great and real kindness here.[72]

In the same month, Boole told MaryAnn that he had heard from a variety of sources that his classes were among the most popular with the students in the college.[73] In addition to his regular lectures on mathematics, it was decided in April that he should also take on the teaching of astronomy. Boole was pleased with this as he felt it would give an additional interest to his usual lectures. In the same month, he did not attend a public dinner in honour of the president, Sir Robert Kane, as he was on holiday in Ballycotton for the week, and also missed a dinner at the home of Major Ludlow Beamish, one of the local magistrates. He told MaryAnn:

> It is really a pleasure to escape these things. I am obliged to people who invite me but I am resolved not to sacrifice my quiet comfort and self-respect, together with the hopes of real distinction, to the demands of society.[74]

As the first academic year of QCC drew to a close in May 1850, he wrote:

I am going on very comfortably working hard during the day and seeing a little company in the evening. Sometimes I ask a few of the students to breakfast with me. I like to have the young about me. Nothing can be more agreeable to me than my duties. They are exciting and I feel fully master of them and know that my labors are appreciated. Thus I live on the best terms with my pupils and on the best terms also with my colleagues in the college.[75]

In July 1850, Boole visited Augustus De Morgan in London. He told MaryAnn that he was resigned to a solitary life devoted to scholarship:

As to myself, I feel more and more devoted to a life of science and my recent holyday will I hope only send me back to my old pursuits with greater ardour. I have such great objects to work for both in the prosecution of my own studies and in my college work that I do not think I am likely to complain of the dullness of a solitary life. De Morgan was urgent with me to publish some of my speculations without delay.[76]

Boole often appeared worried about his sister's welfare. He was concerned that she was confined at home looking after her mother and stressed that recreation was necessary for her.[77] He wrote to her while she was on holiday in August 1850:

You must consider it your duty now you are all together to be happy, and everything like dullness, moping or melancholy must be considered not simply as misfortune but as an offence – a violation of the social contract, an invasion of the rights of your fellow citizens and subjects in the community whose kingdom extends over Mrs Forge's parlour and garden – as in short I am overpowered with the rash of thoughts which come upon me while meditating upon the enormity of the crime against which I once for all lift up my solemn protest.[78]

In a postscript to another letter in 1851, he added:

I have been thinking whether an occasional ride in a pony carriage would not do you and mother good. Ask Mr Collins about it and let me know. I think it might be accomplished without much trouble. The expenses here are small. The proper way would be to have the carriage and pony kept at Mr Leversedge's and engage someone to drive it. The spring is coming on and you might I suppose have a good deal of enjoyment in this way. Remember I should not mind the expense at all.[79]

During the summer vacation of 1850, Boole's friend and colleague Mr De Vericour had published a book entitled *An Historical Analysis of Christian Civilisation*. De Vericour's book was critical of the papacy's involvement in secular affairs and it was placed on the Catholic Church's list of forbidden books. What proved controversial was that De Vericour had written 'Queen's College Cork' underneath his name on the title page. He also recommended the book as a textbook for history students. As a result, De Vericour was suspended from his professorship in July 1850 and from the deanship of the Faculty of Arts which he was due to hold for the next session. In Lincoln, Boole wrote to MaryAnn on 14 August 1850:

> This morning I heard from De Vericour. He is as you may suppose much grieved and surprised at the charges against him … I have heard also from Sir Robert Kane. He says that De Vericour was not censured for the contents of his book but from connecting it with the college. He expressed himself as very sorry for the necessity.
>
> I hope that matters will yet end well. I shall write to them both today and try to mediate between them.[80]

De Vericour was subsequently re-instated as professor of modern languages but did not take up the deanship.

On 22 August 1850, Cardinal Paul Cullen, the newly appointed Archbishop of Armagh and Primate of Ireland convened the Synod of Thurles. This was the first synod of the Catholic hierarchy in Ireland held since the Middle Ages. The Queen's Colleges at Belfast, Cork and Galway were formally condemned at the synod and the laity was warned to shun the colleges as 'being dangerous to their faith and morals'.[81] Up to Thurles, the bishops had not condemned the colleges outright but had insisted that Roman Catholic students could not attend lectures in history, logic, metaphysics, moral philosophy, or anatomy unless those subjects were taught by Roman Catholic professors. Sir Robert Kane and Dr Denis Bullen were the only two Catholic professors on the academic staff of twenty-one.

Boole returned to Cork on 14 October 1850, crossing the Irish Sea from Holyhead to Dublin. The events of the summer in Ireland had taken a toll.

On his train journey from Dublin to Cork he met a student at Limerick Junction who told him that the college had been denounced from the altar and that as a result he was afraid to return to QCC. In early November, Boole told MaryAnn:

> I have now had a week's lecturing and I am sorry to say that although the total number of students in the college is greater than it was during the last session, yet my own classes are smaller, the increase having taken place in the medical school and the number of entries in the Faculty of Arts being not sufficient to make up for the withdrawals which whether through fear or from some other motive have taken place. There is one advantage attending small classes that they involve the teacher in less anxiety of mind than would larger ones. This is the compensation which I must weigh against diminished fees.[82]

In the same letter, Boole was critical of Sir Robert Kane:

> You will probably have seen or heard something of our president's address which has been praised in the *Times* newspaper. It was generally thought by the professors to be too much exclusively occupied with Catholic questions to the almost total exclusion of another faith either in the college or out of it. I believe that he will get a hint that the principle of religious equality must be respected in appearance as well as in fact.

Boole was referring to the address delivered at the annual prizegiving ceremony in 1850. The president was angry at the refusal of two Catholic bishops to join the Triennial Visitation Committee, a board of independent visitors who were appointed to report on the running of the college. Kane had asked:

> Was it the influence of infidel instruction that induced the Roman Catholic students of this college to fulfil their strictest religious duties in a proportion as had been almost unknown among young men of similar ages? Are these the results of 'Godless colleges'?[83]

Kane proceeded to produce a list of eight Catholic bishops who thought that the Queen's Colleges deserved a fair trial.

Boole began to seriously consider a position at another university. The University of Manchester was seeking a professor of mathematics. James Heywood, the Unitarian MP for North Lancashire, wrote to Richard Dowden in Cork inquiring about Boole. Dowden was a well-connected Cork businessman and was Lord Mayor of Cork in 1845. A Unitarian, he was closely involved with numerous philanthropic and scientific bodies including the Royal Cork Institution and Cork Cuvierian Society. He was a close friend of the Jennings family, who were also friends of Boole. Boole acquired a copy of the letter and transcribed it for MaryAnn:

Extract from a letter addressed by Jas. Heywood Esquire MP of Manchester to R. Dowden (Rd) Cork

'One of your professors in that College Mr Boole is I hear an admirable teacher of mathematics. Perhaps you can inform me where he was educated, whether he is of Dublin for instance or Edinburgh or Cambridge. His name has recently been mentioned as a gentleman who would do well as a professor of mathematics at £350 per annum and 2/3rds of the fees from students. I do not know what the professors receive in Queen's College Cork; if their salaries amount to £300 or £400 per annum besides fees, it would hardly be worth his while to think of Manchester – only he is said to be a very good teacher.'

Boole added this comment:

My dear sister,

I have thought the above worth notice. Let me know your opinion by return of post. There would be more work in Manchester than here but much better pay and it is within three or four hours of Lincoln.[84]

A week later, Boole reflected on his options to MaryAnn:

With respect to the Manchester opening, something may be said on both sides. In favour of remaining in Cork the reasons are these.

1st That the work is comparatively light – two hours lecturing in the morning (on Saturdays one hour) leaves me the greater part of the day to my own pursuits. I can without peril to my health and comfort accomplish quite as much work in addition to my college duties as if I had them not to attend to. I live too in pure country air which appears to suit my health well and have made here some kind and valuable friends. The students are steady and attentive and appear to be attached to me and I enjoy the good opinion and the friendship of all my colleagues and of the president and vice-president, more particularly the latter, who treats me with marked esteem and kindness.

In favour of Manchester are 1st The pecuniary advantages which will certainly be great. It is probable that the income will be greater by £250 or £300 per annum than in Cork. 2ndly The circumstances that Manchester is in England, that by railways one can get from it into the country in all directions and that it is within a few hours of Lincoln. 3rdly That it is a great centre of life and intellectual activity and that the very same course of conduct which has secured me some measure of friendship and respect here, would be likely to do the same through a larger and wider sphere.

The salary here, with fees, is not likely to exceed £300 a year for some time to come. It is never likely I fear to exceed £350 a year. The ill-feeling which is springing up between Protestant and Catholic in England will be likely to affect our success here very much.

The only public amusement that I care for, an oratorio, is a weekly event in Manchester. Here it is rare and never well performed for want of organ and space.

I should have no doubt of succeeding in Manchester. I have paid great attention to method in the teaching of mathematics and know that my labors have given satisfaction both to the students and the authorities of the college. I think I may venture to say that I have acquired the habit of working steadily and systematically without overworking myself and this is of inestimable importance.

I am disposed to think that the high view of the question would be to remain for the present where I am <u>certain</u> of discharging my duties well, certain also of possessing leisure and opportunity for those pursuits upon which my ultimate position in the world should I live and my reputation afterwards will depend. I feel too that I owe some gratitude to those who took me on the strength of my testimonials alone and were willing to overlook the fact that I had never been at a college before.[85]

The higher Manchester salary was clearly tempting for Boole but his growing affection for Cork and his colleagues and students at QCC, plus his satisfaction with his work–life balance, outweighed the financial attraction of Manchester. His belief that the Cork position would allow him to carry out the work that his reputation would afterwards depend on was prophetic. Heywood had assumed in his letter of inquiry to Dowden that Boole had been educated at one of the leading universities of the day. Boole would have been sensitive to this incorrect assumption on Heywood's part and was grateful to have been appointed in QCC, despite his lack of a formal qualification. On 21 November 1850, he told MaryAnn:

> I just write to say that I am to remain here. I addressed a letter to Mr Heywood but did not do more in it than make inquiries upon points which seemed to me of essential importance, such as the nature and extent of the duties, the length of the vacations, etc. and I had a reply last night telling me that they had just appointed a Cambridge gentleman, a Mr Sandeman. It was relief to me to hear this. I had decided or nearly so not to accept the offer if directly made to me. For at present I must have leisure for my own pursuits and no situation of the kind in the kingdom could give me more than my present one. All here seem very much pleased at my staying and I feel that it will be best in the end.[86]

The ill-feeling that Boole had referred to between Protestants and Catholics in England related to the re-establishment of the Catholic hierarchy in England for the first time since the reign of Mary Tudor (1555–8). Boole had asked MaryAnn in an earlier letter in November how the 'popish invasion' was received in Lincoln.[87] He told her that there was in Ireland 'no burning of popes in effigy, no walking of processions in honor of the good old constitutional principles of 1688'. In early December, he referred to it again:

> The papal aggression has excited some feeling among Protestants here but not so much as in England. The Catholics are much divided about it. The violent party are more violent than ever but I see nothing of them. I only judge from an occasional sight of the newspapers. There has never been much of Puseyism in the Irish church, nor has there been much hostility between the establishment and sects of Protestant dissenters here, so that matters are on the whole more quiet and peaceful than one could have expected. Some Catholics I am told disapprove strongly of the papal proceeding. The Synod of Thurles gave great disgust to the more moderate members of the Romish church and this has prevented that

warm feeling from being general among the body which undoubtedly exists in the bosums of many.[88]

In the same letter, Boole told MaryAnn that he was happy with his classes and had heard that his teaching was approved of by his students. He was lecturing on differential calculus to his senior class. He was pleased with his own studies and wrote:

I am I hope improving in the habit of steady (not excessive) application to my studies and hope to carry out literally Melanchthus' maxim 'Nulla dies sine linea'.[89] You must make out this bit of Latin yourself.[90]

By this time, life had settled into a pattern for Boole. He enjoyed playing music in his free time but again hinted at his loneliness when he wrote:

All goes on in the usual monotonous way. I give my lectures, read, write, take a long walk occasionally and once or twice a week go out to tea. This is very much the history of my life from week to week. I think that upon the whole I have worked rather too hard of late but living entirely alone I should suffer more from dullness without it. The pianoforte is in some measure a relief but it would be better with someone else to listen to and to be listened to.[91]

He told MaryAnn:

I have just bought a pianoforte – a very nice one indeed, cottage, sweet toned with a very good touch and the case rosewood, price 20 guineas. It was a second-hand instrument but had been little used. I think it very cheap. You must send me some music.[92]

On several occasions Boole requested that MaryAnn send him over music, including Mozart's *Agnus Dei* [93] and the *Gloria in Excelsis* by Haydn.[94] He seemed confident about his musical abilities:

The music you sent me was very welcome and affords me much pleasure. I think that I can without much difficulty learn to play any of the pieces after a certain fashion of my own, differing in some respects from that sanctioned by some authorities as Dickson and Westland, etc.[95]

A few months later he complained to his mother that he was disappointed at seeing so little in his music book apart from 'old trash' which he had worn threadbare from playing.[96] Boole was also interested in hearing music performed and seems especially taken with religious choral music.

Boole's concerns about money continued to be a regular topic in his letters to MaryAnn. In several letters, he mentions not being able to afford to travel home to Lincoln for Christmas or Easter holidays. In the new college year which commenced in October 1850, he calculated his income for the year would be about £300, but again would be determined by how many students came in the second entrance for the year. MaryAnn appeared to have been pushing her brother on the matter and he told her firmly in November 1850:

> P.S. The authorities of this College have not the power of altering the arrangement of fees and stipend. It is not worthwhile to think any more about it.[97]

Boole urged MaryAnn to visit him in Cork. His invitation must have been tempting for his sister, who was at home in Lincoln looking after their elderly mother. He wrote:

> I now wish to invite you to visit me. As mother is so much better she may I think spare you, and the weather being cold in England a change of air would I think do you good. Here we have days of the most lovely character about thrice a week. Were you here you might reckon on getting rid of all your colds and rheumatisms at once. You might have almost daily an excursion into the country and see, which you have never done before, the grass as green in December as in April. You would meet with pleasant society and go back enlarged in experience and in acquaintances.[98]

Boole remained in Ireland for Christmas 1850 to avoid a 'wearisome and expensive journey' which he could not afford. He spent Christmas night with the Bullens and dined at Sir Robert Kane's house on New Year's Eve.[99] In a letter written on New Year's Eve, it was clear that his mother was not pleased at the prospect of MaryAnn visiting Cork. Boole appeared annoyed and was unusually critical:

As I cannot but think that a visit here even at the present season would do you great good, I am sorry that you cannot come. However, I shall hope to see you here in the spring. That mother should have every comfort that can be supplied to her in her declining years is my most anxious wish but I am not willing that you should be excluded from those innocent enjoyments which are proper to your age and necessary to your health. And I think that mother when she comes calmly to reflect upon it will see that there is no real and solid reason why you should not pay me a visit in the spring. I shall be perfectly willing to remunerate Mrs Lilly for her trouble in your absence.

I was sorry to hear that mother still gives way to that unhappy practice of declaring that she has lived too long when things do not exactly tally with her wishes. Tell her that I think it very weak and sinful and that I earnestly hope she will lay it aside and cultivate a more patient spirit.[100]

MaryAnn finally made her first trip to Cork in early 1852.

In January 1851 Boole calculated that the amount he would earn from fees would not exceed £40, making a total income of about £290 for the year. In another letter written on 23 January 1851, Boole told MaryAnn to keep a 'very exact account of the expenditure'. The income from QCC should be enough and there would not be a need for 'retrenchment', but the only way he could see of increasing his income was to take in boarders. Despite his concerns about money, he continued to be a generous benefactor under more pleasant circumstances. In February 1851 he made the following request to his mother:

Will you be good enough to give Mr Martin five shillings on my account to his little boy newly come into the world and called I am told after me. I have given him the same at the birth of each of his children to be put for them with the Savings Bank.[101]

Boole was by now concerned about the college's prospects for success. He wrote:

There has been grievous mismanagement of which we are reaping the fruits now. Our hope of revival was in getting a good senate appointed. We were anxious to have some of the great names in science and literature upon it. That miserable Lord John was afraid of offending the Dublin doctors and lawyers and he has given us a batch of them to rule over us. This was a Whig job, then there was an architect's job and a president's job and it is well if we survive it all. This of course to you.[102]

Boole was referring to Lord John Russell, the prime minister, who led the Whig government between July 1846 and February 1852. Nevertheless, he still believed that Cork was the best option for him at that point in time. He told MaryAnn on 27 January 1851:

Do not disturb yourself about the income. We shall have enough I am sure. My expenses here are moderate and it is a great comfort to me to think that my income can be so well employed as in making you and mother comfortable. There is a probability that I may get some better appointment in the end. In the meanwhile, this is the very best place for study and I have made I hope good use of it.[103]

He continued the letter:

You must not complain of the shortness of my letters — I have really a great deal of work on hand. I sent off a paper to Cambridge for the *Journal*.[104] This week I am writing another and I have two papers sent to me by the Editor for examination and also a little work to revise at the request of the Bishop of Cork.[105] Beside what I mention I have, since I came, written nearly 200 pages of my book on logic.[106]

In January, Boole sent MaryAnn a letter from William which detailed William's move from Derbyshire to Cheshire, having found a new teaching position there. Boole hoped that the climate in Cheshire would suit his sister-in-law Eliza better.[107] However, in February Eliza died. The circumstances are not clear, but Boole appears very angry at his brother for leaving his wife at the time of her death. He wrote to MaryAnn as follows:

William wrote to me on his way to Lincoln and I was deeply sorry to hear the sad intelligence. I wrote to him intending to offer him money if he was in want of it but destroyed the letter feeling indignant at his leaving his poor wife at the last. If she recovered her senses as is usually the case before death what must her sensations have been at finding herself deserted. In his circumstances too to throw away money upon travelling when a letter would have told all. It is worse than thoughtlessness. If he wants money I will beg you to send him some and I will remit the amount to you but I will not write to him.[108]

In the same letter, he refers again to sending money to Charles:

I am going this afternoon to send £5 to Charles for which he has written to me. This makes £25.[109]

Within a few days, Boole had received a letter from William explaining the circumstances of his leaving Eliza on her deathbed. He told MaryAnn:

William wrote to me this morning explaining the cause of his leaving her. I do not think the reasons he alleges a justification of his conduct but it would be unkind to revert to it and I shall therefore not mention it when I write to him. I promised him a sovereign some time ago. Will you send him anything more if he needs it which you will gather from his letters.[110]

After a few weeks, Boole's attitude had softened and he told his mother on 27 February 1851:

I wrote to William yesterday. Poor fellow he has sustained a great loss in the death of his Eliza but I trust that he will soon in the discharge of his duties recover his peace and serenity of mind. He seems to have fallen among really kind people. This is a great comfort and I should think that the melancholy circumstances of his entrance among them will induce them to show him what friendly attentions they can for a long time to come.[111]

Meanwhile, Boole reported that college life went on 'quietly and pleasantly enough'. In a letter to his mother in February 1851, he wrote happily of his colleagues and students and described the craze in Cork that was occupying the minds of both staff and students at QCC:

I am going today to dine at the vice president's although I have scarcely time to do so being extremely busy with college and extra college work. My classes, which are a little larger than I expected that they would be, require a good deal of attention – but it is a very agreeable species of work to instruct them. Nothing can exceed the attention and good order of the students and I think their progress on the whole highly satisfactory.

Mr De Vericour is very well and desires to be kindly remembered. E. Larken is also well, he has been busy like every other idle gent in Cork in making conundrums for the Wizard of the North, a great conjurer who has offered a prize of a gold watch value £21 to the maker of the best. Some of the attempts which I have heard in this line are truly atrocious – not to be endured by gods or men. I heard however a very witty one from a professor which however should it gain the prize will not I fear benefit its learned author as he will scarcely dare to send in his name.[112]

'The Wizard of the North' was the stage name of John Henry Anderson, a Scottish professional magician who later inspired Harry Houdini. Anderson travelled through Europe, North America and Australia with his show in the late 1840s and early 1850s.

Life in Cork had settled into a rhythm for Boole which he described in a letter to MaryAnn in March 1851:

There is so little variety in my life here that I scarcely know how to find materials for a letter. An hour or two of lecturing in the morning, a walk, then examining papers at home and reading or writing or a little music make up the history of my day from week to week. Occasionally I go out to dine or to spend the evening in company, but there would be nothing very interesting in the details of these evenings. One of my best companions here is Mr Nicoll the professor of geology, a man of very various acquirements and above all a man of sense and principle. He has lived in Germany and is well versed in the philosophical literature of that country.

This forms a point of union between us, as my own speculations on logic etc. upon which I am still engaged render any conversation on such topics with a man of thought and information interesting. Mr Nicoll is a Scotchman and he has a nice little Scotch wife who is very much given to laughing and makes other people indulge in the same wholesome exercise. They live not far from my present residence and I have an invitation to go to tea with them whenever I like and of this I gladly avail myself.[113]

The visits to the Nicolls were appealing to Boole for several reasons; they gave him an opportunity to discuss his thoughts on logic but they also provided friendship for a man who seemed to be longing for companionship. Around this time, Boole was himself reading a good deal of German and found he was becoming very familiar with the language which he liked 'exceedingly'.[114]

However, the storm clouds were gathering again in QCC. Boole told MaryAnn:

> We have had a little dissension in the college lately between some of the professors and the council upon different questions partly of college discipline and partly relating to the interest of one of the body who is absent and who a short time ago under a misapprehension as to the nature of his duties resigned his professorship (Celtic Languages) but now desires to withdraw his resignation … I am thankful to be able to say that I have, although not entirely inactive in these movements, been on good terms with all parties. And thus I hope to continue to live.[115]

A dispute had arisen between Christopher Lane, professor of civil engineering and Sir Robert Kane when the latter complained to the Lord Lieutenant that Lane had neglected his duties by failing to give his students an adequate number of field trips and classes of practical instruction in the use of surveying instruments and map-making.[116] The dissension between the president and Lane dragged on, and Lane eventually resigned in April 1853. However, Boole appears to be referring to a different dispute, between Owen Connellan, QCC's second professor of celtic languages, and Sir Robert Kane.

By the end of March 1851, Boole told MaryAnn that college was more peaceful internally than it had been some time previously. His classes were going 'extremely well' and he was scheduled to teach physical astronomy at the start of the next session. He feared that he would be made Dean of the Science Division of the Faculty of Arts in the next academic year. This would involve sitting on the College Council, which would increase his workload and presumably drag him further into college politics.[117] He was duly elected to the deanship in May 1851.

Boole spent the Easter vacation in Cork. In a letter to MaryAnn written in April 1851, he slipped in a reference to a young lady he had met for the first time:

I must thank you for the news which you have so industriously collected for me. It is very pleasant to hear about Lincoln and Lincoln people ...

You never sent me the music for which I last wrote. The Haydn I particularly want; the *Gloria in Excelsis* which you play. I rather think it is arranged to the *And Glory be to God on High*. I have improved since I got a piano and believe that I could play it with a little practice. There is a young lady visiting at Dr Ryall's who plays very well indeed – a Miss Everest from Gloucestershire with whose father I made the excursion to Killarney.

I don't think I have any news to tell you ...[118]

This was Boole's first reference to his future wife, Mary Everest. Miss Everest's mother, also called Mary Everest, was the sister of Dr Ryall, the vice president. Her father, Thomas Roupell Everest, was the Vicar of Wickwar in Gloucestershire. The family lived in France between 1837 and 1843 after Thomas became the victim of an influenza epidemic. Thomas Everest had a strong interest in homeopathy, mesmerism and clairvoyance and moved to France to be close to Samuel Hahnemann, who is considered to be the father of homeopathy. He was a friend of the Cambridge mathematicians Babbage and Herschel and his daughter Mary was also interested in mathematics. In June 1850, Boole had gone on a trip to Killarney with Dr Ryall and the Rev. Everest.[119] The next mention of Miss Everest in Boole's letters to MaryAnn was not for another year after that.

Religious controversy was never far from QCC, and it had erupted again in May 1851. Boole wrote to MaryAnn on 23 May:

The Catholic university is to be opened it is said in November and MacHale is reported to have carried all his points at Rome. Our colleges are formally condemned by the Pope and they are only waiting the opportunity to thunder at us with the greater effect. Probably most of the Roman Catholic students will leave us but that remains to be seen. At present I am sure that the bulk of the laity are friendly to us and that we have but few enemies among them out of MacHale's immediate party. But what can they do when their church commands. They must obey or quit her communion. In one respect I am not sorry for all of this. It will bring matters to a crisis. Rome must be resisted in the end and then her insolence will hasten it.[120]

Archbishop John MacHale of Tuam had been a vocal opponent of the concept of 'mixed education' from the inception of the Queen's Colleges. He had warned Robert Peel, even before the constitution of the colleges was made public that, 'nothing but separate grants for separate education will ever give satisfaction to the Catholics of Ireland'.[121] MacHale had driven the decrees of the Synod of Thurles and they were approved in Rome in 1851. The hierarchy decided to set up a Catholic university. This placed Kane in a very difficult position, given that he was a Catholic.

Very few letters to MaryAnn survive from the period June 1851 to January 1852. In early 1852 Boole moved to new lodgings. It is not clear from his letters why he left Strawberry Hill. By May 1852, he was living in 5 Grenville Place, a townhouse beside the northern channel of the River Lee, closer to the city centre than Strawberry Hill and about a half mile distant from QCC. The preface of *The Laws of Thought* dated 30 November 1853 was addressed from Grenville Place. Boole's landlord was Mr Unkles, a Cork merchant. Boole lived with the family and appeared to be fond of the children. He told MaryAnn in May 1852:

> Mr and Mrs Unkles and the children are quite well. I took breakfast with them this morning and shall have the little folks in to read and perhaps take tea with me this evening. Next Wednesday if it is fine I propose to take them down the river.[122]

In QCC, frustration with Kane was growing, partly due to his management style and partly due to his failure to relocate to Cork. On 25 January 1852 Boole wrote that he had not heard from Sir Robert Kane, and nor had anyone else as far as he could learn.[123] In February 1852, Boole went to Dublin to be conferred with an honorary Doctor of Laws (LL.D.) by Trinity College.[124] While in Dublin, he met with Sir Robert Kane. He wrote:

> I am happy that my visit to Dublin is I trust likely to be productive of some good effects in our college as I had an interview with Sir R. Kane which will I trust lead to an amicable adjustment of some of our differences.[125]

Boole's optimism was short-lived as yet another controversy erupted in March 1852. A dispute arose as to whether Professor Benjamin Alcock, professor of anatomy and physiology, should have control over the Department of Practical Anatomy.

In May 1852, the first triennial visitation of the college took place. This was a visit by an independent board of six, chaired by Dr Whately, the Archbishop of Dublin. When he inquired as to whether any professor of the college had a complaint to make, Professor Boole said he had a memorial to present on behalf of some members of the Faculty of Medicine which was effectively a complaint against the president.

The issue that Boole presented related to the title and role of Dr Alcock, who denied the authority of the council to appoint an officer subject to their control, but who was to be paid from his fees.[126] The visitors found it to be a difficult case as it appeared there had been omissions in the framing of the statutes of the college. They were unanimous in the belief that the council had not acted with a view to creating any personal injury to any individual professor but had acted to regularise arrangements for the study of the practical anatomy.

Boole was disappointed with the outcome, although he was pleased that it ended on peaceful terms. He told MaryAnn:

Our visitation is over – Alcock carried his point, but our cause which came on after was lost. I shall send you a newspaper. The whole business was far more amicable than was expected. Yesterday I dined at Sir R. Kane's and today with the Bishop. Whately present on both occasions, a very great talker indeed.[127]

Boole elaborated further on the findings in a letter written to MaryAnn two days later:

I have reason to believe that the visitors were pleased with the way in which I brought the affair before them. I don't think the college can suffer much from the publication of the affair. At any rate it was unavoidable.[128]

As the college year drew to a close, Boole wrote to MaryAnn on 30 May, saying that all was quiet in QCC but he thought that was not likely to be 'a permanent quiet'.[129] However, he was relieved to be off the council and planned to confine himself to his lectures and studies in the coming academic year 1852–3. At the end of May, he received a copy of a new book by Sir William Hamilton of Edinburgh, which he told MaryAnn referred to his work 'once or twice in a complimentary way'.[130]

In May 1852, Boole wrote that Mr Everest had invited him to spend a few days with him in Wickwar on the way home from Cork to Lincoln.[131] On 20 July, he told his mother that Mr and Mrs Everest were very kind and hospitable and he was partly repaying their kindness by teaching 'a fine youth' who was home for the school holidays.[132] His stay appears to have been extended as he explained in a letter from Tintern in Wales to MaryAnn dated 31 July:

> I am sorry that I cannot be with you; as I found my health improves almost daily, it seemed to me worthwhile to stay a little longer in the neighbourhood. This morning I set out with George Everest (Mr Everest's only son) to explore the Wye between Chepstow and Ross. I am now as you will see at Tintern and am waiting the rising of the moon for a visit to the ruins of the abbey. I propose walking up by easy stages to Ross. Hence taking a coach to Wickwar and remaining there a day in the middle of the week to meet Dr and Mrs Ryall and then setting out for home.[133]

He does not, however, mention Miss Everest in the letter.

Boole visited the Everest family again in September 1852 and also visited Augustus De Morgan with whom he discussed his forthcoming book on logic:

> I stayed with him till after eleven o'clock and had a great deal of pleasant talk with him and his wife. According to our calculations my book will not cost me more than £100 in publication and he is fully of the opinion that I shall get it all back in a few years from the sales. I am going to see Taylor and Walton today on the subject. De Morgan may also get me some private information which may be of service.[134]

John Taylor and James Walton were partners as publishers and booksellers to the University of London, where De Morgan taught.

In January 1853, Boole again visited Wickwar. He travelled there on his journey back to Ireland after the Christmas break. He told MaryAnn:

> I just write to say that I got here safely yesterday morning and that I intend to set out tomorrow for Chester in the afternoon and spend Sunday with Dr Bury. I am enjoying my visit here very much though the weather is on the whole wet. It is a very delightful family to visit.[135]

In February 1853, Boole gave the next glimpse of QCC politics. He referred to the health of the vice president Dr Ryall in a letter to MaryAnn:

> Dr Ryall has not been and is not well. I think he is harassed with college dissensions which under Sir R.K. I am fully persuaded never will cease. Happily, most happily I am off the council.[136]

At this time, Boole was busy completing his manuscript for his book. He told MaryAnn:

> I scarcely go into company at all except to Dr Ryall's and the Jennings, being most constantly occupied chiefly with my book which is going on very well I think. I mean to get a large part of the MSS sent off to press in a short time.[137]

One week later he wrote that his work on the book kept him going. It most likely provided a welcome distraction from the issues in QCC:

> My book is going on fast. It will be in the press in a month's time and will be out I trust in the summer. I should scarcely be able to get on here without it.[138]

By early March 1853, the situation in QCC had deteriorated and Boole began to consider leaving, following the example of his friend and colleague Mr Nicoll:

> Our college differences are again before the government, having unanimously appealed against the arbitrary conduct of the president under whom I am more and more convinced the college can never flourish. I begin to think more seriously of getting out of it. Mr Nicoll has just got an appointment to a chair in Aberdeen where I hope he will enjoy peace and freedom. He will be regretted here – I am going to give a tea party in his honor this week.[139]

In a letter dated 20 March, Boole was pessimistic about the difficulties the college faced:

The affairs of our college are really I think critical. The local newspapers have now taken it up and I think the government cannot pass the matter over. I will send you a document which will tell you something of what has taken place. Dr Ryall is going up to Dublin to have an interview with the viceroy and I think this must do good. His very look and message will convey the impression that he is an honest and truthful man. But in Ireland there exist chances in favour of politic knavery which do not exist on the other side of the Channel and I am far from sanguine as to the issue.[140]

A series of letters was published in the *Cork Examiner* in March 1853, from Sir Robert Kane, Dr Alcock, the Under Secretary for Ireland Thomas Larcom, and from a Dr N.J. Hobart who had been removed from his position in QCC.[141] Boole told MaryAnn that Dr Ryall was seeking clarification of his statutory position and Professor Alcock may have been seeking the same, given the controversy of the previous year over the control of the Department of Practical Anatomy. Despite the 'vexing disquietness' of the position of QCC, Boole was happy that the teaching and discipline at the college were never better.[142]

The *Cork Examiner* reproduced a damning excerpt from the *Dublin Evening Mail* on 1 April 1853:

We have learned that the present disputes in the Cork College have originated in the resistance made by the Council of the College to certain claims which have been recently asserted by the President, relating to the government and administration of that institution. The chief questions the government are now called upon by the council to determine are two:
1. Whether the President has a right of veto on the resolutions of the council.
2. Whether the President has the exclusive right of controlling, directing and carrying on the correspondence of the college.
In other words, as we cannot but interpret these claims, whether the President is, or is not, to have the absolute direction and uncontrolled dominion over the college.[143]

The article asserted that handing over the direction of the college to one individual would have the effect of turning it into a high school rather than a university, and would convert professors into ushers. The publication of this article both in Dublin and Cork was hugely damaging to the morale of the professors and students in QCC. In a letter dated 19 April 1853 Boole was uncharacteristically tetchy with MaryAnn:

> I send you a post-office order for £3 of which you are to pay Mr Brooke. The rest you can do what you please with. I am not sure that under the circumstances you have done wisely in agreeing to paper the house. I have no intention of asking anyone to spend the vacation with me, and if I had it is not the incumbrance occasioned by any want of papering that would be most felt. It is the smallness of the rooms, and the want of separate convenience within the house. However, I am sure that you have acted for what you thought best.[144]

Further on in the letter, Boole added that on counting his money he did not have £3 to spare and would send only £2. His bad humour was attributed to the ongoing issues in QCC:

> I am perhaps the more disposed to be particular as feeling the great uncertainty of all in the institution. What will be done nobody yet knows but I often inquire of myself whether I was not far happier in my school than in my present life. Since I wrote to you last, Nicoll has resigned having got an appointment in Aberdeen and Lane has gone also having got a rather high appointment in Brazil. They had both been most anxious to leave. Hincks is expecting to go to Canada and Blyth has stated that his great object will now be to quit this place. It is probable that I may soon lose nearly all those with whom I have been in terms of the most intimate friendship. I certainly do not intend to take any such or sudden step but I feel less and less disposed to make this place my permanent home.[145]

Rev. William Hincks was a Unitarian minister and the first professor of natural history at QCC. In 1853, he became the professor of natural history at the University of Toronto. Professor John Blyth, professor of chemistry, did not however leave QCC at that time and is recorded as still being in that position in *Guy's Almanac* of 1871.[146]

Added to the trouble in QCC, Boole reported that some new points in his book were causing some delay. On 4 May, Boole told MaryAnn that nothing had been settled regarding the differences in the college and the rift between the president and the council was only deepening. He was concerned that the departure of Lane would damage the School of Engineering which was his main source of fees and was worried about the introduction of income tax which he thought was just but would fall hard on 'those whose salaries were made low in the first instance on the plea of cheapness of living and freedom from income tax'.[147] Despite the politics in QCC and the introduction of income tax, Boole was upbeat and was not allowing MaryAnn to dampen his spirits:

I am sorry to hear the bad news which as usual your letter contains. I hope that you may soon have exhausted your accounts of the death and sickness of friends which have made your letters for some time past only registers of bad news.

He continued:

Mrs and Miss Everest are here. I dined with them today, took a walk after dinner and gave Miss E. a lesson in mathematics in which, she has, as I have told you an extraordinary quickness of apprehension and solidity of judgement such indeed as I have never seen surpassed.

I am glad that they are here for Dr Ryall's sake. It must be a great comfort to him. Last night we were all at a concert where a new oratorio called Daniel was performed, the composer being present, and afterwards *The Creation* (Haydn).[148] I thought there was a good deal of merit in the former piece, but it was of course eclipsed by the vastly higher merits of *The Creation*. Nothing could exceed the beauty of the latter. Some of the singing was most excellent and the instruments were well played, partly by professional, partly amateur. I have never been more pleased with a concert. It called to mind old days in Lincoln, the Choral Society, friends lost and dead etc. I suppose that I have never but once heard music so good as I did last night – that was in Exeter Hall – but last night's pleased me better …

Spring seems to have fairly set in, though late. My health is pretty good, certainly far better than it was last year. My book is going on and I hope to have the printers at work upon it in a fortnight from the present time. It will make a large volume. The paper is all ready and of the tint sent to you before Xmas for inspection.[149]

It is not clear whether Boole's sense of elation was due to the company of Miss Everest or progress on *The Laws of Thought*, or a combination of both.

Before he left Cork for the summer break, Boole was busy with the end of session examinations and also with Miss Everest. On 5 June he told MaryAnn:

> I shall be very busy indeed with examinations etc. during the next ten days. Dr Ryall and I went out yesterday to Kilcrea Abbey and Castle and were greatly pleased with both. Mrs and Miss Everest went off on Friday. I saw a great deal of them during their visit and was much pleased. I have called at various places to bid farewell and have heard many kind inquiries after you.[150]

Boole's brother Charles married his second wife Millicent Nickolls in Sleaford on 20 June 1853. Boole was slightly put out over the timing of the wedding when he wrote to MaryAnn, but wished his brother well:

> Dr [Charles] Graves has invited me to visit him in Dublin. I propose to do so and see something of the exhibition before returning to England. I don't know whether I shall quite have time to do all I want to do by the 21st of June – however, I shall endeavour to be at home though it would have been more convenient to me had the wedding been a little later as there is an opportunity this year of a cheap tour to Connemara which I would have liked to make before going to Dublin …
>
> I am glad to have such good accounts of everything and hope that Charles will find the present step conducive to his permanent happiness. There seems to be every prospect of it.[151]

MaryAnn must have been concerned that George would not make the wedding on time or would not be appropriately dressed. He had written to reassure her:

> I just wrote to say that I fully intend to be in Lincoln by the 20th inst and that I shall get a waistcoat as you direct.[152]

Boole travelled back to Cork after the summer break in October 1853, stopping in Dublin to use the Great Library there. He reported that the Cork students had done well at the late examinations in Dublin.[153] While each of the three Queen's Colleges in Belfast, Cork and Galway admitted its own students and held its own matriculation examinations, students were required to travel to Dublin to sit the university examinations to be awarded their degree by the Queen's University. Back in Cork, Boole returned to his lodgings in Grenville Place. He still appeared to be pleased with the arrangements there but seemed to be considering a move. He told MaryAnn:

> Mrs Unkles and the family are quite well. They have got the house greatly improved. Both my rooms are beautifully papered, the hall has a new floor and is papered afresh and every part of the house is in first rate order. I shall stay and see how my health and spirits are before thinking of moving.[154]

At this time, Boole was on the verge of completing *The Laws of Thought* and was obviously preoccupied with this work. In late October he told MaryAnn that he had been many hours at work and was feeling tired.[155] On 15 November he wrote:

> My classes this year are much better than I had expected that they would be and they may be larger yet. I believe that college differences are as high as ever between the P and the VP, the former being quite as unscrupulous as ever and the government refusing to interfere. I have nothing to do with the affairs except to sympathise as far as I can with the right ...
>
> The printers are now engaged upon the last lap of my work so that I hope it will be out by Xmas but am doubtful. However, it can not be very long now one would think. I shall greatly miss it when it is over. It has been to me a source of extreme delight – from the first – and has far more than repaid me for the trouble already.[156]

Despite being busy with QCC and his book, Boole found some time to do a little Italian reading:

> I am reading an Italian book by Gioberti; *Del Buono e del Bello*.[157] It is a metaphysical treatise on aesthetics and I find it extremely easy and very interesting – though I think it would not be so to you. I had thought that my knowledge of Italian was a good deal of it gone but I do not find this to be the case. I mention this because you spoke of reading Italian in one of your letters.[158]

In early December he told MaryAnn that the book was nearly ready. The printer would be finished within the week and the binding was to be done in London. He felt that the last chapter would interest her. He also gave her an update on the situation in QCC:

> There is a sort of truce at the college but I have no great confidence in its permanence. You cannot change the character of men and I fear that the P will resume his old modes of procedure. I believe it is only through fear that he has been brought to something like a compromise and wait anxiously for the proceedings of next week. My class is very good indeed and getting on satisfactorily. That is a comfort.[159]

Although Boole was busy at this time, he appeared to be longing still for company and a home of his own:

> We had a pleasant dinner party at Dr Ryall's yesterday and I am going to dine at the good old bishop's again on Thursday. But all this does not supply the place of a home and domestic comfort – to me at least.[160]

Boole did not return to England for the Christmas break, instead visiting Ballymoney in the north of Ireland with Mr and Mrs Shaw. He appeared quite lonely in his correspondence with MaryAnn at the start of 1854 and shortly afterwards apologised to her for this:

> I am afraid my letter last night would make you uncomfortable. It was written in a rather melancholy vein. But I feel much better this morning and hope that in a short time I shall be quite well in health. I have certainly been thinking lately a good deal about my present and past life and there are many things in both which I most deeply regret. I look forward however with hope and resolution to do better for the future. I believe that I should never have felt the melancholy which I have lately done if I had not been living for intellectual pursuits ... However, I ought to be profoundly thankful for all that they have done for me and all that they have enabled me to do for mankind (for I do think that my new book will be in its way remotely perhaps a benefit to the world); but I am at the same time quite of the opinion that I have had far too little to do with other things of equal moment and that on the whole I have not been living to so good purpose as I ought to have been.[161]

Little could Boole have guessed how his work was to revolutionise the world for future generations. The completion of the book probably left a void in his life and gave him more time to reflect on his personal circumstances.

Towards the end of 1853, Boole's letters again contain references to MaryAnn's attempts to set up her own school. By January 1854 she appeared to have found only one pupil for the school and Boole told her that it would not be worthwhile pursuing this.[162] During January, MaryAnn was unwell and Boole was anxious that she forget the idea of the school. He was confident about his prospects in QCC:

> I am very sorry indeed to hear of your alarming illness. I hope you will have no recurrence of it. Let me know how you are going on. Of course you will give up the school idea now retaining the Brocklesby engagement.[163] That will be pleasant and do you good. As for the school never mind. My income here is a little increasing and will I think be £320 this year from the college and it is likely to be better. I shouldn't wonder if it rises another year to be £350. And the dearness of provisions does not very much affect me – not more than a few shillings in the week. Thus I can easily spare an additional £10 or £20 if wanted. And I quite expect it will be wanted this year.[164]

MaryAnn had fallen ill while visiting her brother Charles and his wife at Sleaford. However, George was prepared to foot the medical bills:

> I should think as it was in Charles' house that you caught your illness, he will probably prefer to pay the bill; but I had rather you did not ask him to do so. Simply write to inquire about it and if he does not say anything of the kind, pay it yourself and I will make up all deficiencies.[165]

College affairs appeared calmer. Sir Robert Kane had been away from QCC for about two months but was expected back in Cork on 29 January. Boole's lack of respect for the president was clear when he wrote:

> Dr and Mrs Ryall are quite well and the college affairs are at any rate in a more peaceful if not sounder state than they were. The president has been away about two months but is expected today to a council meeting. My opinion of his conduct and character is such that I do not think that

I shall ever call upon him again or hold with him anything but the merest official intercourse.[166]

Boole's regard for Dr Ryall is evidenced by his decision to dedicate his book to him. He told MaryAnn:

I think my book must be out now but I don't know. I expect to hear every day. I have dedicated it to my friend Dr Ryall as I once intimated to you.[167]

Boole asked the publishers, Walton and Maberly, to send six copies of the book to MaryAnn. These were to be distributed as follows:

Of these, you may keep one, give one to Mr Dickson, one to Mr Larken and the three others go to Charles, to Mr Parry of Sleaford for himself and C. Kirk.[168]

In February 1854, Boole's former colleague and friend Professor Nicoll advised him of the vacancy for the professorship of mathematics at St Andrews University in Scotland. The salary would be between £300 and £400 per annum, and the session would be shorter than that in Cork. Boole decided against applying, as the advantages of St Andrews were not 'sufficiently great' to justify leaving QCC. In addition, he doubted whether the severe climate of northern Scotland would be to his liking.[169] However, Boole was still considering a move. He wrote to MaryAnn on 16 February after dining with his friend James Wilson, the Church of Ireland Bishop of Cork, on the previous evening:

I was at the bishop's last night. He tells me that he means to renew his mathematics a little and study my book. He has two or three times lately expressed in a marked way his good feeling toward me and his hopes that I should meet with some better appointment – though I should really feel sorry on many accounts to leave Cork where I have such attached friends.[170]

In the same letter, Boole was quietly confident about the prospects of *The Laws of Thought*:

It will be some time before the work makes its character. But when it has done this it will have a steady sale, if slow. I enclose a letter from Cambridge.[171]

A review of the book appeared in the *Southern Reporter*, written by Dr Ryall. A favourable review also appeared in a Scottish paper. Boole was not, however, pleased with the review that appeared in the *Athenaeum*, a literary magazine published in London:

The review in the Athenaeum was a very bad one and clearly written by someone who found it easier to compliment the author than to understand the book.[172]

When commenting on a review of the book that appeared in the *Westminster Review*, Boole prophetically remarked:

It will be some time before its real nature is understood.[173]

Boole received a note from Sir John F.W. Herschel relating to his book which he forwarded to MaryAnn. The note does not seem to have survived but must have been complimentary as Boole told MaryAnn he thought she would get pleasure in reading it.[174] Herschel was a polymath, chemist, mathematician and a pioneer of photography. He was an associate of Charles Darwin and Charles Babbage and served as president of the Royal Astronomical Society three times.

In March 1854, Boole returned to Strawberry Hill for a fortnight, complaining of the noise in Grenville Place:

I am going for a fortnight to my old lodgings on Strawberry Hill (Miss Knowles) so that you must direct to me there. I am going for a change of air having not been quite so well lately as usual and also desiring quiet and this house is now a very noisy one, partly from the pianoforte which was never silent and partly from some preparations for two new lodgers Mr and Mrs Harkness, the former one the most estimable and agreeable of my colleagues who are coming to live here. I dare say that I shall find their company a very agreeable relaxation after study. They are very much to be liked in every way and have more of plain English bluntness and hospitality than one often meets with.[175]

In the following weeks Boole wrote of his delight with the peace and quiet and the garden in his 'mountain residence' of Strawberry Hill. By early April he had returned to Grenville Place but doubted he would stay as the noise of the house was not conducive to study. His relationship with the Unkles had turned sour. He told MaryAnn:

I have left Mrs Unkles for good (literally so). I have been for a long time very uncomfortable there from the constant noise, the neglect, and a suspicion which has strengthened into conviction that I was not honestly dealt by. It is not worthwhile to enter into details and I hate re-enacting grievances. Suffice it to say that I at length thought it better to accede to a demand that I should pay to the end of the session and leave than remain longer. I am at least enjoying peace and quiet where I am and have confidence in those about me. Sadly there must be something radically faulty in the Wesleyan system. When I told Mr and Mrs Unkles that I thought them 'unjust people' (the very words I used) a torrent of abuse was poured upon me, which was afterwards excused on the grounds of 'warm temper'. Yet I had been driven out of the house before by the same causes, had incurred the expense of my present lodgings for three weeks – had told Mrs Unkles when I returned that I should have to leave at the quarter's end to which no objection was made – had stopt three weeks beyond the quarter to oblige them, and then had the legal demand forced upon me. And I am sorry to say that I do not think this the worst. However, it is all past now and I think I must be more careful for the future. I certainly have been guilty of great carelessness.[176]

Boole was extremely upset by what he viewed as the Unkles' unfair demands for money, given his desire to treat people fairly and to be scrupulously honest in all his financial dealings.

In March 1854, Boole reported that Professor Alcock had been dismissed. Alcock's dispute with Sir Robert Kane had been running for almost two years at that stage. Boole wrote:

There is nothing much to tell except that poor Alcock has got his dismissal – he has been a foolish man in standing up as he has done for minute points of right but I believe that he has been in the right in the main and that all kinds of dishonesty have been practised against him. I am very sorry for him. It may be against my interests and doubtless will, but I have made up my mind not to call upon the P or accept his invitations, but treat him with official respect and never say a word about him.[177]

The following month, Boole became aware of a vacancy at the University of Melbourne. He described the position to MaryAnn on 2 April:

There is a professorship of mathematics now open at Melbourne in Australia and applications are to be sent to Sir John Herschel. The stipend offered is £1,000 per annum with a house consisting of four apartments and a kitchen. I suppose part of a range for the use of professors. I infer from a passage in the ad that there will be fees also from students. An outfit of £300 and one half of the salary is to commence at embarkation and the full salary on landing. The vacations are equal in length to those here but better arranged – one of about 11 weeks, 2 of a month each and one of a fortnight, so that there is never more than seven or eight weeks continuous work. The report says that the climate is genial. What do you think of this? I have taken no steps at present but think the thing worth considering. Applications are to be sent in by the 10th of June.[178]

Boole was not in good spirits at this time, despite some good news regarding his brother Charles. He wrote to MaryAnn on 14 April:

The vacation has now commenced for a fortnight and I am released from lectures. It is probable that I may go out for a time as I have not been very well, suffering chiefly from loss of sleep and depression of spirits. However, my health is not amiss and I am told that I look well. So you need not worry yourself at all. I rejoiced greatly to hear of Charles's becoming a father. It will give him a renewed interest in life. I hope that he will now enjoy all the peace and comfort to which he has been so long a stranger and which I am sure that he deserves.[179]

In the same letter, Boole was also worried about his uncle William, whom he referred to as 'Uncle Boole'. William resided in the village of Bassingham in Lincolnshire with his son, Robert, and daughter, Jane. It appeared that Boole had been contributing to the upkeep of his uncle's family since his arrival in Cork. He gave MaryAnn strict instructions:

PRIVATE: Let me know when you write if he wants any little comforts and if he does I will send £5 – or you may leave it there and let me know about it. Now mind you attend to this under the penalty of the severest spiritual censure. Remember it will be nothing to you or me a few years hence whether we have £5 more or less – but it would be a sad reflection that he or poor Jane had not enough. I am very sorry that the little which I had given before was not so given to provide for Jane after uncle's death ….

As near as I can tell, uncle has had, including the stationery bills which I have paid, from £15 to £20 a year from me since I have been in Cork up to my visit last autumn when I found it was no longer needed. Now you aren't to speak of this to anyone but John Pacey.[180] But you are to ask him whether under all the circumstances it ought not to induce those who are well off to forego a part of their claims in favour of Jane and Robert, supposing that Uncle has not duly considered these in his will. I hardly know whether I am doing right in mentioning these things but they are to be strictly private.[181]

At the end of May 1854, Boole was still undecided as to whether to apply for the Melbourne position. He assured MaryAnn in a letter that he would not do anything without considering her interests:

I am still undecided as to my course with respect to the Melbourne professorship but you may depend upon my not doing anything without fully considering your interests and happiness. I am most deeply sensible of all that you have done for mother and your life of patient self-sacrifice. As to my course, there is certainly a great deal to be said on both sides. Even if I did not like the place, I might come back in a year or two at least richer than I went. Cork I am now becoming attached to, but I feel that I have been living by myself long enough and that I have no prospect of a provision for age.[182]

It is probable that Boole's developing relationship with Mary Everest was a factor in his decision regarding the Melbourne professorship but he did not specifically mention this to his sister. By early June he had made up his mind:

I have not sent in an application for the Melbourne professorship and I feel pretty certain that I shall not do so, certainly without talking the matter over with you. What I hear of the climate deters me and I don't like the thought of leaving so much that is dear behind me. I have just written to secure, if possible, permission to send in an application in a week's time. To an ambitious person the opportunity would be a great one. I have no doubt that the professors in the Melbourne University will hold a much higher relative position than the sons of learning ever gain here. But I feel no ambition. I should like to be useful in the world – to have a home of my own – and to be able to do somewhat better than I have done for you. It is possible that I may accomplish all these things here.[183]

On a sad note, Boole also wrote of the illness of Mr Albani, the registrar of QCC and Boole's fellow lodger from Castle White, in this letter:

I am deeply sorry to say that poor Mr Albani lies dying and is probably now dead of fever. He was a very excellent person and people now feel his worth and goodness.[184]

A new stage in Boole's life was just about to begin, and Mary Everest was to take centre stage. Boole told MaryAnn:

The weather is so fine that I may very likely come home by way of Bristol. If so I shall stop a night at Wickwar. But I have not determined upon this and at present merely think of it. I am full of business just now.

This letter is the last in the series to MaryAnn in the Boole Archive. Boole's mother died in August 1854 and he married Mary Everest in September 1855. MaryAnn moved to Ireland after the death of her mother. Boole never left Cork for another position but during his time in Cork he achieved his dual ambitions of becoming useful in the world and having a home of his own.[185]

Chapter 4

1849–1855:
TRAVEL AND
SOCIAL LIFE

GEORGE BOOLE arrived in Ireland to assume his post as professor of mathematics in Queen's College Cork in October 1849. The four years prior to 1849 are considered a watershed in Irish history and it is useful to examine briefly this period to set in context the timing of Boole's arrival. The country which emerged from the 1840s was different socially, economically and politically from the one which preceded it. The Great Famine, or the Great Hunger as it is known, had been raging in Ireland since 1845, caused by a potato blight that arrived in Ireland from North America. The potato was the staple diet of the masses and the crop failed each year between 1845 and 1849. It is estimated that one tenth of the population, 800,000 people, died from disease and starvation.

Incredibly, huge quantities of grain were exported from Ireland during the period of the Famine. The government did not impose a ban on food exports. In October 1845, the prime minister Sir Robert Peel attempted and failed to repeal the Corn Laws, which imposed restrictions and tariffs on imported grain which kept the price of bread artificially high. In March 1846, Peel set up a programme of public works in Ireland, but the famine situation worsened during 1846, and the repeal of the Corn Laws in that year did little to help the Irish population; the measure split the Conservative Party, leading to the fall of Peel's government. The measures taken by his replacement, the Whig Lord John Russell, also proved inadequate. Russell's administration refused to stop food exports to England and halted the programme of food and relief works introduced by Peel. Russell's ministry introduced a new programme of public works, which by the end of December 1846 employed half a million Irish people but proved impossible to administer. Charles Trevelyan, Assistant Secretary to the Treasury, who oversaw the administration of government relief, limited the government's food aid programme because of a firm belief in laissez-faire. Trevelyan declared that 'the great evil' was not the Famine itself but 'the selfish, perverse and turbulent character of the people'.[186] The government was prepared to promote public works and to make some financial contribution, but it maintained that Irish poverty must be supported by Irish property, and that the landlords of Ireland should take responsibility for the crisis. Some landlords took advantage of the situation to clear their estates with widespread evictions, which in turn reduced their liability.

During the winter of 1846–7, food kitchens were established by voluntary societies, committees and individuals to feed the starving masses. A leading part was played by the Society of Friends, the Quakers, who set up central relief committees in Dublin and London and their reports enlightened British public opinion on the conditions in Ireland. In early 1847 the government realised that the measures taken to that point were ineffective and that the cost of feeding the people should come out of the public purse. By August 1847, over three million people were being fed in soup kitchens mainly financed at public expense.

Famine was not unprecedented in nineteenth-century Ireland; in 1817 and 1822 it had been widespread in several areas of the country. What made 'The Great Hunger' of 1845 to 1849 unprecedented were its consequences. The most striking long-term effect of the Famine was the widespread emigration which it triggered. Between 1841 and 1845, approximately 50,000 emigrated each year.[187] In 1847 alone, 215,000 emigrated, and between 1848 and 1855, almost two million left.[188] The population of Ireland decreased by close to 20 per cent in the decade 1841 to 1851.

Boole's arrival coincided with a period of enormous change in Ireland. His letters to his family describe his first impressions of the terrible state of the country and he periodically refers to mass emigration from Cork and the extent of poverty in the city. Boole's letter to MaryAnn dated 25 October 1849 following his arrival in Cork recounted the scenes he witnessed on the train journey from Dublin to Cork:

> Of the state of cultivation in Ireland judging from what I yesterday saw while travelling from Dublin, it is impossible to speak in terms too sad. There is over the country an air of utter destitution and abandonment. For miles and miles you see nothing but fields overgrown with weeds and plashy with surface water, vast desolate bogs, cabins few in number and of the most wretched kind, scarcely a tree between you and the horizon, scarcely a human being by the way or a herd of cattle in the fields. I have seen nothing like it. I can conceive of nothing worse. Far better would it be to see the forest and the plain as nature left them than to look upon scenes of sloth, neglect and decay.
>
> At Limerick Junction where we stopped a short time, four of the peasantry, stout healthy-looking men, stood side by side to look at us, each with both hands in his pockets. This seemed to be the favourite pastime. There was an air of defiant idleness about them such as I never saw before. They harmonised well with the scenes we were passing through. A gentleman who came up at the next station told us that he was paying 9/6 in the pound to the rates.[189]

The reference to the rates relates to the poor rate which was introduced in the 1838 Poor Relief (Ireland) Act. Ireland had been divided into Poor Law unions based on the Irish electoral divisions. Each union was obliged to provide a workhouse for their destitute poor. A compulsory rate was levied on landlords and their tenants in each union to finance the system.

In a letter written four days later, Boole told MaryAnn:

I went this morning to church and on my return, went into a street in which was a great crowd of people. It was almost entirely composed of beggars and the sight far exceeded in horror not only that I have ever before witnessed but that I had even read of. As it is impossible to relieve this wretchedness by any private efforts and as the sight of it is heart sickening, I must, I believe, resolve to avoid those quarters of the city in which it obtrudes itself upon us. If it were simply want, simply the inability to get food that drove people into the streets, something might indeed be done. But one cannot help seeing that there is an ostentation of rags and filth and squalor, and an instant calculation on the effect which they will produce which is truly upsetting. I think the state of mendicancy in this country a most serious drawback from any advantages which living in it may possess. Remember however to quiet your alarms, that very little indeed of this is seen in the quarter in which I dwell. This suburb is exceedingly beautiful. I know of nothing like it in any English town.[190]

In early December, Boole visited the Cork Union or workhouse. He mentions it rather casually in the postscript to a letter to MaryAnn on 7 December 1849, inserted between two other references:

Kindest love to mother. Yesterday I went to see the Cork Union. It contains 4,700 inmates!! Is it not an appalling number? I cannot get Mr Dicken's note in.[191]

However, in an address to the Mechanics' Institute in Lincoln on a subsequent visit home, Boole described the pitiful existence of Famine survivors:

You may enter a roadside cabin, without window, perhaps without chimney. Two old women are on the ground, or on stones, stretching their hands over a fire, composed of the dying embers of two sticks.

No furniture, except a small wooden block: no chair or table, or vessel for domestic uses. The only food visible is a couple of turnips which have been appropriated, perhaps, but irregularly. A hole in the wall leads to the bedroom but it is too dark to see how it is furnished. You hear the invariable story of the famine, of husbands dead or gone to seek employment, of deaths of children in the union, ending perhaps with a prayer that 'the Lord would take away the poor out of the hunger, the misery and the sin'.[192]

Yet despite the appalling conditions in Ireland, Boole was surprised at Irish attitudes to England which he encountered. He wrote in a letter to his mother in March 1850:

Yesterday I accepted an invitation given by a gentleman who holds a government office. There were a number of barristers present it being the assizes but I did not much like the company – full of grumbling against England and our government, a thing which I am not disposed to hear without making some effort to defend them.

It is almost inconceivable what notions some of the Irish middle and upper classes entertain of England. You would imagine from their talk that they think that all the measures which the government took with reference to Ireland are prompted by malequity – that England delights to see Ireland miserable and desires nothing so much as to keep her so. I suppose that allowances must be made for an exaggerated way of talking which is rather common in this country and which serves perhaps as a vent for the energy that might otherwise be expended in a more mischievous manner.[193]

His letters to his close family contain only two references to the mass emigration of the period. In February 1851, he told his mother:

All seems extremely quiet. I think I can possibly venture to say that it is a quieter place than Lincoln albeit with six times its population. The departure of emigrant ships is one of the most exciting scenes I believe but I have not yet witnessed it – I intend to do so shortly.[194]

By May 1851, he had viewed the spectacle at first hand. He wrote:

THE EMIGRATION AGENTS' OFFICE.—THE PASSAGE MONEY PAID.

Figure 4.1: Gregory O'Neill's Emigration Agency, 9 Merchant's Quay, Cork (1851), *Illustrated London News*

> Cork is the quietest place on earth. Emigration seems to be its chief business now. While at Monkstown I was continually witnessing the passage of emigrant vessels down to the harbour.[195]

In a letter to his mother dated 1 November 1849, Boole complained of the lavishness of a social event which he had attended:

> Cork seems to be a very hospitable place and entertainments are given in a style which to me appears magnificent and even extravagant. At a dinner which I was present at the other day we began with turtle soup and champagne. Considering the distressed state of the country a more homely style of entertainment would be more suitable and in better taste. I intend to limit myself to the acceptance of one invitation in the week. A night of quiet reading or work is better to look back upon. Life rolls fast enough away.[196]

Boole's attempts to limit his social life to pursue his studies are a constant theme in his letters to his sister and mother. His move from his initial lodgings in Castle White to Strawberry Hill in March 1850 was prompted by an attempt to avoid the distractions of a burgeoning social life and work more steadily. The professors were much sought after as dinner guests in Cork society. On 7 March 1850, he told his mother:

I have spent a pleasant time lately working steadily during the day and seeing some agreeable company in the evening. I think better of the good society of this place than I did, there are many estimable persons whose acquaintance is not readily formed but who are worth a host of ordinary acquaintances. I now know some such people in terms of greater intimacy than I could have expected in so short a time. It is pleasant to be on terms of friendship with such people and this is a pleasure which I think I can enjoy without sacrificing any time and my opportunities of study. Indeed it is impossible to make use of the evening here to be reading or working. We dine late and the true economy of time is to make use of the early part of the day.[197]

In the same month, Boole wrote of standing 'on a closer footing than that of mere acquaintances with worthy and excellent people whom it is a pleasure to meet and to converse with'.[198] He appears to have been most comfortable in the company of the Ryalls and the Jennings, a family with whom he became very friendly from the outset of his time in Cork. In February 1850, he told his sister:

I am going out this evening to take tea with the family of the Jennings. This is the third time I have been asked out to tea in succession and I take it as a good omen. It is so much more agreeable for me to join a family at the tea table than at their dinner parties which are too formal for me. I feel quite sure that I shall in time find myself in familiar terms with a few really estimable families and this will be a great acquisition to my comfort indeed.[199]

The Jennings were a prominent Cork Unitarian family, active in the commercial and cultural life of the city. One family member had been on the committee which campaigned for a Munster College prior to the establishment of Queen's College Cork and Francis Jennings was active in the affairs of QCC in the college's early years. He was a member of the Royal Irish Academy and the Cuvierian Society in Cork and a Fellow of the Geological Society of London.[200] Part of the original site of QCC in the 1840s belonged to the family, and most of the land acquired subsequently, as the college extended to the west, was also former Jennings' land. They owned a factory at Victoria Cross, close to QCC, which produced magnesia, vinegar and mineral waters. In March 1850, when suffering from a bout of toothache and influenza, Boole told MaryAnn in a postscript to a letter:

I must just add that my kind friends the Jennings, hearing of my illness, have just sent me three pots of jam and two large bottles of vinegar, with which I have been recommended to rub my skin, the vinegar being first diluted in warm water before getting into bed.[201]

Given that Boole's social life in Lincoln as a school teacher was probably quite modest and that he was away from family and friends, it is not surprising that he would have felt more comfortable at the tea tables of a few close families than at formal dinners. In an undated letter written around 1853, Boole spoke again about his friendship with the Jennings family:

Mrs Ryall and the Jennings are quite well. I took tea with the latter the night before last. They seem now to expect me as a matter of course about twice a week and if I don't go I get a missive from Miss May with some story about a hot cake or something else of the kind. Their hospitality is boundless.[202]

In several of his letters, Boole mentioned calling at Mr Logan's house. William Logan was a deacon at the Independent Chapel in Cork. In a letter written to his mother in November 1849, he spoke of Mr Logan:

The latter is I think a most estimable man actively engaged in all the benevolent societies of the place which are on a general footing but holding himself apart from those which are exclusive, I think him a very valuable acquaintance.[203]

In a subsequent letter, Boole said that Mr Logan's house reminded him more of England than anything he had yet seen in Ireland.[204] Mr Logan had a family of three sons and three daughters, 'all amiable and sensible young people'. He concluded:

I think it really a subject of pleasant reflection that I have in my short stay in this country established, beside many pleasant acquaintanceships, at least one valuable friendship for so I trust it will prove, for esteem is quite as much at the bottom of it as preference or partiality.

He also mentions visiting an unidentified Quaker gentleman who had a telescope and was 'much devoted to scientific pursuits'. He told MaryAnn:

I spent Saturday evening at his country house and was much pleased with the quiet and order that are so characteristic of the Society of Friends. I have made some other acquaintances which I think will be valuable.[205]

Although Boole moved out of his lodgings in Castle White in March 1850 to concentrate on his studies, he continued to socialise with Mr De Vericour and told MaryAnn in October 1850:

I have been to Mr Jennings to tea and met there Mr De V and Mr Whitelegge ... Mr De V is well and desires to be kindly remembered to you. He is taken much notice of and goes into the best society.[206]

Mr William Whitelegge was a Presbyterian minister in St Luke's parish in Cork.[207] He was a member of the Cork Cuvierian Society which Boole subsequently joined and became president of in 1854.

Boole moved in relatively fashionable society in Cork. He became friendly with the Chesney family, whom he visited with Mr De Vericour. The Chesneys lived in Ballincollig, then a village about six miles west of Cork. Ballincollig Royal Gunpowder Mills was one of three that manufactured gunpowder for the British government and in 1810 an army barracks was built in Ballincollig to protect the supply of gunpowder.

In November 1847, Lieutenant Colonel Francis Chesney (1789–1872) was appointed commander of the Cork district. Chesney was descended from a distinguished Scottish military family. In the early 1830s, Chesney had recommended to the British government a canal cut across the Suez peninsula as the best way of shortening the route to India but the British government preferred the Syria–Euphrates option. However, Ferdinand de Lesseps used Chesney's survey and credited him as the 'Father of the Canal' when construction of the Suez Canal began in the 1850s.

The biography of Chesney, written by his third wife Louisa and his daughter Jane, describes their social life in Ballincollig:

Many friendly families in the neighbourhood of Ballincollig, the garrison itself and the general's staff at Cork, made up a very agreeable society. Chesney's quarters were always open to his friends; he had at all times a place at his table for any young artillery or infantry officer whose limited means were unequal to the cavalry mess, which was the only one in the garrison at that time, while social gatherings, music and little dances, kept their evenings well employed.[208]

Figure 4.2: General Francis Rawdon Chesney

Boole mentions several visits to the Chesneys in late 1850 and early 1851. Mrs Chesney was apparently an object of curiosity for MaryAnn. In a letter dated 9 November 1850, Boole asked her:

Is not the curiosity of the female breast insatiable? Mrs Chesney is all that you have a right to suppose her to be in view of the law of morality that bids us to think the best of those of whom we know nothing. She is clever, good and beautiful. I have put the best quality in the middle. Now are you satisfied?[209]

Boole spent time over Christmas 1850 at the homes of the Chesneys and Dr Bullen. In a letter written in early January 1851 he mentioned having been to two or three pleasant parties over the holidays but planned to limit his dining out so as not to affect his work. Boole was attempting to achieve a healthy work–life balance, in his own words hoping to carry out literally the maxim 'Nulla dies sine linea [*Not a day without a line*]'.[210] Sometimes there is a sense that Boole was playing down his social life to his sister, who was at home in England looking after their elderly mother, telling her that all was very dull and quiet in Cork 'compared with the present life and stir of old England'.[211] Nevertheless, MaryAnn appeared to have a keen interest in social life in Cork, getting regular updates, including the following comment relating to the wife of Mr Shaw, Boole's colleague, professor of natural philosophy at QCC:

> Mrs Shaw I saw yesterday. She is not a 'child wife' as you wrote to Mrs Ryall but I should think well suited to her position.[212]

In two of his letters, Boole mentioned dining with the Mahonys of Blarney.[213] It is most likely that the Mahonys referred to were the owners of a thriving textile business in the village of Blarney, about five miles from Cork. Built in 1823, Blarney Woollen Mills was originally known as Mahony's Mills and provided valuable employment for some two hundred people in Blarney and the surrounding areas. Using a water-powered mill, it produced tweeds and woollens for the home and export markets. The mill closed in 1973 but a successful retail textile business still exists on the site today.

Boole also referred to a Miss Penrose in his correspondence with MaryAnn. After MaryAnn had spent a period of time in Blarney in 1852, he wrote:

> I am very glad that you have met Miss Penrose. She is a very ladylike, sensible and unaffected person and I am gratified to think that she so readily and so kindly offered you her acquaintance.[214]

The Penrose family was descended from Cooper Penrose, a Quaker who settled in Cork in the mid eighteenth century. They owned the Waterford Glass Works at the time and Cooper moved to Cork to develop other elements of the family business.[215] The Penroses were patrons of the arts in Cork and their home at Wood Hill had purpose-built galleries constructed for artists and sculptors. Cooper's son, James Penrose (1766–1845), had at least five daughters and it is probable that one of these daughters was the Miss Penrose that Boole referred to.

Although Boole attended many parties, he does not appear to have been an enthusiastic dancer. In a letter to MaryAnn in April 1853, he related:

I was at Mrs Donovan's last night and we had a very agreeable party and I suppose you will hear that I was forced into a dance. However, I had a very considerate and agreeable partner and got on better than I expected at first that I should do.[216]

However, Boole always enjoyed music and hearing music performed, particularly sacred music. While in London, Boole attended a concert at Exeter Hall[217] in 1851 which he described to his sister:

Last night I heard Mendelsohn's *Elijah* in Exeter Hall with a band of 700 performers. Even with this advantage it appeared to sink below the level of Handel's and Haydn's great oratorios performed by the far smaller and far inferior orchestras which I have before heard. The trios and quartets were very good.[218]

He described some music that he heard in Cork in a letter to his brother Charles in November 1849:

I went to one of the churches today of the city and heard the iconic collect 'Lord of all Power and Might' sung to a strain sweet and solemn, music such as I have seldom heard. The singing in churches here is better than it usually is – and I am told it is good in Catholic chapels.[219]

There is no record of Boole visiting any Catholic churches apart from one reference in a letter to MaryAnn in December 1849:

Next Tuesday evening *The Creation* is to be performed at the 'ancient concerts' here and I intend to go. I am reminded of this by Mr Brooke's inquiry whether I have heard any of the R.C. music. I have heard very little and that only at the preaching of two charity sermons when there was no service. It was very poor. I am told that there is good music at one of the chapels and the musical performances of the fair daughters of Cork are admired. I heard 'Agar's Prayer' and some other pieces of that kind on Sunday evening with which I was much charmed.[220]

Boole visited a variety of churches in Cork during his early years in the city but never was affiliated to any. He read widely on religion, and having difficulty with the concept of the Trinity, leaned towards Unitarianism.[221] In October 1850, he asked MaryAnn to send on his copy of Penrose's work 'Of God etc.' which he wished to loan to a friend.[222] John Penrose was the vicar of Langton-by-Whately in Lincolnshire from 1802 to 1859. He wrote several religious works including *Of God, or of the Divine Mind and the Doctrine of the Trinity by a Trinitarian* (1849), which Boole referred to. Penrose's wife, Elizabeth Cartwright, was a popular writer who wrote under the pseudonym 'Mrs Markham' and his sister, Mary Penrose, married Dr Thomas Arnold of Rugby, the well-known educationalist. Boole and Penrose corresponded in the 1850s and Boole later became acquainted with his son Francis in 1853.

Boole wished to remain a religious free spirit as well as a free thinker. When the Archdeacon of Cork, Cloyne and Ross, Samuel Kyle, offered Boole the use of his pew, he refused. He told MaryAnn:

> This I did not think fit to accept as I am very jealous of any invasion of my Christian liberty on the Sabbath.[223]

He mentions visiting Mr Logan's Independent Chapel[224] and noted that the Protestant churches in Cork were better attended than those in Lincoln.[225]

Despite his religious nonconformity, Boole became a friend and regular dinner guest of the Protestant Bishop of Cork, Cloyne and Ross, James Wilson. His first reference to Bishop Wilson appears in a letter written shortly after his arrival in Cork:

> I told you yesterday that I appeared to myself under the discipline of toothache like a portly farmer. But a friend who came in just after described that I was more like a bishop – an Irish bishop, I suppose. I have seen two Irish bishops, both of Cork. The Catholic being fat, the Protestant thin.[226]

He received his first invitation to dine with Bishop Wilson in November 1850 and remarked that he would be glad to go, not because he was a bishop but because he was sure he would like him. Boole described him as a venerable old man who was much esteemed for his kindness and benevolence.[227] There was a large party present at the dinner. Boole liked the bishop very much and enjoyed a discourse with him on the writings of one of his predecessors, Dr Peter Browne. As Boole was leaving, he met the Dean of Cork, Horatio Townsend Newman, who told Boole that he had met Dr Charles Graves of Trinity College in Dublin and had mentioned Boole to him.[228]

Archbishop Whately of Dublin was also present at a dinner attended by Boole at the Bishop's house in May 1852.[229] On that occasion, Boole met the archbishop's chaplain. He told MaryAnn:

> His chaplain Mr Fitzgerald who was with him and who is a man of high reputation got introduced to me and mentioned that he had made my former work on Logic a subject of lectures in the University of Dublin some years ago. This I had not known.

This must have been very gratifying for Boole to discover. William Fitzgerald (1814–83) was professor of moral philosophy in Trinity College Dublin between 1847 and 1852, and professor of ecclesiastical history between 1852 and 1857. In March 1857, he was consecrated as Bishop of Cork following the death of Bishop Wilson and subsequently became Bishop of Killaloe in 1862. MaryAnn became governess to the Fitzgerald children around this time. The family had six children, among them the scientist George Francis Fitzgerald (1851–1901), who became professor of natural and experimental philosophy, or physics, at Trinity College Dublin. Fitzgerald is known for his work in electromagnetic theory and his name is commemorated in the Lorentz–Fitzgerald contraction, which Einstein used in his Theory of Relativity.

In October 1853, Boole made the acquaintance of Francis Cranmer Penrose, son of John Penrose. He told MaryAnn of their meeting:

> A day or two after my arrival as I was sitting in Dr Ryall's in the evening, a card was handed in to me bearing the signature of Mr F.C. Penrose and in came its owner. He had come to Ireland to select the marbles for the sarcophagus of the Duke of Wellington. I invited him to take abode with me, to which he agreed. I had three or four days of agreeable society. We dined at the bishop's on Sunday (I having dined there on the Thursday previous) and at the Jennings on Saturday. He was much pleased with his visit and I not less so. He made acquaintance with the Penroses here and it appeared that they were distantly connected, coming originally from the same place in Cornwall.[230]

Figure 4.3: Francis Cranmer Penrose

Francis Cranmer Penrose (1817–1903) was an architect, archaeologist and astronomer. While at Cambridge he was a friend of Charles Kingsley, and through Kingsley came to know Frederick Denison Maurice, who strongly influenced Boole's religious beliefs.[231] In 1842 Penrose was appointed travelling bachelor of the University of Cambridge and travelled through France, Italy, Greece, Switzerland and Germany. In 1851 he published the first edition of his most significant work, *Principles of Athenian Architecture*, in which he established that what is apparently parallel or straight in Greek architecture of the best period is generally neither straight nor parallel, but curved or inclined.[232]

In 1852, Penrose was appointed as surveyor of St Paul's Cathedral in London. His appointment was made with a view to completing the interior decoration of the cathedral in accordance with the intentions of Christopher Wren. He designed the crypt of the Duke of Wellington, which was completed in 1858.

The article on Penrose in the *Dictionary of National Biography* mentions Boole:

He was adept at mechanical inventions, and an instrument for drawing spirals won him a prize at the Great Exhibition in 1851. A theodolite which he had bought in 1852 primarily for use in measurement of buildings, he applied at the suggestion of Dr G. Boole to such astronomical purposes as accurate determination of orientation and time in connection, for example, with the fixing of sundials.[233]

Boole enjoyed Penrose's company very much and this helped mitigate his continuing feelings of homesickness and loneliness for his family. He told MaryAnn:

During Mr Penrose's visit I felt how much better society is than solitude. However, being in better health I do not feel the loneliness so much as I once did.[234]

They appeared to have kept in touch after Mr Penrose's departure from Cork. In December 1853, Boole wrote:

I heard from Mr Penrose again yesterday. He enclosed a sovereign for the relief of the sufferers by the late flood.[235] He left a very favourable impression of his own character behind him on the minds of those who met him here.[236]

Penrose was awarded the gold medal of the Royal Institute of British Architects in 1883 and was its president in the period 1894–6.

Boole was also a friend of Alexander Mitchell, inventor of the screw pile lighthouse. Mitchell was born in Dublin in 1780 but was educated at the Belfast Academy where he excelled at mathematics. His sight deteriorated so that by twenty-two he was blind. He started a building business in Belfast and invented several machines, as well as musical instruments, wooden clocks and windmills. He continued in the building trade for thirty years, until his career took a change of direction:

Alexander, being of an inventive mind, often thought that many lives could be saved if a method could be devised of building lighthouses on shoals or sandbanks. This led to his ingenious invention of the screw pile, in which he was said to have been influenced by the corkscrew and perhaps the force necessary to open a bottle of wine.[237]

Mitchell patented *The Mitchell Screw-Pile and Mooring* in 1833, a cast-iron support system which allowed for construction in deep water on mud and sand banks. He applied the same technology to propellers and patented the screw propeller in 1854. Among the lighthouses he constructed were the Maplin Sands Lighthouse (1838), Belfast Lough (1848), Queenstown (Cobh) (1853) and Dundalk (1855).

It was during the construction of the Spit Bank Lighthouse[238] in Cobh that Mitchell's friendship with Boole developed:

> An unlighted buoy had previously marked the commencement of the spit bank near Cobh, but Cork Harbour Commissioners required a more notable structure to take its place. Mitchell won the commission to construct the new lighthouse for £3,450, and moved with his family to Cobh (then Queenstown) in 1851 …
>
> … During his fifteen months at Cobh, Mitchell took trips into Cork city, during which he met with academic staff at the university and forged a friendship with the great mathematician, Boole.[239]

Boole was greatly taken with Cobh, anglicised as Cove. The town is situated on the south side of one of three islands in Cork Harbour, Great Island, approximately fifteen miles from Cork city. Cobh or the Cove of Cork was a busy sea port and its large natural harbour made it an important naval

Figure 4.4: Spit Bank Lighthouse, Cobh, County Cork

centre for the British navy, particularly during the Napoleonic Wars. Cobh was an embarkation centre for convicts deported to the penal colonies in Australia from the early nineteenth century. In the post-Famine years, Cobh was the last departure point for approximately two and half million people who emigrated to North America between 1848 and 1950, and was also the last port of call for the ill-fated *Titanic*. Cobh was renamed Queenstown in 1850 following the visit of Queen Victoria in 1849 but reverted to Cobh following Irish independence in 1922.

Boole's first visit to Cobh was with Mr De Vericour, shortly after his arrival in Cork in October 1849:

> I yesterday went with De V down the river to Queenstown. We had not a very fine day but the scene was such as to satisfy me that there is some ground for the enthusiastic admiration which travellers have expressed for it. Mr De V was continually reminded of the Lake of Geneva – and sometimes of the Scotch lakes.[240]

In May 1852 he told MaryAnn:

> I generally get out once or twice a week by the steamer down to Cove. Nothing can be more delightful than the journey on the river at this time.[241]

During the first years of Boole's time in Cork, he visited many locations around Cork Harbour and sent MaryAnn details of his trips and the sights he encountered. In January 1851, the United States mail steamer the *Atlantic* was driven into Cork Harbour by a storm. Boole told MaryAnn:

> You may have read of the Atlantic steamer 3500 tons being driven by stress of weather into Cork Harbour. I went to see it a short time ago and was filled with wonder at the sight. The central axis of the steam engines of solid iron and about two feet in diameter were broken in two at the fissure of support and the metal at the fracture appeared to be crystallised.[242]

Boole was a regular visitor to the southern side of Cork Harbour also, frequently visiting the villages of Passage West and Monkstown. In May 1850, he wrote to MaryAnn:

Figure 4.5: *Cobh*, W.H. Bartlett (c. 1841)

Had a pleasant journey by steamer to Monkstown and returned in the evening with Dr Ryall and his mother. The house at which I paid my visit stands in a park on the hill overlooking the river and the prospect is certainly finer than that of the Thames from Richmond Hill. I am going to the same place to breakfast some day next week and shall return in time for lectures. I wish you were here for a short time and could see some of the prospects with me.[243]

The Cork to Passage railway had commenced operating in June 1850. In October 1850 Boole went twice by train to Passage West to visit the Royal Victoria and Monkstown Passage Baths, which had opened in 1838.[244] The baths were a very popular Cork amenity at the time, with an estimated 15,000 visitors in 1857. They were believed to be beneficial in the relief of rheumatism, lumbago and similar complaints.[245]

In November 1850 Boole made another excursion to Passage West with Dr Ryall. He described the trip to MaryAnn:

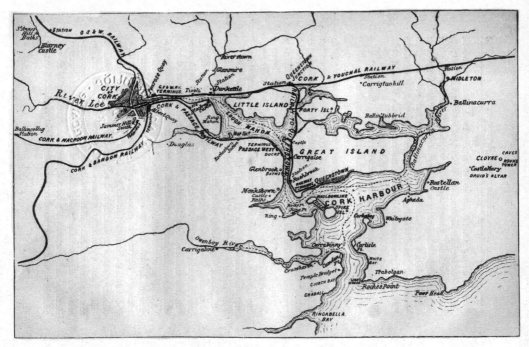

Figure 4.6: Map of Cork Harbour (1891)

Accordingly we set off by train for Passage, took [an] omnibus on to Monkstown and then walked forward along the riverside through a great deal of beautiful scenery, passing the end of one dark wooded glen till we reached a place called Ringaskiddy nearly opposite to Queenstown but somewhat lower down. Here feeling hungry we went into a cottage to buy some biscuits and were asked after doing so to rest ourselves in a pleasant little room looking out over the harbour. Without saying anything, the hospitable woman who kept the little shop sent us in some hot potatoes and butter of which we made a hearty dinner and when at the end of our repast we proposed to pay for what we had just had (the biscuits we had already paid for) she said it would be 'taking down the character of the country' to take anything so that we had to go away contenting ourselves with thanking her for her hospitality. Just before reaching Ringaskiddy we had passed through one of the most beautiful valleys I have ever seen. There was a lake, two ruined castles, a wooded place beyond and the blue water of the harbour at its terminus to the left. This is a region which I mean to visit again before long. The day was splendid – such as I have never seen in the same month in England.

Figure 4.7: *Monkstown Baths Looking up to Passage*, Henry Morgan (c. 1849)

After bidding our kind hostess goodbye we engaged in rowing and sailing in the harbour, boarded a man-of-war which was lying there and through the kindness of an officer to whom we had an introduction we were permitted to see the whole of the interior arrangements. It was a most interesting sight. The space between decks was quite like a town. There were three decks and a steam engine working a screw propeller below. We landed on the opposite side of the river, had a delightful walk beneath the rocks up to the Passage ferry boat where we again crossed and took the train for Cork. I dined and spent the evening with the vice president. I was much more pleased with the scenery I saw yesterday than with anything of the kind that I have before met with in this country. The setting of the sun over the harbour was one of the grandest sights I have ever witnessed.[246]

During the Christmas holiday of 1850, Boole visited the area again alone. He went to Passage and Monkstown by train and then walked about four miles to the village of Carrigaline. From there, he crossed the Owenabue River, or the Carrigaline River as he called it, and walked to its mouth through beautiful scenery. He told MaryAnn:

On Saturday I took a very long walk. Get a map and you may trace my expedition from Cork to Passage and Monkstown by train, thence on foot to Carrigaline, through a very sombre glen which lies about halfway between the two places. At Carrigaline I crossed the river (not the Lee but the Carrigaline River) and walked down to its mouth through most beautiful scenery. At one part the river expands into a lake called Drake's Pool from Sir Francis Drake having found shelter there when pursued by the Spanish Armada. Below this place the river, about as wide as the Trent, winds between hills completely covered with woods to their summits. At one spot you can see nothing but the river and the forest. It seemed to realise my ideas of American scenery. At Crosshaven the mouth of the river I crossed it and walked over the hills to Monkstown whence I returned by a car to Cork. The total distance which I walked was 19 miles and I was glad to find that I could walk so far without fatigue.

Tell W. Brooke that I feel doubtful whether in Scotland he has seen anything finer than the Carrigaline River. If he is sceptical about its beauties tell him that I desire him to come and see for himself.[247]

In May 1851, Boole spent a week in the hotel in Monkstown, for sea air and sunbathing.[248] He wrote:

You will see that I have for the present removed to Monkstown whence I travel by train or by steamer every morning to college. I am staying at the hotel for the week but do not intend to remain longer. Either I shall occupy my lodgings in Cork for the remainder of the session or shall take a lodging here or at Queenstown and travel up and down as at present. The fare by steamer is only 4d, by rail 6d so that one cannot complain of expenses. Nothing can exceed the beauty of the Cork River at this time. The journeys by steamer are among the pleasantest things that have ever occurred to me.[249]

Boole's early years in Cork coincided with the construction of the Chetwynd Viaduct, known to all Corkonians as 'The Viaduct', part of the Cork–Bandon railway line. Boole described his visit to the site with his colleague Mr Nicoll to MaryAnn:

Yesterday I walked with Mr N. to examine a very fine railway viaduct about 105 feet high which they are constructing about three miles distant from Cork. There was a quarry close by and he pointed out among other

Figure 4.8: The Chetwynd Viaduct (1851), *Illustrated London News*

things in it a surface of rock bearing the distinct ripple marks left by the tide of some ancient sea. The markings were as perfect as any that I have ever seen upon the shore. The rocks here are of the old red sandstone formation but almost destitute of fossils.[250]

Another Cork landmark that Boole visited on several occasions was Fr Mathew's Tower. The tower was built in 1846 to honour Theobald Mathew, the Capuchin friar who founded the Cork Total Abstinence Association in 1838. Fr Mathew advocated the taking of 'The Pledge' which was a promise to abstain from alcohol for life. At the height of its popularity before the Great Famine, over three million people in Ireland were said to have enrolled. A further 600,000 took 'The Pledge' in England. The turreted memorial tower was built in Glounthaune, ten miles east of Cork, during Fr Mathew's lifetime by a local merchant, William O'Connor. *The Illustrated London News* reported on the tower's construction and opening in 1846:

> A MAGNIFICENT Testimonial to the exertions of Father Mathew in the Temperance Movement has just been completed at Mountpatrick … The Testimonial is a massive Tower, which has been erected at the sole expense of Mr O'Connor to celebrate the kind reception given to Father Mathew by the right-minded Londoners in the year 1843, upon the occasion of his first Temperance Visit …[251]

4.9: Fr Mathew's Tower (1846), *Illustrated London News*

Boole's only reference to the drinking habits of Corkonians was in a letter written on St Patrick's Day in 1851:

Last night on my return home at about 10 o'clock I encountered a procession of patriotic people who were blowing trumpets and bullocks' horns in honour of the saint and a few of whom I regret to say appear to have been drinking whiskey – also in his honour. I suppose that they would derive authority for the practice from some old song which runs thus I think:

St Patrick was a gentleman
And came of dacent people
His father kept a shebeen shop
In the town of Inniscaple.[252]

Boole visited Fr Mathew's Tower at least three times in 1853. He wrote of his first trip in March to MaryAnn:

Yesterday I took a long country walk. We can now go by a bus two miles down the river for twopence. I availed myself of this and then went some miles further and on my return visit went up to Father Mathew's Tower whence there is the finest prospect near Cork, the vale of the Lee lying stretched out before you.[253]

Boole took several longer trips to the eastern side of County Cork also. The seaside village of Ballycotton, about twenty-five miles from Cork city, became a favourite location of his. In April 1850 he visited Ballycotton for the first time and spent a week there, which he believed brought 'considerable benefit' to his health. In a letter to MaryAnn he touched on the devastation of the shoemaking industry in Cloyne, a nearby market town, in the aftermath of the Famine. This must have struck a chord with Boole, given that his father had been a master shoemaker. *Slater's National Commercial Directory of Ireland* of 1846 listed twenty-two boot and shoe makers in Cloyne, which Boole described as 'an extinguished industry' by 1850:

Friday: Took steamer for Aghada a few miles below Cove, thence outside car to Cloyne, residence of Berkeley and Brinkley, saw a fine round tower there, noticed twelve ruined cabins in a row on entering the town, was told afterwards that they had been the residences of the Cloyne brogue makers, an extinguished branch of Irish industry. Brogues are a kind of shoe made of half tanned leather. From Cloyne to Ballycotton per outside car. Struck by the extreme beauty of the furze bushes on either side of the road, a sheet of golden blossoms. Reached Ballycotton about 7 o'clock pm. Spent the evening at the house of the Protestant clergyman, the Rev. G. Hingston, a very agreeable family consisting of the clergyman and his wife, five children and a very fine young man, brother of Mr H and a student of TCD.[254]

Figure 4.10: Ballycotton Lighthouse (1849), *Illustrated London News*

Boole continued, describing his accommodation and activities for the week:

> Took possession of my house in the village and set up housekeeping with a piece of roast beef and two pots of jam and 1lb of coffee sent without my knowledge by the mother of two of our students who went down with me and took up their abode with the clergyman.
>
> My accommodations are not very good, cleanliness not the household virtue of those who had the letting of the house. My servant Sarah, a barefooted but apparently modest and intelligent maiden, arranged to purchase bread, milk and tea in the village. The village shop, a branch from the establishment of Mrs Riordan (pronounced Reardon) of Cloyne, a very well-to-do matron with whom I had some pleasant conversation in passing through Cloyne touching the 'times'. I should have mentioned that she is the proprietor of the cars which ply in that part of the world.
>
> Saturday morning, took a long walk over the cliffs, scenery very savage, rocks black and sharpened, strata perpendicular and slaty in texture and nowhere rounded but made acute and pointed in the direction of the sea. Found people in every direction collecting seaweed for manure. Great abundance of primroses scattered over every bank.
>
> Sunday: Went to church – a very good congregation and a rather eloquent and very pleasing sermon. Spent the evening at Mr Hingston's.

Rev. George Hingston was the Church of Ireland clergyman in Ballycotton. During the Famine, the Cork Society of Friends supported a famine relief industry at Ballycotton which was jointly supervised by Hingston and Richard Evans, the coastguard officer, to keep inhabitants of Ballycotton from the workhouse or union. Grants of £70 worth of meal, beans, rice and flour were given by the Cork subcommittee of the Society of Friends and £10 was granted by the Ladies' Industrial Relief Association of Dublin. Hemp and fibres were to be made into fishermen's clothing, nets, blankets and fabrics.[255] In his letter to MaryAnn of 23 April 1850, Boole described the industry:

Visited on successive days the houses of the weavers and spinners in the village, inspected some of their native frieze and ordered for myself an outside coat to be made thereof. Those little manufacturies which employ about 90 people were established during the famine years by Mr Hingston with the assistance of some Quakers. Have kept the people out of the union when they could certainly have died and still provide them with a very humble living, the ordinary sustenance being Indian meal. The manufacturers are still under the entire control of Mr Hingston but they are only supported at the expense of great care and watchfulness on his part. Went one day on the sea and visited two islands at the entrance of the bay on one of which a lighthouse is being erected.

The lighthouse at Ballycotton was constructed in 1849 and was first lit in 1851.

Boole also mentions meeting two army officers during his visit to Ballycotton – Captain James Hervey and a Captain Butler. Boole told MaryAnn:

Monday: Received a call from a Captain Hervey, a gentleman who has some place in history having been one of the three men who closed the door of the farmhouse on the field of Waterloo. Had another call from a Captain Butler, a gentleman who had lost a limb in the service of the Queen of Spain under Gen. Evans. Spent an evening at the home of each and was hospitably treated, the remaining evenings at the house of Mr Hingston, the great attraction there being the harp playing of Mrs H, old Irish, Welch and Scotch airs, the sweetest strains I ever heard.

Figure 4.11: *Closing the Gates at Hougoumont*, Robert Gibb (1903)

James Hervey was an ensign in the Coldstream Guards at the Battle of Waterloo in 1815 and played a legendary part in that battle. He is credited with being one of the officers 'who closed the gates of Hougoumont'. The gate was at the entry to a farmyard at Chateau d'Hougoumont, a strategically important site on the west of the battlefield. The British commander, with a small party of officers including Hervey, led the effort to stop further incursions by the French. The Duke of Wellington declared that 'the success of the battle turned upon the closing of the gates at Hougoumont'.[256] In June 2015 Hougoumont was opened to the public on the 200th anniversary of the Battle of Waterloo.[257]

On his return to Cork, Boole received a 'pressing invitation' to return to Ballycotton and spend a few days at the home of either Mr Hingston or Captain Hervey, which he promised to do.[258] He found his health much improved after the visit and returned to the village on at least two more occasions in January and May 1854.[259]

Boole made several trips to west Cork and Kerry. The first was to Glengarriff in June 1850, which took place instead of a planned visit to Connemara with Mr Everest, father of his future wife. Boole explained to MaryAnn:

Figure 4.12: *Bantry Bay*, from Mary F.C. Cusack, *A History of the City and County of Cork* (1875)

The Connemara expedition is given up from want of time of Mr Everest, Dr Ryall's guest. We have therefore come to Glengarriff where we have spent this day and intend to set out for Killarney tomorrow whence we purpose to return to Cork on Saturday. Yesterday we travelled to Bantry over the mountains. It was a delightful day and some of the scenery was very beautiful. From Bantry we came across the bay this morning. Nothing can well exceed the beauty of this part of the bay surrounded by mountains and studded with islands. It deserves all that has been said of it.

The plants of this region would interest you greatly. The little flower called London Pride grows everywhere on the rocks. Spurges of great size are most abundant and ferns and foxgloves line the sides of the roads. The bogs are in many places white with bog cotton, a very pretty plant of which I enclose a specimen, and irises, etc. meet you everywhere. The weather is precisely of that kind which is the most agreeable for travelling – a mixture of shade and sunshine.[260]

In January 1854, Boole recorded a return visit to west Cork when he travelled to the Dunmanway Mountains. The weather was bitterly cold and one of the mountains was peaked with snow. Boole remarked that it was 'a very grand sight indeed'.[261]

Figure 4.13: *Lakes from Kenmare Road, Killarney, County Kerry* (c. 1895)

Boole continued his habit of taking long walks around Cork and took part in some local pastimes. In April 1854 he wrote to MaryAnn:

You must give my kind regards to Charles and Mrs Boole and a kiss to the little one. You must also mention me kindly to the Parrys and Kirks. I wish that they would some of them visit Cork. It is very beautiful this spring and I enjoy much my country walks, one of which I took on Saturday afternoon to a pleasant glen-like valley among the fields about three miles distant where we were shut out from all the world among the furze and wild plants which grew abundantly by a little stream that trawled away through the bottom of the valley. And generally once a week I take a walk of this kind, to the no small improvement of my health and spirits. After our walk we exercised ourselves with throwing a sledgehammer and a heavy weight, in which I need not say that the vice president had greatly the advantage though I succeeded in beating the steward.[262]

In the same letter, he described his expedition to Killarney to MaryAnn:

You have heard I suppose of my trip to Killarney where I spent three delightful days in company with our professor of geology [Professor Nicoll] – seeing the real beauty of that wondrous district of lake and mountain <u>for the first time</u>. I had the opportunity of examining with the greatest minuteness two eagles as they floated for a long time overhead. A small telescope brought out with great distinctness the beak and talons, the white tail, and the long pinions which stretch out beyond the expanded wings like fingers.[263]

The white-tailed eagle, as described by Boole, was the largest bird of prey ever to have existed in Ireland. During the nineteenth century it was extensively hunted and became extinct by 1910. In 2007 a conservation programme re-introduced the white-tailed eagle to Killarney National Park.[264]

There is no record of Boole ever visiting the west of Ireland, despite his attempt to do so in 1850 and his annoyance at the timing of his brother's wedding in 1853 which prevented a trip to Connemara. He spoke of being 'really anxious to see a little of the people in the solitary districts so much talked of yet so little visited'.[265] He did however visit the north of Ireland. In June 1852, Colonel and Mrs Chesney invited Boole to visit them at the time of the British Association for the Advancement of Science meeting in Belfast and he visited Ballymoney in 1853 with the Shaws.[266]

During most vacations from QCC, Boole returned to England. In the summer months, he generally made a detour to other parts of England and Wales on his way to or from Lincoln. His letters to MaryAnn give an account of the places he visited and the interesting sights he encountered on these trips. In July 1850 he visited London and spent an evening with Augustus De Morgan and his wife. He reported to MaryAnn:

> I have seen many interesting sights during my short residence here but the palm must be given among them all to the Nineveh marbles[267] in one of the vaults of the British Museum. I think them quite as interesting as any of the Egyptian remains. Whenever you again visit London you must see them. They and the hippopotamus which I have also seen are the great attractions in London just now.[268]

The hippopotamus that Boole referred to was called Obaysch, who arrived in London in May 1850 and caused quite a stir:

> The great event of 1850 was the arrival of the hippopotamus, the first living specimen seen in Europe 'since these creatures were last exhibited by the third Gordian in the Amphitheatre of Imperial Rome'. This young male was but a few days old when it was captured by a party of hunters sent out by the viceroy. They met with it on the island of Obaysch, in the White Nile, and from that spot the animal was named ...[269]

Figure 4.14: Obaysch the Hippopotamus (1852)

Thanks to the arrival of Obaysch, visitor numbers at London Zoo rocketed.[270]

The following month, Boole visited Thornton Priory, a medieval abbey located close to the small north Lincolnshire village of Thornton Curtis. He was not impressed by the atmosphere there:

> I reached home last night a little after ten o'clock having stopped at Thornton Priory for an hour or two to meditate among the tombs of its monks and abbots and availing myself of a special train in the evening which had brought to the same consecrated spot a body of teetotalers. Never visit a place of tombs with a crowd. All the poetry and devotion of the scene is over. I felt the strangest incongruity between the solemn old ruins and the gay and boisterous crowd which had gathered among them.[271]

In June 1851, Boole returned to Lincoln via Bangor in Wales to see the Menai Bridge which connected Anglesey to the Welsh mainland.[272] In the same month, he travelled to London where he visited the Great Exhibition in the Crystal Palace in Hyde Park in London. The exhibition was intended as a showcase for British engineering, invention, science and the arts but other countries also exhibited their achievements and works of art. It was the brainchild of a civil servant, Henry Cole, but was backed by Sir Robert Peel and Prince Albert. The exhibition was a great success, visited by over six million people in the six months that it was open between May and October 1851, providing the visitors with a unique experience:

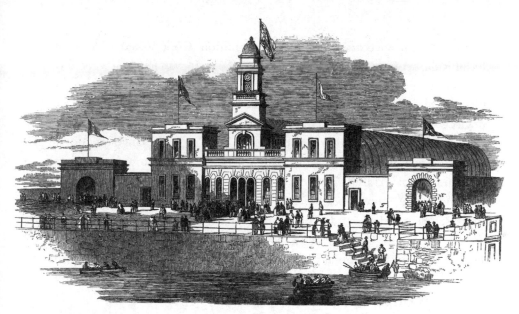

Figure 4.15: The Cork Exhibition Hall (1852), *Illustrated London News*

Within the Exhibition (no dogs and no smoking) visitors found every modern convenience, including refreshment rooms where over a million bottles of soft drinks were sold (no alcohol) and nearly a million Bath buns.

Free comfort facilities were available to all; filtered water was supplied by the Chelsea Waterworks Company and, for the first time, public lavatories were provided for the gentlemen and 'rest rooms' for the ladies ...

... It was the first time that the nations of the world had ever come together in one place, other than on a battlefield and even then not in such numbers or in such variety, and it was a remarkable showcase for the manufactures of Britain and the world.[273]

Boole was suitably impressed. He told MaryAnn:

The exhibition answers all my expectations concerning it. I need not attempt to describe it now. You will soon I hope see it for yourself and will then feel that its merits have not been exaggerated ... The weather here has been extremely hot. In the galleries of the Great Exhibition it yesterday reached 90° but this was not the average heat of the building, nor strange to say was it very oppressive as the ventilation was very good.[274]

Inspired by the success of the London exhibition, Cork hosted a National Exhibition between June and September 1852. It was felt that very few exhibits originating from Cork had been displayed in the exhibition in Crystal Palace and an executive committee in Cork was set up to address this neglect and to stimulate local industry.

The National Exhibition was housed in the Corn Exchange on Albert Quay, on the site of the present City Hall, which was extended to accommodate the number of exhibits. The exhibition included displays of items such as whiskey, ale, porter, pearl barley, 'Norton's Projectile Shells', hydraulic presses, Valentia slate, stuffed birds, wax flowers and Cork ginghams. Most of the major Cork businesses and manufactories participated. The Fine Art Hall of the exhibition contained paintings and sculptures by prominent Irish artists.[275] Prince Albert subscribed £100 towards the cost of the exhibition and Boole contributed ten shillings.[276]

Boole described the excitement in the city prior to the opening of the Exhibition to MaryAnn:

Cork is at this time full of expectation of the pleasure to be derived from its exhibition. I was in the room yesterday and was much pleased with its appearance. We are to have lectures from some distinguished people. Among others Col. Chesney will lecture and the experiments on the new firearms are to be exhibited in Cork Harbour. Whately [the Archbishop of Dublin] is to open the series.[277]

The exhibition was opened by the Lord Lieutenant as part of a four-day visit to the city, which included a visit to Queen's College Cork. Boole told MaryAnn:

The Lord Lieutenant came in this afternoon and the street was lined with soldiers – no great enthusiasm was manifested by the people but a drenching rain might damp the spark. He goes to Bandon to-night and returns thence tomorrow to the opening of the exhibition. We are to be there in costume – the *Hallelujah Chorus, Coronation Anthem* and a special inauguration ode for the occasion are to be sung which will greatly relieve the dullness of the loyal and dutiful addresses. We shall reserve seats with Executive Committee which will be an advantage as none but ladies and official persons are to be admitted to that part of the building during the ceremonial. After it is over the Lord Lieutenant visits the college where we again receive him and present an address. It will be a very busy day and wearisome one to those who afterwards dine with His Excellency in public and then repair to a ball which is to be held on the occasion.[278]

Boole wrote a few days later:

The exhibition is really very far superior to anything I could have expected. The general effect is quite imposing and some of the sculptures and a few of the paintings are really of very high merit. The industrial department too is better than one could have expected. However, I will tell you more when I get home.[279]

In all, over 129,000 visitors attended during its three-month duration.[280]

Once the exhibition ended, the Southern Hall was offered to the trustees of the Royal Cork Institution. The building was dismantled and rebuilt as the Athenaeum on Nelson Place, now known as Emmet Place. In April 1854 Boole reported on the progress of the building to MaryAnn:

They have nearly completed the Cork Athenaeum, a building which contains a large public room, only 17 feet shorter than the St George's Hall in Liverpool. It is to contain a magnificent organ by Telford – I think the one in the Great Exhibition. There is no doubt that in time Cork will be a very fine city. Its natural advantages are very great indeed.[281]

The Great Dublin Exhibition followed between May and October 1853. In May 1853, Dr Charles Graves, professor of mathematics at Trinity College Dublin, invited Boole to visit him in Howth.[282] Boole combined this trip with a visit to the Dublin exhibition.

Boole had visited Dublin previously in February 1852 when he was awarded an honorary LL.D. by Trinity College. He described that visit to MaryAnn:

Yesterday I went to hear John Gregg preach in the morning and in St Patrick's Cathedral in the afternoon. In the evening I called upon Dr Graves with whom I am to dine and breakfast tomorrow. He has still with him the invalid sister, a young lady of whom he spoke in one of his letters. This morning I took an oath adjuring the Pretender and all his posterity and paid £10 for the stamp.[283]

During that trip, Boole visited Howth, a village outside Dublin, with his friend George Allman who held the chair of botany in TCD between 1844 and 1856.[284] Boole told MaryAnn:

I am going down to Howth to enjoy the sea air with a friend, Mr Allman. Tomorrow at one o'clock I am to appear in a doctor's gown. At seven a banquet is to be given in the hall at which the Lord Lieutenant is to be present, also the Archbishop of Armagh the chancellor of the university. I am invited to dine with them. The banquet is given I believe in celebration of the election of a provost or chancellor and I am told that it is to be one of great splendour.[285]

Boole was greatly honoured by the awarding of the LL.D. in 1852 and used the title in *The Laws of Thought*. He wrote to MaryAnn about his trip:

During my visit to Dublin I met with a great deal of kindness and was introduced to a good many people whom I thought it a pleasure to be acquainted with. Had I been able to stay longer I should have seen more of some of them but even during my stay I was prevented by my cold from accepting some invitations. Mrs Ryall has been so good as to make me a present of a plate engraved with my name and new title and a number of cards. These I received this morning.[286]

Mrs Ryall's kindness to Boole is evident from this letter and she appeared to have taken him under her wing.

When Boole visited Dublin for the Great Dublin Exhibition in 1853, he told MaryAnn:

I dare say you may have heard of the famous Hill of Howth, though who Howth was you may not know. Neither do I; but I suppose him to be some fair giant of old days who lived in this part of the world before Saxons were heard of. However this may have been, I write from the Hill of Howth where I arrived last night after spending the greater part of the day in the Dublin exhibition. It is well worth seeing. The pictures, especially the Flemish ones, are magnificent. The general impression is however greatly inferior to that produced by the Crystal Palace in Hyde Park ...

... I am going this morning to walk around the promontory of Howth along the edge of the cliffs. There is a new broad pathway which is said to open up a magnificent scene.

I need scarcely tell you that I am now in the house of Dr Graves. He is in London but Mrs Graves wrote to beg that I would pay her a visit. It is a wild and beautiful spot, the sea breaking on the rocks before the house and the coast much indented with hollows.[287]

In November 1853 Boole witnessed one of the worst floods that Cork has ever experienced from his lodgings in the Unkles' house in 5 Grenville Place, where *The Laws of Thought* was written. 'Cork' is an anglicisation of the Irish name 'Corcach Mór na Mumhan', the Great Marsh of Munster. The city is built around and over two channels of the River Lee so at high tide and after heavy rain, it is prone to flooding. Edmund Spenser described Cork's situation in his epic poem, *The Faerie Queene*:

The spreading Lee, that like an island fayre
Encloseth Corke with his divided flood.[288]

In March 1850, Boole had written:

The wind is still violent, not from the west as I was told but from the SE. This brings in tides which lay a large part of Cork under water. It is a dreadful thing for the poor creatures who live in cellars. Mr F. Jennings described some sad sights which he witnessed yesterday. He had to traverse the streets in a boat.[289]

In November 1853, *The London Illustrated News* reported:

The City of Cork has just been visited by a fearful inundation, stated to have been the greatest calamity of the kind which has taken place in Ireland for upwards of seventy years. The excessive rains with which this part of the country has been visited, added to the violent hurricane from the S.E., which prevailed on Tuesday (last week), and both acting with an unusually high spring tide, produced the most serious floods ...

Figure 4.16: Flood of November 1853 in Great George's Street (now Washington Street), Cork

The waters were dashing under the arches of Patrick's Bridge, carrying chairs, beams of timber, trees, &c. At this instant a terrific crash was heard followed by a piercing shriek, and it was discovered that a great piece of the bridge had given way, carrying down, it is believed, eleven persons. They were borne down the tide and all were drowned, with the exception of one, who was rescued.[290]

Boole wrote an account of this flood in a letter to his mother on 5 November 1853:

My dear mother,
    No doubt you have heard before of the great flood in Cork. To relieve you from any apprehension I write to tell you that myself and my friends are all safe. I was confined the whole day to the upper part of the house, the lower rooms being filled with water and the flood rushing by like the sea. The walls of the quay opposite were washed away and the pavement was in parts ploughed into holes four foot deep. From the top of the house no land could be seen except the hills, and the water in the streets immediately behind us rose to a height of more than six feet.

The principal bridge in the city is nearly destroyed and it is thought that more people perished by the fall of it than are yet known of.

A public meeting was held yesterday to raise a subscription for the relief of the poor, and a thousand pounds were subscribed on the spot. The destruction of property of every kind especially groceries was very great. I am sorry to add that my landlord Mr Unkles will be a loser to a large amount. He had 50 tons of flour and Indian meal damaged – and had to sell a large part of it by auction today.

A foundry standing by the river was washed away and two men who were at work in it were carried off but rescued at a distance of half a mile. In the main streets near this house a house was washed down and in another house a poor tailor was rescued with great difficulty through the upper part of the window. He was floating on his counter near to the ceiling.

It would be impossible to describe the scene that presented itself to the west of the city. The rushing flood might I think be termed sublime. It is said that no flood of equal extent is either remembered or recorded here. The sun shone brightly all the time.[291]

The damage to the city's infrastructure was immense, but fortunately a cholera outbreak following the flood was contained. Boole reported to MaryAnn:

During the fine weather the flood has not so far as I know been followed by illness. I believe too that the cholera has not spread in the harbour. Those who were attacked were chiefly poor German immigrants on whom the change of diet is thought to have had an injurious effect. They have now got a temporary bridge on boats over the river near Patrick's Bridge and are erecting a temporary wooden one also. Estimates of the loss occasioned by the great flood run as high as £60,000 but I think this is too much.[292]

In 1854, the telegraph arrived in Cork. The line from Belfast to Dublin and onto Cork was over ground on poles and an underground system ran from Cork to Queenstown.[293] In April 1854, Boole wrote to MaryAnn about its arrival:

We have new telegraphic communication with London and every day at two o'clock there is great excitement to learn about what the wires reveal respecting the progress of the war.[294]

Boole was referring to the Crimean War which had broken out in October 1853. In the early months of 1854 many Irishmen enlisted for a war which it was believed would be over in a few months, but did not actually end until February 1856. Boole was clearly uncomfortable with Britain's allies, the Ottoman Turks. He continued:

> I confess that I regard the state of affairs with some apprehension. I wish we had a more decidedly unexceptionable cause, or that our cause, good in many respects, were not damaged or degraded by its connection with the (I fear) barbarism of the Moslem population of Turkey. It certainly cannot be propped up long. Reforms forced upon the Ottoman government are not likely I think to work well. Past experience shows this. History however has been compared to a light in the stern of a vessel which illuminates only the waves behind it.[295]

Boole often referred to the climate in Cork and its effect on his health. His letters to MaryAnn mention many minor illnesses during his first years in the city including coughs and colds, lumbago, rheumatism and toothache. But prior to his arrival in Cork, Boole already appeared to have suffered from bouts of ill-health. In July 1849 he had visited Niton in the Isle of Wight for treatment at the chalybeate spring there. The spring water was said to be very beneficial in the cure of many ailments such as indigestion, stomach weaknesses and nervous disorders. Boole probably stayed at the Sandrock Hotel, from which a path led to the spring. He told MaryAnn:

> You have probably seen some of my daily letters to mother and know a little of my doings and adventures since I left home. I shall only add to what you already know that the place at which I am being treated for a few days longer appears to be one of the most delightful in the whole Isle of Wight. I almost daily discover new walks, each more delightful than those before. The sea too is finer, the waves higher, the coast rockier and more broken and the hills higher than in any other part of the island.[296]

His delight at the scenery was tempered by missing his family. MaryAnn appeared to have been unwell also and was staying with their brother William and his wife Eliza at Alfreton in Derbyshire. He continued:

Figure 4.17: The Sandrock Hotel, Isle of Wight

I do not doubt that if pure air and kind nursing and affectionate attendance will do anything for you, you will be better at Alfreton than at any other place. And the scenery of your neighbourhood, though less striking, is not less pleasing than that of the Isle of Wight. It is a great drawback from the pleasure of travelling through or of residing in a beautiful country when you are alone and must enjoy its beauties to yourself. In this respect you have greatly the advantage over me. I wish for my own sake that you, William and Eliza were here.[297]

In December 1849 during Boole's first winter in Cork, he described the weather to MaryAnn:

The weather continues wet, during the last week it was raining constantly. I have bought another pair of strong shoes; it is impossible to do without them. I have also bought a light upper coat chiefly to keep off wet for it is never cold and I was too warm in the one I brought. I have also got a dressing gown to wear in the house. The expedient mother recommended succeeds perfectly in keeping my bed dry. I am told this type of weather continues till the middle of January. I forgot whether I mentioned that my walking stick has become twisted like a corkscrew with the humidity of the atmosphere. With all this my health is pretty good. I am strong and my appetite has improved.[298]

In July 1850 Boole was detained in London due to illness. He told MaryAnn:

I should have returned home today but have got a sudden attack of lumbago through changing my vest for a lighter one just before a change of weather for cold. It is a disappointment to me but I shall travel as soon as I can. I have taken a warm bath this morning and am going to apply some hot flannel and salt which is recommended by one of the men who attend at the public baths and washhouses.[299]

In the following spring of 1851, Boole told his mother that his health was generally good, apart from suffering from some boils and an attack of lameness due to overtight shoes.[300] A few weeks later however he was once again ill. He recuperated on a visit to Monkstown in early May:

In health I am very much better than I was before the change of air. I had been rather seriously unwell. The immediate cause of my illness was a long walk and a long fast in the east wind after too much taxing of the system with work of another kind. The chief symptom of my complaint was an extraordinary sense of bodily weakness after mental application insomuch as I was compelled to lay books aside in a great measure. This is a necessity from which I am now relieved. I have had very little anxiety for myself but a good deal from the thought that if I were taken away you would not be provided for. It is a singular thought that a month or six weeks ago I thought myself stronger than I had been for years.[301]

The winter of 1852–3 was more severe. On 20 February 1853, he wrote:

I have been suffering for the last few days from a cold with a slight attack of rheumatism in the chest, the only species of illness that I have had this session. However, it was not so bad as to confine me to the house or interrupt my lectures and I feel now well again …

We have had frost and there has been skating on the Lough and the weather is bright, cheerful and cold. You can hardly tell how different everything looked during the frost. I felt as if I were enjoying the old English winter once more. The Cork people did not like it. They complained of the cold. But for my part I have never felt half so well in Cork as I did during the continuance of the frost. My cold began on the very day on which it began to thaw. Generally there has been nothing to complain of in the weather since my return.[302]

In March 1853 he responded to a complaint from MaryAnn:

I think you have some reason to complain of the shortness of my letters, but I must try to write longer ones in future. In one point you are mistaken, however. It is not as easy a task to me to write letters. It is always a disagreeable occupation and I have heard many persons not idle and not unpractised in composition say the same thing. I find it more difficult and more fatiguing than mathematics and I am quite sure that my hand becomes weary a great deal sooner with this species of labour than with any other. Very often however I have felt a certain degree of weakness and stiffness in the hand dependent very much upon the state of health and this makes the mechanical occupation of writing letters troublesome. It is very strange that I do not feel this when writing on scientific subjects.[303]

Despite his discomfort, Boole did succeed in writing many letters as well as academic papers which have survived the passage of time.

Chapter 5

DR JOHN BURY

J OHN BURY (1816–67) was a medical doctor in Lincoln who was a close friend and contemporary of Boole's. They became friendly in 1844 through a mutual friend. After Boole became professor of mathematics at Queen's College Cork they corresponded frequently throughout the 1850s and 1860s. Boole's letters to Bury demonstrate a warm friendship between the two men and refer not only to mathematics and logic but also to family matters, sharing intimate details of the health of his wife and children. Boole regularly visited John Bury at his home in Chester on his journeys between Lincoln and Cork. After Boole's death, Bury sent Mary Boole a detailed biographical letter which recorded his memories of her husband's character and interests.

John Bury was born in London in 1816 and studied medicine at the University of Bonn, graduating in September 1843 and becoming a member of the Royal College of Physicians. His wife Margaret was born in Prussia. The couple's first son Edward Thomas (Tom) was born in Lincoln in 1844, followed by their second son Charles in 1846. By 1851, the family had settled in Newgate Street, Chester. Sadly Tom, who had not been a healthy child, died in November 1856 aged only twelve. Bury continued to reside in Chester until his death and his obituary in the *Chester Chronicle* of 20 April 1867 had high praise for him:

> Dr John Bury was born of a very good Lancashire family. He studied medicine fully and exhaustively in the schools of London, Paris, Strasbourg, Dublin and Edinburgh. Some eighteen years ago he commenced practice in Chester and after initial difficulties, built up a considerable clientele, who will attest to his talents, his goodness, amiability, and honourableness of character. Patients will remember his skill, care, and untiring attention, the grave courtesy and ready sympathy they ever met with from the Doctor, and this quite without reference to social position and worldly wealth. Dr Bury possessed an intellect of very high order and he would discourse upon and discuss mathematics, psychology, pure metaphysics, social science, political economy and ethics. Some eight years ago he developed a Theory on the Doctrine of Limits, which was as profound as it was original, and which would have been given to the world had not Mr J.S. Mill, in the latest edition of his Logic, and Mr Herbert Spenser, in the meantime, published the same theory.
>
> Among his close friends he numbered the late Dr George Boole F.R.S. the eminent mathematician …

Figure 5.1: Headstone of Dr John Bury, Overleigh Old Cemetery, Chester

But if his mental qualities were admirable, his social and moral attributes were such that they gained for him the enthusiastic affection and attachment of all who had the great privilege of his friendship. He was unselfish, in fact self-sacrificing to an extent of which the present age affords us few examples … He was a man without guile, without malice; a great lover of literature and poetry, but only of the best; and a man of rare humility.

In him the poor have lost a true friend and helper; Chester has lost a citizen of whom she might justly be proud; and his sorrowing relatives have lost one who cannot be replaced, for it is not given to many to know two such men in a lifetime.

'He was a man, take him for all in all,
We ne'er shall look upon his like again!'[304]

Boole and Bury appear to have lost touch with each other in the late 1840s but contact was re-established in early 1850. Boole received a letter from Bury and replied from Cork on 11 February 1850:

It was a great pleasure to me to hear from you once more. I had often wondered where you had settled or if indeed you had settled and what you were doing and when passing through Manchester thought it would be a pardonable liberty if I made inquiry of your friends. I was glad to find you were still in England and hope that you may yet succeed in establishing a practice sufficient if not to place you in affluence yet to satisfy your modest desires and those of your family. Let me however know whether you have really made up your mind to stay in Chester or whether you desire still to revisit Germany. I should think that unless there is some very important professional object to be accomplished by your return thither it will be better for you to stay where you are and trust to time and perseverance the rest.[305]

The letter continued with praise for his fellow professors:

My colleagues are agreeable and I need really say intellectual men. One of them who lives in the same house with me is a fellow of TCD, and I see a good deal of him. He is a pleasant companion. Among our medical faculty the most distinguished person is Dr Fleming, the author of a work on 'tincture of aconite'. He appears to me to be a very acute and clever man and often spends an evening with me. I should think you know his name and reputation.[306]

The state of Bury's finances and the development of his medical practice are recurring themes in subsequent letters. Boole was never a wealthy man but, as seen in Chapter Three, his letters prove him to have been extraordinarily generous in supporting his family and friends and advancing loans and gifts to those in need of financial assistance. On 5 June 1850, after Bury had set up a practice in Chester, Boole advised:

You must be less scrupulous in receiving fees from friends than you once were.[307]

On 2 December 1850, he offered the family a loan:

I have been thinking of something which Mrs Bury said to me about the furnishing of one of your rooms for the reception of a lodger and I now wish to say that if you are willing to make the experiment I have a few pounds to spare and will lend you what will be requisite to do this in a plain but comfortable way. I can spare £10 to £15 and this would, according to Mrs Bury's account, do. But I must make it an express condition that the money shall really be devoted to this purpose. I had hoped when I visited you a month or six weeks ago to find you doing something of the kind to increase your income till such time as you may not need adventitious help. I must give you my positive conviction that by taking such a step as I recommend, you would not in any degree lessen your social position or diminish your chances of professional success. The majority of people would on the contrary respect you more. And depend on it that your real circumstances are known.[308]

On 19 December 1850 Boole wrote:

My dear friend, I enclose you the sum of three pounds by post office order and sincerely hope that it may be of some service to you. Please to acknowledge the receipt of it and enclose a memorandum of the form 'I acknowledge myself indebted to Mr George Boole in the sum of three pounds value received'. This will be enough between you and me.[309]

On 11 October 1854 Boole responded to what appears to be a direct request for a loan:

I will either send you the money you ask for tomorrow by the post or will contrive to let you have it when I pass through Chester on our way to Ireland.

He added:

I don't know anything that gives me greater satisfaction than to be able to assist you with a little money, but at the same time I feel that it is not less the part of friendship to advise you to overcome that false delicacy which prevents you from asking people to perform an act of common justice in paying you that which you have earned. You will not be offended with me for saying that I think this is really a weakness and under your actual circumstances a reprehensible one on your part.[310]

Boole then goes on to berate his friend in the same tone for several pages, claiming that Bury's underlying problem seems to be 'an excessive fear of censure' which he would be well rid of.

The next mention of money is in a letter from Boole on 15 October 1860 which suggests that Boole's lending of money to Bury had been ongoing, and presumably on an interest-free basis.

> My dear friend,
>   Your remittance which closes the account between us arrived safely and I am much obliged to you for it and at the same time deeply glad that I have been able to render you any aid.[311]

Why did Boole feel the need to lend Bury what were relatively large sums of money for the time in the period 1850–1860? The most likely explanation would appear to be that Bury failed to charge realistic fees or indeed any fees at all to some patients for his consultations. Perhaps in later years Boole also felt that he needed to reward Bury in some way for the consultations given to him and his family over the years.

When Boole married in 1855 and his wife became pregnant, he eagerly sought Bury's advice. On 18 March 1856 he inquired as follows:

> I want to ask you a professional question. My wife expects to be confined about the beginning of July. She has never worn stays and has a great dislike to wearing them. Her female friends who are experienced in such things told her that it is necessary she should now wear stays. I think this advice is chiefly given with a view to appearances, about which we care less than most people. It is added however that if she does not now wear stays she will suffer for it afterwards. I find it difficult to believe this. It seems to me and to my wife that constraints would be injurious to both mother and child. However, I wish to ask you the question. My wife has good health and has always been remarkably active. Mary adds that she is now very careful of herself in every way as respect diet, exertion and whatever else affects her condition.
>   This is all I have to say and an answer at your convenience will greatly oblige me.[312]

The Booles' modern attitude to the health of the mother in pregnancy and their courage in going against conventional advice are impressive. Bury obviously supported their position as is clear from Boole's reply on 29 March:

> I am very much obliged to you for your letter which quite confirms my anticipations. Thus far no one I suppose ever enjoyed greater comfort and better health than my wife has done during her pregnancy and I attribute it and so does she to the freedom from injurious restraints of every kind.[313]

Mary Ellen Boole was born in June 1856 and Boole's letter to Bury on 21 June is surprisingly frank for the Victorian era. His delight in fatherhood is evident:

> I am now a father. My little first-born – a daughter – came into the world two days ago. It is a fine healthy child and its dear mother is wonderfully well. The nurse tells me that she was never present at a more satisfactory case and the doctor confirms her judgement.
>
> I don't know however whether I should have done more than tell you of my new relation if I had not some time ago consulted you about my wife's management of herself during pregnancy. She had the courage, in spite of perpetual forebodings of evil from experienced matrons, to follow out your advice implicitly. She wore neither stays nor corsets nor compresses of any kind. I believe it to have been a consequence of this freedom that she was able to take an amount of exercise very unusual for persons in her situation up to the day of her confinement. Her step remained as light as ever and her motion was unimpeded. Her suffering during labor was less than is generally experienced in a first confinement – nor was it really severe for more than an hour or two. When it was over, she seemed well, talked cheerfully during the evening and slept like an infant the whole night. The next evening her breasts gave milk without any previous accession of fever or uneasiness – and the only symptom she noticed in reply to an enquiry of mine was a little giddiness at the moment when the child first began to suck. She and the child are at this moment as well as it is I suppose possible for them to be under the circumstances.[314]

I thought you would be interested to receive this account. That people who have been in the habit of wearing stays and such like imagined supports may need them during pregnancy is probable enough. But that those who have not worn them previously and who continue to dispense with them are the better for the exemption is a fact, the knowledge of which ought to be diffused. I think that a great deal of suffering, certainly to the mother and probably to the child, is due to the neglect of Nature's plainest dictates.

Perhaps I ought to add that during her pregnancy my wife took no medicine whatever – nor has she taken any since. She has needed none.[315]

The births of Margaret and Alicia followed in 1858 and 1860 respectively and in August 1862 Boole told Bury of the arrival of their fourth daughter:

On Tuesday evening a fourth little girl [Lucy Everest] was added to my family. Mrs Boole seems quite well and so is the little one. I am thankful that all went as well as could be wished. All the children are well. Little Alice is as saucy as ever.[316]

As new parents, the Booles were naturally concerned for the welfare of their children. They were particularly anxious to avoid virulent diseases such as smallpox and courageous enough to consider using new vaccines.[317] On 21 January 1863, Boole wrote to Bury:

I have spoken to our medical man here and he is quite willing to use the vaccine if you will get it for us. If you can do so I ask you must send it soon as we are anxious about the children. Alice is now 2½ years old and every now and then we hear of smallpox in the neighbourhood. Don't forget that you are to come and see us whenever you can. The vaccination of Alice is reserved for your friendship and skill.[318]

In 1861, the son of Boole's friend the Reverend E.R. Larken died of smallpox. Edmund Larken had been a medical student at QCC and had resided with Boole in Castle White in 1849 (see Chapters Three and Seven). The Booles' desire to have their children vaccinated was probably heightened by this untimely death. Again, on 18 August 1863, Boole referred to vaccines when he wrote to Bury from his new house in Ballintemple:

I thank you though late for the vaccine lymph which you sent me for my little girl. We finally had her vaccinated by the village doctor.[319]

Much of the Boole–Bury correspondence is taken up with various other medical matters. Mary Boole was unwell in the early months of 1861. She visited the hydropathic establishment of Dr Barter in Blarney but this did not have the desired effect on her health. On 21 June 1861 Boole told Bury:

Mrs Boole has not been well for some months past and we are thinking of a change of air for her. We propose to go to Bonn [Mrs Bury's home city] for a short time, or perhaps if we like it in all respects, for a couple of months … We should prefer boarding in a German family either at Bonn or near to it … It is probable that we may set off next Friday, so if you could suggest anything before that time we would be obliged to you. Our objects are first to improvement of my wife's health. Secondly, the opportunity of hearing German spoken. Thirdly, the enjoyment of travel and the avoiding of great expense.[320]

The Booles travelled through France, Belgium, Holland and Germany for nine weeks in July and August 1861 (see Chapter Eight). Boole described the last part of their trip to Brooke:

It was a fatiguing journey and Mary was not so well when she reached London as she had been before. We spent three days there, then went down to Chester where we spent one day with my old friend Bury, now I am glad to say a prosperous man, and thence returned after an absence of nine weeks and a few days.[321]

On their return to Cork, Boole reported an improvement in Mary's health. Bury had probably prescribed the cod liver oil that Boole referred to:

I am thankful to say that Mrs Boole is a great deal better than she was in Chester. She is really gaining flesh and begins almost to like the cod liver oil. I am told by all who see Mrs Boole that the change in her appearance is great from the time of her leaving home.[322]

One of the reasons for the strong bond of friendship between Boole and Bury was their common interest in mathematics and particularly logic.

They had met at a gathering in Lincoln where Boole was expounding a theorem in geometry in 1844 and Boole sent Bury the text and page proofs of *The Laws of Thought* for his comments before the book was published. Boole respected his opinion and consulted with him frequently. Bury too seemed to be well versed in mathematics and to have had contact with some eminent mathematicians of the day. For example, there was the famous applied mathematician George Green (1793–1841) of Nottingham, who like Boole was largely self-taught, but who, unlike Boole, did manage to study at the University of Cambridge as a mature student. Boole and Green both had Sir Edward Bromhead as a mentor and supporter, but it is unlikely that the two of them ever met. Green is famous as the father of the mathematical theory of electricity and magnetism and one of the founders of potential theory. He influenced great scientists such as Maxwell and Kelvin and according to some, laid the foundations of quantum theory. In early 1850, nine years after Green's death, Boole wrote to Bury:

> I should like to be in possession of Mr Green's tracts and some particularly of the one on electricity, and if his son (whom I once examined in London at the College of Preceptors) has duplicates of them, I should be very glad to purchase the spare copies. The tract of which some particularly speak was published I believe in Nottingham. I have seen those which appeared in the *Camb. Phil. Transactions*. I have told you how much I admire them.[323]

Bury sent a copy of one of Green's papers to Boole the following month. In another letter in June 1850, Boole wrote:

> Tell Mr Green that I am much obliged to him for thinking of me and that any of his father's papers of which he has duplicates would be valuable to me. I should be happy to remunerate him for them if this could be done in a way that would not hurt his feelings of delicacy.[324]

On 24 March 1851 Boole told Bury:

> I have to acknowledge the receipt of one of Mr Green's papers which you (I presume) sent me some time ago. I am much obliged to you for it and also to young Mr Green if it was to him that you were indebted for it. Anything of Mr Green's is valuable. Cambridge has had in my opinion no other mathematician of equal powers since Newton.[325]

This is an extraordinary compliment that Boole is paying Green, and as he rarely minced his words, there is little doubt that he is quite sincere.

Many incidental details of Boole's attitudes to mathematics and logic appear in his correspondence with Bury, as well as information concerning his progress with publications in these areas in the period 1850 to 1864. On 11 February 1850 he wrote:

> You would not make much of my tract in the *Journal.* I am still working at the same subject [logic] and with great success. My two former essays were premature, not indeed containing any errors, but presenting a very inefficient view of the subject of logic.[326]

On 24 March 1851 Boole wrote to Bury:

> Write a long letter; I would do the same if I were not very busy. The logic has been at a standstill for some time as I have been writing papers for the *Cambridge Journal,* the first part of one of which has just appeared. As professor I feel bound to keep up some correspondence with the purely mathematical public, but my heart is with the Logic.[327]

All through the period 1850–4 Boole bombarded his friend with text and eventually proof pages of the book he was writing, *The Laws of Thought.* Below is a selection of extracts from his letters around this time:

> *26 August 1850* I send you two more sheets of my work but from their imperfect state you will I fear find it difficult to get on with them. If so, don't feel it a duty to read them but wait till the work is out which will not be long. It is about half finished.[328]

> *2 December 1850* I am working steadily at the logic writing something every day and hope in a few months to have the first draft of the work completed. When I have a fair copy of the introduction, you shall see it.[329]

> *23 March 1852* I am working on steadily at the logic and probabilities doing something if but little every day. In a short time, I hope to have it in such forwardness as to be able to decide finally upon the course of publication. The subject loses nothing of its interest in my eyes.[330]

11 July 1853 The copies of my first chapter came late and I am sorry to say that I can only lend you one to read. I think you will like the style in which it is got up.[331]

Boole continued to send Bury pages from his book during the period July to October 1853. However, since we do not have access to Bury's replies to Boole we have no way of knowing what objections, comments or contributions Bury may have made. There is however one intriguing exception. On 24 October 1853, not long before the publication of the book, Boole wrote in answer to Bury's comments:

I have received the sheets and am very much obliged to you for your observations which I have read with attention but upon which having a good deal to do today I cannot now make any remarks further than that if we grant the whole actual procedure of thought to be necessary (and I do not positively affirm either that it is or is not so) still there remains that distinction between right and wrong to which I have referred – a distinction which I differ from you in believing to be absolute and not relative. Here I am afraid we must agree to differ.[332]

One suspects that Bury's contributions may have been directed more towards the philosophical portions of Boole's book rather than those devoted to mathematical logic.

On 2 April 1854 Boole asked Bury:

Write and say if you have received the copy of my book. I have some reason to fear that in one or two instances they have not been delivered.[333]

And on 7 April Boole wrote:

I enclose a review of my book written here by Dr Ryall – which I think very able. I quite agree in your condemnation of the one in the *Athenaeum*. It was evidently written by one who did not understand the subject. There is a well-written notice in the *Westminster* for April.[334]

The Laws of Thought was dedicated to John Ryall as follows:

TO JOHN RYALL LL.D.
VICE-PRESIDENT AND PROFESSOR OF GREEK
IN QUEEN'S COLLEGE CORK
THIS WORK IS INSCRIBED
IN TESTIMONY OF FRIENDSHIP AND ESTEEM

In his introduction, Boole also mentions another mentor:

> To his valued friend, the Rev. George Stephens Dickson of Lincoln, the
> Author desires to record his obligations for such kind assistance in the
> revision of this work and for some important suggestions.

But of John Bury, there is no mention or acknowledgement. It has been
rather cruelly suggested by E.T. Bell that Boole's dedication of *The Laws
of Thought* to John Ryall, the uncle of his wife-to-be, did his matrimonial
prospects no harm at a time when he may have been contemplating marriage
to Mary Everest.[335] On 4 January 1853, in a letter written from Lincoln,
Boole coyly mentioned to Bury:

> I am at present under the necessity of going into Gloucestershire on
> business and it is from thence I shall set out on my Irish journey.[336]

In May 1853, Boole was planning to return to Lincoln for his brother
Charles' wedding in June and proposed stopping at Chester on the way. He
wrote to Bury in bachelor mode:

> There will be time in the interval for a stroll among the hills. Tell Mrs Bury
> that she must get everything ready for us and I am sure she understands
> what poor creatures men are – alone. But it is a piece of knowledge which
> comes to all ladies by invitation if not by experience and I dare not say
> one word against its truth.[337]

The mathematical correspondence between the two men continued after
the publication of *The Laws of Thought* in 1854 and Boole's marriage in the
following year. In the later years letters were less frequent, but on 13 July
1862 Boole wrote:

Two papers which I sent in June to the R[oyal] S[ociety] are to be printed in the *Phil. Transactions* and will be, not before long I think. One of them relates to the theory of probabilities and contains what I think will be considered as putting the theory of the subject contained in *The Laws of Thought* in an established fashion. It is that the conditions of mathematical consistency of the method are precisely accordant with the conditions of probability in the data – in all problems whatever. I have at intervals been trying to prove this generally for many years – but all my previous results were partial. I hope to explain this to you some day.[338]

Some other incidental details emerge from Boole's letters to Bury. Bury had asked him for a reference for Mr Giles, the owner of a school at Netherleigh House, Eaton Street, Chester, in 1849 where Mrs Bury taught. Boole rather pointedly refused to do so and then rather makes a meal of his refusal by moralising about his reasons for not doing so:

> I very much regret that I cannot comply with Mr Giles's request. Will you give my compliments to him and say I have been compelled to make it a rule never to give a testimonial or recommendation of anyone without intimate personal knowledge of the party in whose favour it is given. Mr Giles will I am sure feel that I do not possess sufficient knowledge of his qualifications and attainments to enable me to give my testimony in accordance with the above principle to his fitness for the title of College of Preceptors. He will therefore feel that I do not by thus declining his request intend any disrespect to him. On the contrary, as he is a friend of yours, it would give me the greatest of pleasure to bear testimony in his favour if I felt that I knew him sufficiently to enable me to do so.[339]

Cynically, one might feel that Boole himself had had a great deal of difficulty becoming an examiner at the College of Preceptors, including one false start, so perhaps he felt there was no reason why he should smooth the way for a nonentity like Giles. Incidentally, in another letter to Bury, Boole describes Giles as an 'Antinomian', which turns out to be 'A person holding that the moral law is not binding on Christians, on the ground that faith alone is sufficient for salvation', a belief held by a sixteenth-century German sect. Giles was in fact also the pastor of the Hamilton Place Baptist Chapel, Chester for a time.[340]

The remainder of the Boole–Bury correspondence is rather mundane. Perhaps to balance the number of times that he avails of free accommodation with the Burys in Chester as he commutes from Cork to Lincoln, Boole frequently implores all of them to visit him and his family in Cork, citing the pure air and the scenery as attractions. The death of the Burys' younger son Tom in November 1856 left his parents broken-hearted. The Booles had always enquired after him and they too were deeply saddened by his death. When the Burys' older son Charles became ill in 1862, Boole, who believed strongly in the effects of miasma on health, prescribed a course of pure Irish air for Charles and his mother. They had an enjoyable holiday in Killarney, staying with the Booles in Cork in 1862, but there is no record that Bury, presumably preoccupied with his practice and financial matters, joined them. Charles recovered to lead a long and productive life. The last surviving letter from Boole to Bury dates from March 1864, nine months before Boole's death, and contains a rather sad plea:

> Why don't you either write or come? One would suppose I had given you offence in some mysterious way. It is too bad to cut your old friends thus.[341]

Prior to Boole's death, MaryAnn had requested Bury to record his recollections of her brother in preparation for an anticipated biography. We are fortunate that Bury's biographical letter written a year after Boole's death to his widow Mary Boole has survived and the wealth of detail it contains makes it worth reproducing in its entirety below.

BIOGRAPHICAL LETTER ON GEORGE BOOLE FROM DR JOHN BURY M.D. OF CHESTER[342]

18 November 1865

I became acquainted with Dr Boole by meeting him accidently at the house of a mutual friend to whom he was expounding some proposition in analytical geometry, in Lincoln in 1844, soon after he had obtained a medal from the Royal Society. When we separated, he invited me to his house, and I afterwards spent three or four hours with him three or four times a week till the end of 1846. After his appointment to the professorship in Cork, he has spent several days with me in this city and neighbourhood almost every year, and we kept up a pretty constant correspondence till the end of 1864. It would be highly presumptuous of me to speak, as you desire me, of his character and opinions and of the growth of his mind, but I may say that from his first interview, although I had spent the previous eight years at universities and had seen hundreds of professors, I was so deeply impressed by the greatness of his intellect, with the fact that for the first time I had found indications of genius, and if possible more deeply by his noble moral characteristics, that everything I have observed and gathered relating to him seems to me of the greatest importance, and if not deemed sufficiently important for publication will be I am sure appreciated by yourself and his other relatives.

About three years ago Miss Boole [MaryAnn] requested me to make a memo of anything which I knew which might be illustrative of his character, as she heard from Cambridge that a biography would sometime be required of him, but begged of me not to let George know anything about it, as he would be sure to be highly offended and would put a stop to such a proceeding. Reflecting on his innocence and simplicity, I could never bring myself, although I might be ignorant of it, to do anything he would disapprove of, and so I am obliged to trust to my recollection for the following notes, but am very certain of their perfect accuracy.

He seemed to me, and to everyone who knew him at that time, to know everything and to be able to do anything. Even his scholars were surprised by him taking up their musical instruments – flute, accordion or anything else – and studying them for a few moments and then learning to play them in an hour or two. Knowing that he was a learned and original mathematician occupied with the business of his school, visiting occasionally Bishop Kaye at the Palace to talk over the Greek and Latin fathers, studying German metaphysics and theology and French and Italian literature, I was amazed at finding him as conversant as myself with all the principal doctrines in medicine, transcendental anatomy and physiology, the theories of cellular development and reflex action and with all medical works of any significance with regard to the sciences of pathology and therapeutics. And his friends Mr Hill a solicitor who resided I believe at Hull and the Reverend Mr Dickson were equally surprised by his knowledge of the literature and doctrines of their respective professions. Many times after two or three of his friends have stayed with him in his study till one or two in the morning, have we called at my rooms to talk again two or three hours not on the subjects of our previous discussions but of him and his wonderful character.

In our walks about Lincoln he told me that at twelve years of age he understood thoroughly the first six and the eleventh and twelfth books of Euclid, and that at twenty-one he had read the whole of the *Principia*, had studied all the works of the Greek geometers and every work of any value on the same subjects published in England and other countries.

He often spoke to me in most affectionate and grateful terms of the late Mr Gregory, editor of the *Examples in the Calculus*, who he said had first generously introduced him to the scientific world. While Mr Gregory was editor of the *Cambridge Mathematical Journal*, Mr Boole, then unknown, had sent him a mathematical communication. Mr Gregory replied immediately that the paper was very valuable but not yet written in a manner suitable for publication, but that if Mr Boole would allow him to rewrite it, it would be inserted. Of course Dr Boole gladly acceded to the proposal, the paper was printed and he subsequently became a frequent contributor, and through the aid of Mr Gregory he afterwards obtained the loan of large boxes full of books from Cambridge and occasionally during the university vacations private pupils who were studying for honors. On these accounts the name of Gregory had a peculiar fascination for him, as also I perceived on account of its associations with the late professor of chemistry, Olin Gregory, Dr Gregory the author of the Conspectus[343] and David and James Gregory the friends of Newton, a genealogy to him vastly more interesting than that of kings and emperors. Several of those students have assured me that whatever difficulties they met with in the course of their mathematical studies were solved almost instantly by Dr Boole but almost always by some original methods not to be found in the books.

He often talked with us on the propriety of his going to Cambridge, a course which I always strongly urged on him, but always concluded by saying that he might come out as a wrangler, but not probably as the senior wrangler, for the obtaining of this honor he thought depended chiefly on the possession of a good memory, and that on the whole he preferred staying with his father and mother.[344]

[Insert by Mary Ellen Hinton: His going to college was the cherished dream of my father from the time he was twelve years old. The subject comes up again and again until as late as 1848. It was a terrible disappointment to G.B. that he could not do so, but no doubt he spoke bravely on the subject to his friends.]

I have known him to have been three days and three nights without any sleep engaged nearly the whole time with some mathematical question; but when the investigation had been completed and the paper written and posted he would sleep anywhere. Several times during our walks I have seen him sleep a quarter of an hour sitting on a stile or gate and half an hour several times in the course of an evening party amongst much noise and bustle.

He thought the night in total darkness and silence the most favourable to profound thought, always had paper and pencil at hand and used to write under the bed-clothes, but for some time was unable to decipher easily the writing on account of the difficulty of writing in straight lines. At last he succeeded in making a wooden frame to hold the paper with a contrivance by which he could move along the paper at regular intervals, a straight piece to serve as a guide for the pencil and after that he would think and write through whole nights with this additional advantage that his friends thought that he was resting after the labours of the day.

His intense love of knowledge had led him, I learnt, to read hundreds of books the only use of which was to make him acquainted with the history of opinions and discoveries. Anyone of ordinary capacity, he thought, were his studies properly directed, might get a bird's eye view, and indeed the spirit of every department of human learning. How for example he said a person might become a good mathematician by studying a dozen well-selected works.

To his immense reading he was disposed to ascribe a defect of one eye which caused him some anxiety before he left Lincoln. In 1846 I often found him practising on the pianoforte. On one such occasion detecting I suppose an expression of surprise in my countenance, he said, 'Dr, you know of the defect in my eye. I am afraid the other is beginning to be similarly affected and that I may ultimately become blind. I am therefore paying considerable attention to music, for the ability to play easily on the piano or organ would under such circumstances be a great source of consolation and happiness.' He anticipated pleasure also from the study of the science of music, which he considered imperfect, on account of the conditions which he thought essential to its successful cultivation, considerable skill in performing and a competent knowledge of mathematics being so seldom found in the same individual. His fears with respect to his eyes were fortunately not realised, for years afterwards he told me that his sight had improved.

To me it was one of the greatest of pleasures to hear him play an old chant, psalm or hymn; he played only sacred music. I have heard L [?], Miss Goddard,[345] and Shelberg, but never was so affected by music as when listening to him extemporising grand harmonies, whether on account of their intrinsic excellence or by virtue of associations with the performer, I am even now unable to determine.

Although charitable towards the failings of men, his demeanour, tones of voice, expression of countenance, and short forcible sentences, elicited by any moral obliquity, were perfectly withering in their contempt. Any allusion to his mathematical genius inflicted on him great pain. I shall never forget the intense distress expressed in his face as he once said to a young man whom he was assisting in his studies because he had shown some mathematical taste and who had paid him some compliment, 'Don't I beg of you, my dear sir, let me hear anything of this again.' Yet he manifested no unwillingness to speak, but always with the greatest modesty, on the value of his writings. When conversing with him on his paper in the *Phil. Trans.* 'On a New Method in Analysis', which he had assisted me to comprehend, I ventured to remark that his law seemed to include those of Maclaurin, Taylor, Lagrange, and Laplace, 'Yes,' he said, 'I believe it does.' Well this must be very important. 'Yes, I believe it is,' he said. 'The calculus will probably be made nearly perfect in four or five hundred years, and it is nice to contribute something towards such a result.'

Chapter 6

JOSEPH HILL

O N 13 September 1863, George Boole, while on a visit to Lincoln, wrote a letter to his daughter Mary Ellen (then aged seven). He explained that he was visiting his friend Mr Joseph Hill and gave her the background to their friendship:

My dear daughter Mary Ellen,

I think it is now quite time that I replied to the letter which you sent me while I was at Cottingham and which I read with great pleasure. I daresay that you know that I have been visiting Mr Joseph Hickson Hill who once came to see us at Blackrock, and whom you used to talk about sometimes after he had left us to return home. You must surely remember him a little. He is very fond of children and often invites a great many to his house and tries to make them happy. Of course that means he tries to make them good for one thing, for naughty children are not happy, but he also tries to make them happy by letting them walk and play in his garden, by telling them stories and in many other ways. Mr J.H.H. and I were at school together and we used to sit at the same desk side by side and that is how we came to be friends in the first instance. This was long ago, but we are friends still and I hope we will always be as long as we live. When I used to sit by Mr J.H.H. at school in Lincoln, the place where I now am, he was bigger than I, but now I am bigger than he; also, he knew a great many things that I did not know and used to teach me. Now he knows more about some things and I know more about some things, and so when we meet together he generally teaches me something that I do not know, and I teach him something that he does not know, and that is one reason why we are still so fond of each other …

… I am now quite well; I suppose because I am breathing my native air. I was not well when I was at the house of Mr J.H.H. and I do not think the place agreed with me; it was too low and damp and cold. The great river Humber was only a few miles distant and there were no hills near.[346]

Joseph Hickson Hill was born in Cottingham, Yorkshire on 15 August 1812, the son of John Hill and Mary Hill, nee Hickson. His parents were married in Lincoln in 1804 and lived there for some time. They had three other children: John, Susannah and Mary Ann. In 1835, at the young age of twenty-three, Joseph Hill was appointed a master extraordinary to the High Court of Chancery. He lived in Hull most of his life where he conducted a very successful legal practice with his brother John at 7 Parliament Street. The Hill brothers were solicitors and registrars of marriages and appear to have been well off financially. In 1841, Hill's mother Mary was living at 55 Steep Hill in Lincoln with her two sisters and her daughter. Boole was friendly with all of these ladies and often called to see them. Joseph retired to South View House, Cottingham in the 1880s where he died in 1903, aged ninety.

In the Boole Archive at University College Cork, there are thirty letters from George Boole to Joseph Hill covering the period 1832 to 1852. Doubtless there were many other letters which have not survived. In addition, after Boole's death, MaryAnn Boole requested Hill to write her a 'biographical letter' recounting his memories of her brother. This he did in great style in a document written in six parts over the period December 1865 to June 1868, covering over sixty letter pages.

The first surviving letter from Boole to Hill is dated 26 December 1832 and was sent from Lincoln, telling his friend of his move from Doncaster to Mr Marrat's school in Liverpool. On 23 December 1833 Boole writes to Hill from Lincoln, telling him:

> Our good city is in a state of excitement occasioned by the commencement of the Mechanics' Institution. The merits and demerits of such an institution and the best way of conducting it appear to excite all the interest that was previously bestowed on the cholera or the Bill.[347] There are at present more than five hundred members, but it is very doubtful whether we shall be able to preserve more than two thirds of that number.[348]

The Lincoln Mechanics' Institute was of course to play an important role in the life of the Boole family. John Boole was curator there until his falling out with its management, and George was for many years an unpaid lecturer there on a wide variety of subjects.

In a letter from Lincoln on 22 February 1834, Boole apologises to Hill for the light tone of his letters, especially as they had agreed like philosophers to write profoundly on profound subjects. He goes on:

> I console myself by thinking that at some future period I shall overcome my evil habits and become as grave and solemn, and withal as learned as you could wish your friend to be. I have begun to study Italian. It appears to be a very easy language and I think too a musical and a rich one. It is

perhaps a wild scheme for me to commence a new line of study before I have mastered the difficulties of my former tracks. Ought I not rather to cultivate an intimacy with Euripides and Aeschylus and grow blind over Greek metres and become dry and dusty as a Greek quarto before I bend myself to the light literature of Italy? I shall feel obliged to you for your advice touching this matter.[349]

In later life, perhaps to show his prowess in languages, Boole was to publish substantial mathematical papers in both French and German but apparently not in Italian. Boole concludes his letter to Hill by mentioning that he had just sent solutions to the Prize Question and the one preceding in the *Ladies' Diary* and promising that if he won a prize he would send him a diary. The *Ladies' Diary*, founded in 1704, described itself as designed 'principally for the amusement of the Fair Sex. With an appendix of curious and valuable mathematical research for the use of students'. One suspects it was read by a lot of gentlemen also. Each issue had a prize question, sometimes of surprising mathematical sophistication, which attracted the attention of some of the leading British and even continental mathematicians of the day. Clearly Boole was a regular reader and competition entrant and very probably MaryAnn Boole was a regular reader also. To his delight, Boole received credit for the prize question for 1834, but whether Hill received his diary or not, we do not know. Boole is also recorded as contributing to other questions and answers in the publication. A splendid account of the *Ladies' Diary* and its role in the history of the development of mathematics has been written by Albree and Brown.[350]

Boole and Hill had a great many interests in common – mathematics and logic, philosophy, languages, religion, biblical commentary, and classical Greek and Latin. Indeed, many of their letters to each other are written entirely in Latin and Greek, and the ones in English are peppered with quotations in these languages. On 11 February 1837 Boole writes to Hill:

Every Latin epistle of yours which meets my eye tacitly accuses me of not having made a suitable return. I verily believe that the solicitations of Don Worm would at length have prevailed upon me to write you a specimen of the true Ciceronian, were it not that I have lately been reading Erasmus (*Epistolae Obsturorum Virorum*)[351] which is enough to corrupt and barbarise the Latinity of Cicero himself if he could read and understand them, and secondly that I have not sufficient time. I do intend however when I have more time and when I shall have rubbed off the rust of these obscure gentlemen to atone for all …

… I have lately been devoting my leisure, which is not great, to the study of German. This will I think be my last venture in the region of language and philosophy. All the information I can afford you concerning the language at present is that it bears a very close analogy with our own tongue in its primitive unlatinised form undefiled by Chaucer. How did you get on with Epictetus? I have read very little Latin or Greek lately having been much pressed by business. I have given up all thoughts of learning Hebrew from a conviction of the very great ambiguity and uncertainty of the language.[352]

The reference above to 'Don Worm' would seem to come from Shakespeare's *Richard III* where Margaret of Anjou says to the King, 'The Worm of Conscience shall begnaw thy soul.'

During this period, Boole also had to pay close attention to his main source of income, and that of his family – his school. As well as running its routine day-to-day affairs, Boole also found time for educational innovation and the production of personalised course material. He tells Hill:

I am preparing a tract on grammar and composition for my school. I am at present engaged on the difficult subject of punctuation. I have succeeded in reducing it after a very rigid analysis to a few simple rules concerning which I shall be glad some time or other to have your opinion. I should like to know whether or no you have any system on this subject and if so what your rules and principles are.[353]

Of course, George also had to keep an eye on his scientifically active father John, still deeply involved in the manufacture of technical instruments of various kinds. In the same letter of 11 February 1837 Boole mentions:

My father is now making an electrical machine which I anticipate will be a good one! He has just made a telescope stand on a new and simple construction which appears very effective.[354]

In a subsequent letter to Hill on 30 May 1837 Boole adds:

My father has lately been busied in attempting to make a telescope, and I have spent a good deal of time in calculating the forms and curves of the lenses for different constructions. We shall I think succeed.[355]

The early correspondence between Boole and Hill was frequently conducted at a rather deep intellectual level, not always easy to reproduce. For example, the bulk of Boole's letter of 30 May 1837 is devoted to biblical analysis and commentary, and he makes many observations contrasting the Greek and English versions of the Old Testament. In particular, he comments:

> You have I daresay heard me speak of the variations between the septuagists and the modern versions of the Old Testament. Some of these appear as if they might be reduced to scale and originate I have little doubt in the nature of the Hebrew language. The most usual is the use of the future tense instead of the past. Of this change I will give an instance or two.[356]

Boole then goes on to quote from Isaiah, Habakkuk and Job in both Greek and English, and one can only wonder at his depth of knowledge of both languages and the Old Testament at the age of twenty-one. Equally impressive is the self-confidence of a young man who is self-taught.

In a long and detailed letter to Hill from Waddington on 30 November 1840, Boole characteristically covers a wide range of topics, both gossipy and serious.[357] He relates that during a recent visit to Lincoln he took tea with Hill's aunts, only to learn that Hill had come to visit them in Lincoln without coming to see him in Waddington. In reparation, he demands a long and newsy letter. He tells Hill that he has been reading Gall's system of Sunday school teaching and requests him to read it and report to him on its contents, as he knows that Hill has devoted much energy to the practical experience of this topic.[358] He jokingly adds that in return he will communicate his own views on conveyancing and other legal matters to Hill whenever he arrives at any original or improved conclusions in this area. Boole tells his friend that he has been reading Erasmus's *Life of Jerome* and urges him to do the same so they can discuss the book.[359] Boole is clearly very impressed by the work and describes Erasmus as a genius, 'all meekness and toleration', in contrast with Jerome, 'the most fiery and intolerant bigot of the age of fanaticism'.

In 1840, Boole's mathematical career was taking off, as he reports to Hill:

You will feel interested to hear the fate of my mathematical speculations in Cambridge. One of the papers is already printed in the *Cambridge Mathematical Journal*. Another which I sent a short time ago has been very favourably received and will shortly be printed together with one I had previously sent.[360]

Boole then turns to religious developments in Waddington, just a few miles distant from Lincoln. He writes:

The Baptist chapel recently erected in this place under the auspices of Mr Crass is about to be opened on April 8th. The Revd. Mr Bergue and a Mr Evans of Scarboro are to assist in the ceremonies of dedication and the whole is to be followed by a social tea meeting. The religious world is growing very social and very fond of tea which are two good signs and augur well for a future age. Very probably, if tea had been introduced into Europe at an earlier period, it might have done something for the irritations, and diminish the acrimony of religious differences in less civilised ages. I shall give your aunts an invitation to spend the day with us, but I fear they will not be easily prevailed on.[361]

Boole's teaching career from 1831 onwards was a chequered one. In 1831 he obtained a position as an usher or junior teacher at Heigham's school in Doncaster. In 1833 he moved to Mr Marrat's school in Liverpool, but later in that year he was back in the Lincoln area again. He became a teacher at Robert Hall's academy in the village of Waddington, just four miles from Lincoln. But his income was still small, and certainly not great enough to support his family, so in 1834 he opened his own modest school in Lincoln. However, when Robert Hall died in 1838, Boole returned to Waddington and took over the running of the school. There was a misunderstanding or perhaps even a deception with regard to the lease of the premises from Hall's son, which cost Boole dearly in both financial and personal terms. Accordingly, he moved back to Lincoln and opened a boarding school at 3, Potter Gate, Minster Yard, near the cathedral. Here he remained until late 1849 when he moved to Cork to take up his professorship. We note that at no stage does Boole seem to have received any formal training or tuition as a teacher but this situation was quite common in the nineteenth century and does not seem to have prevented him from becoming an accomplished and highly regarded teacher at both second and third level. This explains the context in which Boole wrote to Hill from Lincoln on 5 May 1840:

My dear friend,

You have no doubt heard of my change of abode. I write to you no longer from Waddington, but from the city of my nativity once more, and from a room the interior of which occupies a very prominent place in your recollection; the very place where you first learned the divine accomplishment of dancing and acquired your relish for sweet sounds and stringed instruments. You must direct your next letter to me to Potter Gate, Lincoln.

You are acquainted with the circumstances which led to my removal from Lincoln, and the expectations which I was induced to form relative to that step. It would occupy me too long to tell you why I have not found those expectations realised and why after two years in attempting to accomplish the object of that removal, I find myself at length compelled on the ground both of duty and interest to relinquish it. The conditions upon which it has finally been agreed that the lease shall be destroyed involve a very considerable sacrifice on my part, perhaps more than I ought to have made; they are such however as I am able to make without putting myself under obligations, and willing to make in order to get out of the business with honour and an unstained character. They were offered by me in writing about two months ago, but not accepted until very lately. I have on this account delayed writing to you on the subject. Before long I hope to see you in Lincoln; you will I think approve of the change I have made, and of the steps I have taken in bringing it about when I have put you more fully in possession of the particulars.[362]
[Note added by MaryAnn Boole: The house was for many years occupied by a dancing master who had instructed all the quality of the town and neighbourhood in the divine accomplishment. Mr Hill had not the slightest relish for sweet sounds, and as little for dancing. George never learned to dance, but he liked to see others dance, and very much admired the geometrical figures of the quadrille.]

Boole goes on to thank Hill for his prompt and comprehensive analysis of Gall's system, but complains that he would prefer to hear Hill's opinions on the absolute merits of the system itself rather than the classification of its elements. He declares that after the close attention Hill had given to the system, he must have arrived at some definite conclusions concerning its advantages and applications. He adds that he has not yet completed his own 'bundle of opinions' concerning educational matters and perhaps never will. Next, Boole advises Hill to expand his 'studies and enquiries after truth' beyond the limits of the exact sciences. This advice is clearly based on his own experience, and gives a good insight into his attitude towards further study and in particular towards the limitations of the exclusive study of mathematics. Here Boole is frankly sharing his opinions with a friend, but he might have been less inclined to publish such views:

> There is a host of subjects, ethical and metaphysical, from which you might derive at least as much pleasure and certainly greater general benefit. The results of the mathematics are valuable as they enable us to trace out the consequences of the laws of nature and put us in possession of truths which we could not otherwise have become acquainted with except by some unknown intuition or revelation. The processes of the higher analysis are also in themselves essentially beautiful and the study to those who pursue it sufficiently far assumes a very high and increasing degree of fascination. Yet on the whole I am compelled to doubt whether its general effect on the mind is beneficial. That it is attended with one advantage and that too of a very important character is generally acknowledged. I mean the tendency which it undoubtedly possesses to introduce method into our mental habits and operations and to strengthen those powers by which we are enabled to classify and analyse. It is I think on this account that a mathematician will generally reason more closely than one who has not gone through the same mental training.[363]

Having listed the advantages of a mathematical training, Boole proceeds, with surprising vehemence, to list the disadvantages of exclusive study of the mathematical sciences:

> If this particular advantage be however subtracted from our general es- timate of the tendencies of mathematical studies, what remains must I fear be placed on the opposite side of the accounts. That they deaden the imagination and destroy the relish for elegant literature and indispose the mind for everything but the bare pursuit of abstract truths is, I believe, as true as any propositions relative to the mental tendencies well can be. Whether these effects are to be attributed to anything in the nature of

mathematical studies, or whether we are able to impute it to the intense thoughts and continued abstractions which they require, it is difficult to decide, but I incline to the latter opinion. And if this opinion be correct, there may be a time when the mathematical sciences shall by the aggregate labour of a multitude of individual minds acquire such a degree of power and simplicity and uniformity in their processes, that what we now estimate a profound knowledge of them may be obtained without any waste of exertion, and without interfering with the due development of the mind in the study of other branches of science and literature. But this we are not to expect although there are in the present state and progress of the mathematics pretty strong intimations that this will ultimately be the case.[364]

Boole then informs his friend about the essential difference between mathematics and other areas of philosophy:

In pure mathematics we seek to investigate the relations of number and magnitude, and are able, partly from the peculiar character of the subject, partly from what has been achieved by the labours of others to carry on our researches to an indefinite extent, and to rely with certainty on our ability to discover new truths. In the speculations to which I would however wish to see you devote some portion of your leisure, the field of inquiry, so far as absolute certainty is limited in every direction, and I have to think clearly on these and to avoid contradictional language and confusion of ideas, is about all we expect to obtain. But the subject is ourselves, our relations to each other, the foundations of moral distinction, the prospects of society and the human race. If on such subjects we could advance no farther than to detect the sources of prevailing error and were altogether unable to arrive at positive truths, the labour however great which it might require to accomplish this would, in my judgement, be at least as well bestowed as in discovering the most abstruse relations of quality, or developing the most important of the laws of the physical world.[365]

He recommends that Hill should devote his attention to areas of ethical and psychological studies, and admits that this advice is selfishly motivated as it would give him the opportunity to correspond with Hill on topics other than philology or the physical sciences.

These strongly expressed views strengthen the notion that Boole sincerely believed that his fundamental interests, and indeed talents, lay in the fields of psychology and sociology rather than in mathematics and logic. Ironically, he made no real progress in either psychology or sociology but his contributions to mathematics and logic were substantial and even revolutionary.

Boole concludes this letter to Hill by remarking that while Hill's letters to him contained frequent mathematical queries, they never mentioned ethical or psychological subjects, as if he thought they were not worth pursuing. Boole also criticises the subject of philology, the study of words, which was a frequent topic of conversation and correspondence between them. He cheekily claims that philologists like to study words just to gratify their curiosity rather than to answer any useful purpose. But he retracts in case he offends Hill's favourite study, adding that their letters would be a lot more interesting and stimulating if Hill were to follow his advice on the choice of topics!

In his next letter to Hill from Lincoln, dated 9 May 1840, Boole comments favourably on Hill's detailed analysis of Gall's system. He goes on to discuss another topic of interest to both of them, namely biography, mentioning that he would like to hear about Hill's recently formulated views on this subject. He shares with Hill his own opinions:

The object of a biographical memoir should be primarily to relate what the individual subject was, under what circumstances he was placed, by what events his life was characterised, and in what relation he stood to his associates and contemporaries and lastly in cases where this third consideration can apply, what claim he possesses to the notice of posterity. The former of these divisions of the object is the most important, and includes the analysis of habits, the estimate of mental powers and faculties, and the critical examination of the sentiments, and the moral character, in short the history of a man's moral and intellectual development. Referred to this object, every other should be regarded as secondary, and the events in his life as merely illustrations. It may remain for further consideration how far the exemplification of the manners of a particular age, and the general state of society, and public opinion, is to be regarded as a separate object, in a particular biography, a question to which, as is evident, no general answer can be given, and such I take to be the true end of biography.[366]

Boole reflects that biography can also be used in a lower and less restrictive sense. For example, a man's life may be worth recording simply from the accidental circumstances of his position without reference to any display of individual talent.

Boole concludes this letter to Hill with a long series of comments on religious biography with which he is clearly very familiar. He bemoans its widely varying quality, which is a reflection of the diversity of talents and opinions of its authors. He pours high praise on Bishop Heber's *Life of Jeremy Taylor*[367] but comments that Everett's *Polemic Divine*[368] bears its condemnation in its title and is both faulty in spirit and vicious in style. The Wesleyan biographies, he claims, are injudiciously conceived, with 'too much excitement and too much tension after the manner of Saint Augustine and Mrs E. Rowe,[369] and too little of the quiet seriousness and holy repose of Christian life'. Again, one can only marvel at the confidence, self-assurance and wide reading of the twenty-four-year-old Boole, as displayed in this letter. He seemed to approach every subject in which he was interested from the same analytical angle, list the relevant parameters, and draw conclusions in a very emphatic manner, almost as if he were dealing with a mathematical proposition.

In a further letter to Hill from Lincoln on 27 May 1840, Boole apologises for its brevity because he is a good deal engaged in a mathematical correspondence which he wishes to bring to a close. He disagrees with Hill's comments that many extant biographies record too many trivial events, and that he would prefer to read Boswell's *Life of Johnson*[370] rather than several volumes about the history of Malta, and that Johnson's *Lives of the Poets*[371] would be far better reading, and that collective biography is preferred to individual. But Boole is prepared to risk upsetting his friend in the interests of truth:

> In these positions I am sorry to say that I cannot agree with you. I believe you to be essentially mistaken, and will very briefly and hastily state my reasons for so thinking. It is very seldom that from an account of the historical events in a man's life you can form any definite judgment as to his character and moral peculiarities. This can be done only by following him from the scene of public labours into the recesses of private life. No one, from a perusal of Swift's life writings, would take him to have been a disappointed and gloomy misanthrope; nor would anyone from an examination of the writings of Sterne suppose that he was an arbitrary

domestic tyrant. The same discrepancy which so often exists between the character of an author's work and his personal character also exists in very many instances between a man's public feelings and opinions. Biography should therefore go into a variety of minor details, whose sole interest may be derived from their bearing upon the moral and intellectual peculiarities of the subject.[372]

Boole goes on to quote a long list of such minor details from Boswell's *Life of Johnson* including conversations with his friends, descriptions of his gross physical person, and seemingly trivial incidents from his life, revealing his character. He then ends his letter with a profound statement:

Truth is sometimes struck out from the collision of different minds.[373]

On 19 January 1841 Boole writes to Hill from Lincoln telling him about his recent educational activities:

I enclose you the notice of a new society, now in course of formation in Lincoln, and of which I have the honour to be a member. The first meeting was held last night, another is to be held after the interval of a fortnight, and a committee is meanwhile engaged in collecting information relative to similar associations elsewhere and digesting a report thereof, to be laid before the meeting at its next sitting. The title of the society is to be 'The Lincolnshire Topographical Society' and its objects are to include topography and local antiquities, etc. in the first instance, and science and Literature in the second. It is to be a society of records; and documents of an interesting character, presented by members and approved by a committee are to be preserved and in some cases published …
    … I have undertaken to provide some information relative to the laws, regulations, and general business of the Philosophical Society in Hull, which has I believe the honour of ranking you in the list of its contributors and supporters.[374]

Boole cunningly asks Hill for a printed copy of the regulations of the Hull society, with a brief account of its workings, accompanied by such remarks and suggestions as may at any time have presented themselves on the subject. This request is made of course if Hill has the time to do so without inconvenience, but with the added stipulation that it might be done before the next Monday, if not by the Monday following. Boole is nothing if not a demanding correspondent. He concludes this letter with a request (perhaps teasingly):

> Could you also spare sufficient time, I should like to hear but on a separate sheet what you are now reading, what thinking, what new classification analyses, nomenclatures, digests, synopses, epitomes, technologies, etc. etc. have recently occupied your attention.[375]

Hill clearly delivered the goods because in his next letter from Lincoln dated 22 February 1841, Boole thanks him profusely for the book of rules and his opinions and experiences on the matter. He adds that the inaugural address of the Lincoln Topographical Society is to be delivered on the coming Tuesday evening by E.F. Willson, and for the 'amusement and instruction of the meeting' there will be some experiments illustrative of the new discovery of the electrotype or the art of producing exact copies of medals, etc. by a galvanic process. These may or not be appropriate for a topographical society but at least indicate the wide range of topics to be covered. Boole then goes on to comment on Hill's suggestions for the contents of an ideal society library. He suggests that Hill might like to publish his thoughts or at least write a preface to a book on this subject. Rather overbearingly, he adds that:

> If you were to divert the course of your serious thoughts from their accustomed channel and devote your leisure and your efforts to the persevering but not immoderate pursuit of some great subjects – history, divinity, metaphysics, political economy, or the philosophy of law and government – you would find the abundant advantages of the change, in the acquisitions of knowledge, solid and useful, of views enlarged and comprehensive in the place of what I cannot otherwise consider than barren speculations. You will pardon the freedom of these observations and if the subject be disagreeable to you, I will promise not to offend you in the same way again.[376]

Boole himself seems at this time to have reached an intellectual and occupational plateau and appears to be content with his lot. He tells Hill that he is currently reading Neal's *History of the Puritans*,[377] a voluminous work but of singular and sustained interest. He reports:

My school this half year is very good and increasing, and I have much cause to be both satisfied and thankful with my present position and prospects.[378]

In a letter from Lincoln dated 29 December 1841, Boole tells Hill that he has some time previously read a paper before the Topographical Society on the subject of mythology and will allow him to peruse it when it has been transcribed. He adds that he has very little interest in politics because of his situation and habits in life. He says that he is currently working on a paper on light and is thinking of following it up by another on physical astronomy.[379] Boole teases his friend on his devotion to the 'midnight gas', *noctes vigilare et serenas*,[380] as he regards it as a most impractical substitute for oil and tallow. He reminds him that poets have written odes to the candle but that he had never heard of a poet apostrophising gas! He suggests that maybe Hill should do so also.

There is a gap now of three years in the available Boole–Hill letters during this time. On 17 February 1844 Boole writes from Lincoln on the subject of Sunday school instruction, which clearly was an important part of his school curriculum.[381] He asks Hill what books he would recommend for the religious instruction of the more advanced classes, adding that he was currently using Lloyd's *Bible Catechism*,[382] consisting of questions to which each answer is a text of Scripture. He has also used a companion to the Bible published by the Religious Tract Society and a little book on New Testament biography. But overall, he is dissatisfied with these books and hopes that Hill can recommend something similar to the companion to the Bible, but more condensed.

On 13 July 1844 Boole is in holiday mood and writes to Hill from the seaside town of Hornsea in the East Riding of Yorkshire, extolling the cliff scenery and the awesome power of the waves. He hopes that Hill may be able to join him there the next day.[383]

By 4 June 1846 Boole is in more serious mood and clearly anxious to get some work done. He writes to Hill from Lincoln:

I cannot accompany you on an expedition into Wales. If you are disposed to spend a fortnight at some quiet watering place I shall be happy to accompany you. I do not mind the place provided that it is far enough from the resorts of fashion and the noise of the great world. My reason for preferring the seaside is that I need quiet and bodily rest and that I have at the same time some books to read and a little writing to accomplish which the intervals of seabathing and exercise would give me leisure to attend to. I fear from this that you would find me a sorry companion – still, I would do my best to be agreeable. Do not however give up any favorite scheme of pleasure on my account. I should be sorry to think of your sacrificing for me that in which I cannot through circumstances participate.[384]

In an undated letter to Hill without a location, but presumably from Lincoln, Boole tells his friend that he has been reading with much gratification *On the Law of Nature and of Nations* by Sir James Mackintosh[385] and recommends it highly, except for its too elaborate style. He is not quite so impressed with Whewell's *Elements of Morality and Polity*[386] lately published, which he regards as a very partial and one-sided performance. Whewell, complains Boole, has a too high estimate of church authority, and like many others, assumes the doctrine of innate ideas, and makes these the foundation of all scientific knowledge. Such commentators simply maintain the existence of truths antecedent to and independent of experience. Whewell believes that the laws of motion and the axioms of geometry are of this class and to the same class assigns the rules of morality, giving the obligations of benevolence, justice, truth, beauty and order an office and a power similar to that of the axioms of geometry. Boole claims that the ultimate blame for such attitudes lies with German systems of philosophy and of a large and respectable faction in the Church of England who argue political, moral and ecclesiastical questions from premises and assumptions different from those which from the time of Locke have been prevalent in England.

The next available letter from Boole to Hill is dated 16 July 1846 and is written from Lincoln.[387] Little seems to have changed in the intervening years; Boole thanks Hill for the kind and cordial manner with which he and his brother received him on his visit to Hull and expresses the hope that their friendship may continue to increase, and that it may be founded more and more on esteem, to the end of their lives. Boole is at this period on the threshold of writing his first ground-breaking book *The Mathematical Analysis of Logic* (1847) so his remarks on his reading and outlook at this time are particularly interesting. He writes:

I have nothing very particular to communicate to you. Indeed our subjects of mutual interest must have been almost exhausted by the long conversations which we have so recently had. I am now reading again Wardlaw [388] and Sir James Mackintosh[389] (on ethics) and hope to be able to make leisure for this kind of reading for some time to come. However much I may be attached to mathematical pursuits, no employment of the intellect affords me such solid gratification as the study of morals. I suppose it is because it appeals to the sentiments and emotions at the same time that it occupies the reason and that the objects with which it is concerned are per se greater and nobler than any relations of material things.

Believe me, My dear friend, Yours faithfully,

Geo. Boole.

PS I think of going to Sheffield tomorrow, having a day through the Peaks of Derbyshire, returning to Sheffield on the Saturday night and home the following week. The idea was suggested by having business between here and Sheffield which I can accomplish on my return.

On 2 February 1847 Boole wrote to Hill from Lincoln telling him that he is very busy, that his school has reopened and is full, but he has no time for books or correspondence. The results of his application for a position in the Irish colleges are still pending, but he has heard nothing but the melancholy detail of famine from Ireland.[390]

In a further letter from Lincoln on 15 February 1847, Boole recounts that he has still heard nothing from Ireland but that:

Indeed I am so happy in every way in my family and personal concerns, and so prosperous in my school that if the professorship for which I have applied were offered to me, it might be well to consider whether I ought to accept it. For my own sake perhaps I ought, as although I am very happy, I have great doubts whether my health will permit me for many years to follow the profession of a schoolmaster, unless indeed I put my favourite pursuits in abeyance.[391]

Boole adds that he has lately been reading Whately's *On the Errors of Romanism Having their Origins in Human Nature.*[392] He observes that it is a book which once mastered is not soon forgotten, and even better than his *Kingdom of Christ*[393] which he has also recently read.

By 14 July 1847 it is vacation time and Boole writes to Hill from Lincoln:

I am proposing to leave Lincoln tomorrow morning by the Gainsboro' coach and to take the packet to Hull. My sister and Matthew Lilly will accompany me, and we shall proceed immediately to Hornsea, Bridlington, or Filey–Filey if the railway should be opened thither but otherwise Hornsea or Bridlington. Now I think that an excursion of this nature might be as useful and as delightful to you as to us, and as the pleasure derived from intercourse with the works of nature is, like all innocent pleasures, increased and not diminished by its being participated in by others, I am so selfish as to wish even for the sake of my own enjoyment that you would go with us. Do try if you can accomplish it. We shall not be altogether idle, but books and work will pleasantly interchange with seaside rambles and shell collecting enterprises.[394]

On the next day Boole writes from the boarding house of Mrs Johnson at Queen's Place in Bridlington, repeating the invitation to Hill. The room in which he is visiting, he tells him, is large and pleasant and looks directly out upon the sea. The party have taken three bedrooms and one is reserved for Hill. And what is more, the rooms are clean and cheerful, so Hill has really no excuse not to join them.[395]

Boole's letters to Hill from Gainsborough on 19 June 1848 and from Lincoln on 21 June 1849 are merely invitations to meet him in Burton Stather, 'to behold your face once more' and to visit the great works at Grimsby docks.[396] But the letter from Lincoln of 13 August 1849 contains some important news:

I avail myself of a couple of minutes' leisure to inform you of my appointment last week to the professorship of mathematics in Queen's College Cork. I expect to have to go in October, but I shall have to make a previous visit to Dublin, to consult with the head of the college respecting my department. You may imagine that with all the business of preparation, I am much engaged. I could not however but wish to inform one of my oldest and best friends of my change of position and prospects.[397]

In a letter to Hill from Lincoln on 30 July 1850 it is clear that Boole has returned home from Cork for his summer holiday. He writes:

I think it likely that I shall pass through Hull with my sister on her way to Hornsea, where she proposes to spend a few weeks. I shall endeavour to see you there, we shall probably get to Hull by the first morning train. Owing to the precarious state of my mother's health I cannot be long from home at once from my sister, and therefore my stay at Hornsea will be short, but I may visit it again, and perhaps you will on my second visit be able to accompany me.[398]

It appears that Boole has not written to his friend for a considerable time:

I hope that our regard for each other has deeper roots than to be shaken by the accident of a neglected correspondence.[399]

Boole's letter to Hill from Cork on 11 December 1850 is quite startling in its assertiveness, and shows that although he has been living in Ireland for just a little over a year, he has already formed deeply held opinions on both Irish politics and its connections with religion. Wisely, he never made these opinions public, as such a step could very well have landed him in deep trouble and controversy and might even have cost him his position, as was very soon to happen to his friend De Vericour (See Chapter Three).[400] The articles he signed on taking up his professorship forbade him from engaging in any religious polemics especially where students were concerned and there is no record that he ever publicly transgressed in this area. But privately, to a trusted friend, and a lawyer to boot, like Hill, it is likely that he felt that he could let off steam, and put his feelings in writing.

The crux of the matter was the Ultramontane Party – those Catholics who felt that 'the man beyond the Mountains', the Pope, should hold sway over governments and kings even in temporal matters. They were strongly supported by the Jesuits and the English Catholic bishops, described as being 'more Catholic than the Pope himself'. In opposition were the Cisalpinists, more moderate lay Catholics who sought to make political concessions to Protestant countries, mostly to achieve Catholic emancipation. Later on, in 1862, there was to be a suggestion that Ultramontanists and their faction were involved in the burning of Queen's College Cork, but this seems unlikely and nothing was ever proved.[401]

There is no doubt on which side of the argument Boole's sympathies lay and with his usual supreme confidence in his opinions, he writes to Hill:

The Ultramontane Party are furious in their papers and journals, but they have always been furious, not against Protestantism alone, but against civil government. The recent declaration of the tablet: 'Every Protestant is necessarily an atheist' is quite in accordance with its former avowals. Two causes have contributed in my opinion to the comparative quiet of this country, at the present time. The first is that men of moderate feelings to whatever party they may belong, dread the lighting of the torch of discord. They do not, they cannot, forget the baleful flames which it has often kindled around them. They stand in mutual fear and are sensible that however England may afford to suffer divisions and rents, Ireland cannot do so without ruin absolute. The preservation of peace, the cultivation of mutual good feeling is the one hope of this country. This is the necessary condition on which the success of all outward efforts – educational, industrial or legal – for escape from the abyss into which she has fallen, must depend. I am sure that any Englishman, who can see the state of the country and calmly reflect upon it, must arrive at the conclusion that whatever cause may lead to divert the attention of men from the overwhelming evils which they have set themselves to the task of endeavouring to remedy, into the field of political and religious discord, must be regarded as fraught with calamity. Another reason why this country is comparatively quiet is that there does not exist here that dissention among Protestants which so unhappily characterises England. There is little of that fear of 'Traitors within the camp' which is so painfully manifest in the Church of England. This reason was stated to me a few days ago, by the Bishop of Cork who is an old and experienced and withal a learned and sensible man, and it accords with the results of my own observation. What is most to be desired in reference to the Church of Rome is that an entire separation should take place between the liberal and ultramontane portions of her members. It is scarcely possible for Protestants to differ more widely than they do. The former are friendly to civil government, to mixed education, to freedom of conscience, and I believe not hostile to the bible. Were they separate from the others they would approximate more and more to the Protestant sect in discipline, in character and doctrine. The ultramontane party on the other hand are, as I conscientiously believe, the enemies of all that is good. I see not how on their principles even moral distinctions are to be preserved. Sooner or later, I believe that these parties must separate. They are not the friends of Protestantism, who by their indiscriminate denunciation of all Catholics endeavour to postpone this most desirable consummation.[402]

This is one of the few instances where he expressed his political and religious views. He concludes the letter by saying that this is most of what he has to say in answer to the question which Hill had put to him, so perhaps Hill is trying to tease out opinions on these matters from his normally reticent friend. Boole adds that he has sought out in vain for Hill local pamphlets and papers on these subjects, and that Irish newspapers print merely extracts from the English ones. Indeed by 1850 Boole was already on good terms with the Church of Ireland Bishop of Cork, Cloyne and Ross, Dr James Wilson, who held the position from 1848 until his death in 1857. Doubtless they had many deep religious and political discussions, and it is clear that Boole sought out in Cork people of intellect with whom he could interact on matters of faith (See Chapter Four).

The final letter from Boole to Hill in the Boole Archive is dated 9 February 1852 and was sent from Queen's College Cork.[403] He excuses his lack of letters by stating that in recent months he has been unwell and is not yet fully recovered, though fast recovering. He rushes to express sympathy to Hill and his family on the death of their ninety-year-old aunt whom Boole knew well in Lincoln and of whom he was clearly very fond. Letters of sympathy are frequently cliché-laden, but Boole comes across with great sincerity, mentioning the lady's great age, her happy life in the company of dear and attached relatives, and her practice of Christian virtues, more especially that one which has been pronounced to be the greatest of them all, in the cheerful and well-grounded hope of a better state to come. 'One who lives thus and dies thus,' Boole says, 'is to be regarded as above the reach of any feeling of pity in those who survive. Regrets are for ourselves and those who suffer the loss of the departed.' Boole regrets that he will never again see a lady who was one of the brightest examples of a cheerful and religious old age that he had ever met with.

Boole closes this letter by mentioning that his sister MaryAnn is at that time with him in Cork, deriving great benefit from Dr Barter's hydropathic establishment in Blarney, but expects to return home refreshed soon to Lincoln to look after her mother [see Chapter Twelve]. Finally, Boole mentions that he has forwarded to Hill a copy of an address he had delivered in Cork the previous October.

By far the most valuable legacy to Boolean studies left by Joseph Hill is the collection of biographical letters he wrote to MaryAnn Boole during the period 1865 to 1868. These are six in number but perhaps it is more correct to describe them as a reminiscence in six parts consisting of over forty octavo pages. They were written at MaryAnn's request, and there can be no doubt that they are authentic and reliable. Around this time also Hill returned to MaryAnn many of Boole's letters to him that have been discussed in this chapter.

In the first biographical letter dated 1 December 1865, Hill promises MaryAnn that he will search for more of her brother's letters and that if he finds any he will send her extracts from them or rather complete copies so that she and her coadjutors may use their judgement as to the passages to be extracted or the matters to be noted.[404] He then goes to give some of the background to a major incident in Boole's life:

> I believe he had a lease of the premises at Waddington but found it inexpedient to retain them till the expiration of the lease and therefore got his landlord to accept a surrender of it though on terms by which Mr Boole sustained some loss. But I do not remember either his reason for wishing to discontinue his school at Waddington, or the terms on which he got rid of it. I have a faint remembrance (though on matters of a defamatory character one ought to speak very cautiously) that he had been induced to take the school by misrepresentation. Amongst the papers relating to business that we have transacted I have a set bearing the name 'Boole', but I did not find any relating to the Waddington lease, which business would have been done by the landlord's solicitor ...
>
> ... Of your brother's patriotic studies I have no recollection. I fear my sister will not be able to furnish any more of Mr B's poetry; but she proposes to write to you on the subject herself. I feel it my duty to afford some aid to the biographers of my late lamented friend, and should have pleasure in doing so if I could supply much useful matter. I feel that a memoir, like a portrait, may require many little strokes, insignificant in themselves, but collectively useful for filling up the picture with suitable shading. Therefore I will, in addition to a few reminiscences that I jotted down a good while since, write as many more odds and ends as I can, and then send you such kind of material for the collection.
>
> In the meantime I will state one thing which certainly does not belong to the class of 'trivial matters unfit for publication' and perhaps may not be known to you. As the matter has some bearing on G.B.'s intellectual character and is an important feature of his moral character, I am sorry that I am unable to state the time with certainty; but I believe it was during the first or second part of his career as a schoolmaster ...

... Mr Boole thought that he had been indulging in his favourite studies, too much for his own gratification, and that he must apply himself to studies from which some good might result, and he therefore thought of turning his attention to ethics. How far he would found his system of Ethics on the law of nature and how far on the divine laws contained in the Bible, I do not know, but no doubt he would study scripture morality, as at least a part of the subject. This may account for the papers he is said to have left containing observations on texts of Scripture ...

... The systems of ethics about which we had conversations were more of Paley and Whewell. Of the former he expressed disapproval; of the latter he stated as to its principles, but I think without exposing his own opinion about the system. As to Paley's *Moral Philosophy*,[405] I think he considered it the least satisfactory of Paley's works. I incline to think he considered Paley's best work to be his *Horae Paulinae*.[406]

Hill then turns to the revival of Boole's interest in mathematics and to his realisation that perhaps after all he had little to contribute to ethics and that he had a better chance of original discoveries in scientific and mathematical areas:

Probably his waning zeal in mathematical studies would revive when he began to see that he could not only be a learner of what other mathematicians had taught, but could enlarge the science of mathematics and become one of the mathematical instructors of the world; and moreover he would find his acquaintance with the higher mathematics more useful to him in the college, than it had been to him in the school. For these reasons I dare say he would discontinue his ethical studies, finding that his mathematical pursuits would not be so selfish in their character as he had thought.

Hill reflects on the genesis of Boole's work in mathematical logic. This account must be regarded as a very reliable affirmation of much that has been claimed by others over the years, being reported by an honest friend of his with no axe to grind, and somebody to whom Boole spoke directly and personally:

Having informed you of a course of study which he discontinued, or at least never matured so as to bring his ideas before the public, I will now state the first origin of that train of thought the development of which has entitled him to be classed with the most distinguished philosophers of modern times. It is often deemed a matter of great interest to trace a great work to its first origin in writing, whether the writing be a draft, perhaps very rough, or some papers partly adopted, partly rejected & partly rewritten, or even a mere sketch or outline. But in some cases it is possible to trace the great thoughts of a great man to their mental origin. Your brother told me that his first idea of using mathematical symbols for ideas not of a mathematical nature occurred to him when he was going down the Witham in a steamboat. Perhaps from his memoir and diaries or cash accounts you may be able to ascertain on what day that would be, and so fix the birthday of the new science of which he was the parent. When he was seen to be silent and thoughtful, how little would his fellow passengers suspect that he was laying the foundation of a science that was to be a connecting link between logic and mathematics, out of which would arise a new system of mental philosophy.

Believe me, Dear Miss Boole,

Yours very truly, Jos. H. Hill.

As early as 1865, and perhaps even earlier, Hill was already aware of the importance of Boole's work in mathematical logic. Whether he came to this realisation of his own accord, or Boole had convinced him of it, is difficult to say.

The next letter from Hill to MaryAnn Boole is dated 20 March 1866.[407] Hill apologises for the delay in writing, saying that he had lost sight of a paper that considered suggestions written at various times as to matters that might be mentioned, but having now found his 'Memorabilia Booleana', he will select some of them for the letter. He describes the background to his own studies, telling her that they have been quite limited, not venturing to sail upon the sea of general literature, but having been content to view it from the shore. At times, he says, he had a strong propensity to mathematics and had fallen in love in turn with Greek, Italian, and astronomy, and had derived amusement and pleasure from scientific instruments. But Boole was much more intense than he was:

I need not wonder then that your brother whose range of study and investigation was of immense extent, should have been propelled in his intellectual voyage by different winds at different times. I will limit the present letter to the fluctuations of his classical taste. At Mr Bainbridge's school I think his grand characteristic, his mathematical bias, predominated, but nevertheless he applied himself, con amore, to Latin and Greek. Before the school closed for the holidays there was a Speaking Day when friends were invited to hear the boys examined and to hear them repeat poetry. On one such occasion George Boole repeated a translation that he himself had made from Greek – I think it was from Meleager's beautiful *Ode to Spring*.[408] I believe he applied himself more assiduously to the study of classical languages when he was assistant in a school at Doncaster. He at one time applied himself with diligence and success to Latin prosody, which seems to me one of the driest parts of classical lore. I very well remember how once during a walk he asked me to ask him questions as to the quantities of symbols, and I asked him many, all of which he answered correctly. But in later life he seemed to turn his back on the literature of the ancients, in order greedily to luxuriate in that of the moderns. When I proposed that we should read Latin to one another he refused it as if it were a thing for which he had quite a disrelish. When I showed him, at Hull, Fry's *Partographia* containing specimens of almost all the languages of the world, a book with which I was then exceedingly enamoured, he turned from it saying he had no taste for languages. He perused instead Watson's *Theological Dictionary*[409] and especially the article on election …

… I had a walk with Dr Boole and Mr Brooke to Skellingthorpe Wood, where we sat down and took tea, having taken a kettle etc. prepared for such a meal. I had put in my pocket one of my favourite books, a selection of Latin poetry from Ovid, Tibullus, and others entitled *Florilegium Poeticum*,[410] thinking it might be very pleasant when we were in the wood and in a rather poetical mood, to read some description of rural scenes by poets of ancient times. I proposed reading something from the *Florilegium*, to which Mr Brooke assented but Dr Boole dissented, so Mr Brooke read from his paper, a dialogue of a serio-comic nature. But then Mr Brooke made a curious proposal that we should speak to each other exclusively in Latin and Dr Boole surprisingly agreed.

Hill goes on to discuss Boole's interest in languages:

After he lost his enjoyment of the ancient classics, he read many books in French, Italian, and German. He admired the German language greatly and afterwards wished his daughters to be instructed in it. He expressed a wish to learn Hebrew, but spoke of its characters as a formidable difficulty; his sight was not very good and he was afraid of taxing it too severely lest he might injure it. He had a great dislike of those crooked characters by which old Greek books are sometimes disfigured, the contractions or ligatures by which one character is substituted for two or three letters. He disliked them not only for their ugliness, but also for their unpleasantness to his eyes.

Hill continues:

I recollect another indication that Dr Boole's taste for languages was less of late years than when he was young. On the occasion of the Great Exhibition of 1851, Dr Tupper composed a 'Hymn for all Nations' which he got translated into many languages. To me it was a great treat to see a book containing an English hymn, with translations into Latin, Greek, Hebrew, French, Italian, Spanish, Welsh, Manx, Gaelic, Irish, German, Dutch, etc., etc. A manuscript Greek version that I had made myself he read with attention, but in the book he seemed to feel very little interest.

The third letter from Hill to MaryAnn Boole is dated 24 May 1866.[411] Hill now turns to the interesting topic of Boole's mathematical activities and in particular his meeting with Charles Babbage at the International Exhibition in London in 1862, at which Hill himself was present. He writes:

When he was a schoolboy on his visits to me, and I think also on my visits to him, our amusements were chiefly of a mathematical nature, mostly algebra, but we did cover other branches of mathematics also, for I remember his lending me a book by Pardies[412] from which I got the only knowledge of fluxions that I have ever possessed.

Hill then jumps over a wide gulf of many years to relate an interesting mathematical adventure which he and Boole had in London in 1862 at the International Exhibition. He writes:

I directed George's attention to Babbage's calculating machine, about which I had in former years had conversations with him. He said he did not understand it. Afterwards, I found a gentleman speaking about

Figure 6.1: Charles Babbage's Analytical Engine

it to a friend (I think a lady) in such a manner that I supposed that gentleman understood it. Therefore I told him of Dr Boole having looked at it without understanding it. He then said he would explain it to Dr Boole if I would fetch him. So I appointed a certain time when I would be in attendance in that place with Dr B. On searching for your brother (whom I understood to be in the picture gallery with my sister), I succeeded in finding him and took him to the calculating machine to receive the promised instruction. After waiting some time for the gentleman I had seen, Professor Boole became impatient, but my sister and I strongly persuaded him to stay longer. Then the gentleman came and commenced an explanation of the machine and Mr Babbage himself shortly arrived and took up the discourse, which with the aid of the other gentleman he illustrated by working the machine, so there was quite a lecture given by Prof. Babbage to Prof. Boole. Several persons gathered about, but probably none but the learned few would understand the explanation of the machine. It was very interesting to see a gentleman who had devoted his whole life to the construction of a machine which should do some of the work of the human mind, explaining his admirable invention to a gentleman who had gained great celebrity by his mathematical discoveries. Who the gentleman was with whom I had arranged the interview, I did not learn, but probably he was some learned professor. The occasion and the scene would have formed a good subject for a painter. As Boole had discovered that the brains of reasoning might be conducted by a mathematical process, and Babbage had invented a machine for the performance of mathematical work, the two great men together seemed to have taken steps towards the construction of that grand prodigy – a calculating machine.

Hill's account of this historically important meeting is a very perceptive one. It refutes for example those historians who believe that Boole was not thinking along the lines of a calculating machine or a computer – just four years after this meeting Hill was thinking along those lines too and his ideas could have come only from Boole. If Boole had lived, who knows what he and Babbage might have achieved together? But there is another curious aspect to this tale. Hill relates that the gentleman who began explaining the workings of Babbage's machine to him was 'speaking about it to a friend (I think a lady)'. Sadly, this lady was not the great Ada Lovelace, who had died in 1852, but it would be very interesting to discover her identity.[413]

As far as inventions are concerned, Boole also had his feet on the ground, and was always prepared to exploit elementary mathematics to achieve an end. Hill relates how Boole used the properties of similar right-angled isosceles triangles to make an ingenious ad hoc surveying instrument notable for its simplicity and ingenuity:

From the grand invention of Professor Babbage I will make a transition to a very simple invention of Professor Boole which impressed me, because it is very easy to understand, very easy to imitate, and very useful; but what makes it especially interesting to me is that he made the invention in my presence. The contrivance is this, to fold a piece of paper at a corner, so as to bring the two edges together, whereby instead of a single paper with a right angle, you get a double paper with an angle of 45 degrees. Then, holding the original edge of the paper in a horizontal position with the corner applied to the eye, look at the slant edge produced by doubling towards the top of a lofty object, and vary your distance till you can, on so applying the paper to the eye, see the top of the object in line with the slant edge of the paper. You then know that your distance from the object is equal to its height, and so by walking up to the object and counting your steps, you may learn the height of it. The occasion on which this lucky thought occurred to him and was forthwith carried into practice was when we were looking at Beverley Minster.[414]

Hill felt that Boole cultivated mathematics as a science and not as an art and relates that once when the pair of them were walking together in Hull, Boole, on seeing a set of geometrical instruments in a shop window, went in and bought them, saying it was unbecoming for a professor of mathematics not to have such a set. As a schoolmaster he would have used them, but they would have been sold as part of the school apparatus to his successor. It seems that as a professor he had found little use for them, as he preferred instructing students with large diagrams drawn in chalk, rather than with small diagrams drawn in pencil on paper. So he remained without them until accidentally reminded of his want. Hill continues:

> Nevertheless, he had some pleasure in seeing mathematical ideas presented to the eye in a visible form for he told me that at one of the great exhibitions he had looked with great pleasure on some curves of double curvature cut out in wood. With respect to mathematical machines, he once told me, I think during his residence at Lincoln, that some clever man in the north had invented a machine for solving cubic equations, but he did not mention it in later times, and unfortunately I did not think of asking about it at the time that Babbage's machine was under consideration. But as to that algebraic machine, your brother spoke of it more as a matter of report, than a matter he was acquainted with.

Boole, it seems, preferred the word 'school' to describe his institution of learning, but felt that 'Boole's School' had an awkward sound to it, and for the sake of euphony called it 'Mr Boole's Academy' instead. Many of his pupils' parents were unacquainted with his mathematical attainments and one even asked him if he could teach Euclid. But the local Drainage Commissioners showed their faith in his mathematical skills by proposing him a problem concerning the dimensions of a drain capable of carrying off a certain volume of water. He was also consulted concerning the rules of a building society which he at first approved but on reconsideration found that they would not work well and warned the people of their error.

Hill then turns to Boole's physical character, his love of walking, his eyesight, and his taste in food:

> When he was a youth he once walked from Lincoln to Doncaster, but he found he over-exerted himself that day. I found in walking with him, when I was disposed to drop into a very slow pace in walking uphill, he

seemed rather to quicken his pace. I thought that in that respect I could perceive an analogy between his physical character and his intellectual character. In either case he was so far from being discouraged by difficulty that it stimulated him to greater exertion.

One thing worthy of observation in regard to his physical character is that his sight was not good. He disliked old Greek books abounding with awkward unsightly contractions, and English books printed in small type, and was deterred from learning Hebrew by the difficulty of reading it. I think he was not shortsighted as he sometimes used a glass in looking at a book, and in using a glass he usually held it obliquely between his eye and his nose, but I never understood the reason.

Some persons can enjoy admirable sights at times when their physical condition would disqualify them from enjoyment. So in your brother I observed how admiration may overcome physical sufferings. In considering a man's physical character we may consider his taste as to eating and drinking, for some persons have curious antipathies. Moreover, the taste of a person as it affects his diet may have some influence good or bad upon his health. The person best acquainted with this aspect of your brother's character, I should think, is his wife. I have nothing to say on the subject, except that he ate a good deal of salt, which caused me some uneasiness, for sometimes when he had taken tea with us, I recollect that we had had no salt on the table, which would be an annoyance to Mr Boole, as he liked salt with bread and butter.

The fourth of Hill's letters to MaryAnn is addressed from Hull on 12 July 1866.[415] He observes that he cannot undertake to write biographical information about George in a regular manner, but can supply only raw material to be cooked by his biographers. He now turns his attention to Boole's opinions and observations relating to persons. Matthew Lilly was a janitor/odd job man at Boole's academy and may have been mentally or physically handicapped in some way:

To Matthew Lilly he formed an attachment when M.L. was a child about five years old, and retained his regard for poor Lilly, I believe till he died (of consumption) a year or two before Dr B. himself. But as to his friendship and kindness towards Lilly, you must know more than I do. I mention it however as a matter which should not be forgotten. He had a great esteem for my last surviving aunt. He once called at our house

Figure 6.2: Elihu Burritt

with the celebrated and learned Elihu Burritt[416] and I believe his motive was not only to introduce him to me, but also to let him see my aunt, a very interesting old lady.

Hill continues:

As to his successor Mr Swift, before Mr S. had actually taken over Mr B.'s school, he told us that he had heard Mr S. examine the boys and from his mode of doing it thought he displayed ability as a teacher. He once spoke with disapprobation of a man who having got on in the world, turned his back on his poor relations, who when Dr B. inquired of him about his former friends found he could say nothing about them, his excuse being, 'You see I have got into a different sphere'. One thing remarkable in Mr Boole's observations about persons was that, when he had need to speak censoriously of people he did so generally anonymously so that he could make use of their faults for moral instruction without damaging their characters. He might occasionally carry this suppression of names too far. A few years since, he had to write to me respecting his transactions with his landlord, but the landlord's name did not appear in any of his letters. I think the reason was that, the landlord's conduct not being fair and honourable, the tenant thought it inadvisable to say who he was. But on the whole I think his practice of suppressing a man's name when he spoke of his faults was a very good one. If such a rule were generally adopted, there would be great freedom in the discussion of the lives and characters of men with very little defamation or discord arising from them.[417]

Here Hill was most likely referring to Boole's dispute with his landlord in Cork, Mr Unkles, the owner of 5 Grenville Place, where Boole wrote *The Laws of Thought* (see Chapter Three). But Boole did not preserve this cloak of anonymity when he wrote to family members, especially his sister

MaryAnn. Hill continues:

> It is a curious fact that I find it easier to recollect my intercourse with your brother when walking in the country than when sitting in the house, and yet he was not so conversational in walking as in sitting ... Once when he told me of a great deal of writing he had been doing in a short time I expressed surprise, because it was a kind of writing that would require much cogitation, to which he answered that he usually did his cogitation before writing. Once after he had called on the father of one of his boys, after a relatively quiet episode, on the return journey he expressed a wish for a philosophical conversation on some profound subject, which would serve as a good intellectual exercise. I thereupon, after observing that some machines (such as watches) work by their own mechanism, whereas others (such as pianos) work according to the mode in which they are acted upon, proposed this question: Is nature in all its departments a machine acting by its own mechanisms, so that it is possible for philosophers to discover its laws and from them to predict its future operations, as they do in regard to many astronomical events; or are there some operations of nature which God guides as it were by His own hand, so that it is impossible for man, being ignorant of the purposes of God, to foretell future events. I expressed my own opinion, that the weather may be regulated by God, not by means of any natural mechanism that it is possible for man to discover, but by His own direct action upon it to accomplish moral purposes according to the scheme of His providential government.

Hill and Boole would no doubt have been fascinated by the modern subject of chaos theory, a recent and fascinating branch of mathematics, which concludes that certain natural phenomena are essentially unpredictable, and that minute variations in measured data can lead to radically different outcomes. Interestingly, one of the first areas to be studied in this context was weather forecasting, so Hill had put his finger, perhaps unwittingly, on a very profound and interesting topic. Boole's reply to Hill's question is interesting, not least because it is phrased in religious terms; whether this was done to please the very religious Hill and to express things in language he could appreciate, or because this is what Boole really felt, is difficult to say:

The reply of my learned friend was to this effect, that he did not regard natural phenomena as resulting from the operation of machinery set in action at the Creation, but he should rather consider everything that happened as effected by the power of God, so that when a body falls to the ground the force which brings it down is a direct act of God operating without the aid of any kind of instruments. I might then have asked how then can some natural operations have so much appearance of the regular operations of a self-acting machine, and how can natural events be distinguished from those supernatural ones which we call miracles and consider to be effected by divine power independently of the laws of nature? But finding his view of nature essentially different from my own, I was afraid and did not feel able to carry on the conversation any longer.

Hill then makes a few comments on Boole's personal philosophy and its implications in religion and physical science:

It might be expected that a mathematician well acquainted with the rigid inflexible unvarying laws by which the planets are regulated in all their movements would look upon nature as analogous to a watch which, though unable to make itself, yet when made and wound up works regularly without needing any person to apply his hand to keep it going. But that he held a different view appears not only from the conversation I have spoken of, but also from his statement of a different time, that he understood the quotation 'God upholdeth all things by the word of His power' to mean that creatures would cease to exist if the Deity merely let them alone without using His power for their preservation. But such notions seem to interfere with principles of natural philosophy, that he must have disunified them from his mind when pursuing investigations in physical science. He once, in speaking of the composition of matter, said that it was becoming the opinion of philosophers that every particle of matter is a system of forces acting from a centre. He did not state that as an original thought of his own, neither did it appear certain that he was convinced of its truth. Another strange idea that he expressed and which was clearly his own opinion (about which he spoke more dogmatically than he was accustomed to speak) was that all that is, is derived directly or indirectly from the Sun – even coals being indebted to the sun for their ability to produce heat, having acquired that ability when they were exposed to the sun as plants.

The fifth letter from Hill to MaryAnn is dated 23 May 1867. It contains little of interest. Hill tells MaryAnn that he has commissioned two poems to be written about Boole.[418] The sixth and final biographical letter is dated 25 June 1868.[419] This is a short letter in which Hill summarises what he has already said in the other letters and places strong emphasis on the division of Boole's life into distinct phases in literature, ethics and mathematics:

I now fulfill a promise that I long since made to send you two poems on the death of Dr Boole, one by Mrs Moulton of Lincoln, the sister of Mr Dixon the Maltster, and widow of a Wesleyan minister, and the other by the late Mrs Corlyon, a very interesting young poetess, the wife of one of my clerks, who died (as might be expected considering her very delicate constitution) at an early age ...

... The lives of men may be compared to rivers in some of which there are many turns and in some comparatively few. Whether we regard the external life of a man, as to his circumstances and mode of life, or his internal character as to his tastes and pursuits, we may find some epochs that may be regarded as turning points. One such epoch in your brother's life was when he turned from the study of classical literature to that of modern literature, about which time he seemed to have weaned himself from the former and to have acquired apparently a disrelish for it. It would be very interesting if in your memoir of him you could distinguish the periods of his life, the classical period, the ethical period, the literary period, etc. The mathematical age or period may be considered to have been coextensive with his life, but even that admits of some distinctions, as he was first simply a student of mathematics, then a discoverer who extended the limits of mathematical science, and afterwards he was engaged in laying the foundation of a new science having some relations to mathematical logic and mental philosophy but not identical of either of them.

Chapter 7

THE REVEREND E.R. LARKEN

GEORGE BOOLE was a close friend and frequent correspondent of the Rev. Edmund Roberts Larken (1809–95), an English clergyman and Christian Socialist. In 1847 they formed a building society, of which Larken was chairman and Boole a director, and they were both involved in the development and running of the Lincoln Mechanics' Institute. Like many other religious thinkers whom Boole admired, Larken was somewhat unconventional in his beliefs and behaviour, espousing radical causes and expressing unorthodox views on social matters. For example, he is believed to have been one of the first parish priests of his time to wear a beard.

Larken's sister Eliza married William Monson, the 6th Baron Monson. Larken graduated with a BA from Trinity College Oxford and proceeded to an MA in 1836. Significantly, while at Oxford he aligned himself with the logician Richard Whately, who had been a professor of political economy there before he became Archbishop of Dublin. Larken later aspired to a chair in that subject himself, first at Oxford, and later at Lausanne in Switzerland. Disappointed in these ambitions, he threw himself wholeheartedly into the campaign for Christian socialism, especially the co-operative movement. He took a leading part in the Leeds Redemption Society which aimed to enable the working classes to work out their own redemption by union among themselves. He was secretary of a scheme for self-supporting villages, president of the first co-op flour mill in Lincoln and served with Boole on the committee of the Female Penitents' Home in Lincoln. Larken often sought preferment but without success, probably because his views were felt to be dangerous. He was ordained deacon in 1833 and priest in 1834. His brother-in-law Lord Monson bestowed on him the living of Burton by Lincoln and he was rector there from 1843 until his death in 1895. He applied to become Dean of Lincoln in 1860 but was turned down, again possibly because of his radical and unconventional views.

Like Boole, Larken was a social reformer, but more radical. He espoused the doctrines of Charles Fourier, in the so-called Christianised Fourierism. In brief, this was an association of Christian principles which proposed, each labouring for all, that the exertions of each would receive their due and proper reward and the weak would be aided and supported by the strong, a commendable if somewhat utopian ideal. Frustrated by his inability to influence government policy Larken dropped out of public affairs but led a full and active life in the service of the church. For example, on most

Figure 7.1: Rev. E.R. Larken (1861)

Sundays he conducted five services, including those in the army barracks, the penitentiary, and the asylum in Lincoln. Larken's lifelong friendship with Boole was based on their common interest in logic and mathematics, and their desire to put their beliefs on social reform into practice.

Larken and his wife Mary (Lawrance) had twelve children in all, of whom four died in infancy. He entrusted two of his sons, Edmund and Tom, to Boole's school in Lincoln where it appears they did well, so that when Boole was appointed professor at Queen's College Cork in 1849, it was decided that Edmund should accompany him and become a student there. In Cork they shared lodgings in Castle White for the first few months. Boole was clearly fond of Edmund and kept a fatherly eye on him. He told his mother in December 1849:

Figure 7.2: Edmund L. Larken as an undergraduate

Edmund Larken is very well. Not so industrious as he should be but not yet a hopeless subject. He may if he likes do great things I should rather say if he will work.[420]

But it appears that Edmund also kept a close eye on Boole and was quick to report all the news back to his parents in Lincoln. For example, on 13 April 1851, in a letter to his mother, he relates:

Mr Boole is reported to have lost his heart again, this time to the vice-president's niece who is rather young, about 19 I believe and very learned; she knows, it is said, more mathematics than all the students put together. I was on an excursion down the river the other day when she was also of the party but I kept a good distance from her. I am studying Botany now …[421]

One wonders if Mrs Larken conveyed this gossip to MaryAnn Boole, and if so, what she made of it.

Figure 7.3: Edmund L. Larken in later life

Edmund studied medicine at Cork and graduated with the degree of MD. After graduation, he went to India to serve as medical officer to the army, but died tragically from smallpox on 19 February 1861 at Byculla, Bombay, aged only twenty-six years. Another son, Thomas Lancaster Larken, died in China in 1870, and Mrs Larken died in 1878. Broken by these tragedies, Larken senior, with failing eyesight, lost his spirit for social action, and retired from clerical duties in 1880. However, he retained a lively interest in current affairs until his death in 1895.

Most of the Boole–Larken letters which we have at our disposal cover only the eventful period 1845–9, but even from this short interval many interesting facts emerge on a variety of topics.

Since Larken had a background in logic and mathematics, Boole was able to converse and correspond with him on these subjects, and Larken would have been aware of the status and importance of the people to whom Boole referred. In January 1847 Boole wrote from London saying that he intended calling on Dr Latham, whom he was sorry to hear was unwell, suffering from a cough which it was feared would terminate in consumption. E.G. Latham,

MD fellow of King's College, Cambridge, was the author of *First Outlines of Logic Applied to Grammar and Etymology* and Boole's work was strongly influenced by his. Boole also called on Augustus De Morgan who procured him a ticket for the reading room of the British Museum for six months. Boole added that it would scarcely be possible to feel dull in London with such an acquisition.

Boole's first book, *A Mathematical Analysis of Logic*, which was published in 1847, features largely in the Boole-Larken letters. On 31 May 1847 Boole wrote:

> Thinking that you might be interested in seeing the rules for the conversion and general transformation of propositions which I mentioned last night that I had deduced, I send you a brief account of them. I must premise that by contraposition of a term I mean changing it from H to not H or from not H to H and I do not suppose this at all to affect the kind of proposition in which the term is found.[422]

Boole goes on to give an example and then gives his three rules for conversion:

> 1. Any affirmative proposition may be changed into its corresponding negative and vice versa. (A into E or I into O)
> 2. A universal proposition may be changed into its corresponding particular proposition. (A into I or E into O)
> 3. In a particular affirmative or universal negative proposition the terms may be corrected.[423]

Boole adds that it appears to him that all known transformations and conversions of propositions depend on these three rules, simple as they are. He then gives a concrete example, commenting that this particular example, a conversion lawful in itself, is not to be found in Whately or Aldrich, although there appears no reason why it should not be. Boole's confidence in commenting on established authors in the field of logic was remarkable, given that he was as yet unpublished in this area.

As the publication date of Boole's first book on logic neared, he writes to Larken on 13 September 1847:

> My manuscript is now in Cambridge ready for the printer. One of the fellows of St John's with whom I have some acquaintance has undertaken

the management of the affair and from what he says I am inclined to think that the book will excite interest and attention. My friend is a very competent judge so as far as the mathematics are concerned, and his opinion fully confirms that of Professor Graves who had the great additional advantage of being a logician trained and practised.[424]

Boole then reverts to his fawning worst on the subject of to whom he might dedicate his book. He writes to Larken:

Now I wish you to do me the favour to ascertain whether Dr Kaye our bishop would permit me to inscribe my work to him. You are acquainted with him and would easily ascertain this. I desire to inscribe my book to him because he is at once a mathematician and a scholar and his character is such as becomes his station and his attainments. With these views and feelings, it would I think be a very proper compliment to dedicate my work to the bishop, but nothing can be further from my wishes than to be in any way intrusive. As the work will be commenced immediately, it is desirable that I should as soon as possible receive the results of this application.[425]

John Kaye (1783–1853) was born in London and graduated senior wrangler from Cambridge in 1804. He was successively master of Christ's College (1814–30), vice-chancellor of Cambridge University (1814), Bishop of Bristol (1820–7), and Bishop of Lincoln (1827–53). Lord Liverpool was his patron and wished him even to become Archbishop of Canterbury if a vacancy occurred. He was elected a fellow of the Royal Society in 1811.

In the event, it appears that Boole did not dedicate his trail-blazing book to anyone. Perhaps Bishop Kaye modestly refused the honour, and to dedicate it to anyone else (Graves, Larken, De Morgan or Whately) might have been embarrassing. Boole coyly ends this letter to Larken with the following request:

While I am speaking on the subject of dedication, may I ask if you will allow me to dedicate to you a little volume of poems and translation which I intend before long to publish.[426]

Sadly, either Boole did not get around to publishing such a book, or if he did, copies do not seem to have survived. Perhaps he thought better of the idea, because such a scheme would have meant exposing to the public view his deepest feelings on love, religion, philosophy, and other subjects which he would have preferred to keep private.

Boole's introduction to his book is dated 29 October 1847 from Lincoln.[427] He is clearly anxious that it should receive as wide a circulation as possible, a hope that eventually failed to materialise. To Larken, setting out for London, he writes on 15 December 1847:

> If you have an opportunity, will you call at the *Athenaeum* office and ask if they have got my book. It is not noticed in the list of publications – nor in the publisher's circular, as I am told … Graves wrote to me a day or two since – he has been very ill. He tells me that he has made an appointment with Whately to discuss the merits of my system – this I did not look for.[428]

Shortly after this time, on 14 January 1848, Boole wrote an extraordinary letter to Larken implying that he intended quitting mathematics for a period of three years. Whether he was disappointed by the poor level of penetration of his book, frustrated by the lack of response to his application for an Irish professorship, or just disillusioned by the subject in general is difficult to say, but maybe it was a combination of all three causes. On the other hand, it could very well have been an elaborate joke between the two men, written in mock legal language. The letter read:

> My dear Larken,
>
> In pursuance of my intention long since formed and never to the present lost sight of, I send to your careful custody my mathematical books; keep them for the space of not less than three years and should I be forgetful of purpose as to ask for them again within that period, tell me that you hold them under a trust which may not be violated and that you will not let them go – and if I be still importunate, burn them even as the books of those which used magical arts were burned in the market place at Ephesus, 'the price whereof was fifty thousand pieces of silver'. And this document to which I set my hand shall be your warrant.
>
> Signed this fourteenth day of January in the year of redemption one thousand eight hundred and forty-eight.
> George Boole.[429]

Figure 7.4: Charles Graves

Larken wrote Boole a glowing testimonial as part of his application for a professorship at one of the Queen's colleges being set up in Ireland in the middle of the nineteenth century.[430] Larken was careful not to mention the personal detail that his sons attended Boole's school. But other interesting details emerge about the application from Boole's letters to Larken. On 29 September 1846, Boole writes:

> I am at present a good deal engaged with correspondence relative to my Irish application and also to the correction of some very troublesome proof sheets of a paper which is now being published … Thomson has sent me a handsome testimonial. He urges me to go for a month to Dublin to see something of university business and promises me his father's influence with Mr Cross, the Secretary of the Irish Education Board, if I determine to go. I don't however see how I can accomplish it. I cannot leave a certain for an uncertain duty. My course seems to be to send in my testimonials and calmly await the result … I cannot allow this opportunity to pass without thanking you in a more direct and explicit way than I have yet done for the very handsome testimonial you have given me. I doubt not that it will be of the greatest service to me and I shall set a high value upon it whether the particular object in reference to which it was written is secured or not.[431]

In a further letter dated 6 January 1847 Boole shows that he is full of anxiety and indecision about the Irish appointment, and that he is tempted to consider other positions closer to home:

I called upon Mr Gill who received me very kindly and showed me the People's College. He states that they are still in want of a principal, but they have an application from a Mr Cannon of Glasgow of whom they speak favourably. If it were not for my Irish prospects I am not sure that I should not offer myself ... But in my present condition I can hardly see how I am turning to account the little learning or talent that I have and the Irish affair is so uncertain. On the whole I am in a painfully unsettled state of mind.[432]

Indeed, we know that on 2 October 1848 Boole actually withdrew his Irish application, until he was persuaded by the Reverend Charles Graves to re-apply in a letter on 8 December of that year.[433]

During this time Boole had also been in constant correspondence with Graves, professor of mathematics at Dublin University, who had written Boole a valuable testimonial for his Irish application and may very well have been on Boole's interview board for the position. Certainly, he was one of the first people to know the outcome and inform Boole. In a letter to Larken on 15 December 1847, Boole quotes an extract from a letter he had received from Graves commenting that he writes with a mixture of gloom and hope about Ireland which was to Boole very touching. Graves wrote:

There is a dark cloud over this country at present under the depressing influence of which thinking men can hardly help withdrawing their attention from abstract matters even though they be in the highest sphere of science and literature and fixing it to no good purpose but as steadfastly upon that concrete trouble and misery that surrounds them. Against this tendency I struggle myself and try to follow my usual pursuits as diligently as I can. But it is impossible to do this as cheerfully as one did in better times. If I did not remember that God has made worlds out of chaos, brought light out of darkness, and is constantly bringing good out of evil, I should despair for this country.[434]

There follows a passage that, taken at face value, appears quite shocking, given that the context is that Ireland was experiencing a raging famine in which hundreds of thousands of people died from starvation and associated diseases. Perhaps what is equally shocking is that Boole does not appear to disagree with Graves' attitude, but then of course Boole had not visited Ireland yet. There is no suggestion that deliberate or public malice is involved, but in a private letter we see the attitude of the upper and privileged classes towards the starving peasantry, appearing to accept the awful happenings as if they were part of the natural God-given order. Graves continues:

> The recollection of these things is the foundation of my trust that He is now accomplishing beneficent purposes for Ireland, purging its social constitution, and bringing it through the crisis of a most painful disorder into a most healthful state.[435]

However, it is only fair to state that Graves was not alone in his attitude. The notorious Sir Charles Trevelyan, HM Treasurer, who was placed in charge of Irish relief schemes, described the Famine as 'an effective mechanism for reducing surplus population and a judgement of God on the Irish peasants for their Catholicism and idleness'. Furthermore, he called it 'a direct stroke of an all-wise and all-merciful Providence, which laid bare the deep and inveterate root of social evil'.[436]

On 24 September 1849, after Boole's appointment to the Cork professorship had been announced, he writes to Larken:

> ... I don't at all know when I shall be called away to meet the authorities of the new colleges in London ... I have conferred with B. Brooke and shall arrange with him what books are to be chosen. Some of my more immediate connections seem desirous that a surplus of a few pounds should be left after the purchase of books to be disposed of in a silver inkstand or something of this nature. To this I should have no objection and as it would gratify my mother and sister, I should be glad if it could be arranged. As to the presentation, I should prefer that mode which is most likely to be agreeable to the subscribers generally. It would give me the opportunity of thanking them for their kindness – also it is probable that there would be a greater number of them if there were no eating or drinking on the occasion. In this and in everything I feel that the simplest way is the best. Of course, I presume that none but the subscribers would be invited – at any rate the general public should be excluded.[437]

Figure 7.5: The silver inkstand presented to George Boole in Lincoln in 1849

In the end, a dinner was organised at the White Hart Inn in Lincoln, and the committee presented Boole with Johnston's *Atlas of Physical Geography*, a set of beautifully bound philosophical books, and a magnificent silver inkstand, valued at £20. This last gift, it was felt, would remain beside Boole on his desk, and hold the ink with which he would write further great works in mathematics and logic, and so provide a physical link with his friends in Lincoln.

The inkstand was inscribed as follows:

Presented to
Mr GEORGE BOOLE
by Friends in the CITY and COUNTY
OF LINCOLN
on his appointment to the
PROFESSORSHIP of MATHEMATICS
Queen's College Cork
28th Dec 1849

The inkstand was for many years housed in the mathematics department of the University of Bristol, courtesy of Boole's great-grandson Professor Howard Everest Hinton FRS, professor of zoology at that university. On his death, the inkstand became the property of his son, Professor Geoffrey Hinton. Through Professor Hinton's generosity, it was displayed at University College Cork for the duration of 2015, the Boole Year 200.

Doubtless Boole and Larken had many religious discussions which have not been committed to paper, but from time to time intriguing fragments appear in Boole's letters to his friend. It is a fairly safe bet that their lasting friendship meant that the two men saw eye to eye on religious doctrine and differed only in details and in the intensity of the application of their beliefs. The next extract from Boole's letter of 29 April 1847 shows that he and Larken engaged in religious discussion with what Boole humorously termed the 'opposition' in a pleasant social setting:

I am expecting E.F. Willson and the Rev. Jas. Simkiss to tea this afternoon. Would you like to see either of them? If so, come in before eight o'clock, or indeed as soon as you can. As they are both Roman Catholics you can consider yourself as representing in conjunction with me the 'Protestant interest'. You know or may have heard of Willson, but not perhaps of Mr Simkiss. I may therefore say that he has as much of the Catholic and as little of the Roman about him as any man that I ever met with in whom the two terms were united.[438]

It is clear that George Boole was a Christian but we know very little about his actual beliefs. However, there is evidence that he read a very wide range of literature emanating from different Christian sects. On 7 October 1847, he writes to Larken:

A respectable old 'friend' called upon me on Saturday having been moved to travel over England and dispose of George Fox's *Journal*. I bought two copies and if you like to have one, you can. There are two octavo volumes each containing above 500 pages for six shillings and there is much in there that is worth reading. The friend told me that he sold many among the clergy and was very anxious to see you and the Bishop (whether to testify in your steeple house or not I don't know) but he had not time to come over.[439]

George Fox (1624–91) was an English Dissenter and a founder of the Religious Society of Friends, also known as the Quakers or Friends. Boole is making a rare joke here because Quakers refused to use the word 'church', substituting 'steeple house' instead. Fox believed that everyone, including women and children, had a right to be ministers, and argued that because God was present in the hearts of his obedient people, believers could follow their own consciences rather than rely strictly on the Bible or the opinions of the clergy. Fox also made no distinction between Father, Son and Holy Ghost, a position that would have greatly appealed to Boole.

In another letter of Boole's, written not to Larken but to M.C. Taylor, a pupil of Boole's at Doncaster, we get a rare insight into Boole's religious beliefs.[440] The two men were close friends at Doncaster and their friendship continued when Taylor proceeded to study at university. From the topics mentioned in the letter, it is likely that Taylor was studying physics but had a continuing interest in philosophy, poetry, religion and 'mental science'. The letter is dated April 1840 and was written from Waddington.

Firstly, Boole recommends to Taylor a treatise on physical science which was published in the *Library of Useful Knowledge*, containing sections on heat, electricity, galvanism, magnetism, electromagnetism and chemistry – to be read in that order. Then he recommends another on instruments for the measurement of heat to be read subsequently. Most of the material was written by Roget, whom Taylor admired as the author of the most philosophical of the Bridgewater treatises. Boole tells him that he had used these works as textbooks in natural philosophy although his first information in physics came from French authors. He emphasises that one perusal is not enough and that the material must be covered again and again until it is mastered and goes so far as to say that pen in hand every student should write a textbook or manual for his own use. This is what he himself had done, almost entirely putting aside the use of the slate. Boole goes on:

> I do not feel surprised that the latent sense of poetry should have begun to manifest itself in you while pursuing the science of mind. Such things which appear anomalous at first sight are not really so ... I conceive that it is impossible that an individual should look with much fixedness of attention on the phenomenon of this inward life and being without the feeling that each obscured fact, each ascertained truth is but one link out of an infinite chain of possible truths of which each may afford matter for more sublime contemplation than can be derived from any of the forms of material grandeur and beauty. The ideas of human immortality, of modes of being infinitely diversified and bearing no relation to our existing senses in the present life of unlimited advancement and continued development, these which are among the reality of our Christian faith, are also among the glorious possibilities of the science of mind. And I am inclined to believe that the study of mental philosophy and the trains of

reflection to which it leads are favourable both to the growth of genuine poetry and the reception and appreciation of religious truth. True poetry has far more to do with man and man's interest than with the babbling of a stream or the glittering of a dewdrop. But it is time to leave this subject for the present. At a future period I will resume it for I have much to say upon it.[441]

Then, rather surprisingly, Boole, for one of the few times that we are aware of, commits some of his thoughts on religion and in particular on Christianity to the written word. Perhaps it is natural to lower one's guard in a letter to a close friend where the likelihood of disclosure is minimal, but there is another question worth considering – was Boole anxious to unburden himself to a trusted former pupil and so relieve the undoubted tension that contemplation of Christianity caused him to suffer? He continues:

> On the subject of religious belief to which you have inquiringly alluded I think it probable that we do not much differ. On the conviction derived from a lengthened examination of the subject conducted with a sincere desire to ascertain the truth, I hesitate not to avow myself in belief a Christian. I place my hopes of future happiness on the great propitiatory sacrifice and above merits of the savior. On minor and unessential parts such as freedom of the human will, I have ceased to think because at a former period I have thought much and earnestly. Here I feel it will be necessary for me to stop. I cannot go on and say to you that in deed and reality I am a Christian. I cannot say that I am advancing or even setting out my own advance …
>
> I doubt whether I am a Christian at all except in mere speculation. And now that I have expressed my opinions more fully than I am in the habit of doing, let me add that I cannot agree to enter into any correspondence on the subject of personal religion. I feel that to do so would on my part be little better than hypocrisy. If you are however engaged or particularly interested in any of the many objects of religious philanthropy and especially in any of those which are connected with my own immediate profession or pursuits, no one would feel greater pleasure than myself in hearing from you on them. In this way and only in this way our correspondence might be of good service to us both. At any rate the separate links of a protracted correspondence should have the same bond of connection as is afforded by the possession of a community of feeling

in some noble and worthy object. Its best ends are advanced when it serves by the collision of different and differently situated minds and the comparison of separate experiences to elicit practical truth or remove errors.[442]

Mary Ellen Hinton notes that the above letter is interesting in being perhaps the only one in which Boole expresses any clear opinion on the subject of Christianity. But she adds that 'religious feeling' is expressed all through his letters. Thus we have a tantalising glimpse into Boole's religious beliefs, which on the surface at least would appear to be leaning towards the agnostic. But one thing does seem certain, that he is happy to consider good deeds based on sound judgement to be perhaps more important an expression of religious belief than explicitly stating the finer points of doctrine.[443]

Early in 1847 Boole wrote a letter to Larken from London containing the following rather cryptic sentences:

> I enclose Mr Roper's acknowledgement of the receipt of the twenty-two sovereigns which you entrusted to my care. I quite forgot until I had executed the commission to consider whether in sending these draconic emblems to the poor living here I was not encouraging idolatry. If so I beg you to take the responsibility upon your own shoulders.[444]

The meaning of the passage is revealed in a letter from Larken to Mary Boole in February 1866.[445] He tells her that the incident refers to some sovereigns which Boole took charge of for Larken to deliver into the hands of a friend in London. They were intended to form part of a remittance to Ceylon, where they sold for the above face value of twenty-two shillings and sixpence each. Whether because of the superior purity of the gold of which they were composed, or because they were an original issue bearing St George and the Dragon on the reverse, these sovereigns were the only ones the natives of Ceylon would accept. Boole is joking that the reason is the oriental tendency towards dragon worship.

Boole and Larken were lifelong friends at both family and personal levels. They had very much in common in terms of their religious beliefs, their ideas about social reform, and their interests in languages, logic, mathematics, science, and learning in general. The tragic loss of Larken's son Edmund bound them together. Boole's premature death was yet another cruel blow to the Reverend E.R. Larken, which marked the beginning of his decline.

Chapter 8

WILLIAM BROOKE

WILLIAM BROOKE (1797–1872), a bookseller and printer, was a friend and lifelong correspondent of George Boole's. The surviving letters from Boole to Brooke indicate an extremely close relationship, with Boole usually using the salutation 'My dear friend'. While most letters to his immediate family cover the period between 1849 and 1854, letters from Boole to Brooke are written mostly in the later period 1855 to 1864, following Boole's marriage and ending just before his death. These letters provide a window into Boole's personal life in the latter years, and give an account of his travels in Ireland, England and Europe during that period.

William Brooke followed the trade of his father and worked with his brother Benjamin in the family printing works in Lincoln. He was a well-read man of letters who never married and lived with his sister Sarah for most of his adult life. He was for many years the Lincoln correspondent of the *Stamford Mercury*, a provincial newspaper, and later contributed to the *Mercury* under the nom de plume of 'Senex'. He was also an expert on local Lincoln history, and his obituary in the *Mercury* noted that he 'undoubtedly knew more of the history and traditions of his native city than any other living person'.[446] Brooke appears to have been an avid letter-writer and was also the principal Lincoln correspondent of Boole's pupil Charles Clarke after he emigrated to Canada (see Chapter Nine).

Boole knew Brooke initially through his father. John Boole and Brooke were both involved in the foundation of the Mechanics' Institute in Lincoln, and George was sent to Brooke for lessons in Latin. In a letter to his seven-year-old daughter Mary Ellen dated 13 September 1863, Boole described his relationship with Brooke:

> I suppose you know that I am stopping at the house of a very old friend of mine named Mr Brooke. I knew him when I was a very little boy, and he was so kind as to teach me Latin, and that was how we got to be such friends. He still teaches me when I see him, a great deal about old things such as old churches, old customs, old manners and habits of life; what people did and thought here in Lincoln a great many years ago. Some people care more about old things than new ones and Mr William Brooke is one of such people though he does care about new things when they are good and worth caring about. The difference I think is that he cares about old things whether they were good or bad. Of course I do not mean that he would wish to have old bad things back again in this world

after they have gone out of it, but he likes reading about them and likes to compare past times with present times and to see how the world is getting on, whether as God would have it be or not. I think the best way for us to mend the world is to try to do our own duty in it as well as we can. For although we cannot do much we can do something; because we are ourselves a part of the world, that is a part of the men and women now living in the world. There will be a time when we shall have gone away to give an account to God of what we have done; and then other people will live, and will have their work to do as we have had ours.[447]

In her biography of her brother, MaryAnn attributes Boole's first instruction in Latin to Brooke, but Brooke told MaryAnn:

I had quite forgot I ever gave him any help in his Latin till he once himself reminded me of it. It must have been but for a very short period of time. I have an indistinct notion of its being on Valpy's *Delectus*[448] and of our sitting together at the round table in our back shop, which we then called the library. But he must have shot far beyond his teacher. His mastery of the classics though little noticed by those who look up only to his mathematical character is very remarkable in one with so few opportunities and one could hardly touch on a branch of knowledge without finding he had been there and gathered all the best fruit, and so quietly and noiselessly done. So it is with the greatest minds.[449]

In 1845 Boole dedicated his lengthy poem on the British Association meeting at Cambridge to Brooke, and Brooke produced a beautifully printed version of Boole's application and references for the professorship of mathematics at Queen's College Cork in 1846. Following Boole's application for the professorship, Brooke humorously retorted with a poem of his own:

Thy heart if on Milesian bogs far away
There are thy young barbarians at play
Whom thou fondly hopest to set all to work
Don't you wish you may get it! But they'll give you a welcome at any rate ...

Hail Hibernia! Mournful maid!
Sighing on a Shamrock shade!

Wipe thine eyes and lift thine head
Lincoln cometh to thine aid …

And poor Colonia[450] is heard to mutter sotto voce
What has that Hibernia done
Thus to steal my favourite son?
Very well of them to shout him
But what am I to do without him …[451]

William Brooke told MaryAnn that after Boole's death he had destroyed many of Boole's letters in a fit of depression, fearing that they could fall into the wrong hands, as he did not have children to leave them to.[452] There is a gap in the correspondence during the five years following Boole's arrival in Cork. However, Boole's letters to MaryAnn are peppered with references to Brooke, mentioning their correspondence and invitations given to Brooke to visit Cork. Brooke, like Boole, was an enthusiastic walker. After a long walk around the villages of Monkstown and Carrigaline near Cork in December 1850, he told MaryAnn:

Tell W. Brooke that I feel doubtful whether in Scotland he has seen anything finer than the Carrigaline River. If he is sceptical about its beauties tell him that I desire him to come and see for himself.[453]

In early 1854, Boole wrote to MaryAnn regarding the distribution of copies of his newly published *Laws of Thought*. Boole was glad that she had included Brooke in the list of recipients.[454] The surviving correspondence from Boole to Brooke resumed around that time, with Boole commiserating with him on the death of his sister Mary and encouraging Brooke to attempt a series of sketches and stories about Lincoln.[455]

Despite having been in Cork for five years by October 1854, Boole still considered Lincoln home and missed it greatly. On his return to Cork for the new academic year, he was glad to have MaryAnn with him, telling Brooke that her presence made 'a great difference to his comfort in every way'. He continued:

Oh! That the Greetwell fields[456] and those with whom I have so often walked them could be transported here. My thoughts are more in Lincoln than they ought be.[457]

In June 1855, Boole again invited Brooke to visit Cork, quoting a popular Cork verse:

You ought certainly to come and see me. I most heartily wish that you would. I think instead of telling you of the pleasantness of the land and the geniality of its people I ought to adopt a wholly different course, reveal to you the miseries of exile and put it upon your faithfulness as a friend and old companion to come over and cheer the lonely hours of captivity. Be it known to you then that unless you do make up your mind to cross the salt sea on friendly thoughts intent I shall proclaim you a recreant knight in every court of friendship that still exists. I adjure you by the 'fen' and the 'hayth' by Skellingthorpe Wood[458] and the memory of Swanpool, yea finally by the little hostelry at Fiskerton in which you once read me Swift's 'Polite Conversations' that you come and see me here at Cork – 'Sweet Corke' as Spenser somewhere with imagination more poetical than true describes it. Who knows but you may leave it singing

> On thee I ponder
> Where'er I wander
> And still grow fonder
> 'Sweet Cork' of thee.
> With the bells of Shandon
> That sound so grand on
> The pleasant waters of the River Lee.

And truly whatever Cork may be it is I firmly believe the best place in Ireland.[459]

Boole appeared to have settled into a comfortable existence with MaryAnn in Cork. Although he had spent time in the company of Mary Everest in the preceding three years, he made no reference to her in the same letter when he spoke of the death of her father:

My sister is pretty well. I have got a little boat and have become skilful in the management of a pair of oars and often take her out on the water. She will probably go to Bristol in a short time and spend a little time with the Turners, formerly of Lincoln. The V.P. is well but he has been suddenly called to England by the death of his brother-in-law Mr Everest. He set off last night.[460]

Either Boole was being extremely coy with Brooke about his relationship or he had no idea at that stage that the end of his bachelorhood was imminent. Mary was twenty-three at the time and not in good health. Boole was approaching forty and had previously told Mary on a visit to her home in Wickwar that he was too old to ever consider marrying but that he would, if she liked, be her friend and would direct her education.[461]

Unfortunately, there are no surviving letters to Brooke which explain the chain of events that lead to the marriage of Boole and Mary Everest in Wickwar on 11 September 1855.[462] Despite its unexpected beginnings, the relatively short marriage which followed was happy and successful. Brooke wrote of it to MaryAnn shortly after her brother's death:

So happy a home – so well fitted a pair – so singularly and exceptionally fitted to each other – one might think Providence had brought them together to do a long work as well as a good work in the world – and they were to walk hand in hand cherishing each other and many more blessings for years to come – and see their children's children. But so much was not to be …[463]

The couple honeymooned in Wales. Boole wrote to Brooke from Tenby, urging him to visit them in Cork and demonstrating that, despite her youth, Mary was making her mark on her new husband:

Mary not only permits me to write to you but urges me to do so at once. I believe at my request she has a little postscript of her own to append. As to writing she says I may write anything but poetry. This she forbids, having a theory that the poetry which is in a man ought to be for home consumption and ought not to evaporate in words. Hence it is she says that professed poets are dull and prosaic people in common life. I am disposed to think that she is right.[464]

The correspondence continued after the couple settled into married life in Cork. In June 1856 Boole wrote to Brooke and took the opportunity to express his disgust with Sir Robert Kane and the administration of the college:

Relieve your mind about me; I have nothing to do with the present row in the college. It merely relates to a professor refusing to re-examine a class when directed to do so by the council, there having been some suspicion of unfairness in the examination at the lithographer's office by a member of the class. I think the professor in the wrong in the matter and am sorry that while there are such real and deep evils in the college, trifles like this should be made an occasion of dispute. I suppose I ought not to tell you of the cause of the dispute for it is not known I believe out of the college. But you are a safe friend.

Of K.[ane] I think as I ever did that he is a man utterly without principle. I do not know any one of his duties that is not either neglected or mismanaged. He spends but a month out of the year on an average in Cork and this would be a relief were it not that he holds, and rigidly guards as his own, rights which can only be exercised for the good of the college by one resident on the spot, e.g. the appointment, control and dismissal of the college porters and the regulation of their pay. We have now a college steward who is a hopeless drunkard, a registrar who scarcely ever issues a notice without betraying his ignorance of orthography, a bursar who cannot keep accounts, and a number of porters whose business of keeping the college rooms clean could probably nowhere in Europe be with impunity so much neglected as it is in Ireland. Judge whether I am captious in feeling dissatisfaction with such a state of things and in holding aloof from the servile herd who flatter the man who holds as a sinecure the office upon which so much depends and who is personally responsible in my opinion for nearly all the evils that we witness in the college. Three men only out of twenty had the manliness to refuse to join in giving him a public dinner some time ago as a testimonial (so it was represented in the papers) to the admirable manner in which he had governed the college.[465]

Boole continued that he could not believe that one of his colleagues who had agreed with him regarding the general neglect in QCC should then propose at the college's council meeting a resolution praising the conduct of Kane. He went on:

The only college affair in which I have moved for a long time was an attempt to get an increase in salary for one of the most deserving of the porters – the one who has charge of the library. His business is to keep the account of the books lent and returned and to hand books from the shelves to students. There is enough here to keep him occupied during the day and it is a higher kind of labour and there is more of it; yet the pay is the same – 12/- per week. When chairman of the Library Committee a year and a half ago I brought the subject forward and a resolution asking the president to increase the pay of the library porter was passed. It was presented but beyond vague promises nothing came of it. Some months ago I again inquired into the case and determined to wait personally on the president and ask him to do something for the poor fellow. Again vague promises and nothing more. This is a case of small importance perhaps compared with many others but it has led me to feel very strongly that the plainest considerations of justice and expediency are of no avail here in little matters or in great.[466]

Boole's efforts to address the unfair working conditions of the porter were undoubtedly due to his strong sense of justice but they may also have been motivated by the poor treatment that his father had received when he was curator of the Mechanics' Institute in Lincoln and which forced his resignation from that position in 1835. He continued his rant against Kane:

I often think that if the legislative union between England and Ireland were only repealed the flagrant jobbing which characterises all official and political proceedings here must come to an end. The strength of K. is that he belongs to a party – the Anglo Catholic party, as it is called. And it enables him to retain an office for which he is morally as unfit a man as could be found – even in Ireland.[467]

In an earlier letter to Brooke written in 1855, Boole had wondered whether the terrible mismanagement of the college put him under a moral obligation to expose it and suffer the consequences.[468] In 1856 Boole took that course of action and aired his criticisms of Kane publicly in a series of letters to newspapers. A Royal Commission was subsequently set up to investigate the conditions of the Queen's Colleges. The report of the commission was published in 1858 and found that the controversy and mistrust would not have arisen had Kane been resident in Cork. Residence was made a condition of holding the office of president. Boole was less than optimistic about its findings:

Our report is out but I have not read it, having decided to wait until the book is finished. I am told however that the commissioners speak well of me. Of other things I scarcely know anything as yet. I still retain most strongly my conviction that if the old system is allowed to continue, the college is gone. From all that I can learn the dissatisfaction is deep and general here. Unfortunately politics and faction make it difficult for a government to act justly even when they can get at the truth and know how. Of course I quietly avoid the subject when brought up – simply saying that I have not read the report and have determined not to read it at present.[469]

Despite his dislike of Kane, Boole was very complimentary towards his son, who became a student in the Faculty of Arts. He told Brooke in December 1859:

One of my best pupils in the second year's class is the son of the president – a very honest-looking lad, and I believe a good lad in every way.[470]

Away from the controversies of QCC, home life appeared happy and was about to get busier. Boole's letters convey his pride in his new wife. For example, in 1857 he wrote to Brooke's brother and business partner Benjamin, asking him to persuade Brooke to visit Cork. He wanted to allay any concerns that their business would be neglected during the visit and offered Mary's services to assist in this regard:

As to one part of William's business, the correction of proof sheets – I have already told him that provided the delays of postage are not too great, that may be very well done here. There is a pair of the sharpest eyes in the world in this house ready for his service and accustomed to the work.[471]

Mary accompanied Boole on his trips around Cork Harbour and he described one trip in June 1856, taken just one week before the birth of their first daughter:

Mary and I feel much benefitted by the change of air and scene that we have just had. We had yesterday a long excursion in a steamer over some of the more secluded parts of the harbour behind the island on which Queenstown stands. Q. itself we do not like. It is hot and dusty and a great part of it – all the old part – is ugly enough. They are about to introduce gas after long opposition on the part of the inhabitants. I am told it was at length only agreed to under a promise that the lights should be put out at ten o'clock. You will understand the reason. Smuggling is said to be carried on there to a large extent.

I had one long walk during my stay at Ringaskiddy. I crossed the hills to the Atlantic and had a ramble on the rocky beach. Very pleasant indeed it was. The drawback on all these coasts is that there is no sand. A few little beaches we found near Ring where there was good bathing. But generally the shores are either covered with stones or are formed of jagged rocks. There is great profusion of ocean life of all kinds, weeds and zoophytes etc. and a microscope which I had with me afforded us great pleasure. My eyes as you will understand from this are well.

Ringaskiddy is not an Irish-sounding name. Mary who adds to her other accomplishments a knowledge of Swedish and Danish traces it to one of these languages, I forget which. She derives it from 'Ring', a circle, and 'skyd', protection. I quote from memory of what she said. She often speaks with great admiration of a poem of Tegner's called *Frithiof's Saga*, I think.[472]

Impressive as Mary's knowledge of Swedish poetry was, what was more striking was a nine-month pregnant Victorian lady exploring the beaches of Cork Harbour. Boole finished the same letter affectionately saying:

My dear wife's time of trial is now drawing near. She is in good health but I feel as you may well suppose very anxious. She has a fine and healthy though not a robust constitution and her age is in her favour so that I am hopeful, and feel that there is little real cause for dread. Still it is after all a trying time. What Miss Tyler heard of her in London was only the truth and so you will say and feel too if you ever have the happiness to know her. And I hope you will yet.[473]

One week later, Mary Ellen Boole was born on 19 June 1856. Three days after her birth, Boole wrote to Brooke thanking him for his letter of congratulations. He told his friend:

Mother and child are doing as well as they can possibly do. For the well-being of the latter the great requisites seem to be milk and warmth and these the mother can abundantly supply. It is a pleasure to see them together.

You will be curious to know if the baby resembles its father. I think not. But it is strikingly like my late Uncle at Bassingham.[474] It has that wonderful expression of placidity for which his countenance was so remarkable. And I have two or three times half fancied that I had a little miniature copy of him before me. The resemblance struck my sister also who came over on Sunday to see the little stranger. It is evidently a very healthy child and the few who have seen it have settled that it is a beauty. It does not strike me that this is the case in any other way than as the quiet aspect of health and placid enjoyment when associated with infant life is always beautiful. This I think is a fair account of the baby and an impartial one though from its father. We must contrive in some way or another to let you see it before the end of the year. Indeed it ought to be, so that if we do not get to Lincoln you must come to Cork.[475]

A few weeks later, Boole wrote of Mary Ellen's progress to Brooke:

All is going well here, baby is growing prettier every day, but some little childish ailment which the nurse I believe predicted and called, I think, the 'snuffles' is making her a little fretful and uncomfortable. She is however very quiet and good-natured on the whole. Is it fancy or is it not, but once I caught quite in a startling way my father's expression on the child's face? More usually it is that of my Uncle.[476]

By May 1857 Mary Ellen was starting to walk. Boole told Brooke's brother Benjamin of her newly developed skill:

I am thankful to say that Mrs Boole and the little woman that is beginning just now to develop most wonderful and unheard of powers of locomotion equally adapted to the parlour carpet, the nursery floor and the lawn in front of the house – are quite well.[477]

Brooke finally visited Cork in 1857 and appears to have been very taken with Mary Ellen, also known as 'Puss' or 'Pussy'. Interestingly, Queen Victoria's first daughter, Victoria Princess Royal, born in 1840, was also nicknamed 'Pussy' by her parents. The following August, Boole gave Brooke an update which initially appears to be scientific but does not disguise the delight and amazement of a father besotted with his two-year-old daughter:

Pussy or, as you prefer think to term her, 'the excellent Pussy' improves in speech, stature, intelligence and favour. I have made curious observations at different times lately on the peculiar features of her intellectual progress, but I can only recall one or two. That peculiarity of advance by sudden starts which I have before mentioned to you continues, though in a less marked degree. Thus she instantaneously took to the use of the personal pronoun 'I'. No doubt the germ of some consciousness had been slowly developing in her before, and found expression at length in the 'I'. It is always I fancy a marked epoch in a child's life. She articulates with great distinctness, especially new words. After a time she grows somewhat careless and does not pronounce them so distinctly. On showing her a book of pictures of animals every quadruped was a horse or dog or donkey, such being the range of her previous experience. Cook mentions something of this kind about the South Sea islanders. She is remarkably fond of animals and often when walking around the garden stops to watch the progress of a snail or the flight of a butterfly, adding observations that would make you smile: 'Oh the snaileen! Poor fellow, go and get your breakfast.' The diminutive 'een' she frequently applies. Thus a little dog which we have got for her to play with and which is called Jumper she sometimes addresses as 'Jumpereen'.

When sitting at breakfast with us her great anxiety is to see me properly attended to and I go through a regular course of petting. 'Get your Toffee, Georgie'; 'Mama, Georgie wants some more coffee', etc., etc. If I take up a book it is 'Mama, Georgie's saying his lessons' or 'Mama, Georgie has got his lesson book' and so on; my doings and my comfort etc. being the great object of her thoughts at that time.

'Whom do you love' I said one day to her. 'Georgie – and everything' was the reply. I sometimes wish that I had kept a sort of psychological record of the different stages of her progress. It would be a very curious one. I think it singular that I have never met with anything of the kind. All these are trifles to most people – but I think you begged to be furnished with any such and therefore I send them.

One little thing more I must add. If she is at all ill – happily it does not often happen – her mother completely supersedes me in her affections and regards. She will go to no one else.[478]

By this time, Boole was living in 'Analore' on Castle Road in Blackrock, about four miles outside Cork city, and was clearly enjoying life there with his young family beside the river. He wrote:

Meanwhile there is nothing to be complained of in my position here at Blackrock. It is a delightful summer residence and there is the great advantage to me of sea-bathing or something as good every day at high water.[479]

The house had a lawn at the front and a garden at the back which was used to grow vegetables. Boole explained:

This is remarked as a year of great abundance here. Potatoes in particular are abundant and excellent. We have been living for the last two months or more (as far as vegetables are concerned) on the produce of my garden and I am called off from my books every morning to 'dig the potatoe', or if it is the cook who calls me it is to dig the 'praties'. The excellent Pussy accompanies me with a little wheelbarrow to collect the crop as they are turned up.

Boole then goes on to apologise to Brooke for the tone of his letter and tries to revert to more serious topics. However, he lapses into doting father mode again several lines later to finish with another anecdote about Mary Ellen:

This has been a very gossipy sort of letter and such as I should not think of sending to anyone but yourself.
    I think you sent me some time ago copies of the *Manchester Guardian*. I was interested in the academical discussions they contained and must thank you for them if I have not done so before.
    I have been trying to get some sheets containing pictures of animals for the album you gave her and such I have seen in Infant schools in England – but they are not to be had here – or I do not know what to ask for. And after all I am disposed to think that the young lady would at present be most pleased with her familiar friends the donkeys, etc.
    Oh, I must not forget to say that on seeing a picture of Lincoln Minster[480] she said after a pause, but with an air of doubt, 'A Pacific!'. We could not make out the meaning of this at first. At length it occurred to us that the Pacific steamer which used to pass this house a few months ago was distinguished from the others by two chimneys – and this was the only thing she had seen analogous to the towers of the cathedral.
    Give my wife's kind regards to your sister with mine and believe me
        Yours ever
        G. Boole.[481]

On 26 August 1858 Boole told Brooke about the birth of his second daughter, Margaret:

I have just had an addition to my little family of a daughter. Mary is very well indeed under the circumstances. And the child is strong and healthy and wonderfully quiet. So that there is room for thankfulness on all sides.[482]

In a subsequent letter, Boole described the newborn as being 'more grave and serious of character than the volatile Pussy'. He predicted that she would be a child of remarkable character.[483]

Boole reported in December 1859 that he was teaching Mary Ellen to read and that she was getting on very well and was evidently enjoying it very much.[484] In the same letter, Boole wrote to Brooke about MaryAnn, who was at that time working as the governess to the children of William Fitzgerald:

We hope that she will spend Christmas with us, and I would that you could also. She seems very happy and looks well. The children are very nice and easy to manage. We had them here one day last week to get a country lunch and see the microscope and very pleased they seemed to be.

There were six Fitzgerald children, including George Francis Fitzgerald who later worked in electromagnetic theory and after whom the Lorentz–FitzGerald contraction is named. The Lorentz–FitzGerald contraction was an integral part of Einstein's special theory of relativity. George would have been about four at the time of his visit to the Booles' home but perhaps his experience of the Booles' microscope may have helped encourage his scientific endeavours in later years.

In late June 1860, Boole's third daughter, Alicia, was born. Boole announced her arrival to Brooke in early July:

An event has taken place in my family of which you ought to be informed – so thinks the principal person concerned. It is that she – the principal person, my wife – has been obliged to retire for a time from the more active duties of life and to confine her cares to one small element of humanity, a little girl that last Thurs morning, to adopt the account of the matter given, after repeated questionings, to my eldest daughter, was 'sent by God from the other world'. 'But I wonder, mother,' was the reply, 'that God was not afraid to send such a little thing such a very long way.' And I believe this is still a subject of wonder and speculation to your little friend Pussy ...

Mary is wonderfully well and will get up tomorrow and dine with me on Thursday – if all be well. She sends her very kind regards to you.[485]

Boole had hoped to attend the meeting of the British Association in Oxford which began on 30 June but Alicia's birth was later than expected. He wrote:

This prevented my going to Oxford. We had expected that all would be over before the great scientific gathering began. What I more regret is that Mary could not accept with me an invitation which we both had to spend the week there as the guests of one of the professors – whose wife, however, when made acquainted with the cause for declining said, while expressing many kindly regrets, that she was 'forced to admit the sufficiency of the reason'.[486]

The meeting of the British Association that Boole missed became famous for a debate on the theory of evolution whose contributors included prominent British scientists and philosophers of the day including Thomas Henry Huxley and Bishop Samuel Wilberforce. Charles Darwin's *On the Origin of the Species* had been published seven months earlier causing wide debate and controversy. Boole does not refer to Darwin in his correspondence with Brooke but in the context of this topic he does mention James Martineau, a Unitarian minister and educator, who was an influential theologian and philosopher. The Martineau family were friends of Dr Ryall, and Harriet Martineau, sister of James and a political writer, had visited the Ryalls in Cork in 1852.[487] Boole asked Brooke:

Do you ever see the *National Review*? There is an article in the April number which goes quite as far as the *Westminster* ever did in the way of discrediting the historical value of scripture. I see it referred to in the *Inquirer* which you sent this morning and for which I thank you. Do you know anything about the writers for the *National*? Martineau is one I know, and there is a good article by him in the present number on 'Bain's Psychology' – but the article to which I referred before is not at all in his style of composition. I am sorry to see the *National* admitting articles of this kind. It argues a change of some kind in the management.

How very curious and great a change has taken place in at least the leading minds of the Unitarian body. Priestly[488] held more literally the historical parts of scripture, miracles, the resurrection of the body, etc. but in his philosophy he was a materialist, a sensationalist of the extreme school. Martineau is the very opposite in both respects. He seems to have given up wholly the theory of inspiration in its usually understood sense and at least undervalues if he does not wholly disbelieve the miraculous statements of the Bible – but he is as far removed as possible from being a materialist. His religious dogmas might be said to be philosophical and his philosophy religious. The course of Maurice in the church has been very similar in its general character.[489]

After Alicia's birth, Mary suffered from a period of ill-health. In the following March, Boole told Brooke:

Mary is not very well and yesterday consulted our famous hydropathic and Turkish bath physician to whom MaryAnn owes the restoration of her health.[490] He gives her a good hope of improvement. She is not very ill, but for a long time past has been unwell more or less. One thing she suffers from is an enlargement of the uvula which may ultimately affect her speech.[491] Though it has not done yet.[492]

Mary had not recovered by the summer and it was decided to take a trip to the Continent to give her 'a change of air'.[493] The trip was a great success and the couple spent over nine weeks in France, Belgium, Holland and Germany. Boole gave Brooke details of the trip in a long letter in September 1861. As far as we know, this as Boole's first and only trip to mainland Europe. His impressions of Germany and the German education system are worth quoting in detail:

We saw Ostend, Antwerp, Ghent, Brussels, Cologne, Bonn, Frankfurt, Mainz, Darmstadt, besides the smaller towns on the Rhine at which we stayed. I saw also Mannheim and Heidelberg. I mean that we saw these places in a satisfactory way, rambling about them so as to make ourselves acquainted with more than the guide books tell us of. We had the opportunity of conversing with a good many educated people, some of high cultivation and, what we did not expect, we found ourselves able after a sojourn of a week or two to talk with the peasantry, the keepers of small wayside inns etc. I need not say to you that the glimpses we have had into the real life of Germany have been full of interest. I cannot but feel that in a great many respects the Germans are both a more civilised and a better people than ourselves. During the whole of our residence among them I saw but one drunken person, and he was not a poor man. I witnessed not one act of cruelty to animals as disgraces England, and still more this country. The compulsory state education is against our received notions of freedom, but the language of all Germans with whom I spoke on the subject was uniform. You, they said, do not understand true freedom; if you did you would both compel the parent, when compulsion was needed, to send his child to school, and you would absolutely take away from him the power to support himself by his child's labour.[494]

Prussia had introduced a modern compulsory education system in 1763. The Prussian system of education included free primary schooling for the poorest children and had extended the school year to facilitate the children of farmers. Teaching was recognised as a profession and specialised teacher training colleges had been established. State funding was provided for the building of schools. This model spread to other German states and was copied in other European countries. The United Kingdom fell far behind its European neighbours and education was used as a means of preserving the privileges of the upper classes. Compulsory education was not introduced in England and Wales until the Elementary Education Act of 1870 which established school boards to set up schools in places that did not have adequate provision to do so. In 1880 education was made compulsory to the age of ten.

During the trip Boole met a professor from Silesia in Brussels and travelled to Cologne with him afterwards. He described him to Brooke:

He was a thorough German and even his accent was that of the common people though he was a professor in Silesia – not indeed in a university but one of those gymnasia which prepare for the university. We were much indebted to him for information, and also once for his assistance when we got into some confusion about the perplexing money systems of the continent. I was struck with the extreme readiness with which he at once formed acquaintance and entered into conversations and even disputations, for he was as fond of an argument as Dr Johnson with any whom we met, talking to persons of whatever rank just as if he belonged to that rank.[495]

On his return to Cork, Boole received a letter from the professor which contained two annual reports from the gymnasium at which he taught. Boole was very impressed. He told Brooke:

These were prepared by the director of the institution, but to each of them was prefixed an essay by my friend. It seemed to be the rule that with each annual report an essay by some one of the professors should be published – the subject being one of some general literary interest and not connected with the report or the institution. This seems very different from our English practice and notions. I thought also the subjects of the essays remarkable. They were
    'World history as a vestibule to the Kingdom of God'
    'The two examples of patience – Job and Ulysses'.
I have read them both and really with great pleasure and interest. They are beautifully written – profoundly religious – but the criticism of the Book of Job is totally unfettered by any theory about the origin of the book. In England the place of the writer would be among the essayist and reviewers by the side of Jowett.

I think this shows very strikingly the difference between England and Germany. We may certainly say that with us the discussion of the Hebrew and Greek idea of patience would not excite any positive interest – would not by a professor in a government institution be tolerated. The interest which the German feels in the subject of the book is with us confined to a theory of its origin – as respects too many.[496]

In Cologne, Boole visited the cathedral as it neared completion. Its construction had commenced in 1248 and finally ended in 1880.[497] As a native of Lincoln, he was very familiar with an impressive Gothic cathedral, but was highly taken with Cologne:

The cathedral of Cologne so far as completed is I can well believe the finest Gothic building in the world. From the gallery corresponding to the triforium[498] in our Minster the view of the choir and the clerestory [499] surpasses all that I have read or conceived. The windows of the clerestory are I think 80 feet high, all painted glass. Between the arches of the choir in the position occupied by the angels in our Lady chapel are pictures of angels by some great German (living) artist which as a whole are of the most wonderful beauty and power. I obtained special leave to remain in this gallery and I think Mary and I spent quite an hour and a half there. Many I fancy go to Cologne and do not even learn of its existence. The view from the floor of the choir is to me spoilt by the extreme height of the interior (at least 160ft), for as the clerestory is the lightest and in every way the most beautiful part and is of such vast dimensions, the impression arises that it is really the cathedral and that you are looking up at it from a crypt below.

The Byzantine churches of Cologne and nearly the whole Rhine district produce a very peculiar impression, quite different from that of a Gothic building. I have seldom felt the influence of place and association more than when sitting one Sunday afternoon in the gallery of the old Byzantine (now Protestant) church at Bacharach[500] listening to the long solemn strains of a German hymn sung by the congregation (as in Germany alone they can sing) below.[501]

Mary stayed in Darmstadt and Boole journeyed through the Rhineland alone. He found the ruins of the castle at Heidelberg were more impressive than any castle ruins he had seen before but felt they did not have 'that air of grey antiquity which gives so solemn a charm' to some of the Welsh ruins that he had seen. He described the countryside to Brooke:

The diversity of the scenery of the Rhine constitutes a very great charm. In some places a lovely foreground of fields and vineyards lies between the river and the hills, in others the river is bounded by steep walls of rock which admit of either no cultivation at all or only that of terraced vineyards. In other places, as between Bingen and Mayence [Mainz], the Rhine spreads out a noble breadth averaging a mile, and in one part I believe extending to three, and you pass on as through a beautiful lake from the surface of which rise lovely wooded islands.[502]

Boole spent an evening in Oberwesel in the Rhineland in the company of some German students. He told Brooke:

Figure 8.1: The Golden Corkscrew, Oberwesel

The evening with the party of German students in the inn at Oberwesel (The Golden Corkscrew) was worthy to be chronicled. Wild boar's flesh was a part of our viands, and there was no less generous drink than pure Rhine wine. I was very much struck with the grandeur of the first song sung by them in full chorus, in which to the best of my poor ability I joined. As I have it before me I send you a rendering of the first three verses, omitting a line or two:

Are we met in the good hour
A strong choir of German men?
Then from the German mouth
Breaks forth the soul in prayer.

To whom shall our first thank sound aloud?
To God the great and wonderful
After our long night of shame
Rose before us in flames
Scattering with lightning the boast of our enemies

Who renews our strength!
Who sits above the stars resting
From eternity to eternity!

For what shall our second wish peal forth
For the glory of Fatherland?
Perish all who scorn her!
Hail to him who dedicates to her his love and truth!

In the nineteenth century, *Zum goldenen Pfropfenzieher* or The Golden Corkscrew was a favourite haunt of travelling writers, poets and artists. The inn is still in business today.

Boole visited Germany during the time of the German Confederation, a loose union of thirty-nine states which had been founded after the fall of

Napoleon at the Congress of Vienna in 1815. By the middle of the century, Prussia dominated the Confederation, having expanded its territories and industrialised rapidly. The growing nationalism was clear to Boole, but he was not sure that it would be advantageous. The open access to the pursuits of education and leisure for even the poorest classes in Germany greatly impressed him but he was not sure if unification would destroy this. He continued:

> The strongest feeling in Germany seemed to me to be the desire for union and especially for union as would enable them to assume a proud, defiant position towards France.
>
> I am of the opinion that though they would gain much by the merging of the smaller states in one great one, they would also lose much. Some of the small capitals are real centres of civilisation. At Darmstadt the capital of Hesse they have, and all through the activity and enlightened benevolence of one sovereign, 1^{stly} a broad-streeted, well-paved, perfectly drained town which the cholera has never visited. 2^{ndly} schools and gymnasia in which all can receive a good education, and the children of the poor from 7 to 14 a gratuitous one. 3^{rdly} a free library of 200,000 volumes, with museums and picture galleries. 4^{thly} public gardens. 5^{thly} public woods and forests, or I should rather say forests open to the public, and with such guide posts along all the principal tracks and alleys that you may walk for twenty miles without losing yourself. 6^{thly} a public swimming pool covering probably 20 acres. I could go on increasing this list. It would be simply impossible to establish in any English or American town such a set of institutions in any single life.[503]

German unification was achieved in 1871, engineered by Otto von Bismarck, who became foreign minister of Prussia in the year following the Booles' visit.

The Booles left Darmstadt in late August and returned via Cologne, Aix la Chapelle (Aachen) and Calais. Mary found the journey very tiring and was not feeling well when they reached London. Overall, however, Boole saw a great improvement in his wife on their return to Cork:

> You will be glad to hear that the journey has worked wonders for Mary's health. She has recovered her appetite and strength and is stronger than she has been for years. From what we hear of the dreadful weather in

Ireland during our absence I am really inclined to think that if Mary remained here her life would have been in danger. She seemed to gain appetite and strength as soon as she got into the sunshine of the Continent – and sunshine it was – such as I have never seen before. It is not the mere scenery that impresses an Englishman most. There were days on which there seemed to be no shadows – but the whole scene before us seemed to be bathed and steeped in light.

We found our children quite well on our return home – the youngest had during our absence learned to walk and seemed to have passed from baby to childhood. That is the greatest change we noticed.[504]

It is not unreasonable to wonder whether Mary was suffering from depression, possibly post-natal depression. In the space of a short number of years she had lost her father, married quickly after his death, moved to Ireland and had three children in quick succession. While Boole appeared to be a loving and devoted husband, he must have been extremely busy and this cannot have been easy for his young wife. In May 1860 he had written to another friend saying that he had spent the last three or four years constantly occupied in writing books and papers,[505] and he also had his duties in QCC to attend to. In the period 1859–60 his last two books, *Differential Equations* and *Finite Differences,* were published.

While the Booles were away, their landlord had added an extra storey to their house in Blackrock. The trip to Europe was probably planned to coincide with these renovations. Boole told Brooke:

My house is now nearly ready for our reception. My landlord has raised it one storey and it will be commodious and pleasant. There will be quite room enough for English friends and especially for Lincoln friends, whenever they may feel disposed to come and sojourn by the Lee.[506]

The extension to the house was fortuitous, as the family continued to expand and to welcome visitors from England. The Booles' fourth daughter, Lucy Everest, was born in August 1862. However, the family moved to a larger residence in the spring of 1863, 'Lichfield Cottage' in Ballintemple, which was a mile closer to Cork city.

In April 1864, just before the birth of their fifth daughter, the wife of Boole's brother Charles visited the family. At the time of Millicent's visit, the steamer *The City of New York* was shipwrecked in dense fog off Daunt's

Figure 8.2: *The 'SS City of New York' Struck on Daunt's Rock 1864* by H.A. Hartland

Rock in Cork Harbour, thankfully without loss of life. The Booles made an excursion to witness the wreck before it sank:

> My brother's wife is now with us. She is a plain sensible good woman and we enjoy her company. We all went a few days ago to visit the wreck of the great steamer which is on a sunken rock three miles from the harbour mouth in the open sea. It was a melancholy sight. The long high sides of the vessel like iron walls enabled us by their fixedness to appreciate the enormous size of the ocean waves which washed them. A large number of men were at work on the wreck trying to take cargo for removal. The captain I am told is in a dreadful state of mind, as well he may be. The rock is like a vast table rising to within about eleven feet of the surface at low water so that the little steamer in which I was went over it without any danger. Mary and Mrs Boole (from Sleaford) accompanied me.[507]

Ethel Lilian was born one month later, on 11 May 1864. Boole told Brooke:

A time of some anxiety is just over. My dear wife brought a little girl into the world on Wednesday. Both are well.[508]

The family was now complete but the strain of having five children in eight years had taken its toll on Mary. In July, Boole told Brooke of the new nurse from London who had been employed to help Mary:

Children are all well. The new nurse is likely to suit well. That will be an immense relief to Mary who has too much upon her mentally and bodily.[509]

But by late October 1864, in the last surviving letter to Brooke, the nurse had given notice to leave, having heard of another position with a very wealthy family in the area. She changed her mind when a dispute arose with her new employers about her pay:

She then gave us notice – but when she went again to the place after an interval of some weeks they declined to have her. I would still have kept her to save my wife the trouble and anxiety of a change, but she had got thoroughly dissatisfied I think with the country and settled to go. I paid her expenses hither from London and you will hardly believe that she asked me to pay her expenses back too though she was leaving my wife without a minder and with an infant still at the breast.[510]

During the summer of 1864, Boole spent seven weeks in London, leaving Mary in Cork with their five young daughters. His visit took place at the time when the rebuilding of the Palace of Westminster was nearing completion. He clearly enjoyed the trip, which gave him peace and solitude for research:

I have spent seven weeks in London fully occupied in making researches in the library of the Royal Society and to a small extent in that of the B. Museum. I did not leave London during that time except for an evening with Mr F.C. Penrose[511] at Wimbledon where he lives and for two days with Mr Justice Willes at Otterspool.[512] I was asked to accompany the visitors of the observatory at Greenwich in their usual inspection which was the immediate reason of my leaving home but it was necessary also for me to go through a certain ceremony of admission into the R[oyal] Society which had been put off for several years. I had also long wished to study the great series of original memoirs by Leibniz, Clairaut, Euler, Lagrange, Laplace for the subject of my book, those which established the science, and I found such comfort and facility for doing this at the RS that I stopped on working for longer than I had intended. There was a large room full of mathematical books and looking out on a stately garden of the old style. There I sat undisturbed. The cleanliness, order, solid goodness (all in the old style) of everything about me made it quite a luxury to work there, and there was at my command, without having to trouble anybody, one of the best scientific libraries in the world. I lodged at Euston St Strand near Charing Cross and used in the evenings to go pretty often to the exhibition of pictures of the R[oyal] Academy or walk on the footbridge beside the Charing Cross railway over the Thames from which there is a wonderful prospect – one I suppose hardly to be equalled elsewhere – of Westminster Bridge, Hall, Abbey, the new Houses of Parliament, the great clock tower etc. all being near. And when the moon shone down, or the last rays of the setting sun pierced through the smoke of London & brought all these in outline the effect was very solemn indeed.[513]

On the return journey to Cork, he met a number of past pupils, one from his school in Lincoln and others from Queen's College Cork. He was struck by the diverse paths they had taken and described them to Brooke:

The first, John Giles, son of Mr Giles of Branston Heath an architect (very successful) in London – the second about to set off, as a government engineer, to India, the third going as an assistant engineer on a railway in Spain (Seville to Madrid) – the fourth British Consul at Tientsin in China – the fifth an Oratorian Father at Brompton. The two last accosted me on the Holyhead steamer. The contrast between these in appearance was as remarkable as in fate. The consul,[514] short, comfortable, somewhat too fat, self-possessed with a pretty young wife whom he had lately married hanging on his arm – the priest tall, thin, macerated by fasting, cheerful however and I should think proud of his position. He was covered with the dust of travel and I brushed his long coat and made him a little more presentable at the dinner table where he expressed his intention of 'walking in' to the good things – a kind of thing which he had not done for some time before I imagine.[515]

Boole's kindness to his old student, a Catholic priest, is typical despite his misgivings about the Catholic clergy in Ireland. In an earlier letter to Brooke in July 1855 he had referred to his Roman Catholic servant attending the 'Popish Masshouse'.[516] In a letter to another old Lincoln friend, W.A.J. Turner, written in January 1860, he commented:

> The Roman Catholic priesthood seem to have been doing all they can to preach disloyalty. Between them and a bigoted Calvinistic Protestant population, this is a country which does not on the whole present the most favourable picture of Christianity.[517]

He despaired of actions taken in the name of religion in Ireland and told Brooke:

> You have heard of the appointment of Lord Wodehouse as Lord Lieutenant of this country. I hope he will get on well; but he will have a difficult task. Animosity between the different religious sects does not diminish and a friend of mine quoted today the famous line from Lucretius 'Tantum religio potuit suadere malorum. (To such heights of evil are men driven by religion.)' That is often forced upon me here.[518]

When referring to a lecture given by William Fitzgerald, the Bishop of Cork, he blamed the lack of educational resources available to the masses on the fractured society that existed in Ireland. However, on a positive note he did mention the low crime rate in the country at that time:

> The bishop is going to lecture on Erasmus at a society here similar to the London Christian Young Men's Association. Protestant and Catholic alike have societies of that kind here in which clergymen expound their views of the universe – and I believe make sad work of geology sometimes. There is no Mechanics' Institute, no library accessible to the multitude and I suppose it would be difficult to establish anything of the kind in so divided and embittered a state of society. It is singular withal how little crime there is. Burglaries are never heard of – I must except a sacrilegious burglary which has just taken place at a country chapel and in which the thieves carried off – what do you think? The vestments of a statue of the Virgin Mary![519]

In October 1864 Boole travelled to Dublin to act as an examiner for candidates in Dublin Castle. While in the castle, he spotted Sir Robert Peel, who held the office of Chief Secretary of Ireland between 1861 and 1865, and was the son of the late prime minster Robert Peel. He told Brooke:

> Today while studying in the entrance hall I saw Sir R. Peel come into the castle. A rather large stately man I thought. An official speaking of him and his brother Fred (in the Treasury) said that they were sometimes designated as 'Impulsive Peel' and 'Repulsive Peel'.[520]

Boole was critical of the examination system in operation for the Queen's Colleges. He complained that examinations did not provide the best measure of a good education:

> I am strongly inclined to think that the matter of examinations is greatly overdone in the present day. For the university examinations there are to be no less than eleven papers set (in pure mathematics) beside mixed mathematics. I do not mean that every student who takes mathematics will have all these to answer, but the examiners have to set these. The engineers have four to answer, the arts students five of them, three others two and so on. All this is bad for students and bad for examiners. Fortunately, there are three of us to divide the labour of the mathematical examinations. The present forcing system of examination must tend to destroy originality and I think to stifle genuine love of knowledge. It comes I believe to this – that the best kind of education does not admit of definite measures of its success that only a secondary and very inferior order does, and that if for competition for the public service, for honours and so on you must have the definite standards, you must put up with the inferior article which admits of being gauged and measured with some accuracy – but that only approximate.[521]

While engaged at the examinations in Dublin, he took the opportunity to hear the new Archbishop of Dublin preach and to view the renovations to St Patrick's Cathedral in Dublin. He found neither impressive:

> On Sunday I went with a friend to hear the new Archbishop of Dublin Dr Trench[522] preach at a village a few miles distant. I thought his manner

very bad and his utterance was so indistinct whenever he became excited that is was impossible for me to hear a considerable part of the session …

The old cathedral St Patrick's is being restored by Mr Guinness,[523] a rich brewer of porter, who has expended I believe £40,000 on it but some parts of the restoration seem bad and the painted glass in particular so tawdry.[524]

After the examinations ended, Boole visited County Wicklow with Dr Ryall. He described the scenery they encountered on what seemed to be quite a physically demanding trip:

After the examinations were over Ryall and I agreed to have a couple of days in the County Wicklow before returning home. We set off from Dublin last Monday week, went to Bray by rail, thence by car about 14 miles to Roundwood, a small walk in the neighbourhood of some beautiful lakes which we went the same day to explore (on foot) and returned in the evening to the inn after a march of about 11 miles. Next morning to Glendalough the seven churches of St Kevin's and their famous scenes and thence in the evening to Avoca, the following morning on foot to Woodenbridge and down the beautiful vale of Arklow to the town of the latter name where we parted, I returning to Dublin in order to take the train on my return ticket to Cork and R. forward to Enniscorthy whence by cars and steamers and railways he made his way to Cork.

Wicklow scenery is certainly much finer than Derbyshire, and it was on the whole grander and wider and with less of soft loveliness than I had expected. There was one scene which made a deep impression upon us both and R said that he had never seen anything like it. It was a lake on a mountain overlooked on one side by awful cliffs of granite and bounded on the other by a bog over which we had to make our way to get to it; but fringed all round with spectral looking rocks of snowy whiteness formed by a granite decomposed and honeycombed by the action of the bog water. There was no vegetation in the lake and the bottom was composed of rocks and stone of the same colour and texture. What, said I to R, does it seem to you like? I could fancy it a scene in a moon on a planet. 'And I,' said R, 'was just going to say that it reminded me of what we read about the desolation of the moon. These are ghosts of rocks.' I suppose this strange scene is not often accessible for we had to cross a mile and a half of bog to get to it – this year comparatively dry. We descended along the bed of a mountain torrent.

All well at home. I hope you, dear friend, are too. Let us hear about you soon. I shall be immersed now in examinations for some time and then lectures begin but I have had a good long rest and must not complain.[525]

The trip to Wicklow took place less than two months before Boole's death. He mentions having had a good long rest but he did have serious health issues in the summer of 1864. In July he had visited his brother in Shropshire on the way home from London and was very unwell. He wrote to Brooke on 20 July after he returned to Cork:

I reached home yesterday morning. I had been very ill while at my brother's, more so than I remember to have ever been in my life and when I looked at myself in the glass after getting home I seemed to be at least 10 years older. I had for some time in London had a cough, but it became aggravated probably from the great heat on my arrival at my brother's and was accompanied with severe headache, a quick pulse, rheumatic pains in the face and a fetid discharge both from the head and throat. The room in which I slept was very small and hot and there was one of those old bedsteads with hanging curtains which seem to smother you. I felt what the lot of the poor must be when sick and dying in their own abode, but I could only hope that their nervous organisation is not except in very rare circumstances like mine. For I remember when a boy how restless I was under heat and restraint and my poor uncle at Bassingham with whom I once slept when about nine years old said that he never got so kicked in his life as by George. I left Shropshire on Monday doubtful whether I should be able to get beyond Chester and seriously thinking of taking a lodging there, sending for a doctor and telegraphing my wife. But the journey which I had to make in an open country cart about 10 miles before reaching Wolverhampton seemed to revive me very much and I felt quite able to travel. Then the fresh breeze of the sea on the deck of the steamer put new life into me so on reaching Dublin I determined to go by the night steamer to Cork ...[526]

A week later he reported that he was still feeling unwell but had improved somewhat. He resolved to visit the Turkish baths in Dr Barter's establishment in Blarney if the feeling of influenza persisted.[527] In late August he referred to his cousin's physical appearance and his surprise at seeing his own photograph:

I must pay a visit to Bassingham I think while in Lincolnshire. I have not seen my relatives there, Robert excepted, for many years. You know that R. spent a day or two with me in Derbyshire. He is almost white-headed and looks very old. He is but one year older than me. We certainly read in others our own changes. How curious it is that we do not really know our own personal appearance – at least I do not. I had my photograph taken in London and I am sure that if I had seen it in a shop window I should not have known it was meant for me.[528]

Hence in months prior to his final illness, Boole had not been physically well. The illness he had suffered in the summer of 1864 must have weakened him and made him more susceptible to the final bout of pneumonia which took his life on 8 December in that year.

Brooke was devastated when he wrote to MaryAnn following Boole's death. In his letter, he acknowledged the close bond MaryAnn and George had enjoyed, similar to his close relationship with his sister Sarah:

How little we thought when we last exchanged correspondence of so sad a subject for our next. But it is so ordained and to an old man like myself heavy as such blows are yet I see the wise hand of providence as one cherished object after another is cut off, we become less eager for life and more willing to go – and all better assured that we must go. But alas and alas for the younger mourners, for the young wife, for sister and brothers, God knows I have thought of you and felt for you. You were all, I know, a loving and united family – but still you and George were specially companions and must have 'grown' more to each other. It was so with my dear sister and me – not that Benjamin loved her a whit less – but that a daily hourly habit that is on a sudden so rudely stopt and so terribly – brings its reminders with regrets daily and hourly too.[529]

Brooke refers to the fact that MaryAnn did not get to see her brother before he died. Having read Annie Gibson's letter (see Chapter Twelve) on Boole's final illness and death, he suggested that perhaps she should be grateful for not seeing him suffer. Brooke recorded the widespread grief among Boole's relatives and friends in Lincoln, including the Chaloners and the Parrys. He went on to express his concern for Boole's widow:

I confess being very anxious after reading the letter in which she told me all was over. True indeed it was calm – there was a holy calm about it, and yet I should have been more at ease had it been a burst of agony, but not as it works in common minds. God give her strength to bear it as it thickens on her memory day by day. It is her five girls that will be her stay and her safety valve and God will temper the wind to the poor shorn lamb.[530]

Brooke's final description of Boole's character is a touching tribute to the talents and humility of his old friend:

Now that he is gone it is the sweetness of his character that comes to mind and dwells in the memory. He was made up of an exquisite reality and simplicity – not the shadow of a sham about him – conscious, he could not be of his true position, for in these exact sciences, so fine a student must know where he stands – how far he has reached and how far others have reached – but who that saw him could have suspected where his real standing was – that he was one of the great authorities in Science and a Lawmaker indeed – one to whom great celebrities would give way at once. How little of all this he carried about with him – while yet yielding no inch of his self-respect. One lingers and lingers on such a character and scarce knows when to leave off – but we must close the budget for it is swelling fast.[531]

Chapter 9

COOPER AND CLARKE

URING THE LATE 1830S, two popular reform movements emerged in England which called for political reform and the repeal of the Corn Laws, namely Chartism and the Anti-Corn Law League. The Chartist leader Thomas Cooper (1805–92) was related to Boole by marriage. Like Boole, Cooper was a schoolmaster and they had a common pupil, Charles Clarke (1826–1909). While George Boole was not overtly political, he was undoubtedly a proponent of social reform and strongly influenced Clarke. Clarke became an important political leader in Ontario after he emigrated to Canada in 1848. His memoirs, written in 1908, are very informative on life in Boole's schools.[532] He corresponded with MaryAnn Boole after her brother's death in 1864, and his letters provide a detailed picture of life as a pupil of Boole's.

Before examining Boole's relationships with Clarke and Cooper, it is useful to look briefly at the political climate in England in the first decades of Boole's life. The end of Napoleonic Wars in 1815, the year of Boole's birth, led to a reduction in industrial demand. The import of foreign grain at cheaper prices into England led to the introduction of the Corn Laws in 1815 which led to tariffs being levied on imported grain in order to favour domestic producers. However, as industrial demand slumped, wages also fell but food prices were inflated by the effect of the Corn Laws. A series of bad harvests in the period 1816–19 inflated grain prices further and fostered discontent in the large cities in particular.

The Whig government of Lord Grey came to power in 1830 and eventually succeeded in passing the 1832 Reform Act. This granted seats in the House of Commons to cities which had grown during the Industrial Revolution and removed seats from 'rotten boroughs', electoral boroughs with very small electorates which were dominated by a wealthy patron. The act introduced a system of voter registration, courts for disputes over voter qualifications and, most importantly, it extended the franchise to small landowners and tenants who held leases under certain conditions. But it did little to empower the working classes, who did not possess or lease property.

A working-class movement for political reform known as Chartism subsequently developed. The movement was called after the 'People's Charter' which was published in 1838 by a committee of six members of parliament (MPs) and six working-class leaders, demanding suffrage for males over twenty-one, a secret ballot, the removal of property qualifications for members of parliament, the payment of MPs, equal constituencies allowing for the same representation for equal numbers of voters and annual parliamentary elections. Support for Chartism was strongest in the industrialised areas of the north of England, the East Midlands and South Wales. Mass meetings were held in Birmingham, Glasgow and other cities in 1838 and a petition signed by over 1.3 million people was presented to the House of Commons demanding reform. MPs voted by a large majority not to consider the petition. In 1839 a confrontation between marchers and soldiers in Newport in Wales became known as the Newport Rising and other abortive risings took place in Sheffield and Bradford. In 1842 a second petition was presented to parliament with more than three million signatures and was again rejected. In the same year, a series of strikes and demonstrations erupted in protest against wage cuts imposed by employers. This led to the arrest of several Chartist leaders and the imprisonment of one, Thomas Cooper.

The Anti-Corn Law League also emerged in 1838, which sought the repeal of the 1815 law that had imposed a tariff on foreign grain. It was founded by Richard Cobden and John Bright, who maintained that repeal would reduce food prices, allow the working classes more disposable income and hence access to manufactured goods, which would in turn improve the prosperity of manufacturers. In addition, it would improve the efficacy of English agriculture by stimulating more demand in urban areas and would also introduce a new era of international peace and fellowship. The Anti-Corn Law League was primarily a middle-class movement, with many Chartists suspecting that it had the support of many employers so that cheaper bread prices would enable them to cut wages. Charles Clarke became an active member of the League. The Corn Laws were eventually repealed in 1846 in response to the Irish famine.

Thomas Cooper's concern for the poor working conditions experienced by hosiery workers in Leicester drew him into the Chartist movement in 1840. Cooper was born in Leicester in 1805, the illegitimate son of a dyer. His father died when Cooper was three and his mother moved to Gainsborough with Cooper and his half-sister. The family lived in poverty as his mother struggled to support and educate her children working as a dyer and box maker. Cooper was an eager student and an avid reader and became a teacher's assistant in a day school for boys in 1816. The school was patronised by the sons of tradesmen and better-paid workers who lent their books to Cooper. In 1820, he became an apprentice shoe maker. He attempted to teach himself the rudiments of Latin, Greek and Hebrew, and read history and poetry, rising at three or four each morning and studying until seven.[533]

Eventually his health failed and he abandoned shoemaking to open his own school in 1828. However, Cooper soon tired of the 'unwelcome drudgery' of teaching and dealing with parents and lost his passion for education. In 1829 he became a Wesleyan preacher and on a trip to Lincoln to hear a Methodist speaker in 1829 he met his future wife, Susanna Chaloner.

George Boole's paternal aunt Susannah (1772–1825) had a daughter, Susanna (1801–80) from her marriage to Thomas Chaloner. In his 1872 autobiography, Cooper described meeting Susanna for the first time:

> But I may now say that I saw the dear one who has now been for thirty-seven years my companion in life, at Christmas of 1829, while on a visit to Lincoln, and conversed with herself and her sister, in the house of her brother. The family were all born Methodists, so as to speak, and I went to Lincoln on a Methodist visit, as I may say, for it was to see and hear the revivalist John Smith. Yet although my heart said 'This is the woman I should like for my wife', I spoke not one word about it. And when I saw her brother, in the following year, he told me she had lain months on a sick-bed, and was never expected to recover. In the year following I heard that she was really recovering, and I went over to Lincoln, and on the 1st of July, 1831, offered my heart and hand, and was accepted.[534]

Cooper also met George Boole on his visit to Lincoln in 1829. He described their first meeting:

> My wife's mother was a Boole and was sister to Dr Boole's father ... Young George came to see his cousins, one day, in that Christmas week of 1829, when I first went to Lincoln as a visitor. He was then a boy of fourteen; had mastered Leslie's *Geometry*, under his father's teaching; was learning Latin, and thinking of Greek; and almost overwhelmed me with inquiries about the contents of books he had not read.[535]

The couple married in 1834. Cooper left Gainsborough after falling out with some of the Methodist community there and took a position as a schoolmaster in Lincoln. He became an active member of the Mechanics' Institute in Lincoln and was elected to its first committee. He continued with his own education, resuming his study of Greek, French and Italian. During this period, Boole taught at various schools in Doncaster, Liverpool and Waddington and returned to Lincoln to start his own school in 1844.[536]

Cooper's next meeting with Boole was in February 1835 at the Mechanics' Institute when Boole delivered his address on the 'Genius and Discoveries of Sir Isaac Newton'.[537] Cooper wrote in his autobiography:

I heard often of his intellectual progress during our courtship; but never saw him again until, in the first year of our marriage, he came to Lincoln, and read an encomium on Sir Isaac Newton, before a crowded audience, in the Mechanics' Institute. The first Earl of Yarborough, who was present, had given a marble bust of the immortal one to the institute; and it was unveiled before George began to read his paper. The writing showed how his mind had expanded; but I drew a far larger conclusion, as to the growth of his intelligence, when he called to see his cousins (my wife and her sister), and I could converse with him.[538]

Cooper and Boole had much in common, both were self-taught men from humble backgrounds, running their own schools in Lincoln. However, they did not become close and Cooper appeared to regret this in later life. He wrote in 1872:

There was one with whom I ought to have been better acquainted. I lament, greatly, that I did not try to draw him nearer to me. But sometimes the slender ties of half-relationship create family likes and dislikes that prevent the formation of what might otherwise be really valuable friendships. I allude to one whose memory is already honoured by the very foremost mathematicians and deepest thinkers, but whose name will become truly illustrious in the wiser future, the late Dr George Boole, professor of Mathematics in Queen's College, Cork.[539]

Cooper appears to have been an abrasive character. The lack of closeness between the two may also have been exacerbated by Cooper's efforts to acquire the curatorship of the Mechanics' Institute after the resignation of John Boole from the position under awkward circumstances in December 1835. MaryAnn described that period as a 'most painful chapter' in the family's life,[540] and Cooper's pursuit of the position was most probably unwelcome. When Cooper failed to secure the appointment, he lost interest in the society and eventually was removed from the committee for non-attendance.[541]

Cooper and Boole shared a common friend, Gilbert Collins, who became manager of the Hull Bank in Lincoln. Boole later referred to Collins in a letter to MaryAnn in 1850 regarding the financial position of her school.[542] Collins was also a student of languages and decided to attempt to learn Arabic with Cooper, until Boole poured cold water on the idea:

> Collins one day bought an old quarto *Arabic Grammar* which had been tumbled about for years in an old bookshop. There was a considerable vocabulary of Arabic words at the end; and the whim seized us both to set on and learn Arabic. I copied the words from the vocabulary, in what we thought very pretty Arabic writing; and we were much taken with our project, when, one evening, George Boole suddenly stepped in, and found us earnestly bent over our new toy. He examined the quarto book with interest; but seemed to have difficulty in restraining his laughter when he saw our Arabic writing and heard us gravely say we were determined to learn the language.
>
> 'But where will you get your Arabic books?' asked George, 'and how can you read them without a dictionary? You could not get a copy of Richardson's dictionary, I should think, under some twelve or fifteen pounds.'[543] We felt ashamed of our thoughtlessness and laid the project aside.[544]

Cooper described his relationship with Boole at that time:

> I saw him now and then; but he was shy and formal. I think I could have brushed away all his shyness, if I had set myself to do it. But I, proudly, let the shyness grow between us, till it reached estrangement. In after years, he called on me in London, and talked freely and friendlily; and I then felt he had distanced me so far in his reach of mathematical science, and in his knowledge of languages – in fact, in all knowledge – that I was but a dwarf in his presence. My acquaintance with some facts of his private life, and knowledge of his tenderness towards his parents and care of them in their age, warrant me in saying that he was as good as he was great. I shall increasingly regret, to my life's close, that I did not strive to draw him towards me as a near and intimate friend. I might have done it, if I had set about it aright.[545]

By 1836 Cooper had given up his school and had become the Lincoln reporter for the *Lincoln, Rutland and Stamford Mercury*. He wrote a series of articles called 'Lincoln Preachers' which critically examined the activities of the cathedral clergy. This may not have sat well with Boole, who appeared to be on very good terms with some of the clergymen attached to the cathedral.[546] Cooper and Susanna moved to Stamford and London before settling in Leicester in November 1840 where Cooper became a reporter for the *Leicestershire Mercury*.[547]

Leicester was the centre of the hosiery trade in England and the city became a Chartist stronghold in the early 1840s. Cooper found the matters on which he wrote in the *Mercury* 'very trifling' until he was sent to report on a lecture at a Chartist meeting. He had been aware of the doctrines and demands of the Chartists and nothing at the meeting surprised him. On leaving the meeting, he was shocked to see the windows of the houses of the stocking makers lit and to hear the sounds of the stocking looms so late at night. His companions detailed the poor pay and conditions of the workers. He wrote:

> We walked on in silence, for some moments, for they said no more, and I felt as if I could scarcely believe what I heard. I knew that in Lincolnshire, where I had passed so great a part of my life, the farmers' labourers had wages which amounted to double the earnings these stockingers said were theirs. I had heard of the suffering of handloom weavers and other operatives in the manufacturing districts, but had never witnessed it. What I heard now seemed incredible; yet these spirit stricken men seemed to mean what they said. I felt, therefore, that I must know something more about the real meaning of what they had told me. I began to learn more of the sorrowful truth from them; and I learned it day by day more fully, as I made inquiry.[548]

Cooper started to write for the local Chartist journal, *The Midland Counties Illuminator* and was given notice to leave the *Mercury* shortly afterwards. He became editor of the *Illuminator* and within a short time established himself as the leader of Chartism in Leicester.

In July 1842 Cooper toured England, speaking at public meetings with the Chartist leader Feargus O'Connor. A wave of strikes broke out in August in the industrial areas of the north of England and Scotland in response to wage cuts imposed by employers. It has been debated whether the strikes were inspired by Chartism or whether members of the Anti-Corn League had deliberately closed mills to stir up unrest among the workers. In August, Cooper left Leicester to travel to a Chartist conference in Manchester.

In Hanley, Staffordshire he called for support for the People's Charter but did not expect the outbreaks of violence and property destruction that followed. Queen Victoria wrote to the prime minister Sir Robert Peel on the day after the outbreak ended. Peel recorded:

The Queen thinks everything should be done to apprehend this Cooper.[549]

Cooper was arrested and stood trial twice. He was acquitted on the charge of arson in October 1842 and returned to Leicester after his release from gaol. He was tried again on the charge of seditious conspiracy in March 1843 and was imprisoned in Stafford Gaol for two years.[550] While in prison, Cooper composed an epic political poem with 944 stanzas called *The Purgatory of Suicides* which was published in August 1845. He was released from prison in May 1845.

Boole corresponded with the Reverend E.R. Larken about Cooper in 1847. He wrote rather caustically:

I saw Cooper yesterday and had a long talk with him. I mentioned your opinion of the defects of the *Purgatory* (concealing your name) and he says people constantly make the same remark but that they always fail in their instances. Those which have been pointed out to him as examples of rugged or unskillful style are the most polished and artistic in the poem. Are you disposed to find fault now?[551]

In a subsequent letter to Larken, he appears to have felt guilty about his comments regarding Cooper:

I am afraid that in my account of Cooper (judging from the impression it produced in your mind) I scarcely did him justice. It is true that he is vain and perhaps pedantic, but after all he has a good deal that might justify vanity, if anything could in such creatures as we are, and then he is so honest and sincere and open that perhaps his vanity may not be greater than that of many who are not thought to be at all conspicuous for that quality, but only more exposed to view.[552]

After his release from prison, Cooper abandoned radicalism and turned to writing and lecturing and settled in London. While on a visit to London in June 1849, Boole wrote to his mother of his intention to see Cooper.[553]

Figure 9.1: Engraving of Thomas Cooper by J. Cochran (1872)

However, their relationship deteriorated in the following year. During Cooper's imprisonment, he had also completed a historical novel, *Captain Cobbler: His Romance*. The novel was a long and complicated story set at night at Stonehenge, inspired by the novels of Walter Scott and Edward Bulwer-Lytton.[554] It was published in 1850 and Cooper dedicated the novel to George Boole without his knowledge. Boole was not pleased. He told MaryAnn:

> You are right in supposing that Cooper inscribed his book to me without my consent. I knew nothing of it until I a few days ago received a copy of it by post with a letter to which I have not yet replied. I know nothing of the merits of the book scarcely having opened it but be what they may I cannot help feeling that he has taken a great liberty. I believe that Cooper's ruling passion and that with all his pretensions to a high morality, he has never taken a single lesson in that species of justice which respects the feelings of others. I mean to tell him in what respects he has erred.[555]

Boole was probably embarrassed at the dedication from a well-known radical such as Cooper, particularly considering his appointment to the professorship of mathematics the previous year. He made Cooper aware of his displeasure. After Boole's death in 1864, Cooper referred to the book and its dedication in a letter to a friend:

Reckon the *Captain Cobbler* also your own – only let me keep it to go on, now and then, with its corrections; it was so horribly ill-printed. Not that it is of much importance whether it be corrected – for it is a very crude affair. My high-minded cousin, just dead, was really indignant when I dedicated it to him; and I don't think he ever forgave me. I did him injustice when I put his name before it. But I did so because the principal part of it was either written or conceived in dear old Lincoln (his birthplace) years before a line of the 'prison rhyme' was composed. And when I recast it in the gaol, it was as a relief to the sterner composition of the poem; and I over-jaded myself in writing it. The antiquarian information in it cost me a deal of minute search – but as a story it is worth less than nothing and can never be re-printed.[556]

After Boole's death, Cooper wrote of his passing:

Dr Boole, my wife's cousin, has died at Cork – one of the foremost mathematicians and one of the best human beings that ever lived. He died on the 8th inst. – Milton's birthday (as you affirm). My darling has been downcast all the week. He leaves 5 female children. He was 49 years old. His father was a Unitarian – but George rejected his father's unbelief and accepted <u>real</u> Christianity – thank God![557]

Cooper spent the last thirty years of his life as a Baptist preacher, refuting the ideas of Darwin. Charles Kingsley used Cooper as his model for the Chartist poet in his novel *Alton Locke*. Cooper's autobiography, completed in 1872, was widely read. Prior to his death in 1892, Cooper received a government grant in recognition for his 'literary talent and influence as a moral teacher'.[558] Both Cooper and his wife are buried in Lincoln.

Figure 9.2: The grave of Thomas Cooper and his wife Susanna in Lincoln

While Boole was not as interested in politics as Cooper, he was, prior to his departure for Ireland in 1849, highly involved in several local organisations in Lincoln that promoted social reform. Boole became deeply involved in the Lincoln Mechanics' Institute as a committee member and teacher.[559] He was a director of a building society which aimed to help middle- and working-class citizens to buy their own houses.[560] He was a founder and trustee of the Female Penitents' Home in Lincoln which opened in 1847 and was also connected with the Lincoln Early Closing Association which successfully agitated for a ten-hour day for all shop assistants, apprentices and other workers.[561]

Both Cooper and Boole had a significant influence on their pupil, Charles Clarke, who became an influential figure in political, social and cultural spheres in the Canadian province of Ontario. Boole's links with Clarke were initiated through his father. John Boole was highly politicised and was part of a radical circle which emerged in Lincoln in the 1830s. MaryAnn recalled that her father regularly met a group of friends at the Falstaff Inn in Lincoln to read political articles in the papers and discuss their content.[562] In a letter to MaryAnn, Clarke described him:

> He was an habitué at Parsy's and before the Reform Bill excitement, and in the parlor there, was the best reader of those who undertook the delivering over again the speeches of Brougham and Grey. Mr J. Boole was an ardent radical, a thorough democrat of days when the name meant more and risked more than now. He had a small black bust of Sir Francis Burdett which figured on a bracket in his living room.[563] The smoke of the Reform agitation passed away, Sir Francis fell, and his bust was discarded from the post of honor and found refuge in one of the back premises where it was often seen but little valued.[564]

Charles Clarke's father, Richard Clarke, may have been part of this circle, as was William Brooke (see Chapter Eight).[565] Richard Clarke was the mayor's officer in Lincoln at the time of Charles' birth in 1826. His mother, Jane Drury Clarke, was assisted at Charles' birth by George Boole's mother, Mary. In a biographical letter written to MaryAnn after George's death, Clarke commented on the closeness of the two families:

> I don't distinctly remember that event, but when I entered the world a kind soul tenderly washed and dressed me, and the good matron was the

mother of George Boole. The intimacy existing between our families was, you may presume, very close, and I cannot look upon the time when I didn't know Mr and Mrs Boole and Miss Boole.[566]

In 1835, Richard Clarke died prematurely and Jane Clarke later remarried John Lincoln Kirk, a shoemaker who had previously worked for John Boole.

Charles Clarke became a pupil of Thomas Cooper at his school in Lincoln sometime between 1834 and 1836. Clarke later became a pupil of Boole's, firstly at his day school in Lincoln, later at Waddington between 1838 and 1840 and finally at Potter Gate in Lincoln in the period 1840–1. In his 1908 autobiography, Clarke described the routine of his days in Boole's school in Waddington:

After leaving the Cooper school, I became a pupil of George Boole, subsequently a well-known mathematical professor of Queen's College, Cork, who opened a seminary in Lincoln, and afterwards became the proprietor of a large boarding-school in the village of Waddington, near Lincoln. Again I was fortunate in my surroundings, for George Boole was even more devoted to his work than was Cooper. The school had an average attendance of about sixty pupils, and these were well and thoroughly taught. At Waddington this was assured by the constant supervision of the master during school hours, and the actual presence of two ushers at all times. The school proper was in a building of the Elizabethan era, and its long windows, like large parallelograms with stone casings and leaded glass, and having iron rods as protection, took the imagination of the pupils back to a period when Shakespeare made a name and 'good Queen Bess did rule this land'. Our refectory occupied about a third of the length of one large room, used as school or dining room, the remaining space being utilised for desks and 'forms', at which we sat to study. Either end of this hall held a huge fireplace, in which, during the winter months, fires constantly burned during the day, and until, at the hour of nine p.m., the pupils retired to their dormitories. A healthy mind and a healthy body were regarded as the normal condition of a Waddington lad, and an epidemic was a thing unknown during the reign of the presiding master …

In our schoolroom the furniture was plain, and there were few of the extra comforts of an ordinary home. The food supplied to the pupils was plentiful and wholesome, and with meat, milk, bread and potatoes as their bases, the means were suited to the capacity and requirements of growing lads and were served at regular hours. Breakfast, consisting of bread and milk, was partaken of at eight; dinner was called at half-past twelve, with a well-known bill of fare, distinguishing each day of the week; and 'tea', of bread and butter and coffee, at six o'clock. At half-past eight we had a collation, termed a 'supper', when we were given bread and cheese or bread and treacle, as we preferred, and every night we were polled to ascertain how many rations of cheese were required, or how many 'treacles' were called for, and it was seldom that the vote fell short of the total number of voters.

Above the schoolroom were the dormitories, in each of which were six or eight beds, an objectionable feature being the fact that there were two boys for every bed. We rose at seven in winter and at half-past six in summer, and retired at nine all year round. Our lavatory was on the lower floor, where basins, the usual sinks, and an abundant supply of water sufficed for our toilets, each boy furnishing his own soap, towels, brushes and combs. Our ablutions were pretty thorough, for we were stripped to the 'buff' and sponged and soused under the superintending eye of a vigilant usher. We had baths, used on Saturdays, and at other times when requisite and we kept about as clean as we felt necessity for. Prayers and the reading of a portion of Scripture followed our morning scrub and preceded our retirement at night. Our studies were as thorough as regular supervision could enforce, and were commenced by half an hour's work before breakfast, proceeded from nine to twelve, were resumed at two and continued until five, and were kept up at night from seven to half-past eight.[567]

Due to the length of time Clarke spent with Boole in both Lincoln and Waddington, he felt that he knew more of him than any other pupil under his care.[568] He described Boole as follows:

George Boole was a born teacher, largely self-taught, and standing in the ranks of the people. Of refined taste, liberal ideas of vast width and depth, he won love, commanded respect, and was successful because thorough, persevering, and well equipped for the work which he set out to do. And to him the schoolroom was his home, while his exacting duties were a labour of love.[569]

Clarke was struck by Boole's huge fund of knowledge and teaching style:

> In his system of teaching he departed from the long-trodden paths of 'learning by rote' and used the blackboard, trusting more to our retention of ideas than words. This tried the man more than the pupils – made ten times work for the teacher – and compelled his thorough acquaintance with all he had to impart.[570]

He provided his pupils with reading materials which Clarke judged to be far beyond those used by the average teacher and which aimed at the 'elevation of taste and cultivation of the mind'.[571] The boys were tested with compositions to ensure that they could express their ideas in writing. Clarke described Boole's pupils as being from middle-class families in Lincoln and its surrounding villages, of average intelligence and of varying age and capacity. Some pupils were aiming for careers in law and medicine, others were destined for farm work or commercial life and one, 'a special wonder', was studying for the naval service and was well versed in trigonometry.[572] He encouraged his pupils to study mathematics, pushing his pupils to work through problems and driving them to try and solve problems for themselves:

> We were taken to the threshold of mathematics but mere lads of from 10 to 13 as most of us were, could not be expected to go further. How he did work at us, how he yearned to pull us on if we would. He told us of the uses of the study, how great discoveries had been made by its aid, how no man could be a really great mechanic without a knowledge of it, how it strengthened the intellect, how robust the mind became under its influences, how no man could claim to be educated if deficient in it.[573]

Boole used dictation as a way of imparting knowledge to his pupils. He would call out a common English word and walk up and down the classroom calling out synonyms which the class transcribed. Punctuation and grammar were taught in a similar manner.

Natural phenomena were used by Boole to illustrate his lessons. Clarke recalled one of these occasions:

> I remember the whole school being turned out one summer evening to witness an approaching thunderstorm, from the brow of Waddington

Cliff. We could see the lightning flash far over and beyond Nottingham-shire, and faintly hear the distant thunder. Watch in hand, he stood for more than an hour, calculating the approach of the storm, until the heavy rain drove us to the house. No boy present will forget the difference between the rate of travel of light and sound.[574]

Boole's father contributed to the boys' scientific education also with his kaleidoscopes, microscopes, telescopes and camera. Clarke described his memories of John Boole:

Boole's father was a clever optician and I have clear and pleasant recollections of several Sunday afternoons spent in a darkened room, which enabled us to greedily drink in the wonders produced by lenses of a solar microscope of great power. I remember, still more vividly, the occurrence of a total eclipse of the sun, and the exhibition of its moving shadow, thrown upon a sheet by means of a telescope placed in one of the shutter-darkened windows of the room. At totality, the pupils present were taken into an adjoining garden to see the closing of the flowers, to hear crowing chanticleers, and to watch jackdaws winging home to roost in the lofty cathedral towers at Lincoln.[575]

On Friday afternoons, the boys were allowed to select a topic on which Boole prepared a lecture for the following week. Clarke continued:

The subject selected, he faithfully read up until he was conversant with every detail, and for an hour, and often for a longer time, would he debate upon it in every aspect, and give us freely and abundantly that which the world would gladly now treasure up. He had ideas as well as facts. One week we would follow Alexander from victory to victory, another Cyrus would be our hero – again, Napoleon would be exhibited to us, in light and dark – military heroes being the boys' choice, if not Mr Boole's favourite subjects. He delighted to dwell upon natural philosophy. Pneumatics and optics were often dwelt upon, and evidently with a liking for them. Electricity was a subject in which he was at home. His father constructed a powerful electric machine and we had experiments which we relished better as spectators than participants. I thought it a grim joke to stand up in a circle and have my elbow-joints torn asunder – or feel as if they had been subjected to some such operation. I can remember Mr

Boole startling us all by telling us that electricity was the great motive and life-giving power – that the world didn't yet believe but some day would. That it was the source of heat, of life, of motion, that it was the root of all, the beginning of all, and it was the one natural agent by which the Creator performed his great work in the universe. I don't pretend to recall his words; his ideas I have faithfully expressed I know. In his recent lectures he took us into the heavens, and into the bowels of the earth, sketched a railroad, a steam engine and a coal ravine, exhibited the plant from the started seedling to the ripened fruit, or gave us a glimpse of natural history, described the races of man and opened a page in physical geography or dwelt upon the importance of good morals, good manners, and godly living. His soul was in whatever he did in this way, and he did it well. How he must have lectured before his classes at Cork upon his favourite subjects I can readily imagine.[576]

School finished early on Wednesday afternoons and there was half-holiday on Saturdays. During these periods, the boys were occupied with different sports and physical activities. Clarke described them from a Canadian perspective in his autobiography:

Games were fast and furious. There were 'seasons' for all of them, and passing waves of shinney, tops, marbles, fox and hounds, prison bars, paper chase, football, bull in the ring, burn-ball, foot races, jumping leapfrog, and the various other amusements which fill up the play hours of young John Bull, followed each other with a regularity which was pleasing in its kaleidoscopic characteristic. But cricket was with us as a 'stand-by', and ball games always had a preference. In those days baseball was unknown, except as rounders, and hockey on ice was a sealed book to the English lad. The games, however, helped to develop pluck, courage and strength just as surely then as do the sports of today, and I like to think that it was the game itself, even more than the hope of victory that appealed to us.[577]

Boole encouraged reluctant pupils like Clarke to take part, telling them of athletics and the 'Olympian Games'. On occasion, he joined in the games himself and Clarke described his efforts:

I had a secret source of satisfaction in seeing his endeavor to play cricket on chance occasions. He was as great 'a butter fingers' as myself and was nowhere. The first ball would scatter his wickets. He would beg another and that was generally enough for him.[578]

Boole was a proficient swimmer and Clarke described seeing him swim in the River Witham at Waddington as 'though to the water born'. The boys were rarely allowed to swim for safety reasons but they did have an annual fishing party.[579] Other holidays were negotiated with the boys using a merit system:

Every Friday we wrote letters before lecture-hour 4pm and the attention he paid to these must have been productive of good fruit in many instances. A well-written letter received a liberal reward in the shape of tickets, and they in turn had a specific value in a shape which boys appreciate. A half-holiday cost 20 tickets. If the boys in the school got up a petition for holiday, as they did whenever they thought they could pay for it, Mr Boole fixed his price and we subscribed to pay for it. If we had 40 scholars, he might agree to give us an afternoon for 600 tickets, letting us have the article cheaper by wholesale rather than by retail. If a few wished for an afternoon he would not reduce the price, and sometimes increased it. You may imagine the scheming, bargaining and coaxing to procure the necessary tickets from those who had a super-abundance by those who always had a deficient ticket exchequer. And you would have been amused had you seen the air of self-importance with which we marched up with our slate-full of the little cardboard representatives of good behaviour, and bought our three hours' freedom. This holiday selling was a greater incentive to hard work than all the gilt prayer books which were ever given to favourites at vacation and should be more generally adapted than it is. Of course the tickets were given for proficiency in any branch but were not lavishly bestowed. You earned them before you received them.[580]

The school at Waddington also had a weekly newspaper and a debating society. The boys were taught public speaking and had their own court of justice:

Among the other things taught at Waddington was the power of conducting public meetings, and we were called to bring up culprits against our own laws for trial by jury. On these occasions, Mr Boole would take his seat as Judge, a counsel was appointed, and the jurymen were bound upon their honor to give a fair and impartial verdict. On one occasion a steel bar was broken by one of the boys, and the owner brought an action for damages. The case was heard. The value of the bar was 1/-. After a long and careful hearing of the case, and due deliberation of the Jury (who were locked up in an old store room with a constable at the door), a verdict was given which ordered the defendant to keep the largest half of the broken bow and pay 10 pence, and give to the owner the smallest portion of the bow as an equivalent for the remaining 2. Our judge laughed heartily when he received the verdict, and told us it was a much fairer decision than many full-grown men would have given. It tickled him and he often referred to it when lecturing us upon right and wrong.[581]

Boole did not tolerate fighting in school and a fight was a punishable offence. Clarke recalled an altercation which he was involved in:

Will Maltby and Will Rudyard, now estimable citizens of Lincoln, no doubt, went to the Waddington school. Maltby's father was a butcher, and Rudyard's a miller. Rudyard was therefore, many degrees higher on the social scale than Maltby, and took opportunity to let Maltby know this. I took up cudgels for Maltby, and silenced Rudyard after a few rounds. An appeal to Mr Boole was made, and each culprit, Rudyard and myself, was ordered to write 100 lines and go to bed. My 100 lines took the shape of a letter setting forth the provocation I had received, and so on, and was sent into Mr Boole in his sitting room. The letter was returned with a gratuity of 2 pence as a reward for good composition, but I had transgressed the rules by fighting and must complete the sentence by going to bed. The 2 pence was a salve to my wounds, and I retired with a sort of consciousness that fighting was not such a very bad thing after all.[582]

Boole abhorred cruelty and brutality. Clarke recalled a debate as to which was more cruel – catching fish or robbing birds' nests. Boole settled the debate by telling the boys that the pain of the fish was more transient, but the pain of the birds lasted for some time. The only time that Clarke recalled Boole losing self-control with a pupil was over a bird-nesting incident:

He had an abhorrence of bird nesting, and nothing annoyed him more than the wholesale robbery of which some boys were guilty. I never saw him more excited than once upon the detection of a repetition of this offence by a boy called Rogers. He had warned him again and again, but Rogers cared not. He stole all the eggs he could get at and had accumulated nearly a hat box full. The box was brought down into the school and placed upon the floor. Mr Boole's face became livid with rage. He jumped up and crushed the box and its contents by dancing upon it until every egg was broken. Then he turned to Rogers and gave him the severest beating he ever administered during my sojourn with him. It was the only occasion upon which I saw him lose self-control, but what he regarded as the cruelty of the lad was more than he could bear.[583]

Many years later as a Member of Provincial Parliament of the Legislative Assembly of the Province of Ontario, Clarke introduced a bill for the protection of insectivorous birds. The bill prohibited the capture, purchase or sale of protected species, as well as the taking of their eggs, nests or young. The Act for the Protection of Insectivorous Birds and Other Birds beneficial to Agriculture was passed in 1877. The act's focus was on stopping the destruction of birds and set out a scale of fines for those who violated the act, especially with young boys in mind.[584]

In addition to recording memories of Boole as a teacher, Clarke recorded his impressions of his personality and his interests:

There were two features of Mr Boole's character which struck me even as a boy: his intense love of study, and universality of talent. He was always thinking and seemed to know a little of everything. At Waddington we boys walked out daily, and he often accompanied us; we were ordered to 'break off' immediately after clearing the village boundaries and then he would follow rapt in study, and wander after us, his head leaning to his shoulder, until we had long exceeded the time allotted for the walk. Often were we thus able to steal an hour more of fun than was intended for us, until the word 'Home' was shouted by the absent-minded master. In the school, when we settled down to our tasks, he would pace the floor with hasty strides, head aside as usual, and his lips moving rapidly, his eyes bent on vacancy, until a laugh or commotion would call him back to Waddington and its school. Sometimes he would pace the playground in a similar fashion, but he felt, as we did, that he was encroaching upon forbidden ground, and more often to take himself into the garden which gave him room and verge enough. When he did unbend, he must have been a genial companion, with an almost childlike love of fun and frolic.[585]

Clarke was struck by his teacher's love of the classics, poetry and music:

Another feat of which he told used to excite my envy, I remember, and made me wonder why I wasn't blessed with the same ability. When a lad, he began a study of Latin, at a very early age, and after he had made some progress, he fortunately became possessed of a copy of Virgil, what a novel was to me – he had caught me reading 'Tom Jones' – Virgil was to him. He used to set down upon his Saturday half-holiday to translate a set, 50 lines. He loved the work, the 50 grew into 100, 100 into 200, and sometimes more, before he used to go to play and then the afternoon was spent. He must have been passionately attached to Helen – his first love, maybe.[586] I fancy he really cared more for the study of Greek than of Latin. He had prayers twice daily, with a chapter, and he frequently used his Greek testament instead of our authorised version. I used to look on and listen with a sort of awe, as he rolled out passages occasionally in Greek, when he met with one of more than ordinary difficulty, but as a rule he read his chapter through without a trip, and in such tones as I have seldom heard. He was musical and had a voice remarkable for its tone and depth when he was thoroughly aroused. Next to his Greek testament, Milton was his choicest reading. He formed a class of the big boys after he returned to Lincoln, with Milton's writings as our only reading book. I can recall the very tones and gestures with which he read off page after page to us, and how he then coaxed us to attempt an imitation, we tried and tried again but felt how immensely inferior was our effort. He felt every word, entered into the feelings of the poet, threw himself into the work, and would have made the *Paradise Lost* a popular book could he have been induced to read before public audiences as he did to the small class which he gathered around him on the stair head leading into the school room at Potter Gate. I said just now that he was musical. Did you ever hear him play the flute? Charles Boole was an exquisite player upon the piano.[587] George was as much at home, although he seldom performed upon the flute. He could breathe out an old melody in such plaintive tones that you almost imagined the words.[588]

Clarke gave his impressions of Boole's religious beliefs in his letter to MaryAnn. He felt that Boole was a Unitarian, an opinion with which Mary-Ann strongly disagreed in her biography:[589]

> Mr Boole was really religious, I feel convinced, but there was no trace of cant about him. But he was more religious, i.e. went to church more often in Lincoln than Waddington. The persons in the village were prosy;[590] in Lincoln we attended the cathedral. When I was a very little boy he took me, one Sunday afternoon, along the Greetwell Fields of which I spoke in my last letter. The ministry bells were ringing in for afternoon prayers, and I told him that we should be late for church. He smiled and told me we were in church, a church built by God himself and not by men, and asked me whether God could not be worshiped as well among the trees and in the fields as in houses made of stone? I did not altogether understand him but he conveyed an idea which I have not yet altogether forgotten. My impression is that he was inclined to Unitarianism although upon this point you must be much better informed than I.[591]

Despite the influence which Boole exerted on his pupil, he was unable to persuade Clarke to stay on in his school as an usher:

> His desire, as my mother's ambition, was that I should be educated as an usher and be employed by him when old enough for that purpose. I knew that he gave extra attention to me on this account, but my very soul sickened at the thought of the drudgery (as it seemed to me) which must be entered upon and borne for many years, and I coaxed my mother to let me off and apprentice me to the drapery business. I left Mr Boole therefore just at the age which would have shown the man more thoroughly to my understanding instead of the master whom I had only known.[592]

Clarke's new master was 'Calico John' Norton, a well-known Lincoln Radical and another founding member of the Lincoln Mechanics' Institute.[593] Norton was a friend of Cobden and Bright, two of the prominent members of the Anti-Corn Law League. Clarke joined the league and wrote a pamphlet entitled *To Our Young Men* which he sent off to Cobden. Clarke wished to harness the energy of youth across all social classes to unite and overthrow the Corn Laws. While the pamphlet had no historical effect, as it was returned

Figure 9.3: Hon. Charles Clarke, Speaker of the Ontario
Legislature, 1880–86 by J.W.L. Forster

by Cobden to Clarke, it is significant in demonstrating the fifteen-year-old
Clarke's political development.

The appeal of the drapery business quickly diminished and in 1844 Clarke
followed his mother, stepfather and sister to the Niagara district of Upper
Canada where they had recently emigrated and purchased a farm. Four years
later, the family sold the farm and moved to the village of Elora. Clarke and
John Kirk became general merchants and by 1850 Clarke was back in the
retail business once more. Around the same time, Clarke began writing for a
local newspaper from the nearby town of Hamilton, *The Journal and Express*,
under the pseudonym 'Reformator'. His articles were published in other
reform journals also and in these Clarke called for a wider franchise, the
secret ballot, and other parliamentary reforms aimed at abolishing privilege
and monopoly in the politics of Upper Canada. Clarke's writings attracted
the attention of the 'Clear Grits', a political movement and party which had
arisen in opposition to the administration of Robert Baldwin, the premier of
the Province of Canada (modern Quebec and Ontario).

Clarke became secretary of the Reform Association of the electoral
district the North Riding of Wellington. He held office as a member of the
village council of Elora and served two periods as 'reeve' or mayor between
1859 and 1864. He represented the riding of Wellington Centre and later

Wellington East at provincial level, winning six general elections. He was a hard-working MPP,[594] drafting private member's bills, raising questions and chairing committees. In 1874 his legislation to introduce the secret ballot in provincial elections was enacted, marking the high point of his legislative career. In addition to his involvement in local and provincial political life, Clarke promoted horticulture, ornithology and natural history in Elora. He believed that these were civilising pursuits which countered the materialism of the age he lived in and advanced the general intelligence of the people.[595] He helped form the local militia, the Elora Volunteer Rifles, in 1861, and rose to command it during the Fenian raids of 1866. He was known locally as Colonel Clarke.

Clarke became speaker of the Legislative Assembly of Ontario in 1880 for six years, and chaired the public accounts committee between 1886 and 1891. In 1891 he was appointed clerk of the Assembly, a position which he held for fifteen years. The clerk was the speaker's chief executive officer, advising the speaker on matters of precedence and order and ensuring that the assembly ran smoothly. He compiled a members' manual in 1893 which was essentially a parliamentary handbook for MPPs.

On his retirement in 1907, Clarke was described by the Canadian national newspaper *The Globe* as a 'veteran Canadian statesman, who has had to a wonderful degree the characteristic of perennial youth' and looked back to his arrival in Canada as a young 'English Radical', many of whose proposed reforms were subsequently implemented.[596]

As well as having a very full professional and cultural life, Clarke had a very busy family life. He married Emma Kent in 1852. The couple had four daughters and one son. Emma died in 1878 and in 1881 Clarke married Rose Ellen Halley, an eighteen-year-old Roman Catholic. They had two sons and one daughter. Clarke died in Elora in 1909, at the age of eighty-two, a year after his memoir, *Sixty Years in Upper Canada with Autobiographical Recollections*, was published.

After Clarke emigrated to Canada, he and Boole had a limited amount of correspondence. MaryAnn Boole subsequently explained her brother's reluctance to write in a letter to Clarke:

My brother was never a good correspondent, he disliked letter-writing and used to say it wearied him infinitely more than hours of private study. This would account for his seldom writing to you. I have frequently heard him speak of you and you were a favourite pupil. He was always pleased to hear from old pupils and took real interest in their welfare but he always avoided entering into active correspondence with them and, without intending, it gave offence to some in consequence.[597]

In the last known letter from Boole to Clarke dated August 1848, Boole gave Clarke some advice which appears to have guided him through his life in Canada:

I will conclude with wishing you a prosperous, useful and happy life – that you may contribute to the happiness of your fellow creatures and make the Right, the Just and the True the unfailing rule of all your actions. In every part of the world and every situation of life there are influences to draw us aside from the cause – in England a too great regard to the distinctions of society, in America the too eager pursuit of wealth. But upon the whole the advantage is I think in favour of the land of your choice to those who possess a sufficient strength of mind to think for themselves and of character to act for themselves. I hope that you will make a due use of your advantages.[598]

Chapter 10

MISCELLANEOUS CORRESPONDENTS

G EORGE BOOLE was somewhat isolated both in Lincoln and Cork but overcame this by writing frequent letters to his personal friends. Only a few of Boole's letters of this kind have survived, but we do have access to many of the replies, and to many of the important biographical letters his friends wrote to MaryAnn Boole and to Mary Everest Boole both before and after his death. From these replies, it is often possible to glean the contents of Boole's original letters.

Boole valued personal friendships a great deal and especially those with his fellow teachers, his pupils, and his third-level students. Apart from his wife, Mary Davis was probably his closest female friend, and one can speculate that their friendship may have been a little more than platonic. George Boole was susceptible to females, had a strong sentimental streak and fell easily in love, but there is no suggestion that he ever strayed from his marriage vows.

We have already devoted several chapters to Boole's correspondence and friendship with major figures in his life such as Bury, Hill, Larken, William Brooke, Cooper and Clarke, and Chapter Eleven will concern his correspondence and friendship with several mathematicians to add to the list containing Cayley, De Morgan, Thomson and Graves. In this chapter we discuss Boole's correspondence and friendship with some other colleagues, friends and students.

THOMAS BAINBRIDGE

George Boole left primary school in the summer of 1828 when he was in his thirteenth year. What little secondary education he received was at the Commercial Academy of Thomas Bainbridge situated at Fish Hill (now Michaelgate) in Lincoln. Bainbridge's establishment was not so much a secondary school as an institution to give its young pupils a grounding in commerce and so prepare them for a career in business. Its owner, a Methodist layman, was very impressed by the young Boole and allowed him to take classes and mark exercises, a valuable free training for a teaching career. As early as 1852, MaryAnn Boole had asked Bainbridge to record his memories of his most famous pupil, and he responded as follows:

George Boole, now Dr Boole Mathematical Professor in Queen's College Cork, commenced his studies under me on September 10th 1828 being then between 12 and 13 years of age. He had then made competent progress in vulgar and decimal arithmetic and also in the rudiments of Latin. I placed in his hands Euclid by Leslie, Valpy's Greek Gradual,[599] and a Virgil. He was very diligent, seemed thoughtful beyond his years, but highly delighted with the course to which I introduced him. I marked the development of his powers, and to the best of my judgement gave suitable direction and encouragement. In Latin and Greek he rapidly proceeded through the usual authors, seeming greatly to relish them and retaining everything he had once mastered. I consulted with his father* (since deceased) that we might concur in the course his son should pursue until Christmas 1830. By this time he could read with little difficulty any Greek or Latin author, had made himself familiar with the greater part of Euclid and had answered a vast number of questions in algebraic equations. After this he continued his studies and assisted me in giving classes and looking over exercises until he was about fifteen years of age.

In 1831 a situation as junior tutor was obtained for him at Doncaster, after which time I saw him only at intervals during his vacations. From the first, I observed in him strict uncompromising principles – filial piety and unwearied perseverance in prosecuting his studies without the least dash of affectation or pedantry. He never played with his school-fellows but had one or two friends of congenial minds, one of whom, Mr Hill, lawyer now of Hull, remains his friend and correspondent to this day. From the first I entertained high hopes of Mr Boole which have been gloriously realised.

*The late John Boole who was an excellent self-taught accountant and mathematician. He told me that at some period of his life a copy of Euclid fell in his way and that he read and understood it with little less difficulty than an ordinary author.

Thomas Bainbridge,
2nd December 1852.[600]

Naturally anxious to share in the glory of his illustrious pupil, Bainbridge may have exaggerated his influence on Boole a little. Mary Ellen Boole Hinton, in an addendum to a copy of the letter above which she very probably transcribed and typed, wrote that George finished Leslie's *Geometry* before he was twelve years old, while still under his father's tuition. She adds that he may have gone through it again with Bainbridge and that her impression was that the young G.B. owed more to home and friends and proportionately less to school than Bainbridge claimed. George, she claimed, knew a good deal of Latin and Greek before he went to Bainbridge's school.

Boole's friend and correspondent William Brooke was not impressed by Mr Bainbridge either and recalled an amusing incident in a letter written to MaryAnn in January 1864:

Poor Bainbridge, he did right little to form the future Professor, we may be sure. I remember your brother's relating his amusement at a strange misapprehension by that rather puzzle-headed man. G.B. had proposed for the Mechanics' Institute a work of KANT – a favourite of his I think. T.B. taking up the proposing book read aloud the entry which concluded with 'by Emanuel Kant' and then turned to G.B. saying in a tender, reproachful way 'Oh George, George, I did not expect that from you!' considering it seemingly as a shaft at himself in his Wesleyan capacity – but why so interpreted it would be hard to say.[601]

THOMAS DYSON

Thomas Dyson was a fellow teacher of George Boole's at Mr Heigham's school in South Parade Doncaster in 1831 where Boole had his first job as an usher or teaching assistant. Dyson was a contemporary of Boole, born in the village of Drax, near Selby in Yorkshire in 1816. It is interesting that MaryAnn Boole wrote to Dyson in Gainsborough as early as 1853, more than ten years before Boole died, asking him for his impressions of her brother. Although Dyson was only a little younger than George and the two of them became friends, George made him his pupil, as Dyson recalls:

I have reason to recollect Mr Boole's coming to Doncaster as his advice and example gave the first impulse to those literary pursuits that have been my chief solace throughout life. I imbibed something of his spirit and have followed him – *sed longo intervallo* (but at a long interval) – in some of those pursuits which the ancients said gilded the prosperous years of man and cheered him even in adversity. I have since reminded him of the advantage I derived from his presence and example and he was delighted to learn that his mind had exercised a general influence on the mind of another.[602]

Boole prescribed him Paley's *Natural Theology*,[603] and for the 'purpose of acquiring a taste for true poetry', Milton's *Paradise Lost* also. Dyson dated his love of reading from this advice. He relates that George, away from home

Figure 10.1: Thomas Dyson

for the first time, worked very hard to improve his pupils and to perfect his teaching skills, but at the same time spent a great deal of time acquiring knowledge for his own education. On their walks and on other leisure occasions he was busy studying French – he had received a few lessons while at home from a young friend, to whom in return he gave some instruction in Greek. But Boole it seems was studying French not for its own sake, but to enable him to read Lacroix's book on the differential and integral calculus, which he studied again and again until he thoroughly understood it. Dyson then paints a charming picture of Boole supervising the boys but completely absorbed in his own studies.

> ... It is the writing hour, but he has nothing to do with the writing. Seated at his desk with the well-known green shade over his eyes, deeply absorbed in study, at times mechanically saying 'hush, hush', when there was not the least noise, to our great amusement, he being perfectly unconscious of what he was saying.[604]

Boole's sense of humour shows through at times also. One boy used the phrase *Domum, dulce domum* (Home, sweet home) in an essay, and Mr Heigham, who was 'in blissful ignorance of all classical acquirements', asked Boole to adjudicate if it was good Latin. Boole replied that it was not classical, but it was 'Monkish Latin'. The boy reported to Mr Heigham that Boole had told him it was 'Monkey Latin' which offended his dignity until the error was discovered and explained to him.[605]

MaryAnn included some extracts from Dyson's letters in her biography, but there is one incident not included there which seems worthy of note:

> At Lincoln, George had been in the habit of bathing. On one occasion a youth got beyond his depth and some of the other young men left him

Figure 10.2: The view from Burton Hills, Lincolnshire, a favourite reading place of the young George Boole

to his fate exclaiming 'Look at Clegg, look at Clegg'. But Mr Boole said in a rage 'You fools' and rushed in and rescued Clegg from his danger.[606]

Other incidents which Dyson recounts include Boole's early publication of translation of Greek verse in the newspapers[607] and the romantic composition of a reply to a Valentine poem. While at Doncaster, Dyson had received a Valentine card from two young ladies, one of whom was a preacher's daughter. The words 'Ne m'oubliez pas' (don't forget me) were written at the end of the sheet. Dyson asked Boole to pen a reply, which he did with great ease:

Reply to a Valentine (ne m'oubliez pas)
Worried with the jarring noise
Of five and forty stupid boys;
When my patience just was spent
Three sweet words in pity sent
Bid my bewildered senses shine
'Ne m'oubliez pas' Valentine.[608]

The two young men read and quoted poetry together in the evenings when their pupils had gone to bed. Even at this stage Boole was very fond of music and played several airs, chiefly of the plaintive kind, on the German flute and occasionally on the violin. He had the greatest regard for his parents and his father's scientific acquirements, as well as his native city of Lincoln and its surroundings. He spoke longingly and lovingly of a favourite tree where as a boy he had perched on its branches reading the heroic novels of Walter Scott.

But there was trouble on the horizon. Heigham's was essentially a Methodist school where more attention was paid to 'converting' the boys rather than educating them. There were frequent prayer meetings, revivals, and other methods of increasing the numbers of the 'chosen'. It was felt that Mr Boole, who was known to read mathematics books during service, was in need of conversion and would be a very valuable acquisition to the ranks of the chosen. Dyson described the incident:

> One youth named Smithies from York, at one of the meetings prayed 'Lord! Convert Mr Boole. Lord! Convert Mr Boole'. A loud volley of 'amens' and 'hear our prayer' issued from every part of the room. When Boole heard of the incident, he said privately to Smithies that he was very much obliged for his good wishes, but as he could know nothing of his (Boole's) religious views, he hoped that he would abstain from mentioning his name in any meetings in the future. The lad apologised, and his prayers, at least publicly, ceased on Mr B's behalf.[609]

The Smithies in question was Thomas Bywater Smithies (1817–83), who became a radical publisher, temperance campaigner and supporter of animal rights. In 1855 he founded *The British Workman*, a broadsheet periodical which was published until 1892 to promote the welfare of the working classes.

Dyson concludes one of his letters with a number of observations on Boole's preferences and activities. He wrote a great deal of verse and translated several of the Psalms into metre. These he read to his friend with much feeling. He preferred the solemn and the grand to the pathetic and the sentimental – the heroic rather than the lyric or the pastoral – and the music of verse had a great charm for him. In science he preferred the abstract to the experimental; at the same time he was familiar with the results of experimental science from his reading. He was immensely proud of the magnificent Lincoln Cathedral, and would stand for long periods gazing at its splendid west front. He never passed that noble pile, in Dyson's words, without stopping to admire it, and the more he looked, the more he admired it.

Finally, Dyson reports some of Boole's comments on the influence of mathematical textbooks on his early researches. It was from Lagrange's *Calcul des Fonctions* that he was led into that trail which resulted in those mathematical papers on which his fame rests.[610] He regretted that he had not been led to use books other than Lacroix, which he later considered very unsuitable for a beginner. Later, he veered towards the Cambridge publications.

In a further letter written to MaryAnn in November 1865 after Boole's death, Dyson was quite critical of Boole as a teacher and attributed his shortcomings as a contributory factor in his departure from Mr Heigham's school:

> He was a most excellent teacher when he had a pupil who could appreciate him, and he had one or two such of that type …
>
> … But with the vast majority of boys who have no such application and required drilling again and again in the same subject, he was the worst teacher I ever was with. Instead of explaining he lost his temper and let the pupil off the spot – the lad too glad to escape the lesson altogether. They showed him each other's work, the same work several times over, and on their word that it was all right he gladly passed it again to be absorbed in his own book. I think you know well enough that this was always his failing. His brother William could not learn from him, he was so impatient if the pupil could not see the reason why as soon as he did. This was the second cause of his leaving.[611]

Dyson's disenchantment may be due to Boole's refusal to provide an endorsement for his younger brother William (Dyson) when he was planning to open a school in Bradford in the early 1850s. William Dyson appears to have been employed in Boole's school in Lincoln after Boole's departure for Cork in 1849. On two occasions in his correspondence with MaryAnn, Boole referred to the requests received from Dyson for testimonials and his reluctance to provide them. In February 1850 he referred to being unable to provide a strong testimonial 'on account of his weakness and frivolity of character'.[612] In November 1853 he told MaryAnn of the requests received again from Dyson:

> I enclose two letters which I have from W. Dyson. He wishes me to give him a testimonial before his commencing as a schoolmaster, but I feel

very doubtful about it. His abilities are very slender, his character weak, and he has a great deal of conceit and is not on the whole the person I could confidently recommend as a master though I think him likely to be very useful as a subordinate under a good master. However, I wish you to answer truly these questions:

Did he behave well after I left England to you and mother? Did he encourage or induce Mr Swift to adopt the flogging system and depreciate the one I had pursued? Did he exert a bad influence over Lilly? I had an impression that you had some complaints about him from Miss Minceft but I do not know. I gave him a testimonial for his present situation in which he seems to have done well.[613]

Thomas Dyson referred to the matter in his 1865 letter to MaryAnn.

He [William Dyson] asked Mr Boole to certify that he was capable of conducting a school and he refused, as he had a perfect right to do of course. I believe (I say so because all I know of the matter is from a few words of my brother) that a sharp letter or two passed between them.[614]

The next time Dyson saw Boole in Lincoln he reported that when Boole saw him coming he turned on his heel and walked at full speed in the opposite direction. A notice appeared in *The Bradford Observer* on 29 June 1854, advising that William Dyson, B.A. of the University of London, formerly with Dr Boole of Lincoln, and for four years classical and mathematical tutor in Wesley College, Sheffield, was planning to open a school for boarders and day-pupils in Bradford.[615] Dr Boole, professor of mathematics at Queen's College Cork, and the Reverend E.R. Larken of Burton by Lincoln were included among the numerous referees. Despite Boole's misgivings about William Dyson's suitability as a master, the school appears to have been very successful with over one hundred and twenty pupils, allowing him to save £5,000 in ten years.[616]

Dyson attempted to pour cold water on MaryAnn's desire to write a biography of her brother, as he felt so much had already been written in the local press. He continued:

I am afraid the publication of a memoir, so long after his decline, when the interest has subsided, will be a serious sop to the editor's reliabilities. That is merely my opinion and it is to be taken for what it is worth.[617]

Over thirty years later, in 1884, when Mary Everest Boole was collecting materials for a biography of her husband, she too wrote to Dyson for his impressions. Dyson appears more positively disposed to Boole at that point in time but covers much of the same ground as in his previous letters to MaryAnn. However, in this much longer communication, several new facts emerge.[618] Dyson lauds the scientific prowess of John Boole and relates that George created quite a stir by bringing to the Doncaster school a camera obscura that he and his father had built. The young Boole liked to read the Waverley novels of Sir Walter Scott while seated in a high tree in the Monk's Leys. All his life, it seems, George had a strong weakness for apples (shades of computers to come?) and spent an inordinate proportion of his income on them. He liked too the rice puddings cooked by his landlady Mrs Heigham, but when the omniscient young George pointed out that the laurel leaves she flavoured them with were in fact poisonous, they suddenly disappeared from the menu.

Boole played very nicely on the flute and Dyson took up that instrument too, but they upset the school management by playing secular tunes and were advised to confine their repertoire to approved Wesleyan hymns. Boole, it seems, was quite shortsighted and on one occasion reproved the school's new English teacher, Thomas Hughill, over breakfast one morning for not having 'finished his toilet', when all the unfortunate man was guilty of was of wearing a white tie! But Dyson adds that this was the worst sin he ever knew him to commit, and in fifty years he had never heard anyone accuse Boole of any worse fault.

Boole's religious beliefs caused him some problems in Doncaster and his Unitarian observance in Lincoln was known, but his conduct was so exemplary and judicious that his position was unassailable. Despite this, some of the parents of the pupils put pressure on the management of the school for his dismissal, claiming that 'the dangerous principles of Unitarianism have no place in a Wesleyan establishment'. Of course, Boole was careful not to enter into any discussion on religious or moral matters in public; he felt it would not be pleasant to defend heterodoxy, so he remained silent. But naturally, Boole and Dyson discussed religion in private, but infrequently and in the early days of their acquaintance. Dyson, a strict and traditional Wesleyan, got the impression that Boole, even at this stage, believed in and had a strong faith in a 'Benevolent Deity' but no more beyond that, Dyson never did learn what his creed was. Boole joined in the family prayers or at least was present at them, and also regularly attended the Wesleyan chapel and never asked to be excused. But during the long sermons he worked out many a problem that was on his mind at the time.

Dyson recalled that he and Boole next met in 1841 though they corresponded infrequently in the period in between – Boole sometimes helping him with mathematical problems. Boole was by now immersed in the mathematics of Poisson and Lagrange, and indeed had published papers in the *Cambridge Journal* improving on the results of Lagrange. He told Dyson that he had 'something in contemplation that would surpass all he had ever done', his paper *On a General Method in Analysis.* He predicted that its content would supersede the usual methods of differential calculus and would include all of them, and accomplish more than could be effected by any previous method. And in answer to Dyson's predictable question, 'Why are your whole faculties devoted to the transcendental mathematics which seemed to be of so little practical utility?' he replied prophetically, 'They would be wanted sometime.'

Dyson knew that Boole had read Whately's *Elements of Logic*,[619] but did not inform him that he had made any original investigation on that subject until 1846. On a visit at midsummer, he gave him an intimation of his method in symbolic logic. Dyson describes the occasion rather poetically:

> I well remember the day on which Boole wrote the first pages of his first work on logic. He was on a visit to me at Gainsboro. We went down the Trent by steamer to the lovely Alkborough Hills. After admiring the beautiful scenery and strolling about for an hour he desired to be alone. He sat under the shade of a huge bush until I disturbed him to announce the hour of return. At night he read to me what he had written, and expounded his system, which was published the following year. Shortly afterwards he informed me that he regretted having published so soon, and proceeded to amend and enlarge his system, which resulted in the publication of *The Laws of Thought.*[620]

Dyson relates that while in Lincoln Boole always went to church with his pupils, frequently to the minster, and always occupying one spot from which he had ascertained the anthem could best be heard – the apex of the acoustic triangle. Boole was very critical of the clergy of the Church of England, saying that there was little hope that Christianity could become the religion of the country de facto from the manner in which it was preached by them. The whole management, he claimed was a muddle, the canons deplorably inefficient and mainly intent on emoluments. He never took part in any religious or political movement but concentrated on philanthropical activities such the Mechanics' Institute or the Young Men's Improvement Society with his friend the Reverend E.R. Larken.

Dyson and Boole met again in Oxford in 1847 at the meeting of the British Association. Dyson, Larken and Boole attended church together on the Sunday to hear Samuel Wilberforce, newly made Bishop of Oxford, preach his famous sermon 'Pride, a hindrance to Godliness'. When asked to comment afterwards, all Boole would say was, 'I thought it was very agnostic.' Dyson closes his letter with a telling remark that his teacher De Morgan made to him. 'I shall miss Boole,' he said.

MARY DAVIS

Mary Davis was the niece of Robert Hall of Waddington, in whose school Boole taught, and she came to live on the school premises there shortly after Boole arrived in 1833, possibly assisting Hall with school duties and looking after the pupils. She was one of Boole's few close female friends, and while their relationship appears to have been platonic, the tone of their correspondence suggests that they may have had unexpressed deeper feelings for each other. On 13 August 1849 Mary Davis was one of the few people that Boole informed by letter that he had been appointed to the Cork professorship. He wrote as follows:

> My dear Miss Davis,
>
> I avail myself of a couple of minutes to tell you that I was last week appointed professor of mathematics in Queen's College, Cork. An intimate friend of mine, Mr De Vericour, who is now visiting at Lord Mavern's nearby, is appointed to the chair of modern languages in the same college. This will be very pleasant for me. My mother bears it very well and I am quite of the opinion that for her and MaryAnn the change from busy to quiet life will be a very beneficial one. I hope to be able to spend about five months in the year with them. You may suppose that I am now very busy and have not much time for letter writing. I however take the earliest opportunity of informing you of my changed position and assuring you of my undiminished esteem.
>
> Ever yours sincerely,
> George Boole.[621]

Clearly Mary Davis regarded Boole as a confidant and wrote to him for advice with regard to her personal problems. Her letters to Boole do not seem to have survived, but Boole's next letter to her, from Lincoln, dated 2 October 1849, gives a good indication of the closeness of their friendship:

My dear Miss Davis,

The advice I should give you without hesitation about the M's is to take no notice of them, not even to think of them, but quietly discharge your duties as if they were not. I see no other course for you. Avoid especially the appearance of resentment (the passion itself I am sure does not find place in your breast) and if you ever are unavoidably thrown in their way, behave towards them with that general kindly regard which a Christian shows to all men. But everything special should be avoided. The best rule is to think much of our duty and little of other people's regards and opinions. We may be sure that even as respects the estimation of the world, a 'patient continuance in well doing' is, though pursued with a far different and higher object, the more likely means to secure it, at any rate so much of it as is worth securing. There is certainly a great deal that is not worth securing. In this category I reckon the esteem of parties, coteries of all kinds, whether political or fashionable or religious. As to myself I am here now but do not know how long I shall remain. Whether I shall have to come up to London before the opening of the Cork college or not, I am equally uncertain about. If I do I will try to get to see you and will then talk to you more at large upon your affairs and mine. Accept my mother's and sister's kindest regards and believe me,

Yours very sincerely,

G. Boole[622]

The next available letter is addressed from Lincoln on 21 August 1854 when Boole sends a letter edged in black to Mary Davis telling her of the death of his mother:

My dear Miss Davis,

You will scarcely be surprised to learn that my dear mother died on Saturday last. She had been seriously ill for about a month or six weeks with that form of dropsy which often follows protracted illness and commences with swelling of the feet. I am most thankful to say that her disease was unaccompanied by pain and that her mind was calm and perfectly resigned to the will of God. In these and in many other things, our great affliction has been made easier to bear. At the same time, it is impossible not to feel that one can only once lose a mother. My sister will write to you before long. She unites with me in kindest regards. Let me add that I hope to hear a good account of your position and prospects in which I always shall feel a strong interest.

Believe me to be, My dear Miss Davis,

Yours most sincerely, George Boole.[623]

No other letters between the couple seem to have survived, but after George's death, MaryAnn included Mary Davis in the list of people she requested to write biographical accounts and memories of her brother. Mary Davis complied willingly and frankly, and although her reply is long and detailed, it is worthy of quotation in full, not least for the light it throws on Boole's character and behaviour, and the tenderness of her feelings for him. Her letter, addressed from 2, Albert Terrace, Anerley Road, London, is dated 29 March 1865:

My dear friend,

I have been thinking much of you lately – you will feel assured it has been with sympathy in your great sorrow and bereavement. I dare say you realise your loss now more deeply than you did at first, when your mind and time were so fully exercised by outward demands – I imagine you are again at your work in Killaloe – I hope with some degree of chastened composure and resignation – you must, you ought to mourn such a brother, and I know you do so deeply and uninterruptedly. Thank God it is with 'hope'. In looking over my letters, I met with a very characteristic one and enclose it – when I was ill I destroyed all from everyone that contained any domestic allusion or other matter that one would not have every or any one comment upon, or I could have given you more.

During one of his visits to London he spent a Sunday at St Hill; in the morning he went to the Moravian chapel and returned charmed with the simplicity of the service especially the hymns they sang – I enclose it for you – in the evening he went with me to the Newington Wesleyan chapel. I asked him to remain for the sacrament – he declined. When I reached home, he sat gazing earnestly and devotionally at the sky in the twilight and scarcely noticed my entrance and turning in his quiet serious way so peculiarly his own, he said, 'I am glad I was never a university cloistered man. I should have been very strait', and then spoke like himself as united in spirit and hope with all who had the faith of the Gospel. I need not enlarge on his large-heartedness and liberality of spirit. You and I can but have sentiments in unison – you ask me for dates – I am not sure I can give them. My uncle would die about August [18]37 – I imagine George went to Waddington first about [18]32. I can procure the date of my uncle's death if you need it. After that event I never saw him till he came to see me in apartments in Dalston in June [18]47. I asked him to read in the evening and selected Job 1st and rather emphasised from the 9th to the 15th verse; the selection was keen because he knew that I had had my fears lest he was not quite orthodox. On that occasion I saw no change from the George Boole I had known at Waddington. I have often wondered how it was that I, who am so shy, so reserved, was, with very superior intellects, never reserved; never in the least afraid of him. I attributed this to the truly brotherly feeling he manifested towards me. The last time I saw him was here on Saturday September 8th [18]60. Referring to my pocket book for that year I find this entry: 'Dr Boole dined – is this the last interview on earth!!' I felt it probable, I think he did also – I never for a moment thought he would be the one taken, so it is; omniscience cannot err, and he told me what a 'recreation' – his own word – teaching his little girl was. I have been tried lately in disposition among the children and yet I am wonderfully sustained through the toils of life. It is I fear late, it is gone ten, I must conclude. It is a brief and unconnected epistle – I am too weary to lengthen it and may not have leisure for some days to come and I want to hear of and from you. I trust you have abounding consolation – as also I hope the poor widow – my heart aches for her. She will more and more realise her loss. Remember me very kindly to her.

Accept my love and believe me ever and affectionately,

M. Davis.[624]

But it was in the next part of her letter to MaryAnn, written shortly afterwards, that Mary Davis really expressed her feelings for George Boole. One wonders if MaryAnn was surprised, or if she knew all along, and if she would have preferred her brother to settle down with a friend of hers, instead of taking a post in Ireland and marrying someone of whom she did not really approve. But all of that was in the past now, and any tender feelings expressed for George could be viewed only in a positive light. Mary Davis continues:

... I was not at Waddington when Mr Boole arrived. When I joined my relatives there he was in the best of their admired and beloved – especially by my dear uncle, who has often remarked of all his assistants he never had one who so entirely behove him and responsibly condescending to the meanest capacity and youngest pupil with unwearied patience. My own first recollections of him are as a grave, serene, winning-looking young man (but being exceedingly retiring and looking with some awe upon mental greatness I rather shunned exchange of words and table courtesies with him or I might have known him far more intimately then – time did arrive when not a tinge of fear or reserve existed). He was pleasant, affable, easy, and kind – we all found him a valuable acquisition to the family circle, as well as a most conscientious helper in the general welfare and success of the establishment ... there was always affection in my uncle's manner towards him as he never manifested beyond his children and myself. He very often applied the epithet 'my lad' to him, used in tenderness only ... We were charmed listeners – the old gentleman and boy tutor were endeared to each other by these little great things, till the affection became parental and filial. Often, I have heard my uncle extol the mental and moral excellence of his young favourite and finish by saying 'If I had no lads of my own, I'd make him go to college and put him there.' He deeply regretted the abandonment of the college by Mr Boole, but when the latter stated the reason, he not only approved and most cordially acquiesced in its being given up and assured nothing could prevent the development of Mr Boole's mental and scientific powers; his being a renowned man, this brought into action what had before been professed, the true disinterested feeling existing between the two. Mr B. was intending to open a school of his own four miles only from his present employer. Mr H[all] unhesitatingly advised the step and so far from any interruption of good feeling, it was cemented by the necessity of the step – Mr H went to see him requested by myself and his daughters to do so – remembered his birthday with interest and on one occasion took a personal interest in inspecting some little token of preparation to be sent in remembrance of the day to 'his lad in Lincoln'. It was something of potted meat. I only name this little circumstance as it proves a feeling. Here I must remark out of order, which you must omit or arrange, that I never heard of or saw any act of violence or severity with his numerous pupils at Waddington, young as he then was. There was in his mild remonstrance a command or rebuke all yielded to without questioning. His reading the scripture, as it was his office to do at family prayer, was then most impressive and we were often surprised at the suitability of the selected parts to sing, existing, or passing circumstance, or remark previously made; he was not what society terms a polished youth, but the natural kindliness of his heart made him a truly polite one. Acts of kindness were natural to him, resulting much from his entire self-possession and composure …

… My own closer intimacy with your lamented brother is of a later date – we renewed it about the year 1846 or 1847 when he visited London. I was then quite surprised to find him so little altered in mind and manner, the same 'child of nature', true to its own noble impulses. I was at that time in circumstances of difficulty. His sympathy, advice and offer of aid were steady and noble. I found him a valuable adviser in some difficulties requiring great judgement and promptitude – pressed as he was, it was always at hand by the post requested. He never disappointed me of his opinion however briefly given …

… The last time I saw him was in Hull two and a half years ago I think. He walked from Cottingham and dined with me alone. I then found him the same easy, unaffected, unsophisticated man and admired him greatly. His conversation was free, friendly and confidential. I went into the hall with him, and while putting on his coat I said, 'Perhaps this is the last time I may see you on earth'. He gave me a cheerful smile and said, 'Oh no, I may come to England to live', and went quickly away. I thought he mentally admitted the possibility, being then much out of health, little supposing that he the strong and young would go, and so verify my prophetic feeling. Seeing life as you observe so uncertain I have thus far at once complied with your wishes – tell me if I can give you this in any other form and I shall most gladly trust my attestation to the worth of a life so uniformly good and great.

Ever affectionately yours,
M. Davis[625]

WILLIAM ATKIN

The kindly side of Boole's nature emerges again when we consider his youthful friendship with William Atkin of Lincoln, a friendship which grew into a lifelong one. Atkin was yet another of those requested by MaryAnn

Boole to submit his memories of her brother soon after his death. This he did with a long and flowery letter from which we present some extracts that contribute to our knowledge of George Boole's character.

Atkin reveals that he was 'an invalid' when he first met Boole, who was then about sixteen. Boole induced him to take long country walks and his company was so valuable that it made Atkin forget his weariness. Boole used these sessions to instruct his friend in a variety of topics and recite poetry to him, Byron's *Childe Harold* being a favourite of both of them. Boole, it seems, like many of his contemporaries, was a great admirer of the poetry of Mrs Hemans, and repeated her poem *The Sounding of the Sea* many times.[626] Other favourites of Boole's were *The Diver*, *Ode to the Joy* and *The Wounded Hussar* by Thomas Campbell.[627] He liked too the compositions of Elenora Elliot and regarded the fifth book of Milton's *Paradise Lost* as among his finest work. Atkin continues:

> I remember some of his own compositions which I had copied in a scrapbook which I regret to say is lost and I can only call to mind the subject on which they were composed. One was an address to spring, at any time worth perusing. There was a beautiful translation of Petrarch's *Sonnet on the Death of Laura* and the *Death of Saul*, which if they were now in my possession I would indeed put a high value on them.[628]

Atkin recalled that George used very often carry to the local theatre the bell belonging to the town crier for the use of the manager when any particular piece required it. He was allowed free admission for his trouble but often used to laugh at the foolish nonsense he saw on the stage.[629]

Atkin had finished his formal education and was unable to work because of his physical condition, but on country rambles with Boole he received excellent tuition from the most enthusiastic and knowledgeable of teachers – botany (ox-eye daisies and trembling spangles), geology (unnoticed pebbles on the pathway) and many other scientific and literary topics, delivered with a boyish enthusiasm, yet with the confidence of a master. Atkin recounts too that he received a moral education from his friend:

> He always hated and detested everything of a lewd and immoral tendency; low degrading thought or words he abhorred, and his principles of Honour and Integrity were highly sensitive, uncompromising, and solid as a rock. His natural diffidence kept him out of all society, except a few

friends, and those who had tastes and pursuits in unison with his own. Trifling and frivolous company he could not endure – he preferred the pleasurable solitude of his own excellent mind ...

... His affections were strong, his professions sincere, he was free from guile, and never aspired to be what he was not...

... His talent had no display connected with it, it shone out of himself, and then but when time and place demanded or circumstances compelled to drag him as it were into public notice. He honoured his father and his mother, loved with enduring affection his brothers and sister, and all whom he knew or had the least acquaintance with him and whom in after life he never forgot. I had much pleasing correspondence with him during the time he was engaged at Doncaster as a tutor in a school and when in the same capacity he was at Waddington. I frequently walked over to see him, and when returning he would accompany me about a mile distant from the village, enquiring after his acquaintances, beginning with his own relatives and sending to them the most warm-hearted greetings.[630]

We have seen that George Boole was a generous man, even from his earliest youth. Here was a poor young schoolmaster, almost completely responsible for the financial support of his parents, brothers and sister, unable to provide for his own further education or even to buy the textbooks on which his career depended, yet who was quick to help out almost anyone in distress. Atkin's genuine gratitude to his friend is very touching:

During the time he was at Waddington and became master of the school where he had been previously tutor, having lost my mother under very unhappy circumstances, being overwhelmed with grief and pressed with difficulties of a pecuniary nature, quite unexpected on my part, he came to visit me and having walked over from Waddington expressly to visit me and sympathise with me, he would not leave until he had extracted from me and made himself acquainted with all my circumstances which are on recollection too painful to relate, and then with open hand and heart he proffered his assistance by a loan of money of which I then stood in great need, which loan I received a few days after from him. Whether his friends ever knew of this I do not know. I was saved through this act of kindness and benevolence from what is generally considered unpardonable and discreditable.[631]

Boole was thus able to save his friend from debtor's prison, and avoid the fate his father had suffered. Atkin was then forced to move to London to seek work and the pair lost touch, both being busy with other things. But fate conspired to bring them together again. In Atkin's words:

Some years later, strange to say, I met with him in London in the National Gallery, gazing intently at a picture of the dead Christ by Fransceso Francia,[632] then placed in one corner of the third room in the gallery where we most cordially greeted each other and afterwards spent some part of the day together. He was particular in his inquiries after my personal welfare and put many questions to me respecting the state of London society and the character of the people, their morals and pursuits. The time we spent together was short but very sweet …

… The next day I dined with him and yourself in Country Street, Leicester Square. About that time he was expecting to be appointed to the professorship at Queen's College Cork.

Some few years elapsed ere I met with him again, by a singular coincidence, but I did at the very same spot at the National Gallery, gazing at and admiring the very same picture. I very quietly approached him unobserved, touched him on the shoulder, he turned and was doubly joyful at our meeting, for the spot seemed to be hallowed by friendship and we both heartily laughed at the idea of meeting again under the same circumstances …

… He had then got the appointment at Cork, as he mentioned some unpleasant things he had to contend with from the Roman Catholic priesthood, but I do not remember the particulars of what they were.[633]

The next sighting of Boole by Atkin is interesting as it provides one of the few descriptions we have of Boole and his wife Mary as a married couple, when Atkin saw them in London:

I think that about three years ago I saw him in town, he and a lady I took to be his wife were strolling through the Pantheon Bazaar, she having hold of his arm tried to draw attention to the toys and articles exposed for sale, but which I could see had no attraction for him whatever; being at that time myself very unhappily circumstanced, I could not and did not make myself known, but I followed them out of the bazaar into Oxford Street thinking I would watch where they might go and I would venture to call upon him, but I lost sight of them in the moving crowd of the bustling part of Oxford Street.[634]

Boole and Atkin did meet a few months later in Lincoln after Boole had just spent six pleasant weeks in London working on a research project. Boole suggested that in his absence Atkin should go over the old walks they had taken together to revive old memories. Atkin did so but missed the comforts of London life. This was their last meeting, but even at this stage, Boole reminded his friend that in any case of emergency or difficulty to be sure to apply to him for assistance. Atkin relates that a few months later the news of Boole's death 'came like a thundershock upon me, and pained my slumber for several nights successively. The cold and solemn truth lay heavily on my spirit.'[635]

CHARLES KIRK

When George Boole was applying for the professorship of mathematics at Queen's College in Cork in 1846, he submitted testimonials from several of the leading British mathematicians of the day, including De Morgan, Thomson, Cayley, Charles Graves and Ellis, as well as character references from the Mayor of Lincoln, and from no less than five magistrates and two clergymen. But he also wisely included the following:

> From Charles Kirk Esq., Student of St John's, Cambridge
> I have read during the present long vacation, and on previous occasions, with Mr George Boole, and can testify with entire confidence to his unvarying kindness and attention as a teacher, and to the great ability which he possesses in the explanation and removal of difficulties.[636]

Charles Kirk may have been a former pupil at Boole's academy in Lincoln, but it is more likely that he was a private pupil from the nearby town of Sleaford whom Boole coached in mathematics and science subjects to help him gain a place to study mathematics at the University of Cambridge. Charles Kirk (1825–1902) was the son of a successful builder and architect, Charles Kirk (Senior). He also became an architect and ran the family firm after his father's death.

Boole and Kirk became good friends, sharing many interests, and corresponded frequently in the period 1846–9. Doubtless there were many other letters between them that do not seem to have survived. In the first available letter, dated 10 August 1846 and written from Lincoln, Boole, writing in an uncharacteristically flowery tone, congratulates Kirk on reaching the age of twenty-one.[637] He apologises for the smallness of his gift but assures him that the esteem and friendship of which it is a memorial are great. He apologises profusely that he cannot at that time be with him in his bodily presence to join with him on this 'long-looked for, most festive, and never-to-be forgotten occasion which love will write with friendship and mirth with wisdom, to strew flowers beneath the dusty wheels of time'. Boole continues:

> But in another sense, think of me as of one not entirely absent. Imagine that in the empty chair, at the remoter corner of the table, you behold me responding to every sentiment, applauding every toast, laughing at every jest, and never once indulging in those philosophic but unsocial mutterings, which by a too severe judgement, have been charged upon me. When the shades of evening descend, I shall in a sober cup of tea, drink to you, health, wisdom, length of days, a sound mind in a sound body, putting upon a heathen's prayer a Christian's interpretation.
>
> My mother, father, and sister, and the dear boys unite with me in compliments and congratulations, part of which are due to your excellent parents and amiable sisters.
>
> Believe me thus to remain with every assurance of continued regard, my dear Kirk,
>
> Yours faithfully, George Boole.

In the next letter, written from Lincoln and dated 30 April 1847, Boole mentions the letter of introduction he gave Kirk to the mathematical economist J.B. Cherriman, known for his work on Cournot (1857).[638] Boole describes Cherriman as a pleasant and agreeable fellow. This letter also shows that even at this late stage, Boole still harboured thoughts of going to study at Cambridge. This is one of the few times he reveals his true feelings on the subject:

> What I now have to say to you is confidential. My father has been very ill. A day or two ago we thought that he could scarcely survive the week.

While he was in this state he took the opportunity of strongly urging me to enter myself at the University of Cambridge. He said that he had been thinking very seriously of it for some time, and was even quite sure that there was no obstacle in the way of my doing so. My sister and my brother Charles second him in this advice, and although I have not given my consent to the plan, the considerations they urge have determined me to deliberate upon it. At present I am in doubt whether, should I ever decide upon entering a university, Cambridge would be my choice. Oxford is amid pleasant country, and Dublin, I expect, has greater advantages for every study except that of classics. If I should finally fix upon Cambridge, I should prefer one of the smaller colleges, not of course an aristocratic one. I should like to turn my mathematics to some account but would certainly not make them a principal pursuit. I should not like to spend more than £80 or £100 per session at college, unless I could in some way make up the difference. Would you be kind enough to give me your opinion? The main consideration for me would be in what way I may look for the greatest opportunities, not of emolument, but of usefulness. I think that I know enough of my own tastes, feelings and principles, to be sure that no considerations of mere personal advantage would weigh with me against that duty which I owe to society. The thought which reconciles me to the quitting of my present restive sphere is, that under the most vigilant and conscientious management, the amount of evil that grows up spontaneously among boys shut up together in a boarding school is almost greater than the good that you can implant.[639]

Reading between the lines, it would appear that Boole is bored of running a school and teaching boisterously behaved young boys and would much prefer to become a mature student at Cambridge or even Oxford or Dublin, where he could enjoy a more relaxed lifestyle, dabbling in mathematics and other subjects such as logic, philosophy, psychology, and maybe even languages. But his financial situation is still critical, and even if MaryAnn, Charles, and the other teachers could continue to run his school, there is no guarantee that he could find the additional money to cover his university fees and living expenses. So this letter to Kirk is very probably in the realms of fantasy.

On 9 August 1847 Boole writes again from Lincoln to Kirk to congratulate him on his birthday. The letter is again a very flowery one, full of exaggerated comparisons and language, and unusually familiar in tone.[640]

He also encloses a letter for Cherriman which he requests that Kirk deliver for him in Cambridge. But on 15 November 1847 Boole sends Kirk a more down-to-earth missive telling him that although his father is ill and growing weaker, he himself is well and prospering:

> I am very well and more busy than ever, having formed a class of young men, whom I teach at my own house three times a week, besides having two private pupils. With these things and others I am very fully occupied, but I am very happy in these occupations and am more truly satisfied to work on in this situation and to be doing a little good in life's short hour than I have been.[641]

We have seen that Boole is still hankering after a place at Cambridge. Perhaps realising gradually that this will never come about, in his next letter to Kirk from Lincoln on 3 January 1848 he indulges uncharacteristically in a bout of sour grapes. He writes:

> I begin to be doubtful whether I shall get to see you in Cambridge. I am not this vacation going up to London as I once thought. The secretary of the College of Preceptors writes that they are 'so very short [of funds]'. I have even directed him to credit my lost expenses as 'subscriptions in advance'. This being the case, I really don't think I can afford to spend my money on a visit to the learned vanities of Cambridge …
>
> … To tell you the plain truth, were I to come to Cambridge, it would be only to see you and Cherriman. The university does not enlist very many ardent sympathies of mine. I don't like DONS – I hate CRAM – I detest, from the bottom of my heart, the cold pride of useless scholarship …
>
> … You need not show this letter to anyone as I don't want to be classed with those who are perpetually grumbling at 'our glorious constitution in church and state'. I am not a grumbler, but I love quiet and simplicity and as far as in me lies, shun the heights of life.[642]

In the next letter from Lincoln on 21 March 1848 Boole excuses his delay in writing on the grounds that he has not been very well. He commends Kirk's study of German which he describes as a noble language and the key to a no less noble literature, saving some extravagances and affectations. He trusts that Kirk has been able to look with equanimity on the backs of his mathematical books which he found it so difficult to contemplate without a sigh in his previous letter. Boole adds, with a rare flash of humour:

> ... like the Israelites, I suppose, sighing after the fleshpots of Egypt or the prodigal desiring to return to the husks which the swine (no allusion to anything in Cambridge) did eat.[643]

It is of course 1848, the Year of Revolution, and Boole now turns his attention to what is happening abroad, again in the rather flowery language he seems to reserve for Kirk:

> People are speculating on the progress of affairs abroad. That wonderful revolution of events that is still going on in France, Germany, and Italy, whose beginning we have all witnessed, but whose end no one can foretell, occupies men's minds to the exclusion of all the minor topics of public interest. I should think that the fruit of these things has penetrated even into the shades of Cambridge, and that pale young men, intent upon Greek accents and double integrals, lift up their heads, and speculate upon the world, whose existence they had almost forgotten.[644]

In a further letter from Lincoln dated 26 May 1848, Boole asks Kirk:

> Will you oblige me by calling as soon as the journal is out at Macmillans for a parcel for me – open it and take out two copies of a paper of mine on Logic for yourself and Cherriman, and send me by post a dozen more, bringing the rest when you come.[645]

This paper would have been *The Calculus of Logic*, Boole's excellent exposition of his theory of symbolic logic, which reached a far wider audience than the 1847 *The Mathematical Analysis of Logic* and increased his reputation in the mathematical community.

Boole was now coming to terms with the fact that his first book on mathematical logic had failed to make the impact he had hoped for. In the final letter to Kirk that we have available, written from Lincoln on 24 January 1849, we see something of the bitterness and disappointment that many authors experience when what they consider to be their magnum opus is rejected, or worse still, ignored, by its target readership. But there are some glimmers of hope and optimism in Boole's words:

My dear Kirk,

Will you oblige me by calling on the Macmillans and asking them to let me have the account of the sale of my book. I wrote to them nearly a month since but have not had an answer. It was their own proposal by letter to send me the account at Xmas …

… I am glad to hear that you have made some application of my method. I have applied it, during the vacation, to the analysis of many complex terms with the greatest success. I had an Oxford tutor here a short time ago, who spent two or three hours with me in discussing the subject, and certainly made all the admissions I could desire as to the defective condition of the old logic, and the practical value of the new. I should gather from his remarks that my book is elsewhere totally unknown. This I am not sorry for as I hope to accomplish something so much better. The interest of the subject grows upon me beyond what I have ever found in any previous investigations, but I have not much hope of making it generally interesting; seeing that the mass of educated persons take their opinions upon authority. Never mind all this – the pursuit of truth is enough of itself.

Believe me yours very faithfully,
George Boole.[646]

Boole's optimism was quite justified. In 1854 he published *An Investigation of the Laws of Thought*, a very much more extensive work, superior to *The Mathematical Analysis of Logic*, and which extended his methodology to cover the mathematical theory of probability also.

T.W. MOFFETT

Thomas W. Moffett (1820–1908) was professor of logic and metaphysics from 1849 to 1863 at Queen's College Galway. In 1863 he became professor of history, English literature, and mental science there until his retirement in 1897, as well as being registrar (1870–7) and president of QCG (1877–97). Moffett was born in Dublin and was educated at Trinity College, from which he graduated as senior moderator in ethics and logic, winning gold medals for logic, metaphysics and Greek, as well as prizes in divinity and modern history. In 1852 he was awarded an LL.D. degree by Trinity and he later received honorary D.Litt degrees from both the Queen's University in Ireland and Trinity. He was knighted in 1896.[647]

Figure 10.3: Sir Thomas Moffett by Walter Osborne, RHA

Moffett and Boole appear to have been quite close friends, though surviving correspondence between them is scanty. The two men shared several interests. Logic was of course of fundamental importance to them both and Moffett was full of praise and admiration for Boole's work in symbolic logic. Each had a passionate desire for the welfare of animals and Moffett published an extensive pamphlet on the subject. But what seemed to bind them together most was their shared love of the countryside, scenery and rambling, in which they communed with nature. Moffett visited the Boole family in Cork, became friendly with Mrs Boole and adored the Boole children. In a letter dated 6 September 1864, Moffett thanks Boole for his kind invitation to Cork, but cannot accept because of his wife's serious illness.[648] However, he proposes that they tour the Wicklow Mountains south of Dublin on their next trip. In another undated letter to Boole around this time, he wonders if they might persuade QCG professor of physics George Johnstone Stoney to join himself and Boole on a trip to some 'quiet sequestered part of England'.[649] Stoney was an eminent scientist and the man who first named the electron.[650]

In the same undated letter, Moffett also sends regards to Boole from two other QCG professors, George Allman (mathematics) and William Nesbitt

(Latin and Greek). Boole had always been full of admiration for the standard of mathematics in Galway. For example, he had ordered for his library at QCC a copy of *Principles of Modern Geometry* by Corkman John Mulcahy, professor of mathematics at QCG (1849–53).[651] Boole had been of the opinion that there was too much emphasis on geometry at Trinity College Dublin, but, maybe as a result of Mulcahy's book, later modified his views, 'with a view to intellectual benefit'. When Boole was appointed examiner in mathematics for the Queen's University in 1856, he generously conceded that two Galway students, John Atkinson (later a Queen's Counsel) and T.H. Harrison (later a civil servant in India) had merited the highest marks in mathematics ever awarded by the Queen's University in Ireland and that their answering surpassed anything previously seen.

Of course, when Moffett wrote to Boole late in November 1864 he was not to know that Boole was now seriously ill. Moffett wrote enthusiastically of proposed touring trips to Dublin, Wicklow and England, of suitable accommodation for excursions which were never to be; of new appointments, increasing student numbers, and academic progress in Galway; of family matters, his own and Boole's; of a new edition of *The Laws of Thought,* and of the *Collected Works of Robert Leslie Ellis,* lately arrived in the QCG Library.

When the news of Boole's death broke, Moffett was distraught. On 16 December 1864 he wrote to John Ryall:

> I cannot tell you how painfully the melancholy tidings affected me, for I cannot express how much I owe to the great and good man so prematurely lost to the world and his friends. It was impossible to associate with him without finding the intellect enlarged and the moral nature purified and elevated. He honoured me with his friendship for many years, and I can say with truth that his conversations and letters opened to me views and inspired me with feelings which no books could impart; and all the time he seemed absolutely unconscious of his own worth and wisdom.[652]

Moffett, like many others, was very concerned with what he believed was the precarious financial state in which Mrs Boole and her daughters had been left, and continued:

> I have been speaking to some friends and we all feel that the government would readily and gladly place Mrs Boole's name on the Pension List (which is filled up from year to year) on the proper representation being

made to them. I believe the regular course is to send a memorial to Lord Palmerston; but it would be expedient if not indispensable to secure the support of the Irish government. Mr Cardwell too had a high regard for our friend and would, I have no doubt, give an application his influent support, as would also, I think, Sir R. Peel.[653]

Unfortunately, Ryall took exception to Moffett's suggestion and similar ones from other sources, and asserted that Mrs Boole and her daughters were not 'destitute' and would be looked after by himself and her extended family. Moneys already contributed by several people (including Hamilton and De Morgan) were returned, but Boole's widow did receive a government pension of £100 per annum within a year.[654]

Naturally, Moffett was one of those written to by Mary Everest Boole seeking memories of George, and in December 1865 he responded to her request.[655] He was extravagant but sincere in his praise of Boole, and his letter is probably the finest eulogy that Boole received, as the following extracts indicate:

> I feel a melancholy satisfaction in complying with your desire that I would communicate to you some reminiscences of one with whom a long-continued intimacy was my privilege and whose memory I shall ever cherish with affection and veneration ...
>
> ... His nature was eminently genial and social and his conversation strikingly original and suggestive. Nor did mathematics by any means present itself as his chief or even favourite topic. He seemed most to enjoy discourse when it took a literary or philosophical turn. Indeed, great as he undoubtedly was as a mathematician, he was quite as much a philosopher. 'A philosophical mathematician' he was truly described by some of the highest authorities of his day. Fully appreciating the great and comprehensive utility of the sciences, he yet loved rather, with Plato, to regard its nature and function as a means of intellectual discipline and as subordinate to a moral purpose. Hence he delighted most to discuss the principles of investigation, to test the sufficiency of received methods, and to ascertain the ultimate grounds and the philosophical relations of results already known – *The Laws of Thought* being the perfect example ...
>
> ... His reading was extensive and varied, for his taste was by no means exclusive. He seemed to possess a thorough knowledge not merely of the great philosophers, but also of the great poets of ancient and modern

times. Of the former class, Plato, Aristotle, Leibniz, and Berkeley were his favourites; he was familiar too with the principal works of the fathers and the schoolmen; amongst the latter, he particularly esteemed the treatises of St Anselm. Of the poets, I am disposed to think he most admired Virgil, Dante, Milton, Young, Wordsworth, and Tennyson. Shakespeare I need not name; but he had an unusually intimate knowledge of the other old English dramatists also.

To controversy he was much averse: truth he believed to be the result of meditation rather than of argument; and mutual conversation he seemed to regard, with Bishop Butler, as an 'entertainment; as something to unbend the mind; as a diversion from the cares, the business and the sorrows of life'; and not as an anxious trial of skill, or a fierce contest for superiority …

… I believe that no person who enjoyed even a casual acquaintance with him could fail to be attracted by the manly simplicity and frank cordiality of an address that revealed a character of perfect truth, reality and courtesy. Not a few of us, more intimately associated with him, will retain indelible impressions of the instruction and delight we experienced in our intercourse with him; and while we deplore its premature close, and often, 'in the moonlight of memory', strive to recall the familiar hand, and voice, and smile; and doubtless feel that, highly as we had appreciated and honoured him, we yet had scarcely honoured him to the full measure of his merits.

He had an exquisite sensibility for natural scenery, and often spoke of its restorative influence, its tendency to calm and purify the heart, and its power even to suggest some of the deepest truths and realities of the universe. The parallelism or correspondence which he conceived might be found to exist between intellectual operations and the movements of external nature – between the laws of the understanding and the actual constitution of things – was a favourite subject of speculation with him; and as pointing to a unity of cause and a unity of method in the system of the universe, and suggesting a dim realisation of some of the highest aspirations of the reason, it seemed to him a theory of much interest and importance. 'To no casual influence', he says, 'ought we to attribute that meditative spirit which then most delights to commune with the external magnificence of Nature, when most impressed with the consciousness of sempiternal verities, which reads in the nocturnal heavens a bright manifestation of order; or feels in some wild scene among the hills, the intimations of more than that abstract eternity which had rolled away ere yet their dark foundations were laid.'

It was at the same time observable and characteristic of him that the beauties of scenery often seemed to produce on him an impression of a complex kind, in which sadness was mingled in a larger proportion than joy. Was it that the soft and smiling aspect the 'Great Mother' found such little accordance in the serious and stern realities of life? Or that the perdurability of the objects of nature was so strongly contrasted with the transient phases of frail mortality

'For men may come and men may go,

But I go on for ever'?

The fact is that, though there was nothing that can justly be called gloom in his nature, yet, as with all men of deep sympathies, there was a large element of melancholy. I believe he possessed in a higher degree than most men two powers which usually weaken one another – the power of close and abstract thinking and the power of intense feeling – at once a lofty philosophic spirit and a hearty affectionate sympathy with the homely cares and concerns of everyday existence; and while the features of the landscape impressed his imagination and taste, 'the still, sad music of humanity' struck on the deeper chords of his nature ...

... His benevolence was of the most active and self-denying kind: many persons might think their obligations sufficiently discharged by a pecuniary subscription – he devoted time and attention to the examination and relief of the wants of the distressed.

In all public questions he felt a keen interest; in the amelioration of the physical and moral condition of the labourer; the advance of political and social reform; the questions of peace and war; and the great issue – then undecided – of the slavery struggle.

Nor was his sympathy confined to his own species. 'Broad and general as the casing air', it extended to every sentient being. The condition and destiny of the lower animals' painfully heightened for him (as for Arnold and other thoughtful minds) the awful mystery of life and aggravated the perplexity which hangs around the question – what it is and what it all means. Tenderness to those creatures, whom we may wrong with impunity, seemed to him the surest test of a humane character; and the wanton cruelty which we so constantly witness, a tremendous proof of the unlimited freedom of action allowed to man. The august relation in which man stands to the lower species – a relation, it may be almost said, habitually ignored – involved, in his judgement, solemn responsibilities and duties which ought to be systematically enforced from our pulpits and chairs of instruction; and the lessons derived from the gentleness and faithful service of many of them to us, 'The feeling of affection great, beyond all human estimate', should be instilled into the minds of the young with all the persuasive influence of parental training. He interpreted the writings of St Paul to imply that as these creatures have suffered with man, with man too they may find ultimate deliverance. The reiterated inculcation of this duty by Wordsworth, Southey, and Coleridge (the moral of whose *Ancient Mariner* he often quoted) greatly enhanced his admiration for their writings. He mentioned in one of his letters his intention to write an essay on this subject, on which he had deeply and painfully meditated.

He was passionately attracted to his native county, and more particularly of his birthplace, and he told me it was his intention, in the event of his attaining his sixtieth year, to return and spend the remainder of his days in England. A native of the same county that had given birth to Newton and Tennyson, he seemed to partake of the characteristics of both his illustrious fellow-countrymen – the mingled simplicity and profundity of the philosopher, the tender home-feeling, subtle thought, and refined sentiment of the poet.

Corresponding to the depth and truth of his moral nature was the earnestness and simplicity of his faith. Religion was no isolated part of his character. So well were the various elements – intellectual, moral, and spiritual – combined, his whole nature, resembling the cloud of the poet, 'Which moveth together, if it move at all', exhibited an individuality and directness, which might at once account for its leading characteristics – strength of insight, energy of will, and freedom and range of speculative thought. A sense of the divine government of the world and of the high destiny and responsibility of man was with him an ever-abiding motive of action; but while this had always been the habitual tone of his mind, his friends, I believe, could not fail to observe, during his latter months, that his religious feeling had become still more fervid and energetic; that there was, it might almost be said, a visible growth in those qualities which are most connected with the thoughts of another world …

… In a letter which I received from him in the autumn of 1863, he spoke of the last conversation which he had with his father. He described the scene of the interview, in sight of the towers of Lincoln Cathedral;

and told with what calm assurance the good old man spoke of a life beyond the grave, where partings are unknown. He also spoke of the feelings excited in his mind by a visit which he made (accompanied by his friend Mr Todhunter of Cambridge) to the grave of a man whom I believe he resembled much in genius and character—Mr Leslie Ellis. (I may observe in passing that he considered Ellis to be the 'most variously accomplished scholar he had ever met'.)

To dwell on such scenes characteristic of the pensive tone of thought to which I have referred, death was indeed, I think, a frequent subject of his contemplation. He once alluded to a saying – 'Every beautiful thought has death in the background'. The idea of that great event presented itself to his mind, I believe, not as involving any essential alteration in character, but only as a change in the mode and sphere of the soul's operations; our faculties not being 'unclothed but clothed upon' – that, to use words of Butler, 'Death may immediately, in the natural course of things, put us into a higher and more enlarged state of life, in which our capacities, and sphere of perception and of action, may be much greater than at present' …

… I shall never forget the tone of deep earnestness with which he bade me farewell on our last meeting. Shortly after came the last of those letters which were always sure to suggest high thoughts and feelings. Its purpose was to fix our place of sojourn at our next annual meeting in Dublin. 'A house not made with hands' was already opening its doors to receive him.[656]

CORRESPONDENCE FROM FORMER STUDENTS

After Boole's death, several of his former students wrote to Mary Everest Boole, probably at her request, giving memories of their teacher not just in the classroom, but also with regard to informal meetings and even visits to the Boole household. Mary Boole later wrote that she knew 'every undergraduate who had any special aptitude for mathematics, and many of them very intimately' and sincere familiarity and affection are often evident in the letters she received from her husband's former students.[657] Among those correspondents were R.A Jamieson, a diplomat in Japan and later a newspaper editor in Shanghai; J.F. Popham, studying at Downing College Cambridge; E.J. Warmington, principal mathematical lecturer at Brighton

College, and H.S. Ridings, an engineer in London. These occupations give a good indication of the types of employment taken up by Boole's students, and he probably wrote references for them with regard to their mathematical ability and character. We see from their letters that they held Boole in very high regard both professionally and personally, and they wrote of him eloquently, glowingly, and even lovingly.

R.A. JAMIESON

R.A. Jamieson was a a student of the Faculty of Arts at Queen's College Cork and the Lincolnshire Archives contain some letters he wrote to Boole.[658] He describes his travels en route to Japan and his work and studies of Chinese. Boole's interest in Chinese in the 1860s may stem from his correspondence. The affection in which Jamieson holds Boole and his family is evident. He refers to the eldest daughters, 'Pussy' and Margaret, and thanks Mrs Boole for her letters. We learn that they had sent him a telescope and stand; that Mrs Boole had acquired a sewing machine with which to make clothes for her little girls, and that he was writing a book on Chinese society which he intended to dedicate to Boole.

After Boole's death, Jamieson wrote to Mary Boole from Shanghai on 13 April 1866:

… It would be impossible to measure him by any standard which passes current among ordinary men. His warm-hearted hospitality sprang from the genuine and unselfish love for his fellow creatures which animated all his conduct … There was in his nature a certain undercurrent of sympathy which from time to time manifested itself that made me, and, I have no doubt, many others, look on him as most fit to receive confidences which would otherwise have never seen the light, and come to him for advice under circumstances of difficulty or embarrassment. I fear few of those who gathered around him attached due value to the religious element which gave a tone to his conversation when discussing scientific subjects, but there is some excuse for us in the fact that he ever depended more on infusing a devout spirit than on directly teaching religious lessons. What always struck me as the most noteworthy peculiarity of his style was the absence of any assumption of that superiority which would so readily have been conceded to him had it not been that he seemed to shrink from even a hint of the reputation he bore …

… His conversation on philosophical subjects took always more or less the form of a lecture, for few ventured to criticise his opinions or suggest modifications in their expression. But although this was, from the nature of the case, unavoidable, it was never noticed until after the discussion had closed and we thought over the contributions, few and far between, that we had made to the conversation. His object seemed to be to elicit the opinions of others and modify them by attrition with his own. This was the course he adopted with me, and to the long conversations which filled up the happy summer evenings at Blackrock, I owe many lessons of wisdom which since I have come into daily contact with the world have stood me in good stead. Liberality was his motto, and well he maintained it even at a time when the admirers of freedom of thought were few and widely scattered.

You, my dear Mrs Boole, have often seen one or two of his favourite pupils sitting as we may imagine the disciples of the old sages sat at the feet of their masters, and you too will bear witness to the energy with which he entered into all the plans, whether remote or near, whether for profit or for pleasure which suggested themselves to us …

… I hardly know whether I rather loved him as a friend or reverenced him as a teacher. One little trait I shall never forget – his sensitiveness to any incorrectness in speaking or writing. Unfortunately, I was, as all Irishmen are, often an offender in the matter of 'will' and 'shall', and to his good-humoured badinage I owe it that I am now free from that particular fault …

… My personal experience extends over three years during which I attended in turn his junior, senior and extra mathematical class. As might have been expected, his lectures became in every respect more valuable as we advanced from the junior to the senior classes. It was indeed drudgery to attempt to drive the elements of mathematics into the dense brains of many who day after day sat around him, and often an irritated glance would betray the disappointment that he felt when some unusually stupid question or remark proved that upon one or another his minute and conscientious explanations had been thrown away. To tell the truth, this seldom happened, for he was not one to be trifled with. Not that the students were afraid of him, but they were afraid of offending him …

… The secret of his success, I think, with the senior classes, and to a limited extent with the junior, is that he never seemed to be repeating or reproducing what he had himself once learned – he always appeared to be discovering the results he educed, and his students were generally carried along with him, and as it were, shared in the honour of his discovery ...

... His books are the best testimony of his powers of mind, just as the grief of his students at his loss is the best testimony to his goodness of heart. Those who best knew him are now scattered widely, and thus all over the world there were sorrowing hearts and moistened eyes when the news of his death was announced. For myself, I felt that I had lost a master, a friend – almost a father.[659]

J.F. POPHAM

John Popham was from Cork city and was an arts student in QCC, where he won several scientific prizes between 1857 and 1860.[660] Afterwards, he attended Trinity College Dublin, where he was awarded honours in physics, logic and metaphysics. After Boole's death, he sent Mary Boole his recollections of her husband:

I was very young, not above 14 years of age, when I was first introduced to Dr Boole as a scholarship candidate, and I cannot soon forget the interest which my extreme youth, perhaps with other causes, led him to take in me, so that I had the pleasure and great good fortune of his personal friendship during the whole of my academic career. Without showing any injustice to the general body of his pupils, of whose claims upon him as a teacher he had the most scrupulous sensitiveness, he was in the habit of selecting some students of each class as his most intimate friends, inviting them to his house and assisting them and encouraging them in their studies; but yet when he became their examiner for any position of honour or emolument he never suffered any private feeling to bias him in the slightest degree for, or against, the candidate. Any honour to be obtained from him must be won by real merit and by open and fair competition. On the other hand, when the object of the student was solely to pass the examination, Dr Boole generally set up a minimum of answering and if this was not attained he unhesitatingly plucked the unlucky pupil. Yet such a general belief existed in his perfect fairness and impartiality, that no one ever thought of questioning his decisions. He used to observe that it would be unjust to the student himself and his parents, and to the design for which the Queen's College was instituted to let young men quit their college with its honourable imprimatur upon them, having acquired an amount of knowledge much greater than their deserts and thought that students were often seriously injured by an ill-advised laxity on the part of their examiners …

… But no examiner was ever more anxious to encourage it, and delighted to reward success, than Dr Boole, when he was able to do so conscientiously.

In connection with the subject of honours and rewards for the encouragement of study, Dr Boole rather looked down upon them. He had such an exalted opinion of the true profit and pleasure accruing from the study of philosophy, and particularly of his own noble science. He considered, perhaps a Utopian idea, that his pupils should study it with the same fervour, the same disinterested zeal and affection, which he showed towards it himself. Indeed his pupils used to be not a little amused when their teacher, seeing the eagerness with which the substantial advantages of a competitive examination were sought by them, would reprovingly shake his head, and sigh over the degeneration of taste which sought the honour rather than the knowledge itself …

… Should any instances of juvenile levity occur, and they were rare, he checked them at once by appealing to the gentlemanly feelings of his hearers, and from the high respect in which he was held, the appeal was never without its effect. It would be a great omission not to testify to the total absence of all self-laudation in his lectures, not through ignorance of the importance of his discoveries, for the high estimation in which his works were held in the great seats of learning was known to, and prized by him dearly, but his modesty of disposition was such that any appearance of ostentatious display on his own part, or of adulation on that of others, was distasteful. Upon particular occasions however when some well-merited compliment had been paid him by learned bodies, he was deeply moved, and the writer of these remarks had the pleasure of witnessing two of these occasions: one of them caused by the highly favourable notice in an Italian journal of one of his scientific works as a most original production: and the other, when the degree of DCL was conferred on him by the University of Oxford …

… He used frequently to express his marked dislike of the process of grinding or stuffing as more calculated to make a student an expert answerer than a good mathematician. The substance of his oral lectures was seldom found in any of the ordinary textbooks; indeed, if his lectures could be criticised at all, it could only be said that he was so much occupied with the higher branches of mathematics, as not at all times to descend sufficiently to the more hackneyed subjects necessary for pass pupils.

... His mode of teaching was the professorial as carried out in the Queen's College, i.e. lecturing from the blackboard. He was usually very careful about his figures which he drew with great neatness. He usually set examples on the theory which he explained, and his opinion of a student was chiefly based on the facility with which he solved them. He always used the English textbooks (especially Todhunter's works) preferring them to the French, for he said that the French books, though good in theory, were very deficient in examples.

On setting examination papers, he studiously avoided all those intricate little questions, familiarly known as cruxes, and which generally show a pettiness of knowledge in the examiner. He used to give about an equal number of book and original questions which though not difficult in their way, yet required a good knowledge of the subject.

His great devotion to the analytical method in mathematics he carried with him to the lecture room and hence his pupils knew the calculus and algebra better than conic sections or Euclid.

Dr Boole possessed in a remarkable degree that valuable property of complete concentration of the mind on a given subject, which has been noticed in great mathematicians ... It is a current story that upon one occasion he entered the lecture room to deliver his usual lecture and put on his gown, the room at the time was filled with students, but he was so intensely buried in thought that he walked up and down the room wholly unconscious of their presence, and finally to their great surprise, doffing his gown, he retired and walked home apparently under the impression that none of his class were present. There was no one who would be more amused than himself at such an occurrence.

Dr Boole was gifted by nature with a most intellectual countenance, and when interested in his subject, its deeply contemplative expression was frequently noticed by his pupils. As Wolfe said of a great mathematician, 'Reason seemed to have expelled all the passions and to reign uncontrolled upon his brow'.[661]

On 20 December 1864, shortly after Boole's death, Popham cheekily put himself forward as a candidate for the professorship of mathematics at

Queen's College Cork. He stated that it would be fitting for one of Boole's former students, the son of a distinguished Cork physician, to be his replacement and that some preference should be given to those seeking a chair in their own *alma mater*. His application was not successful.

E.J. WARMINGTON

E.J. Warmington was a student of the arts faculty of QCC and subsequently studied at St John's College Cambridge. In a letter dated 2 December 1865 he stated that he was principal mathematical lecturer at Brighton College, and was about to be ordained. Mary Boole had written to him requesting information for a biography of her husband. Warmington replied:

> … I well remember my first impressions of the doctor. He was in his thoughtful mood and every feature passionless as stone except, when the working of his mind for the moment half revealed itself, and then his giant thought seemed to veil his countenance in huge varying shadows, deep and distinct. But suddenly the cloud broke up, and beneath was the man himself, gentle and calm and kind, with easy manner and a most penetrating eye which instantly struck me …
>
> … He always had a special recognition for me which presently quickened into a manifest personal interest. But he was a man that always retained, even in his holiday moments, the greatest dignity of manner intact; so that from this and other causes I used to notice whether in the heat of work, or in our more familiar meetings, our sense of regard for him prodigiously increasing day by day the more we saw of him.
>
> I remember a group of us were attending his extra tuition at Queen's College. One day the professor was absent. His class, assembled at the usual hour, were discussing the wonder and with concerned faces hoping for the best. But soon a note arrived – the professor was too unwell to attend but trusted to see us at his house instead, to yet recover the half-lost opportunity …
>
> … No man could ever mix up things great and small to better edification. He seemed to me to dote on principle and final causes of things and without indulging in any useless abstraction he kept wonderfully clear of unnecessary entanglements. No one with a mental power and clear-headedness less than his could else have entertained his hearers with so much new light on such an old picture.[662]

H.S. RIDINGS

Henry Sadlier Ridings qualified as an engineer at QCC and worked as an astronomer in Ireland and later as an engineer in Wales, India and South America. In two letters written to Mary Boole in November 1865 he recalled his days as a student of Boole's:

> There was one deep-rooted feeling in the minds of the students with reference to Doctor Boole which in a great measure accounted for his success as an instructor, namely that their professor was their friend. The most careless of them could not be proof against his kindness, and against the intense interest which he so evidently took in their advancement, morally, intellectually, and physically.
>
> His influence morally with the students was very great, even with those who knew but little of him privately. This influence was of two kinds, the one of example, resulting from his known high moral principles; the other the result of precept, as he was most unflinching in his condemnation of every evil habit, and that not merely as a bar to their own happiness, or as an offence against college rules or against society; but against God. One occasion he uttered a most eloquent warning to some who had swerved from the straight path. At such times he was much depressed, and happily they were but rare.
>
> The doctor's interest in the intellectual advancement of the students shewed itself in unremitting labor for them and with them. His labors for them in the study were evident from the immense number of carefully prepared papers of examples and problems, which in regular sequence from the lowest to the highest branches of mathematics he had printed off from time to time, and some of which he gave every week to the students. He used to repeat that unless these examples were worked, but little advancement would be made, and that little would soon be forgotten. 'Nothing like working numerous examples for impressing mathematical truths on the mind' was his frequently reiterated statement ...
>
> Certainly it was a treat for a lover of algebraic analysis to see the way in which some great principle in mathematical science was gradually evolved as board after board was covered with his calculations – as each successive stage was reached towards the final result, his face beamed with satisfaction and particularly when to his eager inquiry of 'Can you follow me thus far?' there was a ready answer in the affirmative. But

if the reply was 'We don't understand this or that point', there was no ruffling of his temper. Patiently he went over and over it endeavouring by a supplemental analysis, or by a diagram if the problem allowed of such, and by every means at the disposal of one who had a perfect mastery of his subject, to make it as clear to others as it was to himself ...

... His chief strength lay in the method of algebraic analysis – not that he undervalued strictly geometrical methods where available, but analysis was believed by him to be a much more powerful instrument. Though a lecturer on abstract science, Doctor Boole gave a practical turn to his lectures by showing the bearing of mathematics on common everyday matters, as well as on the highest walks of science and art ... the impatient question 'What is the use of this?' was seldom, or never, heard in his classes. That Doctor Boole's desire was not to see the students devoted to mathematics to the exclusion of other branches of learning was evident from his frequent enquiries as to their progress in other classes, and also from the mass of information imparted by himself on every subject, religious, moral, literary and scientific.

He also had an interest in the physical development of the students. He was no advocate of excessive study, and soon noticed the pallid countenance and weak step; immediately recommending cessation from work and the engaging in some innocent amusement. The caring for them was peculiarly manifest prior to examinations, when his cautions to hard workers and his encouragements to the nervous and diffident were frequent.

Dr Boole's whole demeanour was that of a Christian gentleman, and he had a sprightliness and a geniality of manner which went very far to take away from the dryness, thought especially by the juniors invariably to belong to the study of mathematics. His interest in the students did not cease when they graduated. Glad was he to be able in any way to help in giving a good start in life, as so strikingly exemplified in my own case, and glad always to hear of the wellbeing of those who had once been under his instruction.[663]

In his second letter, Ridings continues:

There was nothing oracular about Doctor Boole's style ... He appeared to lower himself to our standards for the time being and having thus gained our sympathies he rapidly rose and carried us along with him.

... Scarcely a lecture was delivered during the course of which some original ideas did not strike him. Occasionally while working out such ideas on the blackboard he would appear to forget our presence altogether so absorbed did he become in the problem...

Dr Boole's was never a naked or lifeless statement of facts, as he appeared to give warmth, colour and life to everything in connection with science.[664]

Five years after Boole's death, Ridings' father passed away and was buried beside George Boole in the cemetery of St Michael's Church in Blackrock, Cork.

Chapter 11

CONTACT WITH MATHEMATICIANS

D UE TO HIS HUMBLE ORIGINS and lack of a formal third-level training in mathematics, in the early days of his career George Boole was not in a position to meet many professional mathematicians. From the age of about twenty, however, he took it upon himself, humbly but firmly, to contact by letter many prominent mathematicians, especially those at the University of Cambridge, informing them of his original mathematical ideas and research, and testing the waters before submission for publication. Among those who responded quickly and generously to his letters were William Thomson, Augustus De Morgan, Arthur Cayley and Charles Graves. Indeed, these men and several others went on to become his personal friends – he visited them and stayed with them. Recently further correspondence with other mathematicians has come to light and we now examine Boole's contact with these individuals.

DUNCAN GREGORY

Figure 11.1: D.F. Gregory

Duncan Farquharson Gregory (1813–44) was born in Aberdeen and was the great-great grandson of one of the most famous of all Scottish mathematicians, James Gregory (1638–1675), the discoverer of a series for the evaluation of π. His father, also James Gregory (1753–1821), was professor of medicine at Edinburgh University, but died when Duncan was just seven years old. He was educated at home by his mother Isabella until he was ten and then at Edinburgh Academy, where James Clerk Maxwell also went to school. He studied mathematics at Geneva and later at Edinburgh University where he showed a great talent for chemistry and experimental science also. In 1833 he proceeded to Trinity College Cambridge where he graduated fifth wrangler in 1837 (ahead of him were Green and Sylvester) and he was conferred with an MA in 1841. He retained an interest in a wide range of scientific disciplines including chemistry, astronomy, physics and botany. In 1840 he became a fellow of Trinity, and from then onwards devoted himself almost entirely to mathematics. In 1837, assisted by R.L. Ellis, he founded the influential *Cambridge Mathematical Journal* and became its first editor. It is indicative of the poor state of mathematical research in Britain at the time that many of the early papers in the *Journal* had to be written by Gregory himself.

Gregory suffered from lifelong ill-health, and this led to his turning down the offer of a chair in mathematics at the University of Toronto in 1841. He returned to Edinburgh where he was an unsuccessful applicant for the chair of mathematics there. He died in Edinburgh at the tragically early age of thirty in 1844.

Duncan Gregory may be regarded as one of the true founders of modern algebra. In 1830, Peacock had written:

> Symbolical algebra may be defined as the science which treats of arbitrary signs and symbols by means of defined though arbitrary laws: for we assume any laws, so long as our assumptions are independent and therefore not inconsistent with each other.[665]

Peacock almost got as far as formal algebra but faltered just before the final step. He believed that algebra was pointless unless the symbols are interpreted and insisted that the laws chosen for algebra should mirror those of arithmetic, using the principle of permanence of equivalent forms. Gregory saw this as a weakness or even a flaw in Peacock's approach, but his definition, superficially resembling Peacock's, is more daring, and goes a great deal further along the road to abstraction:

> Symbolical algebra is the science which treats of the combination of operations defined not by their nature, but by the laws of combination to which they are subject. We suppose the existence of classes of unknown operations which are subject to the same laws.[666]

Boole was in almost total agreement with Gregory's approach. Indeed, during his self-education in mathematics, he had worked through Gregory's textbook *Examples* and had not just learned a great deal from it but had picked up much of the flavour of his approach.[667] Gregory had a very strong influence on Boole's mathematical development, which Boole was quick to acknowledge. In a footnote to his paper *On a General Method in Analysis*, Boole writes:

> Few in so short a life have done so much for science. The high sense which I entertain of his merits as a mathematician is mingled with

feelings of gratitude for much valuable assistance rendered to me in my earlier essays.[668]

Indeed, the opening lines of Boole's first book, *The Mathematical Analysis of Logic* read like a perfect echo of Gregory's sentiments:

> Those who are acquainted with the present state of the theory of symbolical algebra are aware that the validity of the processes of analysis does not depend upon the interpretation of the symbols which are employed, but solely upon the laws of their combination. It is upon this general principle that I propose to establish the calculus of logic, and that I claim for it a place amongst the acknowledged forms of mathematical analysis, regardless that in its object and in its instruments it must at present stand alone.[669]

Gregory thus gave Boole the courage to develop the calculus of logic as a viable and independent branch of mathematics and therefore deserves great credit for the development of this area.

Boole first contacted Gregory in 1839, sending him a parcel of his researches with a view to publication. At this stage, Gregory was already in a poor state of health, but responded warmly and positively to Boole's work, treading a fine line between enthusiasm and the need for precision, clear proofs, and clarity of expression. He always remained conscious of Boole's position as a schoolmaster outside of mainstream mathematics, and phrased his criticisms in very gentle language while lavishing praise on correct work. On 4 November 1839 he writes:

> I conceive that your language is likely to mislead a person who does not read your paper with very great care and it is better if possible to avoid such mischances. I think your explanation of the connection between the problems of rotation-axes of elasticity and the diameter of surfaces of second order is clear and satisfactory. If you think my criticism well founded and feel inclined to make any corrections accordingly in your paper, I shall be obliged by your transmitting these at your earliest possible convenience, that your paper may be sent to press.[670]

One can hardly imagine a more positive and welcoming environment for the encouragement of an unknown amateur mathematician by a member of the establishment; would that more of today's editors were that friendly and courteous. It helped that the two men had already met in person in Cambridge, which is not far distant from Lincoln. Gregory writes:

> You spoke when I saw you here of some investigations in the calculus of variations which you were inclined to publish. If you still desire to do so I shall be happy to give them a place in *The Journal.*[671]

In a further letter of 15 December 1839, addressed to Boole at Academy, Waddington, near Lincoln, Gregory continues in the same tone, offering to make corrections at the proof stage and again gently adding, 'You appear to me to have fallen into an error regarding the stability of the eccentricities in the remarks you have made.'[672] On 5 February 1840 Gregory apologises to Boole because of the fact that the numbers of the *Journal* in which his papers have appeared have not reached him, realising that this is an important milestone in the life of any young research mathematician, and promises to investigate the problem. Ever anxious to fill the pages of his journal, he tells Boole:

> I should like to see the investigation concerning linear differential equations of which you speak. I have sometimes thought that there ought to be some simpler method of arriving at the final result without the long process of integrating by parts, but I have never been able to find one.[673]

Later in February 1840 Gregory expresses a strong interest in Boole's method of separation of symbols and draws his attention to his own paper of 1838 and the work of Lagrange with regard to the symbolic form of Taylor's theorem. He tells him that the 8th number of the *Journal* containing Boole's paper on analytical transformations is due out the following week and that his paper on the calculus of variations will appear in the next number after that. Boole must have been tremendously excited and gratified by the opening paragraph of Gregory's next letter dated 16 February 1840. Gregory writes:

> Your method of simplifying the solution of linear differential equations with constant coefficients is exceedingly ingenious, and I think reduces the problem to the greatest degree of simplicity of which it admits. Every part of the process is now dependent on the ordinary theory of algebra except the theorem
>
> $$\left(\frac{d}{dx} - a\right)^n = e^{ax} \left(\frac{d}{dx}\right)^n e^{-ax}$$

This is all that can be desired, and I conceive that no further improvement is likely.[674]

It emerges that Boole's paper on the subject had previously been rejected by the *Philosophical Magazine* and Gregory explains its non-insertion very frankly on the following grounds:

I do not think it was due to any other cause than this – that the editor is ignorant of mathematics, and is very unwilling to risk the publication of any mathematical communication, unless a previous knowledge of the author gives him some security for the correctness of the paper.[675]

Gregory's reasoning was probably correct and helped to ease the hurt that his paper's rejection caused Boole. He goes on to say that he will be very happy to insert the paper in the *Cambridge Journal*, but gently points out that there are still imperfections in Boole's method of exposition; for example, treating specific examples when a general solution is just as easy using the method of separation of variables. He even goes so far as to offer to rewrite Boole's entire paper in a form best suited for publication and send it to him for inspection. Gregory closes by saying that he will be glad to hear that Boole has made progress with the more difficult and important problem of the solution of differential equations with variable coefficients.

The next letters of March and May 1840 are concerned mostly with the possibility of Boole's applying for a fellowship to formally study mathematics at Cambridge. In these letters it is sad to see financial and social considerations forming a barrier to important developments in mathematical research.[676] Gregory draws a line under the discussion, saying:

It would be impertinent of me as a stranger to offer any advice with regard to the propriety of your coming here as a candidate for a fellowship. I have stated as fairly as the general nature of the subject allowed what I conceived to be necessary to gain success here. It is for you to judge how far what I have said may suit your own case. If however you should at any other time wish for any further information I shall be happy to give it.[677]

Communication between the two men continued. Boole submitted virtually all of his work to Gregory and he published all he received. In May 1840 Boole mentions that he had applied general differentiation to the evaluation of definite integrals; Gregory tells him that the same idea occurred to him some time ago and gives a number of worked examples.[678]

In a letter of 24 May 1840 Gregory acknowledges Boole's remarks on a theorem of Liouville and says he has had similar thoughts himself and also with regard to Fourier's work. Very curiously, Gregory admits that he has excluded proof by the method of generating functions from his journal because when using it he never felt certain of all the steps and preferred the method of separation of variables as Boole had done. The letter closes with a discussion of validity and evaluation of improper integrals.[679]

As time went by, Gregory's health deteriorated rapidly, but he and Boole stayed in touch by letter, while the mathematical topics they considered became more and more advanced – triple integrals, gamma functions, and improper integrals, for example. Gregory continued to encourage Boole by lavishing praise on his efforts. On 11 February 1841 he writes:

> I have been much pleased with the ingenuity of your method and the great skill which you have shown in treating it. As far as my own reading extends I have not seen any researches which anticipate yours and I believe that your method, if properly followed out, would become of much utility in various parts of analysis.[680]

Yet Gregory still continued to exercise a restraining hand on Boole's efforts and never got carried away by his admiration. In the same letter he adds:

> You will allow me however to say that I think your memoir is not quite as clear as I should have wished. I found considerable difficulty myself in following the thread of the argument, and on giving it to a friend to look over, he made the same complaint.

The paper in question, in which Boole laid the foundations of a new branch of mathematics, nowadays called invariant theory, appeared in two parts in the *Cambridge Mathematical Journal*, November 1841 and May 1842, and consisted of thirty-three pages in all. It was entitled 'Exposition of a General Theory of Linear Transformations'.[681] The two men continued to trade punches in citing many continental mathematicians such as Lebesgue, Lagrange, Laplace, Cauchy, Lacroix, Euler, Poisson, Fourier, Liouville and others, and they seemed quite familiar with the works of these authors, especially with regard to integration. But then they came from the same tradition – Gregory under the influence of the Cambridge Reformers, and Boole through his gut instinct, facilitated by his fluency in continental languages.

In October 1841 Gregory reveals that he and Boole share some other mathematical interests, finite differences and functional equations.[682] Gregory praises Boole's method of summation of series using finite differences as 'very ingenious'.[683] He also expresses a wish to see Boole's applications to partial differential equations. In another letter, he lauds Boole's theorem on the expansion of $(1 - 2r\cos\theta + r^2)^{-n}$ which he describes as 'very elegant' and says it is analogous to the Legendre functions treated by Robert Murphy in his work on electricity.[684]

In a letter from London dated 19 June 1843, Gregory tells Boole that he has not yet recovered from a serious attack of illness.[685] Indeed, he had not long to live – he had left Cambridge in the spring of 1843 and he died in Edinburgh in February 1844. It was a huge loss to British and world mathematics. But before he passed away, he advised Boole to have his paper printed in the *Philosophical Transactions* of the Royal Society in order to avoid expense and gain more exposure for it.[686] Boole followed this advice and his paper of 1844 was awarded a gold medal by the Royal Society. Sadly, Gregory added:

> My own solution of the equation of differences is much simpler than that which you propose; but I am not in a fit state to enter on the subject at present.[687]

Duncan Gregory had a profound influence on the development of modern mathematics, and one can only speculate on what further progress he would have made had he lived. His emphasis on abstraction, separation of variables, and the calculus of operators showed him to be an innovator of the highest order and there can be no doubt of his positive influence on Boole in these areas. He enthusiastically promoted continental methods in calculus, all the time emphasising the historical context. His work as editor of the *Cambridge Mathematical Journal* helped to drag British mathematics out of its slumber, and Boole in particular benefited from having his papers published there with Gregory's generous editorial help. But above all Gregory will be remembered for his extremely amiable disposition, his disinterested kindness to all his contributors, and his unselfish willingness to share with others his inventive ideas and his vast store of learning.

Figure 11.2: Robert Leslie Ellis

Robert Leslie Ellis (1817–59) was an English mathematician, linguist and classical scholar, and was accomplished in many other areas also. He was called to the bar in 1840 but never practised law and he wrote on subjects as diverse as etymology, bees' cells, Dante, and a proposed Chinese dictionary. With Heath and Spedding, he edited *The Works of Francis Bacon*[688] and in 1837 he co-founded the *Cambridge Mathematical Journal* with D.F. Gregory. His most important contributions to mathematics were in the areas of differential equations, functional equations, and the theory of probability. In 1844 he defended an objective theory of probability against a subjective one and therefore probably had a strong influence on Boole.[689]

Ellis was privately educated in mathematics and entered Trinity College Cambridge in 1836, graduating as senior wrangler in 1840, and he was elected fellow of Trinity soon afterwards. He was a sickly child and suffered all his life from ill-health and depression which made it difficult for him to meet and mix with his fellow mathematicians; but he had private means derived from his father's extensive estates in Ireland and was able to indulge his academic interests in several directions.

Around the time of Gregory's final illness and death in 1844, Ellis effectively took over the editorship of the *Cambridge Journal*, so it is likely that his contact with Boole began around this time. In January 1844, he writes to Boole:

There appears to be some difficulty in filling up the forthcoming number of the *Journal*. I have therefore ventured to address myself to you and to express my hope that you will be willing not only to relieve us from our embarrassment, but also to give a higher character to the number than it would otherwise acquire, by contributing any fragment of your researches which may be readily detached from the general system. You will perceive that in the next issue [February 1844] I have ventured to give a demonstration of a general result to which you were led by considerations of a different nature from those of which I have made use.

> Mr Gregory, I regret to say, is detained by illness in Edinburgh; in his absence I have taken a share in the management of the *Journal*, which must be my apology for addressing you.[690]

Shortly afterwards, Boole submitted his paper *On the Inverse Calculus of Definite Integrals*[691] which startled Ellis by its level of difficulty and the fact that it posed questions rather than giving answers – he was afraid that Gregory might not approve. Playing safe, he requested Boole to send him some 'mathematical notes' instead.[692] For information, Boole sent him a prepublication copy of *A General Method in Analysis*[693] which he was about to submit to the Royal Society. Ever intent on filling the pages of his *Journal*, Ellis coyly suggested in June 1844 that Boole might submit to the *Cambridge Journal* 'an account of this paper which might induce people to read it who might otherwise be deterred from attempting it by the appearance of difficulty and want of interest in the subject'.[694] Boole does not appear to have risen to the bait.

But in the same letter Ellis also comments on Boole's paper in the *Cambridge Journal* on the theory of linear transformations[695] and points out that he has left one of the most remarkable of his results undemonstrated. He tells him that the result had excited a great deal of curiosity – in particular, Cayley had said that he was convinced that Boole had reached the root of the matter with respect to linear transformations. This is a very significant remark in light of the fact that although Boole had laid the foundations of invariant theory in this paper, the subject was developed by Cayley, Sylvester, Salmon and others. 'Would it be too much trouble,' Ellis asks, 'to make out a demonstration of it for the next number?' adding, 'Cayley and I, and I am sure many others, would look upon it as a very important contribution.'[696]

William Thomson, later Lord Kelvin, was soon to take over the editorship of the *Cambridge Journal*, under whom it flourished. Ellis had noted Thomson's immense talent for mathematics while he was still an undergraduate sitting the tripos examination in 1845, saying to his fellow examiner Harvey Goodwin:

> You and I are just about fit to mend his pens.[697]

Boole and Ellis corresponded infrequently in the following years and more often than not concerning philosophers such as Spinoza, Hegel and Pascal, but in 1846, when Boole was applying for the professorship of mathematics in Cork, he felt confident enough to ask Ellis for a testimonial. Ellis duly obliged with a glowing reference:

> I have much pleasure in stating that Mr Boole's earlier contributions to the *Cambridge Mathematical Journal*, of which I was for some time editor, convinced me that his mathematical abilities were quite of the first order and that the opinion which I had thus been led to form has been fully confirmed by his subsequent researches, among which I may particularly mention his 'Essay on a New Method in Analysis', for which he received a gold medal from the Royal Society.[698]

Boole had been too modest to mention this last fact in his application, and naturally it sounded much better coming from Ellis. He concluded:

> I have recently had the pleasure of becoming acquainted with Mr Boole and from what I have seen of him, believe myself justified in saying that he is not merely an excellent mathematician, but that while his attention seems to have been chiefly given to science, his conversation bears manifest traces of varied and original talent and of a mind at once active and well-cultivated.[699]

When Boole obtained the appointment in Cork, Ellis was one of those people he thanked personally, and Ellis in turn sent him a letter expressing congratulations and delight. And when in 1854 Ellis read Boole's *Laws of Thought* his admiration for his friend reached new heights. He included a comment on it in Bacon's *Works*, which he was editing at the time:

> Mr Boole's *Laws of Thought* contains the first development of ideas of which the germ is to be found in Bacon and Leibniz; to the latter of whom the fundamental principle that in logic $a^2 = a$ was known (v. Leibniz, *Philos. Works*, by Edmann, 1840, p. 130). It is not too much to say that Mr Boole's treatment of the subject is worthy of these great names.[700]

Robert Leslie Ellis was a true friend to Boole, helping him along with a judicious mixture of praise and admiration and facilitating his publishing career. Perhaps he was not as influential as Gregory had been, but Boole admired him greatly, and he had initiated problems which Boole was destined to solve.

THOMAS A. HIRST

Thomas Archer Hirst (1830–92) was a British mathematician who travelled widely on the continent of Europe and attended lectures by Dirichlet and Steiner in Berlin and Liouville and Lamé in Paris. He studied chemistry under Robert Bunsen and was also a friend of John Tyndall. He was elected a fellow of the Royal Society in 1860, two of his proposers being Boole and Sylvester. Hirst was a founder member of the London Mathematical Society and first president of the Association for the Improvement of Geometrical Teaching,

Figure 11.3: Thomas A. Hirst

now the Mathematical Association. He held many other important posts and received many honours and succeeded De Morgan as professor of mathematics at University College London in 1867.

Curiously, however, Hirst is best remembered today for the private diary he kept in which he recorded his candid and honest opinions of the famous mathematicians he had met.[701] Here are some examples:

Lejeune Dirichlet (1853) Dirichlet has his peculiarities – one is forgetting time; he pulls out his watch, finds it past three, and runs out without even finishing the sentence.

Michel Chasles (1857) I went to hear Chasles' first lecture on geometry and was far from satisfied with it. Perhaps he was in a bad humour – certainly he did not enter with his whole might into the subject. He hesitated and bungled much, and altogether his lecture formed a sad contrast to his books which are remarkably clearly written.

Joseph Bertrand (1858) I am still in doubt whether his harsh, forbidding, arrogant exterior is a true index of his character or merely a cloak to a better nature. To me it is extremely disgusting, the air he assumes. His manner to me appears to repel you by the announcement, 'What you are telling me may interest you, but as to me, I knew it all before and much more – in fact with respect to mathematics, I may be said to have utterly exhausted that elementary science.'

Augustus De Morgan (1862) A dry dogmatic pedant I fear is Mr De Morgan, notwithstanding his unquestioned ability.

Pafnuty Chebyshev (1864) He is evidently a good-natured man, has a stuttering way of speaking French, and is lame.

William Thomson (1863) I have attended Thomson's two lectures at the Royal Institution on the electric telegraph. More random, unsatisfactory lectures I have never listened to.

Sofia Kovalevskaya (1869) She is a young Russian lady who attends Konigsberger's lectures and is extremely at home in elliptic functions. She belongs to the mathematically gifted family of Schuberts. She is pretty and exceedingly modest.

Joseph Liouville (1879) He has become a little shrivelled, gouty old man and very garrulous. It was with difficulty I broke away from him.

It would be interesting to have the equivalent of Hirst to describe the famous mathematicians of today in these frank and often unflattering terms – surely an opportunity for some budding author. When it came to Boole, Hirst was quite flattering, and there can be no doubt of the truth of his description:

George Boole (1862) I was much pleased with Boole. Immediately after breakfast I stepped up to him and introduced myself. The same day we sat together at the Hall dinner and had some pleasant chat. Evidently an earnest, able and at the same time a genial man.

Hirst and Boole had already exchanged a series of letters around 1859. Hirst had just returned from Italy and brought greetings to Boole from the mathematicians Tortolini in Rome and Tardy in Genoa.[702] Both men were anxious to obtain copies of Boole's paper 'On a General Method in Analysis',[703] but unfortunately he had only a single copy left for his own use. Boole remarks to Hirst:

Of the Italian mathematicians I think highly and always look with interest at Tortolini's *Annali* whenever I have the opportunity of seeing a new volume.[704]

On 5 December 1862 Hirst writes to Boole asking him to fill up a certificate concerning Dr George Salmon with a view to nominating him for a fellowship of the Royal Society.[705] Salmon was a noted Irish mathematician and writer of geometric textbooks – he was duly elected FRS in June 1863. However, it is difficult not to agree with the comments of the great Charles Babbage on the incestuous nature of the Royal Society. Though himself elected FRS as early as 1816, he once anecdotally described the Royal Society as 'a group of people who meet every month to drink sherry and award each other medals'.

In 1863 Boole sent queries to Hirst on the determinant of a system of linear equations and the number of equations which were independent.[706] These questions had arisen in connection with the theory of the differential equations of dynamics on which Boole was working at the time. Hirst responded by sending him explicit references to the works of Cayley and Jacobi and Boole replied saying, 'I know all of Jacobi's papers.'[707]

After Boole's death, Hirst and Salmon were among those involved as 'his brother Fellows of the Royal Society' in seeking a Civil List pension and a Royal Society Literary and Scientific pension for Boole's widow.[708]

ISAAC TODHUNTER

Figure 11.4: Isaac Todhunter

Isaac Todhunter (1820–84) was an English mathematician, perhaps more noted for his textbooks on calculus, algebra and geometry and his books on the history of probability and the history of the calculus of variations than for his researches in pure mathematics. His father died when he was just six, leaving his family in considerable financial difficulty. Like Newton, he was considered 'unusually backward', but he soon blossomed into a fine mathematician. After a short spell as a schoolteacher, having gained a scholarship, he attended evening classes at London University, where he was taught by De Morgan and Sylvester. He financed his studies by teaching at Wimbledon, and graduated as BA in 1842 and MA in 1844, winning a prize for topping the class in mathematics. This led to a place at St John's College Cambridge where he showed his prowess by becoming senior wrangler and Smith's Prizeman in 1848.[709] Like Boole, he studied Latin and Greek, and was fluent in German, Spanish, French, Italian, Russian, Hebrew and Sanskrit. He seems to have had a genial personality and to have been dearly loved by all who knew him.

Todhunter progressed from fellow to principal mathematical lecturer at St John's, but his biggest contributions to the subject were his strong support for Euclid's Geometry and his foundation of the London Mathematical Society with De Morgan in 1865. He had been elected FRS in 1862, and Boole was one of his nominators for that honour. Todhunter's third-level textbooks were some of the most widely translated and circulated mathematical books of all time, and Boole had adopted them for students at Queen's College Cork, claiming they were clearly written, student friendly, and superior to French texts such as Lacroix which he himself had ploughed through.

The Todhunter–Boole correspondence seems to have commenced around 1860 when Todhunter became interested in Boole's book on differential equations; he sent Boole a list of errata and some suggestions for the content and arrangement of a proposed new edition. From time to time he urged Boole to make the exercises and examples in his book more difficult as his students found them too easy. Perhaps what he did not know was that Boole had rewritten the book many times in order that its content was crystal clear to his wife Mary who at the time was not very well versed in the subject!

In a letter from Cambridge dated 8 July 1861,[710] we learn that Todhunter had asked Boole to contribute to a biographical dictionary he was editing; Boole refused on the grounds that one needed an extensive library to engage in such work, and the library at Queen's College Cork was not adequate. However, he did express an interest in writing something on Berkeley, the mathematical philosopher who had been Bishop of Cloyne just across the harbour from him in Cork, only to be told that a clergyman called Napier who was collecting material for a new edition of Berkeley's works was likely to undertake his life too.[711]

Todhunter and Boole then began a long exchange of letters on the format and content of a second edition of Boole's *A Treatise on Differential Equations*,[712] which Todhunter felt amended and possibly in two volumes, had tremendous potential as an undergraduate textbook. Boole very generously offered him co-authorship of the revised volume, but Todhunter immediately refused, saying he was not entitled to the honour and that the glory should belong to Boole alone, adding that the remuneration for such a work was utterly inadequate for the labour of its production, and that it would be robbery for any person to take any of it from the author. Boole repeated his offer, but again Todhunter refused; however, he offered his services to strengthen the examples in the book. Ironically, after Boole's death in 1864, Todhunter immediately offered his services to Mary Boole and Macmillan with regard to the production of the new edition and they gratefully accepted.[713] He did an excellent job and it is this edition that graces many mathematical libraries and bookshelves all over the world even today.

Throughout their contact, Boole asked Todhunter for copies of examination papers from both Cambridge and London with a view to finding questions which he could use in his books. These Todhunter supplied in great numbers, several hundred of them, and he also had a vast personal collection of questions in connection with his activities as a private tutor or coach at Cambridge. Among his pupils were the eminent mathematicians P.G. Tait and E.J. Routh, and Leslie Stephen, father of Virginia Woolf. In 1862, however, he ceased being a private tutor to have more time for writing textbooks.

Todhunter often had perceptive insights into Boole's work. On 26 June 1862, he writes:

> Your great work on *The Laws of Thought* has not found so many readers I fear as it should have done, from the very fact which in my opinion constitutes the great attraction of it, I mean the union of the two parts. I find among my friends that the logic interests some and the probability interests some, but few seem to pursue both subjects. It seems to me remarkable how few mathematicians there are who are interested in anything that looks like metaphysics.[714]

In October 1862 Todhunter invited Boole to visit him in Cambridge. If he came alone, Boole was promised good accommodation on campus, but if his wife accompanied him, Todhunter suggested that he might perhaps be of service in finding an apartment for them in the town.[715] (In 1864 Todhunter married Louisa Davies and had to quit his fellowship and residency in the college as a result.) Boole was well received at Cambridge, which must have been very gratifying, as he had often considered it as a possible step in his own progression. Afterwards, on 18 October, Todhunter wrote:

> I can only say that the days you spent here were among the very happiest I have ever enjoyed. My friends are all speaking to me of the pleasure they have had in forming and renewing acquaintance with you.[716]

He thanks the Booles for their invitation to visit them in Cork but reminds them that he is growing older and was never a good traveller; he expresses the hope that Boole will someday return to England permanently where he will be more accessible. Finally, he makes a cryptic reference to some 'Chinese letters' Boole has sent him and promises to pass them on to Professor Grote who was writing a Chinese dictionary at this time.[717]

In a further letter on 9 January 1863 Todhunter praises Boole's memoir on the eccentric Cork mathematician John Walsh, a copy of which he has just acquired from De Morgan and expresses the hope that he will write a book of interest to non-mathematicians as well as mathematicians. In particular, he hopes that Boole will continue with his plans to write a popular work on logic.[718]

On 23 May 1863 Todhunter wrote to Boole encouraging him to apply for the Sadlerian professorship of pure mathematics, then vacant at Cambridge, but at this stage Boole was weary of such applications and declined; the post eventually went to Arthur Cayley, of whom Todhunter was quite disparaging.[719] It appears that all Todhunter really wanted was for Boole to lay down a marker for a future application. In a further letter dated 10 June 1863, Todhunter again thanks the Booles for an invitation to visit but says he would be unable to do so for at least a year.[720] In the event he never did make the journey.

On 7 December 1863 Todhunter suggests to Boole that the new edition of his *Differential Equations* should become a complete thesaurus of methods on the subject, including symbolical methods. It should consist of two volumes including the work of Jacobi on dynamics and the examples should be at the end of each volume or in a small volume separately. Reference should be made to the work of Peacock, Gregory, Euler and others in the examples.[721] In the event, after Boole's death, as we have noted, Todhunter did edit the definitive edition of Boole's *Differential Equations*.

In a letter written in late December 1863, Todhunter tells Boole of the difficulties he is encountering with Laplace's works on probability in connection with the book he is writing entitled *A History of the Mathematical Theory of Probability from the Time of Pascal to that of Laplace*, which was eventually published in 1865.[722] He has great difficulty, as many had, in understanding the details of Laplace's work, particularly with regard to arbitrary functions and independent variables.[723] Boole's reply is not available, but Todhunter's reaction to it is. On 9 January 1864 he writes to Boole:

Many thanks for your letter which has been of the greatest service to me. I see that in the first question I was quite wrong … The other question has I think great interest and I am glad to find your conclusions what they are … I shall certainly avail of your kind offer and contact you again if I find myself in difficulty.[724]

One is immediately impressed by Boole's generosity, his knowledge, and above all his confidence in interpreting the notoriously knotty points in the works of Laplace.

On 25 June 1864 Todhunter writes to express his pleasure that Boole's revision of *Differential Equations* is progressing and says he has no doubt that the work will prove fully worthy of all the time and trouble he has expended on it. He also draws Boole's attention to a new book on differential calculus published by Bertrand in Paris, part of a work which promises to treat the whole of calculus, including integral, on a very elaborate scale.[725]

In what may be his last letter to Boole written on 2 August 1864, Todhunter returns to probability theory and the writings of a minor mathematician called Mendelsohn, who published a memoir in 1761.[726] While dismissing the book as having 'no value', he concedes that it contains one interesting example:

Suppose two events A and B have occurred simultaneously n times; is there a causal connection, or is it accidental? Mendelsohn says that the chance is $\frac{n}{n+1}$, but gives no clue as to how he arrives at that conclusion.[727]

The example quoted is a nice one: a man drinks coffee and is attacked with dizziness; there may be no connection between the coffee and the giddiness, but it is claimed that the chance is $\frac{n}{n+1}$ that there is such a connection. But how is this demonstrated? This type of question is of great significance in medical probability even today in the analysis of questions ranging from the very serious 'does cigarette smoking cause lung cancer?' to the more philosophical and seemingly facetious 'people die if and only if they drink water – is drinking water therefore the cause of all death?' Boole had considered such problems in the probability section of *The Laws of Thought* (1854) – for example, does going to bed at night cause the sun to rise in the morning? In that book Boole had also begun a discussion on the validity of the work of Thomas Bayes,[728] a debate which is still ongoing today, so it is interesting to find Todhunter and Boole already discussing such questions in 1864. Todhunter suggests that a valid demonstration of Mendelsohn's result would have to resemble the theorem of Bayes. Mendelsohn, it seems, went on to discuss the implication of his example in discussing free will and our reliance on the evidence of our senses, a contribution which Todhunter dismisses as of no value. There follows a curious sentence:

> I could send the book to you, but as I am going away next week and shall not return until after the library is closed, there might be some difficulty in getting the book returned on time.[729]

Did Todhunter engage in the dubious and possibly illegal practice of borrowing books from the library of the University of Cambridge and posting them to friends abroad? But more seriously, he ends with an ominous remark:

> I hope that the fine weather will dissipate the remains of your influenza and enable you to work at the differential equations.[730]

Boole was quite ill and weak all through the summer of 1864 and this very probably contributed to his premature death on 8 December of that year (see Chapter Eight). Like many others, Todhunter was shocked and distraught at the sudden demise of his friend. Having read the sad news in *The Times* of 14 December 1864 he wrote the next day to Boole's widow, describing him as his 'dear and venerated friend'. He goes on:

> The loss of so great and good a man in the maturity of his transcendent powers is indeed irreparable. No one could know him without admiring him and loving him, and the more he was known, the greater was the devoted esteem and affection which he excited … For myself I can truly say that I have always counted my acquaintance with Professor Boole as one of the greatest benefits of my life; and I am most grateful that our acquaintance refined into a cordial intimacy. His generous and unselfish devotion to truth, his deep religious feeling, his varied and profound knowledge, and his vast ability rendered him rather the object of worship than of any inferior homage.[731]

A rapid exchange of letters followed and Todhunter undertook to examine Boole's papers with a view to completion and publication. Mary invited him to Cork but he pleaded the pressure of business. He emphasised that the new edition of *Differential Equations* should be their priority and suggested that the existing incomplete manuscript should be entrusted to Mr Macmillan, who had already invited him to edit the book. He told Mary that Boole had offered him co-authorship of the book and that he was therefore very anxious to do it.[732]

It may seem that Mary Boole was a bit callous in pursuing publication of her husband's works so soon after his death, but she was now an impecunious widow with five children whose ages ranged from eight to under a year, and she must have been desperate to secure an income from any source. Although we have access to only one side of their correspondence, it is obvious from Todhunter's replies that he had to discreetly point out to her that some of her suggestions and proposals were not really viable for publication. For example, she mentions Boole's proposed 'Fragments on Logic'; Todhunter was aware of this work and that it had appeared in Macmillan's advertisements, but he steers her clear of it and her proposed editor, Bishop Colenso, saying he would be 'busy with anxious affairs, and unlikely to have any fondness for metaphysical speculations'. Ominously, he recommends the cleric F.D. Maurice as a suitable person to read the manuscript, but he himself expressed a strong desire to read it also. He suggests that the moral philosopher and friend of Boole's, Professor Grote should be allowed to read the work too. Finally, Todhunter steers Mary clear of contemplating any publication of Boole's thoughts on the ideas of Père Gratry, the French Catholic mystic.[733]

Todhunter advises Mary against any attempt to draw up a long biography of her husband; the brief notice to be drawn up for a deceased fellow of the Royal Society would be sufficient, and he suggests that a short life could be prefaced to new editions of *The Laws of Thought* or *Differential Equations*. And if a full biography was to be written, nobody would be more qualified to do so than Mary herself, when she had recovered and regained her strength. However, we now know that she collected much material for this biographical project but on the advice of F.D. Maurice dispersed and maybe even destroyed much of it.

Todhunter concludes his letter of 10 January 1865 with a final tribute to Boole:

> He always seemed to me like one who had descended for a time from a loftier and purer sphere; and to bear with him the impress of a nature superior to that with which we habitually associate. I feel for myself that to have known such a man is one of the greatest benefits which Providence

has served on one; and I am sure there is a corresponding responsibility to show in daily life that the highest example has not been displayed in vain.[734]

He tells Mary that he will be very glad if she does him the favour of consulting him on every point with reference to his revered friend. Doubtless she did so many times when she returned to England a few months later.

However, in the meantime there was an embarrassing incident to which we have already referred in Chapter Ten. Immediately after Boole's death a rumour circulated that he had died in complete poverty and destitution and a petition was launched in *The Times* inviting subscriptions to be sent to the editor for the relief of his wife and children. John Ryall wrote indignantly denying that this was the case and asking that any subscriptions already donated should be returned. On 3 February 1865 Todhunter wrote to Mary Boole from Cambridge:

Dear Madam,

    I am very sorry the subscription was suggested as it has caused anxiety and pain to Dr Boole's family. It did not originate with Dr Boole's English friends. Letters and money were sent to the editor of *The Times* from various persons in Ireland, and it was under the influence of these that the step was finally taken. I am sure that no shadow of shame could ever have been cast on Dr Boole's stainless name. But the conviction felt here was that from his narrow stipend sufficient resources have been provided for the bringing up of his five daughters. The donations left in our hands have been all returned with a full explanation of the circumstances, so that I am confident no harm will ensue.

Believe me, Yours very truly,

I. Todhunter.[735]

Todhunter was a true friend to George Boole. While realising that Boole was a much greater mathematician than he was, he was not jealous of Boole's superior talent but admired him and helped him in every way possible. He shared with Boole his immense skill in the writing and editing of books to make them reader-friendly and put the resources of Cambridge that he had access to at Boole's disposal. Above all, he gave practical help and much-needed advice to Boole's destitute widow in her hour of need.

Figure 11.5: Francis W. Newman by
Herbert Watkins

Boole had always admired religious mavericks and freethinkers, so it was no surprise that towards the end of his life he made contact with Francis William Newman (1805–97), the younger brother of Cardinal John Henry Newman.

Newman was born in London and obtained a double first at Oxford in 1826, becoming a fellow of Balliol in the same year. He spent a few years as a tutor in County Wicklow and in 1830 he travelled as one of a missionary group to Baghdad on a utopian journey which ended in tragedy and the deaths of several of the members. Accused of heresy concerning the doctrine of eternal punishment, he returned to Bristol as a classical tutor. In 1840 he became classics professor at Manchester New College, an institution designed for dissenters, and in 1846 reached the pinnacle of his career by becoming professor of Latin at University College London where he remained until 1869. He fancied himself as a mathematician and published several papers on the subject, but it is clear that he never progressed beyond the elements. He delved too into oriental studies, especially history and philology, and among the other subjects to which he contributed were logic, economics, politics, Roman history, nutrition and women's rights. Newman was undoubtedly eccentric and described himself as 'anti-everything', including meat-eating, vivisection, and vaccination, and believed that the perfection of the soul lay in 'becoming woman'. He believed strongly in a woman's right to vote, to educate herself, and to ride astride on a horse. He was praised by both Thomas Carlyle and George Eliot, who called him 'our blessed St Francis'. He formally became a Unitarian in 1876 long after Boole's death, but perhaps significantly, though he espoused all his life a sort of 'rational-mystical agnosticism', before his death in 1897 he returned to the Church of England.

It appears that Boole was attracted to Newman by his religious writing, especially *Theism, Doctrinal and Practical*,[736] which detailed his transition from Calvinism to 'pure theism'. Boole wrote to Newman admiring his writings and expressing the hope that they might correspond and become acquainted. Newman was flattered but appears to have mistaken Boole's overtures as praise for his mathematical writing, which was not of a very high standard. Newman requested copies of Boole's papers on integrals and integration and told him that he had read his 'great paper' of 1844 but did not have a copy. He added that he had read his 'beautiful and profound theorems with great delight', but one suspects that he did not really understand them.[737]

Boole sent Newman a copy of his paper on simultaneous differential equations, which was probably completely over Newman's head;[738] indeed, he told Boole in a letter on 17 January 1863 that he could understand it only by giving definite numerical values to the variables.[739] And when Boole sent him one of his papers on probability, he informed him that he had never gone beyond Wood's *Algebra* in that subject.[740] He tells Boole that 'pure mathematics were my juvenile delight, and if I had concentrated my mind on them, I might have perhaps excelled'. But his overpressing circumstances and his numerous other tastes had distracted him. He had long since concluded that his function in life was to interpret and explain the discoveries of others and be a mediator in many things, but foremost in none – an honest self-assessment.[741]

The misunderstanding continued – Newman sent Boole a copy of his Latin translation of *Hiawatha* and apologised for an advertisement for his book *On the Difficulties of Geometry* which appeared on the back cover.[742] Having now diverted the conversation into archaeology and the people of Iguvium, Newman proposed to send Boole some of the manuscripts of books he had written on mathematics. One was on elliptic functions which he had laid before the Royal Society, the only result of which was that it was not returned and he had to rewrite it![743] There is no record that the two men ever corresponded about theological matters, probably because of Boole's embarrassment on the topic.

But Boole was quite serious about maintaining contact with Newman on religious and philosophical matters. His wife wrote:

> There was only one person in England whom he thoroughly liked the idea of becoming personally acquainted with – Professor Francis Newman. He did not exactly agree with all that Mr Newman said, but he had intense sympathy with his way of feeling and seemed to think that it would be possible to come to an understanding with him; only with his usual modesty he doubted whether Mr Newman might care to know

him. I succeeded in overcoming this difficulty and he wrote to propose an interview. The letter received, as I expected, a most cordial reply. On his next visit to England he called on Mr Newman, who afterwards spoke of the interview, in a letter to me, as 'a vision which had been shown' to him.[744]

On 30 November 1864, just over a week before Boole's death, Newman wrote to Mary Boole from London:

I am truly sorry to hear of your husband's illness, which I trust is only temporary. I beg him not to have the slightest care to answer my question which I have asked. As far as practical service to myself is concerned, six months is as good as to-day.[745]

On 21 March 1865 Newman again wrote to Boole, not realising that he had been dead for over three months, but at long last he had seen the point of Boole's overtures to him. But perhaps his confusion was understandable – he had received an offer of acquaintanceship from a famous mathematician, and as he dabbled in mathematics himself, he naturally assumed that the offer was made on mathematical grounds. Newman writes:

My dear Sir,

I have sometimes said to myself that you have an unfair advantage over me. I know nothing of you except as a mathematician, which shows certain peculiar powers, and no more. You probably know something of my mind on other topics. I want to know more of you beyond the fact that you have kindly sought my acquaintance. Have you ever written anything on any of the questions, philanthropic, social, political, religious, which call out men's deeper sympathies? I now take the liberty of sending you an address which I recently made at Margate, directly on the drink traffic,[746] indirectly on organic reform.

I hope you are quite re-established since the illness of which I was sorry to learn from the pen of Mrs Boole.[747]

Boole is now posthumously paying the price of never having committed his deeper feelings, particularly those on religious matters, to paper. Newman is, quite rightly, prepared to judge him on what he has or has not written on the subject. Had Boole lived, it would have been interesting to see how many of his opinions, especially social, philosophical and religious, he would have divulged to Newman.

When Mary Boole wrote to tell him the sad news, Newman was of course apologetic, but not overly so. He pleaded that since he had left University College he was isolated and heard very little news, especially about men of science. But he was genuinely sorry to hear about Boole's death and waxed eloquent about his good personal qualities:

Your late husband's loss must be felt by mathematicians in all Europe. I felt it an honour that he sought my acquaintance and I wondered within my heart whether I should ever call him my friend. His gentle, refined and intelligent manners were very endearing; and I am quite touched to think that such a vision was shown to me for a moment and as suddenly taken away. I felt, upon meditation over the case, that no friendship can ever be formed on a mere knowledge of a man's abstract powers, and that I was profoundly ignorant what were Professor Boole's judgements on any of the questions which move human hearts, display sentiment, or attract abiding intimacy; and I did not know how to initiate a word on any subject without danger of obtruding something from which a sensitive nature might strongly dissent, yet shrink to express its disagreement. This it was which at last prompted the letter received by you in so untimely a moment. It will give me a sad pleasure to receive the 'short lecture' which you announce. I certainly had not the least idea that your husband, when I saw him, was not in perfect health. I should have said he appeared delicate – not even weakly.

Believe me, I have a deep sense of the depth of your loss.

I am, Yours with respectful sympathy,
Francis W. Newman.[748]

Chapter 12

EPILOGUE: THE DEATH OF GEORGE BOOLE

The very pertinacity with which error retains its hold is one of the strongest arguments for the final and eternal establishment of truth.

George Boole, Newton Lecture, 1835[749]

THE WIKIPEDIA ARTICLE on George Boole gives the following details of his death:

> In late November 1864, Boole walked, in heavy rain, from his home at 'Lichfield Cottage' in Ballintemple to the university, a distance of three miles, and lectured wearing his wet clothes. He soon became ill, developing a severe cold and high fever. As his wife believed that remedies should resemble their cause, she put her husband to bed and poured buckets of water over him – the wet having brought on his illness. Boole's condition worsened and on 8 December 1864, he died of fever-induced pleural effusion.[750]

Sadly, this story has gone viral over the years. *The Freeman's Journal*, an Irish national newspaper based in Dublin, included on Monday, 12 December 1864 a lengthy and very complimentary obituary notice taken from *The Cork Reporter*. This referred to the cold-water treatment also:

> His illness was only of a few days' duration and at first appeared to be a mild fever. He was immediately attended by Dr Barter. The cold-water treatment pursued is thought to have brought on pleuropneumonia. When the symptoms became alarming, Dr Bullen, senior, was called in, but it was too late.[751]

Dr Denis Bullen was a surgeon at the North Infirmary Hospital in Cork and was appointed the first professor of surgery in Queen's College Cork in 1849. Boole and Bullen were friends, and Boole spent Christmas with the Bullens in 1850 (see Chapter Three). While Boole's final illness was brief, he had been extremely unwell earlier that year, and this must have diminished his ability to fight the illness brought on by the unfortunate drenching in November.

The myth of the buckets of water was also contained in a letter from Boole's youngest daughter Ethel Voynich to her nephew, Sir Geoffrey Taylor. This letter was written in 1954 when she was ninety. However, as Ethel was less than a year old at the time of her father's death, her recollections are vague and based on hearsay. She wrote:

Now about his only sister, Aunt Mary Anne, who also never married. She was for many years resident governess to the children of Fitzgerald, the Anglican Bishop of Cork (Killaloe) or Dublin, I forget which. I remember meeting her on two occasions and receiving a vague impression of constraint, which may have been due to the bitter rivalry between her and 'the missus' [Mary Everest Boole]. My sister Mary Hinton, who had a friendship with her, and who collected from her various anecdotes about the family, told me that in Aunt Anne's [MaryAnn's] view at least, the cause of father's early death was believed to have been the missus' belief in a certain crank doctor who advocated cold water cures for everything. Someone – I cannot remember who – is reported to have come in and found father 'shivering between wet sheets'.

Now for myself, I am inclined to believe that this may have happened. The Everests do seem to have been a family of cranks and followers of cranks. The Missus's father apparently adored Mesmer[752] and Hahnemann[753] and the Missus herself ran theories to death (James Hinton,[754] Rabbi Marks[755]); also, I remember that she ran theories to death during our childhood. But I do not believe that there is any use in reopening these vague stories now. Of course, no one wanted him to die. He just died.[756]

The 'crank doctor' referred to by Ethel Voynich was probably Dr Richard Barter, the founder of St Ann's Hydropathy Establishment in Blarney. After his arrival in Cork, MaryAnn's health had been a cause of concern to Boole. In April 1851 he suggested she come to Cork to spend time under the care of a hydropathist. He wrote:

All goes on very smoothly and pleasantly here. Shall you get over in the spring? If you could, I should I think put you under the care of Dr Barter, a hydropathist at Blarney of the more moderate and judicious sort who has done a great good to many people especially to delicate females. The situation is very delightful indeed and the terms are moderate.[757]

Richard Barter founded St Ann's in 1844 and it was the first hydropathic establishment of its kind in Ireland. In 1828, Barter graduated with distinction from the Royal College of Physicians in London, and moving back to Ireland, he took an appointment as a dispensary doctor in the rural village of Inniscarra, near Cork. He appears to have been successful and

well-liked by his patients. He became interested in agriculture and self-suffi-
ciency and founded the Agricultural Society of County Cork. His son, also
named Richard, was later knighted for his services to agriculture.

Barter had become interested in the curative power of water during the
cholera epidemic in England in 1832. Hydropathy, now known as hydro-
therapy, involves the use of water for pain relief and therapy. Hydropathy
had been used in the ancient civilisations of Greece and Rome but enjoyed
a fashionable revival in the late eighteenth century in England and Germany.
In 1797 Dr James Currie of Liverpool published a highly popular book on
the use of hot and cold water in the treatment of fever and illness.[758] In
1829, Vincent Priessnitz popularised new methods of therapeutic treatment
in Germany. Priessnitz forbade the use of drugs, urged exercise, provided the
coarsest of food and prescribed huge quantities of cold water internally and
externally.[759] Priessnitz and his followers used wet and dry pack methods of
treatment, a practice of wrapping patients in wet or dry blankets or sheets,
depending on the condition being treated. Patients were also given cold water douches – high-pressure showers of water.

In 1841 Captain R.T. Claridge, an English asphalt contractor and
captain in the Middlesex militia, travelled to Priessnitz's establishment in
Graefenberg in Germany with his wife and daughter and spent three months
there. He was highly impressed by the treatment he and his daughter
received and by the large number of illustrious patients under Priessnitz's
care, which included an archduchess, princes and princesses, military men of
all ranks, professors, doctors and lawyers.[760] Claridge published his account
of the treatment in a book in 1841 which ran to a third edition in 1842. He
conducted a series of lecture tours in England, Ireland and Scotland in 1842
and 1843. His lecture in Cork in 1842 was attended by Richard Barter.

Barter travelled to Malvern and Ben Rhydding in England to witness the
practical application of processes of hydropathy that he had heard about.
In 1843 he opened St Ann's Hydropathic Establishment in Blarney which
became an almost immediate success, despite the opposition of the medical
profession in Ireland.[761] In 1850 David Urquhart published a book called
The Pillars of Hercules which influenced Barter.[762] Urquhart was an MP
and Scottish diplomat who had been secretary of the British Embassy in
Constantinople in 1835. He advocated the use of Turkish baths in his book.
Barter invited Urquhart to Blarney where he supervised the construction of
a Turkish bath at St Ann's. The establishment in Blarney became immensely
popular and grew to an incredible size, becoming one of the largest in the
world.

Figure 12.1: Interior view of the Turkish baths at St Ann's, Blarney, County Cork

In January 1852 MaryAnn was in Blarney for treatment by Dr Barter at St Ann's. Boole teased her about the consequences of the water treatment:

> I was truly sorry not to be able to visit you yesterday, but I hope to do so shortly. Console yourself with thinking that the longer the delay, the greater the astonishment I shall experience at the change in your looks. Perhaps you will get some new appendages between the fingers and the toes similar to those which are said to characterise some of the inhabitants of our native country …
>
> I want to hear the net increase in weight manifested by Saturday's weighing. Mind that due abstraction is made of the weight of water imbibed and absorbed during the day as that cannot be called flesh and blood – also of the diurnal belts, umschlags [wrappings], packing sheets and of the water they contain; also of any swimming apparatus which it may be thought necessary to carry about with you in case of drowning emergencies, etc. etc. etc.

Notwithstanding all this I mean to become a Triton among the Naiads myself before long; in other words I mean to join the other amiable enthusiasts who appear to be so happy in their delusion and their soft Blarney. But this weak fit of resolve will not last if you do not realise all your grand promises of health and amendment.[763]

Boole's reference to the practice of wrapping patients in wet sheets is noteworthy, as it proves that his knowledge and interest in hydropathy predates his marriage to Mary Everest in 1855. In another letter to Mary-Ann during her stay in Blarney, Boole teased her about becoming carried away with the treatment and reminded her that other methods of caring for patients were not without merit, such as those practised by his landlady, Mrs Unkles:

I am delighted to think of your prospect of renewed health …

I suppose that the very treatment will become agreeable to you and that you will look for the daily excitements of the douche and the plunge and the wet sheet and the packing in ice, just as the epicure does for his glass or the smoker of opium does for his pipe …

Depend upon it that although we don't know here all the mysteries of hot cold moist and dry so well as you do at Blarney, we are not altogether ignorant of the science of nursing sick people and making them comfortable. So you are not in your extravagant admiration of Dr Barter to forget the merits of Mrs Unkles. You are not to be infected with the watery notion that hydropathy is the sum total of human science and the wet sheet the only mantle of virtue and heroism.[764]

It is not clear from the correspondence how long MaryAnn stayed in Blarney, but she was back in Lincoln by May 1852. Boole continued to visit Blarney, telling MaryAnn about meeting some of her old friends there on a day trip he made in April 1853. During the visit, he had a vapour bath with cold plunge and douche and felt 'all the better for it'.[765] In November 1853 Boole mentions meeting Mrs Barter in Blarney who inquired after MaryAnn.[766] St Ann's was very busy and Boole told MaryAnn that Dr Barter was obliged to refuse admission to patients.[767] The final available reference to St Ann's appears in a letter to MaryAnn in January 1854:

Figure 12.2: St Ann's Hydropathic Establishment, Blarney, County Cork

I have not been to Blarney since the commencement of the session but I hear that it is quite full of people. If you don't get well we must have you there again. But I hope that you will without any such expensive means.[768]

In March 1861 Mary Boole attended Dr Barter, whom Boole had described to William Brooke as 'our famous hydropathic and Turkish bath physician to whom MaryAnn owes the restoration of her health'.[769] In July 1864 Boole had been very unwell on a trip to England. He told Brooke that after the bout of illness he felt he had aged ten years when he looked in the mirror (see Chapter Eight).[770] Furthermore, he told Brooke one week later that if his influenza persisted, he had decided to visit the Turkish baths in Blarney.[771]

Hence it appears that the belief in Dr Barter and his treatment methods may have been incorrectly and unfairly attributed to the 'missus' and originated from Boole himself and indeed from MaryAnn also. Mary Boole commented some years later:

He [George] was very much attached to the work of the late Dr Barter, who had spent thirty years in the study of non-medicinal therapeutic agents.[772]

Dr Barter passed into the family folklore as the 'quack doctor' and perhaps the villain of the piece, instructing Mary to pour buckets of cold water over her unfortunate husband. Dr Barter himself passed away a few years later in 1870, but the establishment continued to be run by his family. Its popularity was at a peak in the period 1880–1920. The centre closed in 1952. Finally, it is possible that homeopathy has been maligned in this story too. Dr Barter practised hydropathy or water cure but there is no evidence that he practised homeopathy, though it is of course possible that he did so also.

We are fortunate that there is an independent eye-witness account of Boole's illness and death. It was written by Annie Gibson, who lived at 'Northcliffe', Blackrock, Cork, and was a neighbour and friend of the Booles'. 'Northcliffe' was, and still is, a beautiful large house on the Marina in Blackrock, less than one mile from the Booles' home at 'Lichfield Cottage'. Annie refers to getting her parents' consent to stay to assist Mary Boole, so we can assume she was a young woman at the time. *Henry & Coughlan's General Directory of Cork for 1867* [773] lists William E. Gibson at 'Northcliffe'. *Guy's Almanac* [774] of 1875–6 includes Gibson as an export merchant and a member of the subcommittee of the Cork Butter Exchange. In her article 'Home Side of a Scientific Mind', written after her husband's death, Mary Boole refers to one of her 'most intimate friends – a girl who spent many an evening with us in reading poetry or looking at the telescope'. [775] This girl may have been Annie Gibson.

It is clear that MaryAnn Boole was suspicious of the circumstances of George's death and, knowing that Annie Gibson had been in attendance during his last days, wrote asking her for a detailed account of what had happened. This is Annie's reply, dated 22 January 1865:

My dear Miss Boole,

I send you a few particulars of Doctor Boole's illness, according to your request. On Tuesday, the 22nd of November, I spent the evening with Mrs Boole. Dr Boole had walked to town that day to inquire for Dr Blyth who was ill – he seemed tired and was suffering from a bad cough. He lay back in an easy chair a great part of the evening. He spoke of a meeting of the shareholders of the 'local gas company'. Some of the shareholders proposed to divide amongst themselves 10 instead of 8 percent, although they had pledged themselves never to take more than eight. Dr Boole had attended this meeting to enter his protest as one of the shareholders, against this proposed breach of faith. He read several poems for us from a manuscript book of extracts, amongst which was a beautiful sonnet by Blanco White, [776] in which he speaks of the glories which the day conceals, and night reveals and proceeds to say that if the light conceals such glories, which night reveals, what may not life hide, which death will manifest? Dr Boole read it over twice with the greatest apparent pleasure. I tell you these little details because I never saw him again – the poem impressed me very much at the time and now I look on it as his farewell legacy to me; I wish I could get an exact copy of it – if you meet it will you kindly allow me to see it?

Next Friday afternoon, the Doctor was out, but Mrs Boole told me he suffered from cold and cough. On Sunday evening we heard that he was very ill and the servant whom we sent to inquire brought word that he was in his bed and attended by Dr Barter.

On Monday, Mrs Boole told me that Dr Barter had pronounced his illness to be low fever and had said that if he had been using stimulants or high living previously, it would most likely have assumed the character of typhus fever.

On Thursday, it was decided that he would require all the attention of Mrs B. and a faithful servant Hannah and Mrs Everest requested me to stay in the house to try and make Mrs Boole take care of herself as much as possible and to prevent the servants and children from troubling her; as Mrs E.[verest] could with difficulty leave her aged and infirm mother, Dr Boole's earnest wish that Mrs Ryall should not be neglected, decided me on acceding (with my parents' consent) to a request which I little thought would offer the last opportunity I should have of gratifying him. Mrs E. spent part of each day with him until Friday. Dr Barter said the illness should run its course but that there were no unfavourable symptoms. The cough continued very troublesome.

Saturday. Mrs B. did not think him so well and when the doctor came, he looked very grave. Mrs Everest followed him to the door, he said the illness was a serious one and it must run its course. Mrs B. shrank from hearing his opinion but received minute directions as to treatment, and feeling that if she continued to take entire charge of him, her strength would fail before her task was done, she procured the assistance of an able nurse tender, to whom he now made no objection. He was never delirious, but his mind wandered occasionally and lost count of time. He repeatedly asked Mrs B. to 'set him right'. At last she said, 'You must not trouble yourself now dear, think of what I will tell you, viz. Jesus Christ, the same yesterday, and today, and forever.' These blessed words seemed to act on him as a charm, to soothe him to rest and to stay the wandering of his mind. He grew worse as the evening advanced and during the night the crisis seemed to come on, as well as I can judge from what I heard, the fever left him that night, but the oppression increased, and he complained of a pain in his side.

Mrs B., overwhelmed with terror and anxiety, sent at 5 o'clock in the morning for Dr B[arter], and at 7, at the expressed wish of Dr Boole, for Dr Bullen. Dr Bullen ordered mustard blister to relieve his chest and side and substituted chicken broth for the beef tea which he had been getting since Thursday. Shortly after, Dr Barter arrived, and paid his visit. On his return home, he wrote to Dr Ryall, saying as Dr Bullen was in attendance, and it would be useless for two doctors who would not consult together to attend the same patient, and as Dr Boole no longer required active treatment, he would withdraw. Mrs Boole heard this on Monday morning. Dr Bullen continued in attendance, ordered light nourishment and turpentine stripes to relieve the pain and oppression which came on in paroxysms, with long intervals of ease. During the entire illness he seems to have suffered very little pain. He repeatedly said that he had never been so happy in his life, and that his mind had never been so clear, especially on religious subjects, as it was during some periods of his illness. He asked to see his little baby [Ethel] and was much gratified by a few flowers sent him by a friend; he also asked to see Miss Bullen, but was thought too weak. A second nurse was procured in order that while one rested the other should remain with Mrs B. to assist her. Mrs B. very seldom left the room by night or day.

On Wednesday night Mrs Boole left the room about 12 o'clock to try to get a little sleep; about half past one Mrs Harvey (the nurse) saw a great change take place. She went to call Mrs Boole at once, telling her, in order not to alarm her, that Dr B. had asked for her; she went down to his room immediately. They gave him something with whiskey to moisten his lips every ten minutes, but from that time Mrs Harvey gave up all hope.

Up to this time Dr Boole did not appear to think that there was the least chance of the illness proving fatal. Even (Thursday) this morning he spoke of the future as if he expected to have many years here below in which to do his master's will and work. At breakfast Mrs Boole seemed struggling between anxiety and hope. She had sent for Dr Bullen, who arrived early and, after seeing Dr B., came down looking very anxious. Mrs B. had wished to telegraph for the best London doctor; Dr Bullen said it would be useless, as all must be decided before the doctor could reach Cork. He dreaded suffusion on the chest, ordered a blister to be applied and

Figure 12.3: Plaque at St Michael's Church of Ireland, Blackrock, Cork

said its effect would in a few hours decide if he would be spared to us or not. He called again about one o'clock. Dr Boole was then quite aware of his state and told Dr B. he could now do nothing for him. Mrs E[verest], Miss Bullen and I were downstairs and he sent down a request that we would pray for him. Miss B. opened the Bible and read aloud several petitions from the Psalms, and as we rose from our knees pointed out to me the first verses of the 14th of John. The dear doctor's strength failed fast, he was passing away in great peace. The misses said they saw many deathbeds, but they never saw such as his, such perfect peace, they said, 'Heaven came down to receive him.' He was perfectly conscious until about three o'clock, and about five o'clock on Thursday December 8th, he passed away.

'Mask the perfect man, and behold the upright, the end of that man is peace.'

I have taken great pains to be accurate in every particular; still, my dear Miss Boole, you will please to remember that I was never in the sick room and therefore dependent on the report of others, also that it is now some time since the said events took place and that perhaps I do not remember everything in exactly the right order.

Fever was very prevalent when the doctor was ill and indeed is so still. Shortly after he took ill he sent money to the dispensary doctor asking him to give it to those who most wanted it amongst his poor patients who were ill of fever.

Believe me to remain dear Miss Boole,

Yours sincerely,
Annie Gibson.[777]

Even in his last days, Boole's generosity to those less fortunate than himself is notable.

Boole was unfortunate to have been caught in a rainstorm at a time when his health was already compromised and that he and his wife adhered to unorthodox medical theories in which they sincerely believed. There is no suggestion of malice or neglect by his wife, family, doctors or carers. The death of George Boole at the age of forty-nine was deeply tragic and a great loss not only to his young family and community but also to science and mathematics. Who knows what he might have achieved if he had been spared to live out the biblically allotted three score years and ten, and how different the fortunes of his wife and five daughters would have been.

Chapter 13

BOOLEANA

N THIS CHAPTER, which could be considered a Boolean miscellany, we have collected information on various aspects of Boole's life, character and activities, ranging from poetry, science, life in Lincoln and Cork, to personal matters and memorials.

POETRY

William Allingham and George Boole

Many people in Ireland know by heart the lines of the poem *The Fairies*. It begins:

> Up the airy mountain,
> Down the rushy glen,
> We daren't go a-hunting
> For fear of little men;
> Wee folk, good folk,
> Trooping all together;
> Green jacket, red cap
> And white owl's feather![778]

These lovely lines, which are frequently quoted in modern films and stories, were written by the Irish poet William Allingham who was born in County Donegal in 1824 and died in London in 1889. He was a friend of Alfred Tennyson and Thomas Carlyle and many other poets and writers. After leaving school he did not attend university but obtained a post as a customs officer in his native town of Ballyshannon. In 1874 he resigned this job and moved to London where he became editor of *Fraser's Magazine*, a position he held until 1879. During his lifetime, he published several collections of his poems, which had a strong influence on the development of W.B. Yeats.

Allingham knew George Boole, who admired his poetry. Allingham wrote to Boole while he was professor of mathematics at Queen's College Cork asking him if it would be wise for him to go to Cork and go through a regular course of study to enhance his poetic work.[779] Boole advised him not to do so because he believed that a university education would not further the development of his poetic talents. Perhaps he was echoing his own experience.

A Boolean Poem

George 'Daw' Harding is an Irish poet who lives in Blackrock, Cork, close to where George Boole lived. He has published two collections of poetry, *My Stolen City*[780] and *Last Bus to Pewterhole Cross*.[781] This poem, taken from *My Stolen City*, describes the fatal walk Boole took in November 1864 from his residence at 'Lichfield Cottage', Ballintemple to Queen's College Cork in the pouring rain, after which he became seriously ill. He died a few weeks later. The poem contains many references to Boole's life, work and family.

Leaving Lichfield

After leaving Lichfield
his drowning tool became his overcoat.
Immersed in his convolutions
he trekked through Ballintemple
oblivious to the rain hanging heavy
on his shoulders.

On down Dead Woman's Hill
his pocket watch testing durability
he took shelter in the 'Tall Mast'
on the Quay. There inspecting
some solutions of his quandaries
he meditated.

The simplicity of rain
undid his Everest. Mist upon mist
obliterating all resistance.
Base camp will suffice
for gadflies and romance
to glory in.

Dark ages sidled
up through the grey quays.
The language lost in dog-
eared notebooks, but
eventually relayed from tall masts
beyond the moon.

Figure 13.1: Mary Ellen Boole Hinton (c.1900)

Mary Ellen Hinton's Poetry

Mary Ellen Boole Hinton (1856–1908) was the eldest daughter of George and Mary Everest Boole. Her public profile was perhaps less extensive than her four better-known sisters, but she was a published poet. We are indebted to John Fitzgerald, librarian of the Boole Library, University College Cork, himself a prize-winning poet, for the following critique of Mary Ellen Boole Hinton's poetry.

Mary Boole Hinton's *Other Notes* was one of two books of poetry published in 1901 by the Washington DC-based Neale Publishing Company. Four of the volume's forty-two poems had already appeared in print, including one each in *The Atlantic* and *Harper's Magazine*, two highly reputable titles with national circulation and a reputation for selecting excellent new unpublished poetry. In submitting her work to these publications, Hinton was clearly ambitious for wider readership of poetry which was judged by these editors as of exceptional quality by the standards of the day.

Intensely private as a person, Hinton the poet became a more public figure after the publication of *Other Notes*. Its appearance in public must have been of immense personal significance to its author: the title is a reference to one of the book's principal themes, music; and, despite the early challenges to their relationship posed by his notorious bigamy, it is dedicated simply 'To My Husband'. Music features in some guise on almost every page, either explicitly or by allusion. There is an abiding almost mystical sense of music as a superior form of expression, as representing a state of apprehension and knowing that transcends the cares and demands of the everyday material and emotional worlds; and that the poet and the poetry are both striving and aspiring towards this state. The tone is set by the dramatic opening poem 'The Quest After Music' which enacts in swift heroic couplets a dramatic valourisation of music personified as the only true calling in life.

> A voice, a voice is calling through the night.
> Some being calls! Our fathers judged aright
> Who peopled sound of wave and song of wind
> with multitudinous things of spirit kind.
> Some being calls! Some being hides within
> The magic tuning of the violin,
> The glad rejoicing of the golden horn,
> The hautbois mournful as a ghost forlorn,
> The cymbal's sweep that mocks a wild typhoon,
> The gentle flute, the harp, deep bassoon.[782]

Other overtly musical poems include 'Too Close to Music', 'Life and Song', 'Cadence Song', 'Out of Tune', 'Nature's Notes' with its song-like repetition, 'Song on the Petrarchan', 'Credo', and many others. It is interesting to note that all three of the explanatory notes at the end of the book relate to musical topics.

Religion also asserts a presence in the book. While the poet resists admirably her father's well-known tendency for resolution in the all-embracing solace of God, neither is she anywhere dismissive of the Christian faith, which she often celebrates without complication, as in 'Any Daughter to Any Mother':

Mother, in thine a mother's hand
Is clasped to-day across the years.
In the great hand of God we stand,
And smile through tears.

There are instances of the firm grip of reason too, which seems to reprimand the fanciful tendencies elsewhere in the book, as in the single-verse 'Emotion' ...

Emotion is a vice like drink.
Take heed you do not feel.
Jerk off high dreaming in a twink,
If through the soul it steal.
Some erring temper-gust, forthright
Proves you a hypocrite.

... which performs admirably in dialogue with another eight-line poem entitled 'Thought':

Cold crystal! thee I touch.
Thou needst not flinch, close-pressed.
In thee the hurrying passions rest,
That clamoured overmuch.

Other Notes includes a number of short and intensely thoughtful lyrical poems such as 'Idolatry', 'Midsummer' and 'The Seer'. These tend to be the best poems in the volume as they are the least constrained by form and yet achieve admirable concision while managing still to remain always slightly opaque in some way, demonstrating that Hinton was not afraid of obscurity as she wrote from the cusp of late Romanticism and Modernism. These poems sound a curious echo of Emily Dickinson whom it is possible that Hinton could have read, albeit in a form which would have been edited to the style of the time. At least three of Dickinson's volumes had been published and extensively reprinted up to 1896. Hinton's poem 'After Death', which is based on the *Zend Avesta*, is a curious but engaging prayer to poetry. Her other poems about death are restrained and analytical, such as 'Requiescat' with its vivid images of recent death, and 'Body and Spirit' which memorialises human creativity and spirit. These are as memorable as the lyrics and demonstrate a high level of creative competence by any standard.

The collection numbers many poems inspired by love, both parental and romantic, such as 'Any Daughter to Any Mother' and the enigmatic 'Love Song' which the reader may be tempted to treat as autobiographical if read as addressed to her husband:

> Hath anyone taken the bloom off
> Thy love from me?
> Is it entire and single
> On thy life's tree?
> No one has taken the bloom off
> My love for thee.
> It is as God first grew it
> On my life's tree.
> One little bud he set there,
> Green veiled from sight.
> Followed a pure white blossom,
> Thy heart's delight.
> Soon the red fruit must ripen
> In summer sun.
> May the bloom blush on forever
> Till life is done.

A sense of the unrequited, unresolved is evoked by the final two quatrains and lingers without being clarified.

Other Notes is the work of a poet who takes herself and her craft seriously and who is alive to her literary inheritance as well as the spirit of the times. Poems such as 'The Pearl Diver' and 'Revery' show a strong romantic influence with clear references to the established writers of the past, her 'deeper solitude' invoking Wordsworth in particular, whose presence hovers over some of the poems. So too, the love poem 'Elizabethan Lyric' is a carefully assembled graceful and poignant derivation of the age of its title.

The natural world is present throughout the book as a palate for the imagery with the botanical particularly prevalent. Little is known about when Hinton started to write poetry – she makes no mention in her personal letters – but it is possible that this book was written and assembled in Japan where she lived with her husband and children before settling in North America. Her letters from Japan and a journal from that period contain much admiring description of plants and the flora of that part of the world. These accounts also provide the setting for the whimsical poem 'In Far Japan'.

The writing in *Other Notes* is mature and informed and is not afraid to reflect upon itself. 'Sons of the Morning', 'The Little Poet', 'Prelude', and 'Review' all consider the art of poetry in one way or another. The ekphrastic poem 'The Hermit', is an effective reflection on the nature of representative art.

There is a general sense of the poetry in *Other Notes* as coming from a very private person: a wife, mother, thinker and observer of the world pressing language to express her own personal experiences and beliefs. Such as the public acclaim for the book may have been, this, and her achievements and practice as a poet apparently were not enough to sustain Hinton through the difficult times that followed the death of her husband from a sudden cerebral haemorrhage in 1907. *The Washington Post* report of his death mentioned his wife as being '… prostrated at the news and … placed under the care of a physician'. Mary Ellen Hinton went into decline after her husband's death and one year later, despite a brief respite of her interest in life and in reviving the work of her husband, tragically she would take her own life, dying of asphyxiation in May 1908. A brief report in *The New York Times* described her as 'a frequent contributor to English and American magazines' and noted that she had recently commented that 'life is something we have the privilege of ending when we choose. When I think it is time to die, I shall end it all.'[783]

SCIENCE AND SCIENTISTS

Hamilton and Boole

It is surprising that two of the greatest mathematicians who ever lived and worked in Ireland, Sir William Rowan Hamilton (1805–65) at Trinity College Dublin and George Boole (1815–1864) at Queen's College Cork, had very little contact with each other, despite the fact that they were contemporaries and were both effectively working in abstract algebra and experimenting with algebraic axioms.[784] Hamilton was dropping the commutative law $xy = yx$, while Boole was adding the idempotent law $x^2 = x$. Of course, since it was very early in the development of this area of mathematics, neither of them seemed to be aware of the true nature of what they were doing. Hamilton thought he was unlocking the door to the physical universe, while Boole thought he was revealing the workings of the human mind.

There were many differences between the two men – social, educational, financial, religious and national – and one must also include the traditional antipathies between Trinity College and the Queen's Colleges and indeed the rivalry between the capital Dublin and the second city Cork. But a short single publication of Boole's which appeared in the *Philosophical Magazine* in 1848, 'Notes on Quaternions',[785] may have been an additional crucial factor in the situation.

Having put complex numbers on a firm mathematical foundation, Hamilton went on to invent a new mathematical system which he called quaternions in 1843 (on 16 October to be precise), though others – Euler in number theory and Rodrigues in mechanics – had given concrete examples of the phenomenon previously. Hamilton's was however the first abstract treatment of the subject on which he presented a lecture to the Royal Irish Academy in Dublin on 13 November 1843. He went on to develop the theory and its applications in a series of published papers in the period 1844 to 1850 and he published his massive tome – *Lectures on Quaternions* (736 pages!) in 1853.[786]

From reading Hamilton's papers on quaternions in the *Philosophical Magazine*, by 1848 Boole had clearly acquainted himself with the definition and basic properties of quaternions, not as a central interest in mathematics, but probably as an interesting curiosity. His interest may have stemmed from the fact that he had recently published both a book and a paper on symbolic logic.[787] Even at this early stage he showed a remarkable grasp of the nature of quaternions and their properties. What Boole pointed out in his paper of 1848, among other things, was that Hamilton's treatment of quaternions contained some redundancies. These were not mistakes, of course, but Boole proved that Hamilton could have achieved the same results by assuming less, i.e. fewer hypotheses.

We will discuss in a moment exactly what Boole established, but we can at least speculate what Hamilton's reaction was to this paper and its results. Was he annoyed because he regarded quaternions as his own almost exclusive area and that Boole was improving on his results? Did he resent the fact that Boole was self-educated, socially inferior, of working-class origins, a foreigner in Ireland, of a different religious persuasion, living in Cork, and yet telling him, the inventor and master of quaternions, what was what? Hamilton was a difficult and sensitive person, and it is possible that he regarded Boole's paper as a personal affront and maybe even the last straw in an already difficult situation. Perhaps Hamilton was a little jealous of Boole, who had achieved so much with so little help. Hamilton was not used to sharing the limelight with others and may have felt that Boole had gone too far.

We now give a simplified version of what Boole established. His point at the time must have seemed rather trivial to both men, but neither was to know that it would grow into an important topic in the theory of groups, which is itself a major area of modern mathematics. Hamilton's original equations for quaternions, as famously scratched on Brougham Bridge, were

$$i^2 = j^2 = k^2 = ijk = -1$$

However, as Boole remarks, these were usually written as follows, to emphasise the non-commutative nature of the quaternion system:

$$i^2 = j^2 = k^2 = -1;$$

$$ij = k, jk = i, ki = j, ji = -k, kj = -i, ik = -j.$$

What Boole, ingeniously, pointed out was that the last three of these equations were consequences of the previous three and so were redundant. Interestingly, Boole regarded quaternions as operators, but the essence of what he did was as follows:

If $ij = k$, then $ijj = kj$

But $j^2 = -1$,

so $-i = kj$ and similarly for the other equations.

Boole thus appears to have been one of the first people to remove redundancies from a group presentation, and we may add this to his list of innovations in mathematics. Hamilton himself was one of the first people to attempt this process more formally – a little later, in 1856, in his study of icosian calculus, he gave a presentation of the icosahedral group A_5, the direct symmetry group of the regular Platonic solid the icosahedron, as follows:

$$< s, t \mid s^2, t^3, (st)^5 >.$$

In the meantime, in 1853, Arthur Cayley, a good friend of both Hamilton and Boole, had written the first paper on the abstract theory of groups. The general systematic theory of group presentations did not commence until around 1880, stemming from Walther von Dyck, a student of the great Felix Klein. We remark that modern group theorists have produced the following rather beautiful presentation for the quaternion group Q_8 with two generators i and j and two relations between them. This is called a presentation of deficiency zero (= 2 - 2) and can be shown to be minimal. It is

$$Q_8 = < i, j \mid iji = j; jij = i >.$$

No doubt the symmetry of these equations would have delighted both Hamilton and Boole.

The material we have quoted is based on the final paragraph of Boole's paper of 1848, and is perhaps something of an addendum. Earlier in the paper he had confidently commented on Cayley's remarks on quaternions being interpreted as rotations in space, and the conditions that such quaternions must satisfy. He cautions against the free application of quaternions to geometry (and maybe this too annoyed Hamilton) without a careful consideration of the principle 'that the laws of the sign shall constitute in every respect an exact counterpart of the laws of the thing signified'. Finally, he remarks, with supreme confidence:

> I believe that upon examination it will be found that these systems of interpretation are founded upon a principle of naming, as the one which I have proposed is founded upon a principle of operation. And I think it not foreign to the subject to remark, that the symbolical forms of common language exhibited in the calculus of logic may indifferently be referred to the one or other of these modes of conception.[788]

One can almost see and hear Sir William Rowan Hamilton snorting with indignation when he read this!

Surprisingly, Boole was lukewarm on the new algebras that were springing up all around him. He took a mild interest in De Morgan's algebra of triplets and certainly knew about the new structures being considered by John and Charles Graves and Cayley leading to octaves, but perhaps he felt they were just a passing phase. In a letter to Thomson, Lord Kelvin, dated 6 August 1845, Boole wrote:

> They will soon get through their quaternions and triplets, I should think. And, interesting as the subject is, I must confess that I should be glad to see them turning their attention to the integral and differential calculus and to physical science.[789]

This confirms the view that Boole was at heart an analyst, but it is ironic that his Boolean algebra has become one of the most important structures in modern mathematics.

Leviathan of Parsonstown

One of George Boole's earliest scientific activities was astronomy, which he enjoyed with his sister and brothers, inspired by their father. Their laboratory was the heavens and at night they observed the stars and the planets, comets and asteroids, little thinking that one day some of these celestial objects would bear their names. For better observation they needed telescopes and other instruments, and being short of money, they were forced to build their own astronomical equipment, which they did right down to grinding and polishing lenses. Young George was thus led to study the wonderful subject of optics, the geometry of light, and thence to mathematics itself. But John Boole and his family were always willing to share their discoveries with their friends and neighbours, and 'anyone who wishes to observe the works of God in a spirit of reverence' was invited to come and look through the Boole family telescope which they had built themselves.

The Booles were also what might be termed 'experimental astronomers' before their time. A Lincoln newspaper records:

The eclipse was observed with much advantage at Lincoln by a considerable number of persons, through the kindness of the Messrs. Boole, whose attainments in science are well known: a telescope was fixed in the window of Mr George Boole's school-room (which was darkened), and thus the sun's image was projected upon a screen allowing the progress of the obscuration to be watched with ease by several hundreds. The quantity of the eclipse was a full 11 digits, as appeared by reducing the sun's image to the dimensions of one foot in diameter, and measuring the breadth of the bright crescent, which was barely one inch in the broadest part. The diminution of light was not so great as was expected, probably owing to the great altitude of the sun, and the peculiar brightness of the day: the planet Venus was, however, distinctly visible near the meridian for a considerable time, and when viewed through a telescope appeared like the moon entering its second quarter.[790]

Boole continued his interest in astronomy when he came to live in Ireland. His offer to put on extra courses on astronomy for undergraduates was gratefully accepted by Queen's College Cork, and his wife Mary relates that he once invited the members of a 'temperance band' to look through his large telescope in the garden of their house in Blackrock.

The Irish nobleman William Parsons, the third Earl of Rosse, who lived at Birr Castle in County Offaly, decided in the early nineteenth century that he wanted to build the world's largest telescope. The astronomer William Herschel had not left behind any records of how to manufacture the huge mirrors required for the task, so Rosse had to start from scratch. Over a seventeen-year period he built progressively larger mirrors, ending with a 72-inch mirror, which he completed and placed in a telescope in 1845. The length of the telescope was about fifty-four feet; it weighed about twelve tons and it was supported by two fifty-foot walls. The local people of Parsonstown dubbed it 'Leviathan' after the fabled sea monster.

The telescope was a limited success. It could be moved up and down but its range from side to side was restricted. Its location was also problematic. The site was damp, windy and cloudy, and viewing conditions were difficult – even today it is estimated that a maximum of sixty nights' viewing per annum is possible. However, it led astronomers worldwide to consider the problem of the optimal location of telescopes, as well as the methods of their construction.

Figure 13.2: Messier 51 Whirlpool Galaxy

On the positive side, Rosse's telescope was for over seventy years the world's largest and since its restoration in 1999 it is arguably the world's largest historic scientific instrument still working today. The specific purpose of 'Leviathan' was to investigate the nebulae in the catalogues of Messier and Herschel. Parsons discovered that several nebulae had a spiral structure, suggesting their dynamical origins, and he observed the spiral nebula Messier 51, which he resolved into stars. Based on observations using 'Leviathan', Rosse produced a beautiful drawing of the Whirlpool Galaxy in 1845. In his work, Rosse was greatly helped by his wife Mary who was a talented photographer and whose pictures of the telescope were vitally important in its modern restoration. Their son Charles played an important part in the development of the steam turbine, which changed the face of shipping and led to the development of the jet engine.

Birr Castle now houses an excellent science centre built around a restored Leviathan and it is well worth a visit. Given that George Boole began his scientific career with astronomical observations and had arrived in Ireland in 1849, it was perhaps inevitable that he should visit 'Leviathan' at Parsonstown, now Birr. On a hunch, two researchers from UCC, Olivia Frawley and Michael Holland, visited Birr Castle in 2014 and through the kindness of the current Lord Rosse were allowed to examine the visitors' book. They found Boole's signature there; he signed himself 'George Boole FRS, Professor of Mathematics, Queen's College, Cork'. The exact date is not given, but since he signed himself FRS it was probably around August 1857. It is possible that Boole visited Parsonstown on his way back from Dublin where he had spoken on the theory of light at the annual meeting of the British Association for the Advancement of Science.

Figure 13.3: The restored Great Telescope at Birr Castle

On the same page that Boole's signature appears, one can see that a few days earlier another visitor had been in Birr. He signed himself Henry J.S. Smith, Balliol College, Oxford. He was a Dubliner, an eminent mathematician of the nineteenth century, a famous number theorist, though little remembered nowadays. In 1860 he became Savilian professor of mathematics at Oxford, a post for which Boole had allowed his name to go forward, but without submitting any credentials. Ships that pass in the night!

Herbert McLeod's Petition

Herbert McLeod (1841–1923) was an English chemist who worked at the Royal College of Chemistry until 1871 and then at the Royal Indian Engineering College until his retirement in 1901. He is famous for his invention of the McLeod vacuum gauge for the study of gases at low pressure. He also invented a sunshine recorder, consisting of a glass sphere by which the sun's light and heat are concentrated on prepared paper, whereby the duration of the sunshine is measured by the trail of charred paper. Both pieces of apparatus are still in use today. But McLeod had wider philosophical and religious interests. A devout Anglican, he was concerned that researches

Figure 13.4: Herbert McLeod

into scientific truth were, in the hands of some, casting doubt on the truth and authenticity of the Holy Scriptures, when he and many others felt there should be no conflict between them. He and a group of colleagues wrote a declaration expressing their concern in 1864 and circulated it as a petition. It gathered a substantial number of signatures and supporters – many of them from the Royal College. The petition ran as follows:

The Declaration of Students of the Natural and Physical Sciences

We, the undersigned students of the natural sciences, desire to express our sincere regret, that researches into scientific truths are perverted by some in our own time into occasion for casting doubt upon the truth and authenticity of the Holy Scriptures. We conceive that it is impossible for the Word of God as written in the book of nature and God's word written in Holy Scripture to contradict one another, however much they may appear to differ. We are not forgetful that physical science is not complete, but is only in a condition of progress and that at present our finite reason enables us only to see as through a glass darkly and we confidently believe that a time will come when the two records will be seen to agree. In particular, we cannot but deplore that natural science should be looked upon with suspicion by many who do not make a study of it mainly on account of the unadvised manner in which some are placing it in opposition to Holy Writ. We believe that it is the duty of every scientific student to investigate nature simply for the progress of elucidating truth and that if he finds that some of his results appear to be in contradiction to the Written Word, or rather his own interpretation of it, which may be erroneous, he should not presumptuously affirm that his own calculations must be right and the statement of Scripture wrong; rather, leave the two side by side till it shall please God to allow us to see the manner in which they may be reconciled, and, instead of insisting upon the seeming differences between science and Scripture, it would be as well to work in faith upon the points on which they agree.

Proposed by M. Gilman and H McLeod, Spring 1864.[791]

George Boole was one of those to whom the petition was sent, in expectation of his support. However, rather than let the matter die a natural death, which it eventually did, he reacted rather furiously and his reply, which fortunately survives, shows the extreme sensitivity of his views with regard to the connections between science and religion. We must also remember that McLeod was only twenty-three when he circulated the petition and that he might have been less impulsive in later life. Boole's reply was as follows:

Ballintemple near Cork,
July 21st 1864

Sir,

I have been prevented by absence from home and by occupation from replying sooner to the letter which you addressed to me on June 30th, accompanying a copy of a declaration to which you invited my signature, and to which you informed me that upwards of 150 names had already been attached.

I should be glad if I could allow myself to decline by silence this invitation, but in a written postscript you request an answer, and your letter is also of a kind which seems to require one. I feel it therefore to be my duty to state some of the reasons which forbid me to allow my name to be attached to the declaration.

1st. I believe the attempt to influence the course of opinion by the authority of names to be absolutely wrong.

2ndly. I regard the endeavour to force scientific men into party divisions separated by a sharp line of dogmatic opinion upon the subject of the declaration or upon any other subject as a species of treason to science. It is to ask them to abandon that ancient tradition of the fitness of argument alone for the support of truth, which they have received as a sacred heirloom, and which it devolves upon them to deliver unimpaired to their successors.

3rdly. Many 'students of the natural sciences' are so immersed in special pursuits, and many, probably, are so disqualified by want of general learning, that they are unable to pay any critical attention to the subject referred to in the declaration, and have perhaps never even formed a decided opinion upon it. It seems to me scarcely possible that such persons should be induced to take at once a party position on it, on either side without sustaining moral injury; even if the inducing motive be the purest regard to the interests of religion, according to their conception of those interests. But if other motives mix with or take the place of this, such as the desire of standing well with other men, of pleasing the great and powerful, of avoiding the reproaches of that large section of society which judges men chiefly by their professions, then the moral injury is deeper. And therefore, it seems to me that they who put men under the temptation to yield to such inducements, made perhaps stronger by the sense of a dependent position, do in fact tempt them to violate their inward sense of right and to displease God. I must add that I view with profound regret and surprise the fact that in a country in which discussion is perfectly free, men, scientific men, should combine to employ tests and declarations for the advancement of what they suppose to be truth.

History, while it shows how powerless such combinations have ever been to serve the objects which they were intended to promote, shows in its tremendous lessons how powerful they may become to sow the seeds of evil and unchristian passions.

I am, Sir, Your obedient servant, George Boole.

To Herbert McLeod Esquire.[792]

Boole's reply was rather extreme and constitutes one of the few times when he let his strong feelings overcome his reluctance to expose his views on religion. However, it is not difficult to pick holes in some of his arguments. For example, his first contention is that it is absolutely wrong to 'influence the course of opinion by the authority of names'. Perhaps he had forgotten the fine collection of references from some of the best mathematicians of the day that he submitted when applying for the professorship in Cork. His next point is that party divisions of scientists on religious or other grounds is a 'treason to science'. He claims they would be forced to abandon 'that ancient tradition of the fitness of argument alone for the support of truth, which they have received as a sacred heirloom, and which it devolves upon them to deliver unimpaired to their successors'. But what exactly are the unstated principles of the 'fitness of argument alone for the support of truth'? Presumably these are based on a set of axioms, accepted, but consisting of unproven and unprovable statements. Boole is accepting nineteenth-century rationalism, in the tradition of Descartes, Leibniz and Spinoza, as an absolute, while criticising McLeod for adopting a similar stance with respect to the Scriptures.

James Clerk Maxwell on George Boole

Figure 13.5: James Clerk Maxwell

The great applied mathematician and physicist James Clerk Maxwell was an admirer of George Boole. Boole's book of 1847, *The Mathematical Analysis of Logic*, where he attempted to give a mathematical expression to logical forms, had naturally strong attractions for Maxwell.

Some time after Boole's death, at a meeting of the British Association, Maxwell stated:

One of the most profound mathematicians of our time, the late George Boole, when reflecting on the precise and almost mathematical character of the laws of right thinking as compared with the exceedingly perplexing though perhaps equally determinate laws of actual and fallible thinking, was led to another of those points of view from which Science seems to look out into a region beyond her own domain.

'We must admit,' Boole says, 'that there exist laws (of thought) which even the rigour of their mathematical forms does not preserve from violation. We must ascribe to them an authority, the essence of which does not consist in power, a supremacy which the analogy of the inviolable order of the natural world in no way assists us to comprehend.'[793]

Einstein used the work of Boole in his application of invariant theory and that of Fitzgerald through the Lorentz-Fitzgerald contraction but interestingly when he was asked if he stood on the shoulders of Newton, Einstein replied, 'No, on the shoulders of Maxwell'.

Charles Darwin and Mary Everest Boole

On 21 September 2015, a record price for a letter written by Charles Darwin was set at Bonhams, New York at the History of Science and Technology sale. Darwin's very explicit letter, consisting of just a single page confirming his lack of belief in the Bible and the divinity of Jesus Christ, was sold for the astonishing sum of $197,000, nearly three times its pre-auction estimate.

On 23 November 1880, a young lawyer named Francis McDermott had written to Darwin with a blunt request:

> ... If I am to have pleasure in reading your books I must feel that at the end I shall not have lost my faith in the New Testament. My reason in writing to you therefore is to ask you to give me a Yes or No answer to the question: Do you believe in the New Testament?[794]

He continues by promising not to publicise Darwin's reply in the 'theological papers'. Faced with this Boolean question, Darwin replied the very next day giving a surprisingly frank answer:

> Private
>
> Down, Beckenham, Kent
> 24 November 1880
>
> Dear Sir,
>
> I am sorry to have to inform you that I do not believe in the Bible as a divine revelation, and therefore not in Jesus Christ as the son of God.
>
> Yours faithfully
> Ch. Darwin[795]

McDermott kept his word, and the letter has only recently come to light after being hidden for well over a hundred years. Darwin had studied theology at Cambridge, but his true religious beliefs, or lack of them, had always been a matter of speculation since the publication of his ground-breaking book *On the Origin of Species by Means of Natural Selection* in 1859. At the time of his reply to McDermott he was just two years away from his death in 1882, so perhaps he felt that little damage could now be done to his theory of evolution by the admission of his atheism. Afterwards, there were rumours of a deathbed conversion, but these were strongly denied by his family. He had been a reluctant student of theology, largely to please his father, so he always tried to avoid commenting on religious matters, preferring to confine himself to science. In this he strongly resembled George Boole.

According to some accounts, Mary Everest Boole's father, the Reverend Thomas Roupell Everest, was an acquaintance of Darwin's, as was her uncle Sir George Everest, the explorer after whom the mountain was later called. There are dozens of references to Darwin in her *Collected Works*[796] published in 1931. It is likely that in the period 1859–64 up to George Boole's death, he and his wife Mary would have been well aware of Darwin's theories and discussed them at length. In her *Collected Works*, Mary showed a surprisingly good grasp of Darwin's concept of natural selection and other theories, but on the other hand she tended to group them with other phenomena she herself espoused, such as mesmerism, hypnosis, phrenology and hydropathy. But, soon after George's death in 1864, Mary must have felt isolated and insecure without her beloved and trusted mentor, and for her the crux was: could she continue to espouse both Christianity and Darwinism, or were they in conflict? So, who better to ask for advice than Darwin himself, who was still living? Accordingly, she wrote to him as follows:

Private

43 Harley Street
London W.
13 December 1866

Dear Sir,

Will you excuse my venturing to ask you a question to which no one's answer but your own would be quite satisfactory to me.

Do you consider the holding of your Theory of Natural Selection, in its fullest and most unreserved sense, to be inconsistent, – I do not say with any particular scheme of theological doctrine, – but with the following belief, viz:

That knowledge is given to man by the direct Inspiration of the Spirit of God.

That God is a personal and infinitely good being.

That the effect of the action of the Spirit of God on the brain of man is especially a moral effect.

And that each individual man has, within certain limits, a power of choice as to how far he will yield to his hereditary animal impulses, and how far he will rather follow the guidance of the Spirit who is educating him into a power of resisting those impulses in obedience to moral motives.

The reason why I ask you is this. My own impression has always been, – not only that your theory was quite compatible with the faith to which I have just tried to give expression, – but that your books afforded me a clue which would guide me in applying that faith to the solution of certain complicated psychological problems which it was of practical importance to me, as a mother, to solve. I felt that you had supplied one of the missing links, – not to say the missing link – between the facts of science and the promises of religion. Every year's experience tends to deepen in me that impression.

But I have lately read remarks, on the probable bearing of your theory on religious and moral questions, which have perplexed and pained me sorely. I know that the persons who make such remarks must be cleverer and wiser than myself. I cannot feel sure that they are mistaken unless you will tell me so. And I think – I cannot know for certain – but I think that if I were an author, I would rather that the humblest student of my works should apply to me directly in a difficulty than that she should puzzle too long over adverse and probably mistaken or thoughtless criticisms.

At the same time I feel that you have a perfect right to refuse to answer such questions as I have asked you. Science must take her path and theology hers, and they will meet when and where and how God pleases and you are in no sense responsible for it, if the meeting point should be still very far off. If I receive no answer to this letter, I shall infer nothing from your silence except you felt I had no right to make such inquiries of a stranger.

I remain,

Dear Sir,

Yours truly,

Mary Boole[797]

It is interesting to note that Ethel S. Dummer in her preface to Mary Everest Boole's *Collected Works* (1931) relates that Mary's *The Message of Psychic Science to Mothers and Nurses*, written in 1868 but not published until 1883, was based on a series of talks to a group of London mothers, who, finding their religious beliefs threatened by Darwin's new theories, sought Mrs Boole's philosophic wisdom.

The courteous Darwin replied to her letter the next day as follows:

> Down, Bromley,
> Kent
> 14 December 1866
>
> Dear Madam,
>
> It would have gratified me much if I could have sent satisfactory answers to your questions, or indeed answers of any kind. But I cannot see how the belief that all organic beings including man have been genetically derived from some simple being, instead of being separately created bears on your difficulties. These as it seems to me can be answered only by widely different evidence from science, or by the so-called 'inner consciousness'. My opinion is not worth more than that of any other man who has thought on such subjects, and it would be folly in me to give it; I may however remark that it has always appeared to me more satisfactory to look at the immense amount of pain & suffering in this world, as the inevitable result of the natural sequence of events, i.e. general laws, rather than from the direct intervention of God though I am aware this is not logical with reference to an omniscient Deity. Your last question seems to resolve itself into the problem of free will and necessity which has been found by most persons insoluble.
>
> I sincerely wish that this note had not been as utterly valueless as it is; I would have sent full answers, though I have little time or strength to spare, had it been in my power.
>
> I have the honour to remain, dear Madam,
> Yours very faithfully,
> Charles Darwin
>
> P.S. I am grieved that my views should incidentally have caused trouble to your mind but I thank you for your judgment and honour you for it, that theology and science should each run its own course and that in the present case I am not responsible if their meeting point should still be far off.[798]

Darwin is being coy in his reply, and there is little of the frankness we find in his later letter to McDermott. He merely separates science and religion and gives no hint of his own rejection of the Bible and God. But then in 1866 his theories were less than ten years old and he was very anxious for their acceptance and conscious that opposition from religious believers would not be to his advantage. It is ironic that the letter from Darwin would afterwards be worth a small fortune, and Mary received it at a time when she was really struggling to survive and rear her family of five little girls. In truth, Darwin had said little to answer Mary's questions, but perhaps she felt that he had, and she must have been delighted to receive a reply from the great man, because just three days later she wrote to thank him as follows:

43 Harley Street,
17 December 1866

Dear Sir,

Thank you sincerely for your kind letter. You have told me all I wanted to know from you. The criticisms to which I referred were such as seemed to take for granted that all speculations as yours, in fact, as it seemed to me, all independent untheological speculations on creation as we find it, must be incompatible with any belief in a moral government of the world. I have always taken the liberty of telling the people who brought such criticisms under my notice that, in my opinion, the authors of them were simply talking about what they had never examined into. But still, when one is studying alone, and so ignorant too as I am, one gets frightened, and loses faith in one's own principles. And I thought, for my own satisfaction, I should like to have your assurance that moral and religious faith are things quite independent of theories about the process of creation. You have given me that assurance and again I thank you.

With sincere wishes for improvement in your health,
I remain
Dear Sir,
Yours truly,
Mary Boole[799]

One can only marvel at the immediate and frank communication that took place between Mary Boole and Charles Darwin. Despite the advancements of our digital age, it is increasingly difficult for a reader to make direct and personal contact with an author.

Mary continued to mention Darwin in her writings for the rest of her life, but her interpretations of his writings were unorthodox and even tenuous. A few randomly selected passages should suffice to illustrate this. In *The Message of Psychic Science* (1883) we read:

> And if I dared hope that Mr Darwin would care for any thanks of mine, I would express to him my gratitude for making me feel, as no writings but his ever did, the infinite contrast between the size of God's thoughts and the size of mine; and for teaching me to realise, as I never did before, how much truer and more artistic work I should do by carving out faithfully one bit of a moulding or cornice in God's great temple, than by having the material of a thousand worlds in my hands to work out my own devices with ...[800]
>
> ... Anyone tolerably familiar with both phrenological analysis and the details of Darwin's theory would find it an interesting task to try to trace out some of the steps by which the peculiar circumstances of women, and the physical infirmities and faults of character which result from these circumstances, have led to their becoming more 'religious' (or as I would prefer to say, more emotionally and consciously religious) than men usually are ...[801]
>
> ... No one who knows Darwin's works needs to be told that great results for human progress are brought about by the production of enormous numbers of creatures of low type ...[802]

LINCOLN MATTERS

Rules for Boole's Schools

George Boole was always aware of the fact that his surname rhymed with 'school' and of the comic possibilities that fact would present to his pupils. He therefore favoured the word 'academy' rather than 'school' both in the title of the Waddington institution and in his own later foundation. We are fortunate that a summary of the rules he drew up to govern the operation of his own school in Lincoln survives.[803] This summary tells us a lot about Boole's own moral principles which he wished to instil in his pupils. While idealistic and perhaps a little unrealistic as a set of moral guidelines for children and young men, nevertheless the principles are based on sound and practical common sense typical of their times. Naturally they were also designed to appeal to the parents of potential pupils.

Rules and Instructions addressed to his pupils and more particularly to those who are under his immediate care as members of his household

by

George Boole

The general principles by which the conduct of men in all situations should be governed, and by which you are to endeavour to regulate your own are:

1st JUSTICE This requires of you that you should give to all their due, reverence to your maker, love to your parents, respect and obedience to your teachers. You are by the same law required to be industrious in the pursuit of your studies and to be honest and open in your transactions with your schoolfellows, unwilling to take advantage of their ignorance or weakness, and mindful to do unto others as, under the same circumstances, you might reasonably expect them to do unto you.

2nd BENEVOLENCE By this you are required to be kind to all, and to show your kindness both in words and deeds, to study, to promote the happiness of your schoolfellows, to direct them when you think them to be in error, and to encourage them when they are engaged in that which is right, to be courteous to your equals, and respectful to the poor.

3rd TRUTH This requires that you not only speak the truth but act the truth, that you avoid either deceiving or countenancing deceit in any way – that you say on all occasions exactly what you mean and neither more nor less, and that you shun every species of untruth even in jest.

4th PURITY By the law of purity, you are required to shun all impure thoughts, words and deeds, aim to be pure in mind, cleanly in person, temperate in habits.

5th ORDER The law of order requires you to be exact and punctual in the discharge of your duties, careful of your clothes, your books, your instruments, to keep everything in its proper place and to do everything at its proper time. You must bear in mind that the rules of conduct which have now been stated to you do not rest on the opinion or the authority of your tutor. The principles on which they are founded are those by which all rational creatures should be governed. You are not too young to understand and to practise them. You will throughout life be happy in proportion as you honestly endeavour to do this and miserable in as far as you treat them with neglect or contempt.

The more particular directions suitable to your present position are the following:

At school you are required to be punctual in your attendance, quiet and orderly in your demeanour, and attentive to your studies. You are forbidden to leave your seat except on business, to quit the room without permission, or to talk aloud out of school hours while others are pursuing their tasks.

There follow very minute and careful details as to the behaviour at meals and in the sleeping quarters, and instructions on personal hygiene. For example, Boole forbids the using of any other pupil's comb, brush or towel. He then summarises the position:

> As it is the fixed determination of the compiler of these rules to see them as far as possible enforced and obeyed, he will in any case of confirmed and continued disobedience to them, and especially to that portion of them which relate to the moral duties of the young, cause (after other means have failed) the offending party to be removed, and this less by way of punishment than to prevent the contagion of evil example from spreading to others.

This last sentence shows that Boole was a firm believer in the 'rotten apple' theory of contamination among human beings. But at other times he was perhaps more realistic, admitting that there seemed to be no limit to the amount of mischief that young boys could get up to, especially in the confines of a boarding school. And it would have been very illuminating if in addition to writing *The Laws of Thought,* Boole had written a book on the laws of moral behaviour. Writing on such a topic might have been somewhat in conflict with his Unitarian leanings, but it would have made very interesting reading.

An extract from Boole's 'School Arrangements' has also survived.[804] It is representative of the spartan and intensive regime followed in his establishment, and probably not dissimilar from many others of its time throughout England:

Letters to be written by all as early as possible in each month. Some one standard work in English literature to be read by the older boys in each half year. A book for memoranda relative to the business of the school, the particular defects and requirements of each pupil to be kept.

Times of rising: Half past six in February and October; six in March and September; twenty minutes to six in April, May, June, July, August; twenty minutes to seven in November and December. Feet washed in School every Saturday night.

In the above list of rising times, all of the months of the year are covered except January. Was this the only month where there was provision for holidays? If so, then Boole ran his school virtually all of the year round, giving him very little time off – perhaps due to financial pressures?

LIFE IN CORK

Boole's Residences in Cork

From Boole's arrival in Cork in October 1849 until his death in December 1864, he lived in at least six different houses, split evenly between his time as a bachelor and as a married man. His first four known residences were quite close to Queen's College Cork, namely in College Road, Sunday's Well, Bachelor's Quay and Sunday's Well again. His last two family homes were situated in the villages of Blackrock and Ballintemple, which were further from the college but were accessible thanks to the Blackrock and Passage Railway Line which had opened in 1850.

Boole's first residence in Cork was in Castle White, which was close to the college grounds. Boole described the house as being 'in a delightful situation quite indeed like the country'.[805] He told MaryAnn that the grounds were extensive, and the River Lee ran through the grounds in front of the house. The house no longer exists but its site is now part of the campus of University College Cork. A modern student accommodation block named 'Castlewhite' stands on the bank of the River Lee opposite the original house.

Boole's landlord was John O'Brien, whose eldest son was a student at QCC.[806] Boole had a private sitting room, bedroom and dressing room. As well as the family, two other QCC staff also resided there, Professor De

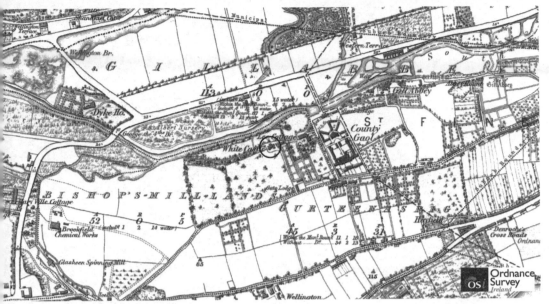

Figure 13.6: Castle White, Ordnance Survey Map 1837–42

Vericour and Mr Albani, the registrar, so the house must have been quite large. As discussed in Chapter Three, he moved from Castle White in early 1850 as his studies were being adversely affected by the busy social life in the house.[807]

In March 1850 Boole moved to new lodgings in Strawberry Hill in the suburb of Sunday's Well on a hill on the north side of the River Lee, overlooking Queen's College Cork. Boole described his rooms in his new lodgings as being southern facing with an 'almost unrivalled prospect'. A very well-kept orderly garden stretched down the hill before the window of his sitting room.[808] Boole's landladies were the Misses Knowles whom he described as three middle-aged sisters who were 'very intelligent and respectable' and highly spoken of by those who knew them. He was very pleased with his lodgings, which were very clean and well cared for.

We do not have much information about the Misses Knowles. Griffith's Valuation of 1852 lists Robert Knowles as being the tenant of a house in Strawberry Lane, as Strawberry Hill was previously known, in the parish of St Mary's, Shandon. City directories of 1863 and 1871 refer to Maria Knowles of Soho Terrace, Strawberry Hill, and an obituary in the *Cork Examiner* of February 1864 refers to the death of Frances Knowles, 'second surviving daughter of the late Robert Knowles'.

Strawberry Hill is still a residential area and continues to be a very pleasant place to live, as Boole found it to be. When the 1837–42 OS map

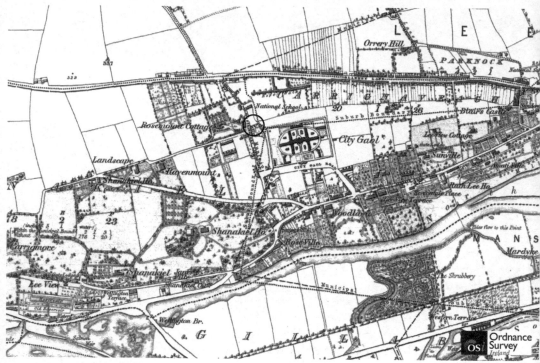

Figure 13.7: Strawberry Lane, Ordnance Survey Map 1837–42, with the likely site of the Knowles' house outlined

is compared to a modern map of the area, it seems likely that the Knowles' house no longer exists. The property circled in Figure 13.7 is the likely location of the house rented by Robert Knowles from John J. McCarthy.

Strawberry Hill runs from north to south in Figure 13.7 above, represented by the dotted line. The City Gaol was located at the opposite side of the hill, beyond a quarry. Boole did not refer to this in his letters when describing his lodgings to his mother and sister.

Boole appears to have remained in Strawberry Hill until some time in early 1852 when he moved to new lodgings in 5 Grenville Place. He mentions the family of his new landlord in a letter to MaryAnn in May 1852 but did not disclose why he moved.[809] The preface of *The Laws of Thought* dated 20 November 1853 was addressed from 5 Grenville Place. The new lodgings were closer to the city centre and to QCC. The house in Grenville Place is in a terrace of six houses situated on Bachelor's Quay on the banks of the River Lee which was built in approximately 1770.[810] The house was large and had four storeys, over a basement. It was situated in what would have been a fashionable part of the city at the time, close to the former Mansion House and facing the fine houses of the North Mall on the opposite bank of the river. The house was derelict for many years, but University College

Figure 13.8: Grenville Place, Cork (The Boole House of Innovation)

Cork has recently worked in partnership with Cork City Council to renovate it and restore it as 'The Boole House of Innovation'.

Griffith's Valuation of 1852 cites the representatives of Benjamin Bousfield as owning houses 1–5 of Grenville Place.[811] Henry Unkles was named as the tenant of the house and was in turn Boole's landlord. The Unkles were Methodists and Henry Unkles was a provision merchant.

On his return to Cork after the summer break in October 1853, Boole told MaryAnn that the Unkles had redecorated, and that every part of the house was in 'first rate order' including his two rooms. A new floor had been installed in the hall.[812] In the following month, Boole witnessed from Grenville Place one of the worst floods that Cork had ever experienced. He described being confined to the upper floors of the house, while the lower rooms were filled with water, which must have severely damaged the newly decorated hall (see Chapter Four). In the floods of November 2009 the Lee burst its banks at Bachelor's Quay, again causing major devastation in the city.

Boole was not the family's only lodger in Grenville Place. In March 1854 further renovations were carried out in preparation for two new lodgers, Mr and Mrs Harkness. Robert Harkness had been appointed as professor of

Figure 13.9: 38 Sunday's Well Road, Cork, previously known as 'College View'

geology in QCC following the departure of Professor Nicoll. Boole found the house too noisy and returned to his old lodgings in Strawberry Hill for a fortnight (see Chapter Three).[813] Following a dispute with the Unkles, Boole returned to Strawberry Hill in April 1854 and that is his last known address in Cork prior to his marriage.[814]

After their marriage in Wickwar in Gloucestershire on 11 September 1855, George and Mary Boole travelled back to Cork in time for the new college term. They rented a house, 'College View', on Sunday's Well Road, a fashionable area largely occupied by the well-off merchant classes of the city, not far from Strawberry Hill where Boole had previously lodged. They were now living on the north side of the River Lee in a lovely house on a hill overlooking the Queen's College and about a mile distant from it. Their first child, Mary Ellen, was born there on 19 June 1856, a honeymoon baby. She was baptised at St Mary's Shandon Church of Ireland on 3 July 1856. Sunday's Well seemed an ideal location for the Booles and their little daughter, on a sunny south-facing hill with a superb view of the city of Cork, a long garden stretching down to the beautiful River Lee, and within easy walking distance of Boole's place of employment.

Figure 13.10: 'Analore', Castle Road, Blackrock, Cork

But despite this, Boole was not satisfied with his location so near the city. He, and perhaps his wife too, seems to have believed in the miasma theory – that foul vapours emanating from rivers and swamps (the name Cork is from the Irish Corcaigh, a derivative of corcach, a marshy place) were not conducive to his health and that of his wife and young daughter. Extreme miasma believers felt that diseases such as cholera, typhoid fever, chlamydia, and even the bubonic plague were caused by 'bad air' or 'night air' from the marshes. The word 'miasma' is an ancient Greek term for pollution coming from rotting organic matter. The theory was superseded in the 1880s by the more modern 'germ theory'. Boole felt that sea air would be a better choice, so early in 1857 the family moved to Castle Road, Blackrock in the Cork suburbs, a distance just over four miles from the college, and quite near Blackrock Castle, a famous Cork landmark. Ironically, the bracing smell of the sea air, felt by many in the nineteenth century to be healthy ozone, is now believed to be just rotting seaweed! The move to Blackrock was probably also influenced by the opening of the Cork to Passage West railway line which opened for service in 1850, and the little Blackrock station was about a mile from the Boole house.

The identification of the precise location of the Boole residence on Castle Road proved to be enormously problematic. Boole, during the period 1857 to 1863 when he lived on Castle Road, always gave simply the address 'Blackrock' in his correspondence, and presumably since he was the only person of this surname in the area, post always managed to find him. But in his letters to various people he drops several hints about his house. For example, in a letter to his former pupil from Lincoln John Larkin, by then an architect in London, dated 27 February 1861, he relates:

> I live at some distance from Cork in a cottage on the River Lee – but am thinking of building myself a house. This may be considered I suppose as in some degree an evidence of prosperity, but you must take it as only a very moderate one. I have three children, girls, the youngest an infant. We live in great quiet, peace, and comfort and are full of thankfulness. Some time perhaps we may return to England. If I had my present lot in England, I think I should have no earthly wish ungratified.[815]

Learning that Boole was planning to build a new house, Larkin soon drew up plans for a new structure and sent them to his former teacher whom he respected and admired greatly. But on 13 April 1861 Boole replied, thanking Larkin for his plans but returning them, as his landlord had offered to extend the cottage:

> I return your designs with many thanks both for your goodness in sending them and for your kind offer as to the building itself. But just before receiving them I had written to tell you of my landlord's offer. All I can now say is that if ever I am in a position to build myself a house I will if possible arrange to have you as my architect …
>
> … When the repairs to my house are completed, you shall make it your house on any occasion of your visiting. At present we do not have a spare room but an attic through the roof of which you may I believe see the stars at night.[816]

When Boole wrote to John Bury in late May 1862 inviting Mrs Bury and her son Charles to come and stay with him, he told them that because of examinations he would be unable to come and meet them at the railway station. He advised them to take a car and alight near Blackrock Castle, adding that they should pay no more than half a crown, with luggage.[817] Elsewhere it emerges that the Boole house had a lawn in front and a garden behind and a view of the majestic River Lee as it widens before entering Cork Harbour.[818]

The search to locate the house took many years. The late C.J.F. McCarthy, Blackrock's distinguished local historian, discovered that the landlord's name was Henry Westropp. For a long time, it was felt that the elusive house could be 'Midsummer Lodge' (afterwards 'Towerville' and nowadays 'Mount Rivers') but a newspaper account of a marriage in 1859 had the house occupied by a Mr John Wheatley. Indeed, Boole did have his eye on 'Midsummer Lodge' as a family home and on 4 August 1862 when it came up for auction he was the only person to bid for the property. However, his bid of £100 was not deemed sufficient and the lot was withdrawn. It is also possible however that Boole wished to purchase 'Midsummer Lodge' to house foreign students attending Queen's College Cork and give them individual tutorage in various subjects. He had expressed a desire to do this several times in letters to friends but it seems to have remained just a hope.

The rate books for the various estates in the Castle Road area for the nineteenth century finally provided the location of the Boole residence. The books included the name of George Boole renting a house, offices and garden from Henry Westropp. The name of the house is 'Analore' on Castle Road and it satisfied all the criteria mentioned in Boole's letters. 'Analore' had been ruled out from the search as it was a two-storey building and Boole had referred to the residence as a cottage. However, on the discovery of newly available research material in the Lincolnshire Archives, it transpired that the house had originally been a cottage and the Booles had resided on the ground floor. In the summer of 1861 their landlord added an extra storey to the house, making it 'commodious and pleasant'.[819] The bigger house next door was called 'The Cottage', and 'Analore' is just two doors away from 'Midsummer Lodge', which came up for auction again in 1866, after Boole's death and the departure of his wife and family for London.

'Analore' has now been restored to its former glory. In 2015 'Midsummer Lodge' changed hands for €900,000, which puts Boole's bid of £100 into perspective. 'Analore', a listed property, was originally built around 1800. After its extension, it had four bedrooms upstairs, two reception rooms downstairs, and a central front and rear hall with a side-slung staircase off it. There was a kitchen with pantry, under-stairs storage, and a ground-floor bathroom. The site of the house has a considerable depth of about 200 feet from Castle Road to its rear lane access; behind is a substantial south-facing long garden about 140 feet in length. 'Analore' still retains some of its classical features such as original sash windows, decorative arches and plasterwork, a front door with stained glass panels and fanlight, and mahogany handrails around the stairwell. The original front gates still survive, as do the spear-headed wrought iron railings and the pink granite nameplate by the front pedestrian entrance. The limestone window sills and the limestone door steps are very likely of local Blackrock origin. All in all, during the period when the Booles resided there from 1857 to 1863, it must have been a very pleasant place to live and rear a young family.

The Booles were to move house one more time in Cork. Early in 1863 Boole, perhaps frustrated by his inability to buy 'Midsummer Lodge' or requiring more space to accommodate his growing family, decided to move

Figure 13.11: 'Lichfield Cottage', Ballintemple, Cork

to the beautiful 'Lichfield Cottage', in the village of Ballintemple, about a mile closer to Cork city along the Blackrock Road. He was now a little nearer the little Blackrock railway station and St Michael's, his parish church, and indeed the Queen's College. 'Lichfield Cottage' is still in a lovely state of preservation and looks very much like it would have been in Boole's day. It is currently occupied by paediatrician and UCC professor Tony Ryan, a pioneer of a procedure called therapeutic hypothermia for new-born infants, which reduces brain injuries.

Sadly, Boole died in 'Lichfield Cottage' on 8 December 1864 after his wife was said to have wrapped him in damp sheets (see Chapter Twelve). Professor Ryan has remarked, 'It was an interesting thought process, he got the right treatment, for the wrong condition.'[820] Boole never did get to build his own house in Cork, and he never got to return to live in his beloved England. Within a year, his wife had left for London and several of their children were farmed out to relatives because of her difficult financial circumstances.

The Cork–Dublin Train

Physical objects play an important role in history. In the case of George Boole, we have some of the manuscript papers he wrote, and many of the original steps and corridors in Lincoln and Cork on which he trod are still there in their original form. Touching these objects gives us a tangible link with the great man and a palpable sense of continuity. In Kent railway station in Cork city, named after one of the executed 1916 revolutionary leaders Thomas Kent, stands the beautifully preserved Engine No. 36 which drew the train on the Cork–Dublin line, and in which George Boole travelled on many occasions, especially when he went to Lincoln and back on holiday.

In 1847, just a year after the Irish Great Southern and Western Railway ran its first services from Kingsbridge station (now Heuston station, Dublin), the company ordered new locomotives to haul their heavier, faster trains over longer distances as the railway expanded towards Cork. Locomotive No. 36, with a wheel arrangement 2-2-2 and a single driving axle of 6ft diameter, weighed in at 19 tons 10cwt and was purchased from the firm of Bury, Curtis and Kennedy of Liverpool and based at Inchicore running shed. The meticulous records of GS & WR show that the No. 36 cost £1,995 and go on to detail her major overhauls and replacement of parts throughout her working life between 1847 and 1874 when she was finally withdrawn from traffic. Boole's first journey by train from Dublin to Cork through famine-ravaged Ireland is vividly described in Chapter Four.

No. 36 was a hard-working machine, hauling passenger trains at speeds of up to 60 miles per hour on flange rails, and when she finally went into well-earned retirement had clocked up an incredible 487,918 miles. As befitted a faithful horse of the iron road, No. 36 was destined not for the scrapyard but instead for a retirement of leisure and stardom. She appeared at the famous Cork Exhibition in 1902, the Railway Centenary Exhibition in 1925, and the bicentenary of the Royal Dublin Society at Ballsbridge in 1930. Placed on permanent display in the concourse of Cork Kent station in 1950 on a section of the original GS and WR flange rails, the locomotive was to have one final outing on show at her old home for the 'Unique Exhibition of Railway Locomotives and Rolling Stock' at the Dublin Inchicore works in June 1958.

Locomotive No. 36 was restored to her former glory by Iarnród Éireann craftsmen and has been on permanent display in Cork since May 2007. She is the oldest preserved locomotive in Ireland and is a lovely physical link with George Boole.

Figure 13.12: Engine No. 36, Kent Station, Cork

George Boole and the Cork Gas Company

George Boole took a prominent part in many community societies and activities during his time in both Lincoln and Cork – educational, religious, scientific, financial, and charitable. While living in Cork he was a very active supporter of the Cork Gas Company and was even one of its shareholders. Doubtless Boole was interested in the practical applications of coal gas in Cork city and its suburbs, but it is very likely that his interest in this area also sprang from his close friendship with Denny Lane, a native of the city and a veritable Renaissance man.

Denny Lane was born in 1818 into a wealthy Cork distilling family. Although a Catholic, he earned an MA degree from Trinity College Dublin and was afterwards called to the bar after legal studies at the Inner Temple in London. He was a friend of the Young Ireland revolutionaries Charles Gavan Duffy and Thomas Davis, and Lane himself was imprisoned in Cork Gaol for his Young Ireland activities. On his release, he became involved in several practical industrial schemes in Cork, including the production of high-quality starch, the manufacture of light beer, the production of electricity from peat, and the extraction of sugar from beet. Though he had no formal training in engineering, he developed a keen interest in projects such as inventing an electric clock and developing a gas incubator for chickens. He was present at the meeting of the British Association for the Advancement of Science in Cork in 1843 when Joule announced the mechanical equivalent of heat. Lane was overawed by this concept and wrote several papers on its practical applications. He was on the board of several railway companies and became director of the Cork Gas Company, which he was instrumental in founding in 1856, and president of the Institute of Gas Engineers in 1887 and 1893.

Lane also had a strong artistic side to his character, being involved in Cork's School of Art and School of Music, and he is remembered by many today for his composition of one of the best-known Irish ballads, *Carrigdhoun*. He was a central figure in the Cork Literary and Scientific Society, and Historical and Archaeological Societies.

Denny Lane died in 1895, having unsuccessfully stood for parliament in the 1876 Cork City by-election. Thomas Carlyle met Lane on his visit to Cork in 1849 and summed him up as follows: 'a fine brown Irish figure, Denny, distiller, ex-repealer; frank, hearty, honest air; like Alfred Tennyson a little'.[821]

Figure 13.13: Denny Lane by Henry Jones

It would seem that Lane and Boole first met in 1850, shortly after Boole's arrival in Cork, at a meeting of the Cuvierian Society of which Boole was later president. Lane had inherited a distillery at Glanmire near Cork and described in a paper to the Cuvierian Society his attempts to utilise to the best advantage the fall of fifteen feet of water at his command by employing the principle of the Barker Mill. He brought to the meeting a number of complicated diagrams, together with a proposal for a machine having 'curvilinear flexure, thus providing a gradual curve instead of the several right angles of the older wheel'. Boole offered to work out the difficult calculations arising from Lane's ingenious proposal.

This incident led to an instant friendship of kindred spirits, and Lane began to interest Boole in the Cork Gas Company. The *Cork Examiner* of 15 February 1864 documented an incident describing Boole's involvement with the company. It took place at the thirteenth half-yearly meeting and was held at the company's office, 72 South Mall Cork, also the home of Denny Lane. Many dignitaries were present including the previous and current mayors of Cork, Sir John Arnott and J.P. Maguire, who was also chairman of the company. A controversial motion before the meeting proposed that 10 per cent of the annual profits of the company, instead of the current 8 per cent, be distributed among the shareholders. For this motion the meeting was declared an extraordinary one. Boole was present and spoke against the motion with great feeling. He said that his shareholding was so small that it was with great diffidence that he rose to speak, and that it was at considerable personal inconvenience that he had managed to attend the meeting at all. He felt strongly that if there was any money left over after paying 8 per cent of the profits to the shareholders, then that money should go to the consumers by way of reduced prices for gas and even investigation into how the quality of the gas could be improved, and that to do otherwise would be to contradict the repeated pledges given to consumers.

After a long and complicated discussion involving the price of gas in London, Belfast and Dublin, the cost of freight of coal to Cork, and the escape of half a million cubic feet of gas from the Cork Lunatic Asylum, the company was sarcastically described as 'robbing and plundering'. A Mr Sugrue[822] proposed an amendment that the dividend be maintained at 8 per cent and Professor Boole seconded, having first desired to have his protest against the resolution recorded. In the event, the amendment received only four supporters, and the resolution was carried by 'an immense majority'. The greedy shareholders prevailed, but the incident demonstrates Boole's concern for the community in which he lived, and his courage to support a minority view, at some personal cost, in the cause of justice.

Incidentally, the Boole–Lane friendship may help to solve a long-standing mystery that has puzzled some people: why in her *Collected Works*[823] did Mary Everest Boole quote in full a poem ('The Flower is Small') by the previously mentioned Irish revolutionary Thomas Davis (1814–45), a native of Mallow near Cork? Indeed, an American historian of mathematics spent a whole year in Cork in a vain attempt to justify his theory that because of the inclusion of this poem, George Boole and his wife must have been supporters of the Irish revolutionary cause and even taken part in it! The real explanation would appear to be that Lane was a close friend of both Boole and Davis, all three of them being poets. Lane may have persuaded Boole to overlook Davis's revolutionary and anti-English feelings and appreciate his poetry instead.

A Language Mystery

George Boole was undoubtedly a linguist and was essentially self-taught in the many languages he learned. At an early age he acquired Latin, and afterwards, without the aid of a tutor, he mastered classical Greek. Next, he became fluent in written and spoken French, German and Italian, all self-taught, and in later life published lengthy mathematical papers in the last two of these languages. At one stage he studied Hebrew but did not persist because of its difficulty and the lack of suitable textbooks.

Language played a very important role in Boole's development of symbolic logic and was a powerful motivation in the development of his laws of thought. He observed linguistic features such as subject, predicate and object, which were common to all of the languages he studied, and noted differences such as whether adjectives preceded nouns or not, and when verbs were to be placed at the end of a sentence. He discovered that there were mathematical structures such as distributivity to be found in all languages and that these were naturally and readily absorbed even by children at their mother's knee without any difficulty, as were the correct usage of the crucial words 'and', 'or' and 'not'.

Boole came to Ireland for the first time in 1849 and died there in 1864. He lived almost entirely in Cork city for that period except for holidays in Lincoln before his marriage in 1855. The Irish language (or Gaelic or Erse as he might have called it) was commonly and extensively spoken in Cork at that time, and within thirty miles there were areas where Irish was the predominant spoken language of the population. Largely for political reasons one suspects, there was a Department of Celtic Studies at Queen's College Cork where Irish was taught to degree level, and a full-time professor, Owen Connellan, though admittedly he had very few students.

It is noteworthy that there is not a single mention of the Irish language in Boole's letters, his books, his papers, his public lectures, his conversations, nor any record that he ever took the slightest interest in this ancient and beautiful tongue by which he was surrounded in Ireland. He had a keen interest in word derivation, place names, religion, history and the structure of languages in general, yet the subject of the Irish language seems to have held no interest at all for him, and not a single Irish word or phrase or a discussion of their meanings or significance is to be found in his extensive writings.

The following reasons may account for Boole's lack of interest in the language:

1. Irish was the language of the poor and uneducated, with whom Boole did not wish to identify. Perhaps there was also a degree of snobbery and typically British anti-Irish feeling involved also.

2. The Irish language was closely connected with the Catholic Church towards which Boole was clearly antagonistic. For example, even basic greetings in Irish such as *Dia dhuit* (God be with you, meaning hello) and the reply *Dia is Muire dhuit* (God and Mary be with you, meaning hello to you) had Catholic implications which he may have been uncomfortable with.

3. There were virtually no books or papers in the Irish language concerning mathematics, logic or philosophy, the subjects which most interested him.

4. Most of Boole's colleagues at Queen's College Cork would not have been Irish speakers.

5. It is likely that Boole regarded Cork as an outpost of the British Empire rather than an Irish city. The language and culture of Gaelic Ireland would therefore have been alien to him.

In Chapter Eight, Boole boasts of his wife Mary's knowledge of Scandinavian languages and her attempts to give a derivation of a local Cork place name 'Ringaskiddy'. She renders the word as coming from the Swedish 'ring', a circle, and 'skyd' protection. Anyone with even an elementary knowledge of the Irish language should see at once that the word comes from 'rinn', a headland, and 'Skiddy', a proper surname found locally, though admittedly Skiddy is believed to have arrived in Ireland from Scandinavia, via Scotland.

Mysterious too is the fact that one of Boole's closest friends in Ireland, Charles Graves – professor of mathematics at Trinity College Dublin, with whom Boole stayed in Dublin and corresponded frequently – seems to have been the person who broke the ancient Irish Ogham code found on gravestones, as early as 1848. One would have expected that Graves – who later became Bishop of Limerick, abandoned mathematics, and devoted himself almost exclusively to archaeology – would have discussed this connection between code breaking and the Irish language with Boole, but there is no record of this.

Sir William Rowan Hamilton also seems to have shown a similar disdain for the Irish language. Hamilton was a prolific linguist, said at the age of thirteen to be fluent in thirteen languages, but seems to have ignored the native tongue of his country completely and there is no record that he ever spoke it.

Similar remarks might be made with regard to Boole's seemingly total lack of interest in Irish music, songs and poetry. There is no mention of them in his letters or publications, although he loved both music and poetry.

MORE FAMOUS BOOLE DESCENDANTS

The final chapter of *The Life and Work of George Boole* discussed some famous and accomplished descendants of George Boole including his daughters Alicia, Lucy and Ethel, Geoffrey Taylor, Howard Hinton, Joan Hinton, George Boole Hinton and Leonard Stott.[824] We can now add further names to that list – Margaret Boole, Sebastian Hinton, Julian Taylor and Geoffrey Hinton.

Margaret Boole

It has been traditionally claimed that of George and Mary Boole's five daughters, three of them – Alicia the mathematician, Lucy the chemist, and Ethel Lilian the novelist – were exceptionally talented and approached genius level. The other two daughters, Mary Ellen and Margaret, are regarded as less famous in themselves, and remembered more for the undoubtedly famous children they produced (see the critique of Mary Ellen's poetry earlier in this chapter). However, recent evidence uncovered by Gerry Kennedy and presented in his book *The Booles & the Hintons* paints a different picture.[825]

Margaret, who was the Booles' second daughter, was born in 1858 and was only six years of age when her father died. Taken to live in London by her mother in 1865, she grew up and was educated there in relative poverty. Luckily, she was able to spend happy holidays in Ireland with her relatives the Ryall family. However, in 1874, when she was just sixteen, the Booles had a stroke of luck. Their maternal uncle, the Reverend Robert Everest, died, and left them £3,000, a large amount of money in the nineteenth century. Mary Everest Boole generously divided the legacy equally among herself and her five daughters and the money enabled Margaret to train as a nurse at the Eye, Ear and Throat Hospital in Cork, which was right beside Queen's College Cork where her father George had been professor.

Figure 13.14: Margaret Boole

Margaret, as befits her ancestry, was no ordinary nurse carrying out routine tasks and obeying orders – she became a highly creative innovator in medical science. While employed as a clinical assistant at the Eye, Ear and Throat Hospital in the period 1875–8, she turned her artistic talents to good use. Charles Babbage (see Chapter Six) had invented the ophthalmoscope in 1847 whereby the retina of the human eye could be viewed and examined for signs of disease. The trouble was that photography at that time was not advanced enough to record accurately what had been seen, and the problem was even more acute in relation to the human ear, so that patients suffered prolonged pain because of lengthy clinical examinations. Margaret developed a technique of capturing a good image quickly in watercolour. When in 1878 Henry MacNaughton Jones published his *Atlas of Diseases of the Membranum Tympanum*, it contained fifty-four coloured illustrations by Margaret Boole. For pictures of these, the reader is referred to Gerry Kennedy's book.[826]

Margaret also studied at the Cork School of Art, and was awarded a prize there in 1879. In the early 1880s she returned to London and worked as an ophthalmological artist, continuing to produce excellent watercolour images of the human eye, published in journal form between 1883 and 1886. She studied at the Slade School of Art where she met her husband Edward Ingram Taylor who became a famous ship's artist. The couple had two children, Geoffrey, the eminent mathematical physicist, and Julian, a distinguished surgeon. Margaret died in 1935.

Sebastian Hinton

Figure 13.15: Sebastian Hinton

Sebastian Theodore ('Ted') Hinton was the son of Charles Howard Hinton (of four-dimensional fame) and Mary Ellen Boole, and therefore the grandson of George and Mary Everest Boole. He was born in London in 1887 and moved to Chicago in 1913 after graduating from the George Washington University as a lawyer. Later he specialised in patent law.

In his investigations into the fourth dimension, Charles Howard Hinton constructed unusual geometric objects made of bamboo rods. One day in 1920 while watching children playing in a park, Sebastian was inspired by these objects and the monkey-like antics of the children to build the jungle gym, also known as monkey bars. The jungle gym consists of a series of cubes so that children in the playground could climb safely in a variety of directions, with plentiful safety ropes to prevent falling and injury. As a patent lawyer, Sebastian designed and patented the jungle gym, now to be found throughout the world in playgrounds and backyards.

In 1916 Sebastian married Carmelita (Chase) Hinton (1890–1983) the educational pioneer who founded the Putney School. Their daughter Joan Hinton (1921–2010) was a famous nuclear physicist.[827] Sadly, Sebastian suffered from severe depression and died tragically in 1923.

Julian Taylor

Professor Julian Taylor CBE FRCS (1889–1961) was a specialist in neurological surgery at University College Hospital in London and later professor of surgery at the University of Khartoum. His father was Edward Ingram Taylor, a ship's artist, and his mother Margaret (Boole) Taylor was George Boole's second daughter. His elder brother was Sir Geoffrey Taylor OM FRS, the renowned physicist and applied mathematician. Julian qualified in London in 1911 and was appointed FRCS in 1914. He joined

the Royal Army Medical Corps and served in France and Macedonia with the 85th Field Ambulance. Later in the war he became the medical officer in charge of the 52 and 43 field hospitals in Salonika. He was awarded the OBE in 1919.[828]

After the First World War, Julian had a distinguished academic medical career as an examiner in surgery for the Universities of Cambridge, Leeds, and London. He held many posts such as vice president of the Royal College of Surgeons. When the Second World War broke out he volunteered for military service as a consulting surgeon, Malaya Command, with the rank of brigadier. After the fall of Singapore, he was captured by the Japanese and became a prisoner of war in Changi prison camp where he worked in appalling conditions with 2,500 wounded soldiers, suffering from starvation, deprivation of all kinds, and a complete lack of medical supplies. This experience scarred him for life and weakened his health, but he never lost his love of humanity and dedication to medicine and saved the lives of many of his fellow prisoners by his unswerving devotion to duty under unspeakable medical conditions. After the war, he was appointed CBE in 1946 and pursued a personal practice in London as well as continuing as a hospital surgeon. After his wife died in 1955 he began a new career as professor of surgery at the University of Khartoum where he made a huge impact on the development of medicine in the Sudan and in Nigeria, Uganda and Ghana also. He inherited the warm and generous personality of George Boole, and though the world wars interrupted his career twice, he rose to the very top of his profession.

Geoffrey Hinton

Geoffrey Everest Hinton FRS, born in London in 1947, is the son of Howard Hinton, the renowned entomologist and thus the great-great-grandson of George and Mary Boole and also of James Hinton, the noted ear surgeon and author. He graduated from King's College Cambridge in 1970 with a degree in experimental psychology and proceeded to study at the University of Edinburgh, where he was awarded a doctorate in artificial intelligence in 1978. As a computer scientist he went on to become one of the world's

Figure 13.17: Geoffrey Hinton

foremost experts on artificial neural networks. He was one of the first researchers to demonstrate the use of generalised backpropagation for training multilayer neural nets and is a leader in the deep learning movement. His aim is to see how the design of artificial neural nets can be adapted to achieve learning without the aid of a human teacher.

He has received honorary doctorates from several universities and awards from learned societies all over the world including the Royal Society fellowship like his ancestor George Boole, as well as having authored over three hundred papers and supervised over twenty doctoral students. He co-invented Boltzmann machines. He is professor of computer science at the University of Toronto, as well as working in a research position at Google. In many ways he is fulfilling the ideals of George Boole, in that he is at the forefront of those scientists currently investigating the workings of the human mind in a machine-based environment. He studies the use of neural networks for human learning, memory, perception and symbol processing, interests very dear to Boole's heart.

In the 1950s the world was shocked by the invention of computer programs that could play chess. At the time, they were regarded as passing fancies, but people began to sit up and take notice when in 1996 the world chess champion, Russian grandmaster Gary Kasparov, was beaten by IBM's Deep Blue computer.

Go is an ancient Chinese board game, vastly more complicated than chess, in which black and white counters are alternately placed on a board with the object of territorial control by surrounding the opponent's pieces. Victory at Go requires something far more than supercomputers and computing power – it requires 'deep learning', using neural networks, almost duplicating the actual neurons of the human brain and progressively learning as it goes along like humans do, seeing patterns, formulating rules and using a type of intuition. Victory by a computer over a top-class human opponent at Go has been regarded as the pinnacle of ambition and the holy grail of computer science for decades.

In 2016 the AI program AlphaGo, designed by Google's Deep Mind team, defeated the South Korean Go grandmaster and reigning world champion, Lee Se-dol, in three games out of four. Foremost in the design and implementation of AlphaGo was Geoffrey Hinton, now considered the 'godfather of neural networks', who pursued and developed the concept of 'deep learning' even when it was not popular among computer scientists. Currently, Geoffrey Hinton and his team are working on computerised speech recognition and are making spectacular progress in this area. Truly, by accident or design, he is walking in the footsteps of his famous ancestors.

MEMORIALS

The Boole Window at University College Cork

On 18 December 1864, less than two weeks after George Boole's death, his fellow professors at Queen's College Cork met and resolved that the institution would provide a fitting memorial to its most illustrious member of staff. They decided that it should take the form of a stained-glass window to be erected in the east-facing wall of the college's Aula Maxima. Coincidentally, in September 1849, shortly after the college was completed, the *Cork Examiner* newspaper suggested that a window of plain glass in that site was totally out of character with its magnificent surroundings. It went on to propose that it be replaced by stained glass to 'impart a mysterious charm to the details of architectural embellishment with its chequered and many-coloured lights'. Furthermore, it hinted that the expense could easily be covered by the new academic staff, at a rate of £50 from the president and £5 from each of the professors.

By 6 February 1865 the impressive sum of two hundred and four pounds and one shilling had been collected. Newspaper reports of the day suggest that the beautiful memorial window was in place by the second anniversary of Boole's death in December 1866. Happily, the window still survives today in pristine order. It contains ten panels with themes and historical figures relevant to Boole's life and work.[829]

However, there is a curious absence of any mention of any official ceremony in connection with the installation of the window, and no record of it is to be found in the university archives, in the minutes of council, or in the records of the Board of Works, who would have been charged with carrying out the task of installation. However, the *Cork Examiner* report on the matter records that the window was erected under the superintendence of Mr R.D. Williams, the foreman of the manufacturers. But a mystery remained for nearly a hundred and fifty years – who commissioned the window? Who designed it and who manufactured it? At the suggestion of one of the present authors, Mr Harry Lande MSc, a mathematical graduate of University College Cork, agreed to research the matter. We are very grateful to Mr Lande for permission to report his findings which appear to settle the matter definitively.[830]

His first step was to send a colour photograph of the Boole window to Dr Nicola Gordon-Bowe at the National College of Art and Design in Dublin. She passed the photograph on to Dr David Lawrence of Lawrence and Company, stained glass manufacturers in Canterbury and Hereford. Dr Lawrence, an expert on stained glass, was very strongly of the opinion that the window was the work of the firm of Hardman and Company of Birmingham, based on its similarity to their other known productions. After a search of the archives of the Library of Birmingham by Ms Rachel MacGregor, it turned out that the Boole window was indeed the work of Hardman and Company. The designer was almost certainly John Hardman Powell (1827–95), the firm's chief designer. He was a grandnephew of the founder of the firm, John Hardman Senior (1766–1844), a member

of an old English Catholic family. Hardman and Company were very strongly associated with the world-renowned architect and designer A.W.N. Pugin (1812–52), the master of the Gothic revival. Pugin, a recent convert to Catholicism, steered the Hardman firm from ecclesiastical metalwork towards stained glass, in which they acquired a worldwide reputation. They made glass for the new Houses of Parliament in London for which Pugin was the interior designer. To cement the relationship further, in 1850 Powell married Anne (1832–97), Pugin's eldest daughter. Sadly, the firm of Hardman closed its doors and ceased trading in 2008.

The Boole window was most probably commissioned by John Ryall, professor of Greek at Queen's College Cork, and uncle of Boole's wife. With his classical background, Ryall was in a good position to choose the themes and figures featured in the window,

Figure 13.18: A panel from the Boole Window, UCC, featuring George Boole at work with Euclid and Aristotle in the background

but it is possible that many of these were chosen by the designer Powell. On 1 February 1866 Ryall wrote to the firm of Hardman as follows:

Queen's College Cork

Gentlemen,

I request you will have the kindness to advise me of the return of your artist Mr Powell as I wish to enter into personal communication with him on the subjects of the design and inscription for the Boole Memorial Window.

I remain gentlemen
Yours faithfully
John Ryall[831]

However, another old friend of Boole's, F.C. Penrose, deserves a great deal of credit for the final design of the window and for the final choice of scientists and philosophers who adorn it. Ryall sent Penrose the initial designs which Powell had sent him on behalf of Hardman and Company, and Penrose replied as follows, echoing some of Ryall's reservations and adding several suggestions of his own:

St Paul's Chapter House
Nov 2 1865

My dear Sir,

I think that Messrs. Hardman's design would have a very rich effect both in colour and play of line. With you, I doubt its sufficient application to Dr Boole. It would do just as well for – say – the Master of Trinity Cambridge. Indeed to individualise is very difficult. It may however I think be made more direct by some alterations. I will refer to the compartments by numbers

1	2	3	4	5
6	7	8	9	10

Leave out 1 and put in a new compartment indicating religion: of course without any RC emblems. You will judge how far this is possible or politic. If no way else it might be combined with music, indicating and naming David.

No. 2 Navigation as dependent on astronomy: STET name Columbus and Vasco da Gama.

No. 3 Fame STET.

No. 4 Take No. 7, naming Hippocrates, Galen, Harvey.

No. 5 Architecture and civil engineering: STET naming Phidias and Archimedes.

No. 6 Astronomy: STET naming Hipparchus, Copernicus, Galileo.

No. 7 Here introduce a group of figures bearing British scientific names: Newton, Napier, {for Ireland} Bacon.

No. 8 Very much as it is naming Euclid and Aristotle with Dr Boole writing *The Laws of Thought*. His name not introduced directly, but some other of his books may be on the ground or shelves with their titles.

No. 9 Here foreign scientific names: Pascal? Descartes? Leibniz. It won't do I think to come to more modern names; you will however easily improve my list.

No. 10 If music has gone to the upper range to indicate by the name David, the religious tendency of our friend, a new compartment will be required here, and astronomy at 6 suggests geography here with the names Ptolemy, Strabo and some other that may occur to you.

You would I presume have an inscription at the bottom of the window, in the glasswork, stating to whose memory and by whom the window is dedicated. The hieroglyphic picture may be supposed to stand for his scientific renown. But the inscription could mention his kind heart, his modesty, and his domestic and social virtue.

These my dear sir are the comments which have occurred to me in looking over this very clever sketch of Messrs. Hardman's, i.e. of their artist Mr Powell whose hand I recognise in it. If they are of any use I shall be very much pleased. I think the Lincoln memorial window is in good train now.

Returning to your window, I think the Royal arms and supporters are rather too big and I would suggest the tracery not being overcharged with ornament. If any reduction in Messrs. Hardman's estimate is desired, I would suggest it in the Tracery rather than in the design.

Yours very truly

F.C. Penrose

I will return the window by book post. Give my best respects to Mrs Boole.[832]

The Boole Window in Lincoln Cathedral

On 11 January 1865, soon after George Boole's death, his friends in Lincoln met in the Guildhall and decided that they would raise a memorial to him in his native city, as good if not better than anything provided in Cork. The meeting was chaired by Alderman Snow and among the attendance were the Rev. E.R. Larken, J.B. Porter, and the Brooke brothers, Benjamin and William. A motion was proposed and passed that the memorial should take the form of a stained-glass window in Lincoln's magnificent cathedral, with a further memorial in the city, if funds would permit. A list was opened for donations and within a few months the sum of £139 and 17 shillings had been collected. However, it was felt that up to £50 more was needed if a window worthy of Boole was to be provided. A pamphlet appealing for further contributions was circulated, very probably written by William Brooke. He eloquently put the case as follows:

No memorial of an inferior character would be tolerated by the subscribers, whether the worth of him who is the object of it, or the fair claims of the august edifice containing it be considered. As a gentleman well known in this district, and of a high professional position, Mr F.C. Penrose, the chapter architect of St Paul's Cathedral, observes: I trust that the committee will not fail to give their best attention to the great importance of putting the execution of their window into the best hands, and that they will not hesitate to choose a small window if the funds are not sufficient to give an ample expenditure upon a large one. They should bear in mind that not only is the beauty of the minster, but the honour intended to the memory of our excellent friend hazarded by an unsatisfactory result.

Figure 13.19: The Boole Window, Lincoln Cathedral

Penrose therefore was closely involved in both the Cork and Lincoln Memorial Committees. Brooke goes on to laud Boole in very extravagant terms with a view to shaming the people of Lincoln to make good the deficiency of funds. He quotes tributes from old friends and old pupils and in particular one from Sir J.S. Willes, Justice of the Court of Common Pleas (see Chapter Eight), when forwarding his liberal donation to the memorial:

> Whether I regard the judgment of the most competent, which placed him in the foremost rank of intellect, or the worth of his exertions (alas but too disinterested) as a professor, or the singular influence of his honourable, pure, and lovely example, I look upon his death as a public calamity. Lincoln may well be proud of such a man, and for her children's, and her children's children's sake, affectionately careful of his memory.

Brooke's pamphlet goes on to mention Boole's domestic happiness, his humility, his care for his pupils and students, his close circle of friends, and his deep tone of religious thought. The plea had the desired effect and over the next few months the desired shortfall was made good. Sadly, there was no surplus of money to provide an additional memorial in the city of Lincoln. In 1869, after a short delay, the window was inserted in the north aisle of Lincoln Cathedral, where it can still be seen today. It was designed by the renowned artists Ward and Hughes. The window consists of three panels or medallions and has become known as the Teaching Window. The lowest and main panel is based on the Calling of Samuel, suggested by Mary Everest Boole as one of her husband's favourite biblical stories. The central panel features the child Jesus with the learned doctors in the temple while the top panel commemorates Christ teaching the verse 'Render unto Caesar the things that are Caesar's and to God the things that are God's'.

Underneath the window is a brass plate with a Latin inscription. In translation it reads:

> In memory of George Boole LL.D., citizen of Lincoln, a man of the acutest intellect and manifold learning, who being specially exercised in the severer sciences, diligently explored the hidden recesses of mathematics and happily illuminated them by his writings. He was carried off by an untimely death in the year 1864.

The Heavenly Booles

Out of Boole's passion for astronomy grew his interest in optics and the making of telescopes and other optical instruments. This led to geometry and further mathematical topics such as calculus and algebra, and eventually to logic. It is fitting therefore that modern astronomers have named two heavenly objects after Boole and one after his daughter Ethel Voynich.

BOOLE CRATER ON THE MOON

Figure 13.20: The Boole crater on the moon

Boole is a lunar crater that lies along the north-western limb of the Earth's moon to the northwest of crater Gerard. Its coordinates are 63.7N and 87.4W, and its diameter is approximately 63 km. Viewed from Earth, it appears quite oblong in shape due to foreshortening. However, in reality the formation, like many other lunar craters, is close to circular, with a wide inner wall that has been worn and rounded due to subsequent impacts. The interior floor of Boole is relatively flat and features only tiny craterlets. Its depth is unknown but is believed to be substantial. Boole is surrounded by nearly a dozen satellite craters of different sizes.

ASTEROID BOOLE – MINOR PLANET 17734

Asteroid Boole – minor planet 17734 was discovered and named by Paul G. Comba on 22 January 1998 at Prescott Observatory, Arizona. When first pictured, it was just past 'Opposition' i.e. at its closest to the Earth (still some 200 million km away); by June 2016 it was at its furthest from us. There are several hundred thousand named asteroids, but 17734 Boole appears to be a typical inhabitant of the main asteroid belt, orbiting the sun between Mars and Jupiter at a distance of 2.4 times that of the Earth–sun distance, every 3.7 years.

ASTEROID ETHEL – MINOR PLANET 2032

Asteroid Ethel – minor planet 2032 was discovered and named by the Russian astronomer Tamara Mikhailovna Smirnova (1935–2001) on 30 July 1970 at the Crimean Astrophysical Observatory in Nautschnyj. Because of her immense popularity as a writer in the Soviet Union, it was named after Ethel Lilian Voynich, née Boole (1864–1960), George Boole's youngest daughter, who was born in Cork. Ethel is a main belt asteroid of diameter 36.31 km which orbits the sun about every 5.5 years.

United Nations General Assembly honours George Boole

On 27 May 2015 a declaration of the General Assembly of the United Nations, signed by over seventy member states, announced that 20 October 2015 was to be designated World Statistics Day, under the general theme 'Better data, better lives'. It recognised the long history of official statistics in the work of the United Nations and acknowledged the fundamental importance of sustainable national statistical capacity in producing reliable and timely statistics and indicators measuring a country's progress, together with analysis and informed policy decision-making in support of sustainable development.

The resolution also noted that 2015 marked the bicentenary of the birth of George Boole whose work on the application of the principles of logic as a form of algebra underpins modern computer science, which makes large-scale data management possible.

The resolution was introduced by Hungary and co-sponsored by the Republic of Ireland. Speaking in New York, the Irish Ambassador to the United Nations, Mr David Donoghue, said, 'At the United Nations General Assembly, the singular importance of the work of Boole in enabling modern computing and the operation of electronic computing was worthy of special celebration this year. Boolean logic is a fundamental foundation of the science of big data which offers immense opportunities for enhancing the lives of humanity.'[833]

The Bust of George Boole

There are many memorials to Boole in both Lincoln and Cork, but during 2015, the Boole 200 Year, it was decided that a bust of the great man be commissioned and given a permanent home outside the Boole Library at University College Cork. It was made of clay and cast in bronze by the Irish sculptor Paul Ferriter, and set on a block of Cork limestone, engraved by

Figure 13.21: Bust of George Boole, University College Cork

Ken and Matthew Thompson. The bust was sponsored by two former UCC students, Shemas Eivers and Teddy McCarthy, who have been very successful in the computer industry. Fittingly, the bust was unveiled jointly by the British ambassador to Ireland, Dominick Chilcott, and Daniel Mulhall, Ireland's ambassador to Great Britain, a former student of mathematics at UCC. In May 2017 Daniel Mulhall was appointed Irish ambassador to the United States of America.

Appropriately, the bust has already become part of UCC student folklore. Manual fondling of the nose of the statue is believed to bring good luck in examinations, while full-blown nose to nose contact (Eskimo style) is obligatory for those who wish to obtain honours!

Google Doodle to Boole

It has been said, perhaps simplistically, 'no George Boole, no Internet, no Google'. If George Boole had not invented symbolic logic and Claude Shannon had not seen its application to switching circuits, then maybe other people would have eventually done so, but the fact is that Boole and

Shannon were the trailblazers in these areas, and thus the instruments by which the internet and Google came about.

On 2 November 2015, George Boole's 200th birthday, Google devoted its daily doodle to Boole, and it is estimated that this tribute was seen by a billion people all over the planet. The interactive presentation was created by artist Leon Hong and cycled through all the ANDs, ORs, NOTs, and even XORs of the Boolean states for two discrete variables. The accompanying blurb acknowledges that Boole brought to a complex world the simplicity of true and false, 0 and 1, and enabled revolutionary thinking, not just in logic and mathematics, but also in engineering, electronics and computer science. Boole is credited with having laid the foundations of the entire Information Age while working at Queen's College Cork. Google itself admits, 'No Boole, No Google!'

The tribute finishes in true binary fashion by wishing genius George Boole a very happy 11001000th Birthday.[834]

Chapter 14

SHERLOCK HOLMES, JAMES MORIARTY AND GEORGE BOOLE

THIS CHAPTER PRESENTS extensive evidence that the character of Professor James Moriarty, the arch-villain of the Sherlock Holmes stories and the nemesis of Holmes, was largely inspired by Professor George Boole. The claim was originally suggested, albeit indirectly, by Dr John Bowers, a lecturer in mathematics at the University of Leeds, in an article in the *New Scientist* magazine in 1989, 'James Moriarty: a forgotten mathematician'.[835] We were alerted to Bowers' work in an article by Isabel Healy in the *Cork Examiner* (now the *Irish Examiner*) entitled 'Elementary My Dear Boole' in January 1990.[836] Our intensive research in this area confirms that the claim that Boole was the inspiration for Moriarty is strong, and far more convincing than the claims of other names that have been suggested.

Fictional characters rarely appear out of the blue in an author's mind, but are often based on real people whom the author has come across, heard about, or read about. On the other hand, it is unusual for a fictional character to be based exclusively on a single person, if only for legal and practical reasons; a character is therefore more likely to be an amalgam inspired by several people to a greater or lesser degree.

Figure 14.1: Sir Arthur Conan Doyle

Undoubtedly the most famous and popular of all fictional detectives is Sherlock Holmes, a character invented by Sir Arthur Conan Doyle (1859–1930). The Sherlock Holmes stories have been immensely popular internationally, ever since they first appeared in 1887, and they have never been out of print since then. They have enjoyed widespread adaptations on radio, stage, film, television and video games. There is even a periodical devoted to Holmes, *The Baker Street Journal*. He enjoys periodic revivals on television, most notably *Sherlock*, starring Benedict Cumberbatch in the UK and *Elementary*, starring Jonny Lee Miller in the US.

Why then were the Sherlock Holmes stories so popular at the time, and have been ever since, throughout the world, and in so many languages? Certainly, they are timeless good yarns and exciting adventures, but so were many others of the time. What did these stories have that caught the public imagination and set them apart? Our belief is that Doyle portrayed the messianic figure of Sherlock Holmes as a superhuman character who used logical analysis and statistical techniques to deduce conclusions. In an age before the automated logic and data processing capabilities of the electronic computer, the reading public imagined the well-nigh infallible Holmes being programmed with facts and data and unerringly coming to the correct conclusion as to who had committed a particular crime and what the motivation and methodology were.

The tradition of the almost infallible sleuth using impeccable logic to deduce correct conclusions lives on today in novels – take Miss Marple and Hercule Poirot, for example. The very popular US television series *Criminal Minds* uses the computer to sift through vast amounts of data to narrow down the number of suspects. Another example of this is the excellent British detective series *New Tricks*, featuring the Unsolved Crime and Open Case Squad (UCOS) detective Brian Lane. However, an episode entitled 'A Death in the Family' featured a present-day UCOS team solving a cold case of a London murder committed in 1851 where one of the suspects gave the false name 'George Boole' to conceal his identity. Brian concluded that the culprit must have been a mathematician, otherwise he would not have known the name George Boole, famous for his work in logic. But in 1851 Boole's name was virtually unknown in London and elsewhere, because his seminal work, *A Mathematical Analysis of Logic*, published in 1847, achieved very little circulation. It was only after 1854, when *The Laws of Thought* appeared, that Boole's name became widely known among mathematicians. The moral of the story would appear to be: when introducing an historical figure into a modern fictional story, be very careful with the dates!

A central theme and motivation in the Sherlock Holmes stories is provided by data, logic, statistics, probability, deduction and proof. In Conan Doyle's autobiography, he states:

The first thing is to get your idea. Having got that key idea, one's next task is to conceal it and lay emphasis upon everything which can make for a different explanation.[837]

These concepts occur again and again in the Sherlock Holmes stories, as the following extracts illustrate:[838]

• To a great mind, nothing is little.[839]

• Eliminate all other factors and the one which remains must be the truth.[840] [This is remarkably close to Boole's assertion that the complement of 0 is 1.]

• I never guess. It is a shocking habit – destructive to the logical faculty.[841]

• You can, for example, never foretell what any one man will do, but you can say with precision what an average number will be up to.[842]

• An exception disproves the rule.[843]

• It is a capital mistake to theorise before one has data. Insensibly, one begins to twist facts to suit theories, instead of theories to suit facts.[844]

• How dangerous it always is to reason from insufficient data.[845]

• Crime is common. Logic is rare. Therefore it is upon the logic rather than upon the crime that you should concentrate.[846]

• Data, data, data. I cannot make bricks without data.[847]

• It's a wicked world, and when a clever man turns his brain to crime it is the worst of all.[848]

However, as Anthony Berkeley has perceptively remarked:

That was the trouble with the old-fashioned detective story. One deduction only was drawn from each fact, and it was invariably the right deduction. The Great Detective of the Past certainly had luck. In real life one can draw a hundred plausible deductions from one fact, and they are all equally wrong.[849]

It is entirely plausible that Conan Doyle would want to pay tribute to pure logic by basing one of his characters on George Boole, the founder of symbolic logic. If Holmes was the messianic logician on the side of law and order, then, if only for balance, or maybe even by Boolean bipolarity, the plot demanded the presence of a formidable opponent, an antichrist of diabolical cunning and evil, who like Lucifer of old had once occupied a high position but had fallen from grace. In mathematical terms, the vector v gives rise to a vector -v, of the same magnitude but opposite in direction, such that when added, $v + (-v) = 0$, and the vectors annihilate each other. To play this role, Arthur Conan Doyle gives us the notorious mathematician Professor James Moriarty, master criminal, and arch-villain.

Moriarty is of course a south of Ireland surname almost exclusively located in the counties of Kerry and Cork. The name is derived from the Gaelic surname Ó Muircheartaigh, meaning 'a person skilled in the ways of the sea'. But it has been suggested that Doyle chose the name Moriarty for his arch-criminal because it can also be rendered as 'mori-arte', one skilled in the art of death. Professor Tadhg Foley of NUI Galway comments that the name Moriarty could be derived from a famous phrase of the Latin poet Horace 'non omnis moriar' ('I shall not all die'). This may be connected with the well-known saying 'Sherlock Holmes will never die, because he never lived'.

It is generally accepted that Doyle based the name of his character on two brothers, John Francis Moriarty and Michael Moriarty, fellow pupils at Stonyhurst College, a Jesuit public school in the north of England. John Francis won the Stonyhurst prize for mathematics in 1873 and Michael won it in 1874. Significantly from our point of view, the Moriarty brothers were natives of Cork. John Francis went on to become a leading if colourful figure in the Irish judiciary and was appointed Lord Justice, though he did end his days in bankruptcy. We note incidentally that the part of James Moriarty in the acclaimed TV series *Sherlock* is played by an Irish actor, Andrew Scott. Recently, the present authors were contacted by John Moriarty who runs an engineering firm in County Kerry. He claims direct descent from the Stonyhurst Moriarty brothers and it turns out that he himself studied mathematics at University College Cork where he was taught by the first author. This is Doyle's description of Moriarty, through the mouth of Holmes:

He is a man of good birth and excellent education, endowed by Nature with a phenomenal mathematical faculty. At the age of twenty-one he wrote a treatise upon the binomial theorem which has had a European vogue. On the strength of it he won a mathematical chair at one of our smaller universities and had to all appearances a most brilliant career before him. But the man had hereditary tendencies of the most diabolical kind. A criminal strain ran in his blood, which, instead of being modified, was increased and rendered infinitely more dangerous by his extraordinary mental powers. Dark rumours gathered round him in the university town and eventually he was compelled to resign his chair and come down to London where he set up as an army coach …

… I seized my thread and followed it, until it led me, after a thousand cunning windings, to the ex-Professor Moriarty of mathematical celebrity. He is the Napoleon of crime, Watson. He is a genius, a philosopher, an abstract thinker. He has a brain of the first order. At the end of three months, I was forced to confess that I had at last met an antagonist who was my intellectual equal. My horror at his crimes was lost in my admiration at his skill.[850]

Later in the Sherlock Holmes stories there is a physical description of Moriarty:

He is extremely tall and thin, his forehead domes out in a white curve and his two eyes are deeply sunken in his head. He is clean shaven, pale and ascetic looking, retaining something of the professor in his features. His shoulders are rounded from much study and his face protrudes forwards and is forever slowly oscillating from side to side in a cunningly reptilian fashion. His soft precise fashion of speech leaves a conviction of sincerity which a mere bully could not produce.[851]

Elsewhere in the stories, we learn the following facts about Moriarty:

• His eyesight was poor.

• Inspector MacDonald of Scotland Yard remarks that he would have made a grand clergyman with his thin face and grey hair and solemn way of talking.

• His annual salary as a university professor was about £700 per annum.

• He had written a book called *The Dynamics of an Asteroid* which was described by Holmes as 'a book which ascends to such rarified heights of pure mathematics that it is said there was no man in the scientific press capable of criticising it'.

• He had a strong interest in practical astronomy, globes, eclipses and reflector lanterns.

• He had designed and built an air gun.

• He had two brothers, one of whom was also called James, incidentally, but this may have been a simple mistake on Doyle's part.

We now aim to demonstrate that the character of Professor James Moriarty is closely modelled on Professor George Boole. Nowhere in Bowers' original article is the claim explicitly made – just cleverly hinted at. But let us see how the known characteristics of George Boole fit the portrait of Moriarty as painted by Doyle:

- Like Moriarty, Boole became professor of mathematics at a small university, namely Queen's College Cork. Curiously, the late Irish playwright Hugh Leonard in his 1987 play *The Mask of Moriarty* places Moriarty as professor of mathematics at the University of Reading in England. Other suggested localities are Durham and Leeds.[852]

- In his twenties Boole had written a paper, deep and extensive, which won the Royal Society gold medal for mathematics, and appeared in its *Philosophical Transactions*. It was entitled 'On a General Method in Analysis' and one of the highlights of this paper was a generalisation of Taylor series extended to operators.[853] The binomial theorem is of course a very special and elementary case of Taylor's theorem, and Doyle may have picked this example because it was probable that readers who had reached any level of mathematical proficiency would have come across it. It also received a mention from W.S. Gilbert in *The Pirates of Penzance* in the major general's song:

> I'm very well acquainted too with matters mathematical
> I understand equations, both simple and quadratical,
> About binomial theorem I'm teeming with a lot of views,
> With many cheerful facts about the square on the hypotenuse.

Of course, Isaac Newton, a native of Lincolnshire like Boole, was one of the first people to prove the elementary case of the binomial theorem which he needed for the differentiation of powers and polynomials. However, professional mathematicians, even of the nineteenth century, would probably be amused at the notion of a treatise on a topic as elementary as the binomial theorem and the winning of a mathematical chair on the strength of it. On the other hand, the extension of the binomial theorem to negative, fractional, irrational, or complex exponents is a non-trivial matter, and perhaps this is what Doyle had in mind. But in the present context, it is significant to note that Boole's prize-winning Royal Society paper of 1844 was a crucial factor in his winning the chair of mathematics at Cork.

• Boole certainly had a phenomenal mathematical faculty.

• Boole was undoubtedly a genius, a philosopher, and an abstract thinker. Indeed, in conjunction with Hamilton and Cayley, many regard Boole as one of the founders of abstract algebra, and Bertrand Russell claimed that pure mathematics was discovered in Boole's book *An Investigation of the Laws of Thought* published in 1854.

• Boole was tall and thin, clean-shaven, and had poor eyesight.

• Boole certainly had the appearance of a nineteenth-century clergyman and we know that he would have liked to become a clergyman, had family circumstances permitted it.

• Boole's professorial salary in Cork was about £600 per annum (half from the Queen's College and half from student fees). This is close to the figure of £700, the annual salary of Professor James Moriarty.

• Like Moriarty, Boole had an intense interest in both theoretical and practical astronomy, inherited from his father. He gave lectures on astronomy at the Lincoln Mechanics' Institute, and was selected, above the professors of physics and natural philosophy, to deliver lectures on astronomy to the undergraduates at Queen's College Cork. Boole also wrote a paper entitled 'Are the Planets Inhabited?'[854]

• In 1851 Boole had written a paper concerning Mitchell's Problem of the Distribution of the Fixed Stars, comparable to Moriarty's *Dynamics of an Asteroid*. Additionally, in 1863, Boole published a paper entitled *On the Differential Equations of Dynamics*. Interestingly, in the twentieth century, asteroids were named after both Boole and his daughter Ethel Voynich. [Conan Doyle is surely having a Homeric nod when he describes Moriarty's *Dynamics of an Asteroid* as 'ascending to rarefied heights of pure mathematics'. Such a book would almost certainly be classified as applied mathematics.]

• Boole and his father built telescopes, beam balances and other pieces of scientific apparatus, comparable to Moriarty's air gun. Incidentally, Boole's son-in-law, Charles Howard Hinton, built the first air-powered gun for projecting baseballs used in practice by the Princeton baseball team.[855]

• The dark rumours gathering around Moriarty could refer to Boole's bitter and public confrontation with Sir Robert Kane, president of Queen's College, Cork.

Figure 14.2: George Boole (1864)

Figure 14.3: Professor Moriarty by Sidney Paget (1893)

- Boole and Moriarty both coached pupils.

- The matter of finding a parallel for the hereditary taint in Moriarty's background in Boole's life is a little problematical. Perhaps Doyle was referring to John Boole's term in prison, though admittedly this was merely for non-payment of debt, or the fact that Boole's mother was born out of wedlock. More plausibly, it could refer to the fact that Boole's brother Charles had strong manic and sadistic tendencies. These were the inspiration for Ethel Voynich's novel *Jack Raymond* based on his cruel treatment of her when she was forced to live with his family after her father's death.

- It is perhaps facetious to mention it, but both Boole and Moriarty met with a watery end, Boole allegedly between his wife's damp sheets and Moriarty at Reichenbach Falls.

- George Boole had two brothers, William and Charles, with widely different personalities.

But perhaps one of the strongest pieces of evidence in our opinion for the Boole–Moriarty connection is visual. The only photograph of Boole was taken in 1864 when he was ill and looks quite different from the flattering portrait one usually sees of him. The Sherlock Holmes stories were first

Figure 14.4: Image of Moriarty superimposed on photograph of Boole

published in *The Strand Magazine* and were exquisitely illustrated there by the artist Sidney Paget. Examining a portrait of Moriarty that Paget drew there, it could justifiably be claimed that he based his drawing on the one and only photograph of Boole. The faces, shoulder and arm angles, and physical shapes of the two men are uncannily alike, down to the waistcoat, long coat, buttons, collar and neck tie. Firstly, we reproduce the two images separately and then superimposed on each other.

Having presented compelling evidence that the character of Moriarty is largely based on Boole, we must now address how and why this could have happened. The answers are based on a long and tangled tale. George Boole's widow Mary Everest Boole (1832–1916) outlived him by fifty-two years. Soon after his death, she moved from Cork to London with her young family of five daughters. She obtained a post as librarian at Queen's College London, the first women's college in England, a position obtained for her by the Rev. F.D. Maurice, whose teachings George Boole had followed. She supplemented her meagre income as a matron, running a boarding house for students of Queen's College while some of her daughters were students there also. She was interested in a wide range of subjects, including psychology, psychic science and Judaism, as well as mathematics, and held 'true logic' classes to which students were encouraged to bring their problems for discussion. Ultimately her ideas were considered 'unstable and dangerous', and the lease of her premises was terminated by the college in 1873.

Mary Boole then became an assistant or secretary to the eccentric surgeon James Hinton and a devout disciple of Hinton's unorthodox and even dangerous theories. In London she kept open house for literary and scientific figures and many famous people attended soirées at her home in Notting Hill. Among these were Henry Maudsley, Wedgwood, Shaw,

Figure 14.5: H.G. Wells

Chesterton, and H.G. Wells. Wells was of course the father of modern science fiction and the author of such masterpieces as *The Time Machine, War of the Worlds, The Invisible Man* and *The First Men on the Moon*. Indeed, *The Time Machine* (1895) makes mention of the fourth dimension and it has been suggested that Wells was influenced on this topic by discussions with Boole's mathematical daughter Alicia and her brother-in-law Charles Howard Hinton.

Wells and Mary Boole were strong supporters of fringe medicine and initially they appeared to have been friendly, but this situation did not last. A bitter dispute had arisen between them, apparently sparked off by some literary matter, and this became personal and quite nasty. Wells' antagonism towards both Mary and George Boole came to the surface and became public. In 1911 Wells published a novel called *The New Machiavelli*, which was in fact a thinly disguised autobiography. The novel contained a bitter attack on the Fabian couple Sidney and Beatrice Webb, but when Wells was advised by his publisher that the Webbs were likely to sue, he made extensive changes in the second edition of the book in 1914. He introduced an extremely unpleasant couple called the Booles and attributed all the 'dirty work' to them. The extent of his bitterness and his dislike for them can be gleaned from some extracts from the book describing the Booles and their activities; and there can be no doubt to whom he is referring, if only because of the rarity of their surname. It is also worth noting that there was considerable correspondence between Mary Boole and Marjory Pease, who was at one time secretary of the Fabian Society.

Sister Rosemary Boole, an Anglican nun and a granddaughter of George Boole's brother Charles, recounts that Mary Everest Boole was a friend of H.G. Wells but that they quarrelled, and he put an 'interesting' character named Boole in his novel *The New Machiavelli* on purpose to annoy her, or so she was told.[856] And here, verbatim, are some of the offensive extracts from that book:[857]

- Then with a real feeling of relief I came across the culprits, the Booles, those queer rivals and allies of the Baileys [= the Webbs]. It was odd I didn't think of the Booles at the outset, but I didn't. [Mrs Boole] was a vulgar careerist aiming only at prominence and perhaps her best quality was a real unreasoning devotion to what she imagined were her great exemplar's interests ... The Booles set themselves with all the loyalties of parasites to disseminate a highly coloured scandal against me.

• I passed at a bound from such monstrous theology to a towering rage against the Booles. In an instant and with no sense of absurdity I wanted – in the intervals of love and fine thinking – to fling about that strenuously virtuous couple. I wanted to fling them into the gutter and make a common massacre of all the prosperous rascals that make a trade and rule of virtue. [This could indicate that Wells was tired of hearing about the virtuous sanctity and perfect behaviour of George and Mary Boole and wanted to redress the balance by denigrating them. Clearly, he was not afraid of being sued by Mary Boole.]

• I was equally unsuccessful with Boole. I caught the little wretch in the League Club and he wriggled and lied. He tried to get past me as though he had not seen me. He couldn't say where he had got his facts, he wouldn't admit he had told anyone. That struck me as mean, even for Boole. I've still the odd vivid impression of his fluting voice, excusing the inexcusable, his shifty face evading me, his perspiration – beaded forehead, the shuffling shoulders and the would-be exculpatory gestures of his enormous ugly hands. 'I can assure you my dear fellow,' he lisped, 'I can assure you we've done everything to shield you – everything.'

• Boole, I found was warning fathers of girls against me as a 'reckless libertine' and his wife, hushed, roguish and dishevelled, was sitting on her fender curb after dinner and pledging little parties of five or six women at a time with infinite gusto not to let the matter go further.

• 'The Booles don't intend to let this matter drop,' I said, 'they mean that everyone in London is to know about it. Damn them, to be separated by people like that. They are organising scandal.'

• Mrs Boole is a person of literary ambitions herself but she writes a poor and slovenly prose and handles an argument badly.

• I went to Mrs Boole and tried to stop her. The woman wouldn't listen, she wouldn't think, she denied and lied, she behaved like a naughty child of six years old which has made up its mind to be hurtful.

Thus, there can be little doubt that Wells had come to loathe Mary Everest Boole and by association her perfect husband George, whom he had never met because Wells was born in 1866, two years after George's death. Incidentally, Wells also included a character named De Booley in his book *The War in the Air* published in 1907. De Booley is described as having mysteriously disappeared while flying an early aeroplane in Paris.[858] Ironically, Wells was one of the people who predicted the modern Internet or World Wide Web. In his book *World Brain* (1937) he put forward the idea of a permanent World Encyclopaedia.[859]

14.6: George Gissing, E.W. Hornung, Arthur Conan Doyle and H.G. Wells in Italy

In the period 1881–3 Wells worked as a shop assistant in Portsmouth and just around the corner from him was the surgery of Dr Arthur Conan Doyle. It is likely that the two men met then, and Wells, who was a lifelong diabetic, may even have been a patient of Doyle's – his boss, the shop proprietor Edwin Hyde, certainly was. In later years they met again through their writing for *The Strand Magazine*. But there is more concrete evidence that the two men were friends and maybe even good friends; a photograph shows them together on holiday in Italy in March 1898 when Wells and his wife Jane were visiting the novelist George Gissing in Siena.

Doyle was accompanied by his brother-in-law E.W. Hornung and the five of them had a holiday, drinking wine, eating Italian food, and travelling in the Campagna and the Alban Hills. Wells and his wife also spent a day in Isola Di Gaiola, at the home of Doyle's sister. In addition, it is known that Wells and Doyle were occasional correspondents on a variety of subjects.[860]

Some details of the life of Arthur Conan Doyle are now relevant. He has been described as a British Celt, Irish by descent, Scottish by birth, and English by adoption. His grandfather, James Doyle, an artist and cartoonist, left Dublin in 1815, the year of Boole's birth. His father, Charles Doyle, was a government official in Edinburgh where in 1855 (the year Boole married) he married Mary Foley, also of Irish descent. Their son Arthur (Ignatius) Conan Doyle was born on 22 May 1859 in Edinburgh, the second of ten children, of whom only seven survived. The family described themselves as 'Irish and Catholic'.

The young Arthur Conan was precocious. When he was only ten, his local library committee passed a byelaw aimed solely at him to the effect that 'no boy shall be permitted to change his library book more than three times a day'. He wrote his first short story at the age of six and although he loved reading and literature, he was not so enthusiastic about other school subjects. At Hodder School, a preparatory school for the Catholic public school Stonyhurst run by the Jesuits, he developed a hatred of Greek, equalled only by his loathing of Latin, ironically two subjects which the young George Boole had taught himself at around the same age. Of particular interest to us is that he also had an abhorrence of Euclid, equalled only by his detestation of algebra. 'Mathematics of every sort I abhor and detest,' he is quoted as saying. 'My education was the usual public-school routine of Euclid, algebra, and the classics, which is calculated to leave a lasting abhorrence of these subjects.' But interestingly, these attitudes did not prevent him from being successful in subjects he disliked. He got the highest marks in the school in arithmetic and he mastered the parabola (but not the ellipse) in geometry. And in June 1875 he reported to his mother that he had done well in Latin and Greek.[861] As a result of his school experience he acquired a lifelong hatred of mathematics, to which he devoted very little time. But while he was reluctant in his studies, his brain was very nimble, and he became very popular with his classmates as a storyteller. He was stimulated by the works of Macaulay and by the novels of Scott, who incidentally was Boole's favourite novelist also.

Doyle entered the University of Edinburgh as a medical student in 1876 and later in his writings based some of his characters on his teachers there, including Dr Joseph Bell, widely believed to be the inspiration for Sherlock Holmes. Doyle had observed that Bell could deduce from a patient's appearance not only what disease he was suffering from, but also his occupation and place of residence. Doyle qualified as a doctor in 1881 and had many menial jobs in various medical practices. He wrote his first Sherlock Holmes story in 1886 and went on to become one of the world's most successful authors. Having rejected his Catholic faith, possibly as a result of his harsh treatment by the Jesuits, he turned instead to spiritualism and psychic phenomena. He was in contact with many of the leading literary figures of his day including Wilde, Barrie, Stevenson, Chesterton, Jerome K. Jerome, George Moore and, of course, H.G. Wells.

Doyle had a reputation as a joker. Indeed, it has been strongly suggested that the first name of his most famous character, Sherlock, was based on that of a classmate at Stonyhurst, one Patrick Sherlock, from County Carlow in Ireland. Sherlock was in fact a distant relative of Doyle's. The joke was that Sherlock was not considered very bright, and one of the least likely in his class capable of making logical deductions.

It is worth noting some curious connections between George Boole and Arthur Conan Doyle:

• Lycett describes Doyle's religious views as 'in a broad sense unitarian'.[862]

• Doyle, referring to his own father's mental state, said, 'Insanity is often the logic of an accurate mind overtaxed,' quoting from the American judge Oliver Wendell Holmes, who is widely believed to be the source of the surname of Sherlock Holmes.[863]

• Both Boole and Doyle had an interest in mesmerism.

• In late life, Doyle began to read the works of Renan, one of Boole's guiding lights.

• Doyle has Holmes say, 'Instead, the detective method is more correctly known as "abduction", which is about assessing various clues and concluding that on the best balance of probabilities, something happened. This is the more creative modus operandi of Sherlock Holmes.'[864]

We have no evidence that Doyle was a guest at Mary Boole's gatherings but he may have been as many of his literary circle, including Wells, did attend. Doyle and George Boole of course never met, but either from Mary Boole or through Wells, Doyle must have heard about the saintly George, his prowess in logic and deduction and his ground-breaking contributions to the higher mathematics. Add to the mixture Doyle's undoubted hatred of mathematics and his paradoxical worship of logic (though in those days logic was not really regarded as a branch of mathematics), his propensity to joking, and Wells' documented hatred of the Booles, then the following scenario suggests itself: Doyle and Wells, either in jest or seriousness, and it is difficult to tell which, conspired to invert and pervert the saintly character of George Boole into that of the arch-villain Moriarty. Boole's genius was retained, but his undoubted goodness became pure evil, and now Holmes had a worthy opponent, equal and opposite to himself. Doyle may even have regarded the portrayal of Boole as Moriarty as a perverse tribute to the founder of symbolic logic.

Inversion of the characteristics of a real person to create a fictional character was in fact a common technique used by Arthur Conan Doyle. Jane Stanford in her book *Moriarty Unmasked* gives three other such instances of inversion in Doyle's works.[865]

And here we must record what may be just a series of bizarre coincidences but may also have a bearing on our claims. William Jackson Cummins MD (1828–93) was a member of a well-known Cork medical family and was at one time Cork coroner. It was he who signed George Boole's death certificate in 1864. Cummins graduated in medicine with a degree of MD from Edinburgh University and also obtained an LRCSE[866] from Edinburgh. This was of course the alma mater of both Arthur Conan Doyle and Joseph Bell. Cummins and his family lived at 'Lichfield Cottage', Ballintemple, Cork, Boole's final residence, just before the Boole family moved in there in 1863. And in 1865, after Boole's death and the departure of Mary Boole and her daughters for England, it appears that the Cummins family moved back again to 'Lichfield', which was then, and still is, a beautiful family home.

Boole and Cummins were acquainted with each other. An undated letter from Cummins has survived, in which he requested Boole's assistance:

My dear Dr Boole,

There is a poor German woman in the North Infirmary who cannot speak a word of English and there is no one who can understand her or speak to her. Mr Gillick asked me today to write to you and request if you have time to call and speak to her as they tell me you are a good German scholar – perhaps you would kindly do so as the poor creature's case is a very trying one.

Yours truly,

Wm. Cummins [867]

Boole obliged and, in her book *Symbolical Methods of Study* (1884), his wife Mary records:

An old German Jewess, whom I visited in a hospital in Ireland, told me that she was ill-used by the nurses and patients on account of her religion. She added, 'My child, there is a Messiah. Whether he has already appeared or whether he is still to come, we know not; but one thing I know; all men who treat each other as brothers, are his.'[868]

Geraldine Dorothy Cummins (1890–1969), a granddaughter of William Cummins, followed a literary career as a novelist and playwright; she was also a suffragette and an Irish international hockey player. But her main claim to fame is that she was a spiritualist medium, producing 'channelled' and automatic writing in a trance-like state, mostly concerning the lives of Jesus and Saint Paul. In 1928 she published a controversial book called *The Scripts of Cleophas*[869] giving details on early Christian activity complementing the Acts of the Apostles and Saint Paul's writings, allegedly communicated by Paul's companion Cleophas. She continued with *Paul in Athens* (1930)[870] and *The Great Days of Ephesus* (1933).[871]

14.7: Geraldine Cummins

Geraldine is relevant to our story because in later life Arthur Conan Doyle became intensely interested in spiritualism and psychic phenomena and Geraldine Cummins was one of the writers on these topics he read and admired. Indeed, when problems arose concerning the publication of her work, he supported her cause in a copyright dispute with F. Bligh Bond, editor of *Psychic Science*, who had helped transcribe the automatic writings of Cleophas. Doyle and Cummins eventually prevailed. We do not advance Geraldine's writings in any sense as a validation of a Moriarty–Boole connection, but one must admit at least that they constitute an extraordinary series of coincidences.

We note that one of the students in Boole's mathematical class in Queen's College Cork for 1851 was named Jeremiah Moriarty, a fact which Doyle could hardly have known. But Moriarty is also recorded as having attended only five out of a possible ninety or so lectures, so perhaps his criminal tendencies were breaking out at an early stage of his mathematical development!

Several other coincidences manifest themselves also. For example, the name of one of Boole's very first teachers as a child was Holmes, and what is one to make of the following fragment of a letter written to his mother by his former student Edmund Larken in 1860 from Aden:

... The man Moriarty whom De V[ericour] mentions is a beast. Dent and I tried to marry him to a nice little girl in Sinai but he escaped our toils. I stayed with him a short time in Broach but didn't like him.[872]

The extremely strong Celtic (both Scottish and Irish) backgrounds of so many players in the Holmes scenario are worthy of emphasis. We may mention Foley, Bell, Sherlock, Moran, Stapleton, Moriarty and three generations of Doyles. Allied to this are the many Irish place names featuring in Doyle's life – Dublin, Waterford, Kerry and Cork – and we feel that to link the mathematician Professor Moriarty with the mathematician Professor Boole, who spent all his professorial life in Cork, is a not unnatural step.

It is interesting to note that Anthony Horowitz, the best-selling author of the modern Sherlock Holmes stories, appears to agree with our claim that there is a Moriarty–Boole connection. In his book *Moriarty* (2014), his character Moriarty writes:

My father determined that my brother and I should be sent to England to complete our education. I found myself at Hall's Academy in Waddington where I excelled at astronomy and mathematics. From there I went to Queen's College, Cork, where I studied under the great George Boole, and it was with his guidance that, at the age of twenty-one, I published the treatise on the binomial theorem which, I am proud to say, caused quite a stir across Europe.[873]

Some quotes from Holmes himself concerning Moriarty would seem to fit very comfortably with the Boole-Moriarty hypothesis. For example:

• When you have one of the finest brains in Europe up against you, and all the powers of darkness at his back, there are infinite possibilities.[874]

• A brain that might have made or marred the destiny of nations. Moriarty seems to be a very respectable, learned, and talented sort of man.[875]

• We balance probabilities and choose the most likely. It is the scientific use of the imagination.[876] [Boole was of course the first person to give an almost axiomatic treatment of the theory of probability in his 1854 book *The Laws of Thought*.]

• You see but you do not observe.[877]

Boole saw significance in ordinary language and elementary mathematics which many others had seen but not observed.

Having presented our case that Boole was largely the inspiration for Moriarty, we feel it only fair to examine the cases that have been put forward for other candidates. At no time do we claim that Boole is the exclusive inspiration for the great villain, and we admit that at least some of the evidence for others has merit.

SIMON NEWCOMB (1835–1909)

A case that Professor James Moriarty owes something to the Canadian-American astronomer and mathematician Simon Newcomb has been made by astronomer Bradley E. Schaefer.[878] The strengths of Schaefer's case may be summarised as follows:

- Newcomb's first research paper, which was never published, was entitled 'A New Demonstration of the Binomial Theorem'. He was just nineteen when he wrote it.

- Newcomb published several papers on the dynamics of asteroids.

- Newcomb was a difficult and intimidating individual who bore grudges and was more feared than liked. He studied mathematics under Benjamin Peirce but became envious of C.S. Peirce, Peirce's talented logician son, and went out of his way to destroy his career.

- Newcomb was Professor of Mathematics and Astronomy at Johns Hopkins University from 1884.

- Schaefer postulates a link between Newcomb and Doyle through a mutual friend named Alfred Drayson, a patient of Doyle's and a fellow spiritualist. Indeed, Drayson himself has been proposed as a model for Moriarty.

However, Schaefer's case also has several weaknesses, among which are the following:

- Newcomb's appearance is nothing like that of Moriarty as portrayed by Sidney Paget. Newcomb was stout, square-faced and heavily bearded.

- Moriarty was professor at a 'provincial university' and the context is clearly the British Isles and not North America.

Figure 14.8: Simon Newcomb

• Newcomb was obviously an applied mathematician and called his autobiography *Reminiscences of an Astronomer.*[879] [Boole was interested in astronomy, but nowhere describes himself as an astronomer.] Moriarty would certainly be described as a pure mathematician.

• There is no evidence of any direct contact or meeting between Newcomb and Doyle although they lived during the same thirty-five-year period.

• Newcomb does not appear to have any Irish connection either by ancestry or by name.

• Newcomb once borrowed a translation of Laplace's *Mecanique Celeste* from the library of the Smithsonian Institution but found the mathematics of the book beyond him. Most of his scientific publications were in the areas of astronomy, economics and statistics. At one stage he declared that flight by heavier-than-air objects was impossible, despite the many birds he presumably saw about him. The evidence indicates that he was a competent but not a particularly skilful or innovative mathematician.

ADAM WORTH (1844–1902)

Figure 14.9: Adam Worth

Adam Worth was a real-life American criminal whom Scotland Yard detective Robert Anderson nicknamed 'the Napoleon of the criminal world'. Since Doyle reports Holmes as describing Moriarty in the words 'He is the Napoleon of Crime, Watson', it is very likely that Doyle latched on to this catchy phrase to describe Moriarty. In addition, the American writer Vincent Starrett reports that Dr Gray C. Briggs once told him that Doyle had said to him that 'Worth was the original of Moriarty'.[880] But what reliance can be placed on such unverified and alleged third-hand conversations is open to discussion. Undoubtedly, Worth was a lifelong and career criminal who operated criminal networks in New York, London and on the continent of Europe, but there any resemblance with Moriarty begins to fade. Worth began as a pickpocket and robber of low-level pawnshops, criminal actions totally unworthy of our arch-villain. Unlike Moriarty, whose forte was masterly organisation behind the scenes, Worth himself took part in his crimes, and was caught and jailed several times, though he did manage to escape on a few occasions. In fact, Holmes commented on Moriarty 'He does little himself. He only plans.'[881]

In 1876 Worth stole a very valuable painting by Gainsborough of Georgina Cavendish, Duchess of Devonshire, from the London gallery of Thomas Agnew. Worth took a fancy to this work of art and decided to keep it, much to the annoyance of his partners in crime. In 'The Valley of Fear',[882] Holmes remarks that a painting found in Moriarty's rooms could hardly have been purchased by a man on a professor's salary. The painting is named as *La Jeune Fille a l'Agneau*, which some commentators have suggested is a pun on the name of Agnew who owned the gallery. This theory is surely tenuous.

There is no hint of any connection with Ireland in Worth's life; he had been born into a poor Jewish family in Germany which moved to the United States when he was five years of age. There is no suggestion that Worth had any skill in mathematics or indeed any academic prowess whatsoever.

He was anything but a genius, a philosopher, or an abstract thinker with a brain of the first order. His photograph indicates that he was short and squat (he was sometimes called 'little Adam') and square-faced with a large moustache, quite unlike the Paget illustration of Moriarty. But one straw in the wind is that Doyle may have based his Sherlock Holmes story 'The Red-Headed League'[883] on a real-life robbery carried out by Worth and his accomplice Charles Bullard which involved breaking into a Boston bank by means of a tunnel from the building next door. Indeed, it has been suggested that the spectacular 2015 Hatton Gardens multi-million-pound robbery was inspired by the same scenario.

In 1997 *Sunday Times* journalist Ben Macintyre published a book entitled *The Napoleon of Crime: the life and times of Adam Worth, master thief*,[884] strongly supporting the theory that Worth was the model for Moriarty. He also claimed that T.S. Eliot's cat 'Macavity' was inspired by Doyle's characterisation of Moriarty.[885]

Macintyre's assumption that Worth is the almost exclusive model for Moriarty has several flaws. For a start, he freely admits that Moriarty is physically very different from Worth – in fact a far cry from the diminutive, moustachioed criminal. Moreover, Moriarty is held responsible for murders, but Worth, while a master at forgery and robbery, prided himself at never having used violence or even contemplated murder. Worth too in his final years had an astonishingly close relationship and understanding with the Pinkerton Detective Agency, which would have been totally out of character for Moriarty.

Macintyre does concede that aspects of Moriarty's character were doubtless drawn from sources other than Worth but the examples he gives are highly implausible. Moriarty's exceptional mathematical ability, it seems, is just a reference to Doyle's friend Major General Drayson, an obscure and at best a minor mathematician. Friedrich Nietzsche is mentioned as the inspiration for Moriarty's being an abstract philosopher. Even Moriarty's surname is explained away as referring to one George Moriarty, a crook who featured in the London newspapers in 1874. Macintyre makes no mention of the mathematical Moriarty brothers at Stonyhurst, Moriarty's professorship, and the many Irish connections. Simon Newcomb too does not feature in his analysis.

JONATHAN WILD (1682–1725)

In 'The Valley of Fear', Professor Moriarty is referred to as a latter-day Jonathan Wild by Sherlock Holmes in these words:

> Everything comes in circles – even Professor Moriarty. Jonathan Wild was the hidden force of the London criminals to whom he sold his brains and his organisation on a fifteen per cent commission. The old wheel turns and the same spoke comes up.[886]

Figure 14.10: Image of Jonathan Wild on his gallows ticket

Wild was a London underworld figure, renowned for playing both sides of the law against each other, posing as a righteous crime fighter and nicknamed 'Thief Taker General'. He received large sums of money for recovering stolen property which he and his gang had in fact stolen in the first place, and for exposing criminals, often his rivals, and he sometimes betrayed his own men when he lost control over them. But his followers in turn betrayed him and he was hanged at Tyburn in 1725. Despite his crimes, he was a folk hero and the inspiration for John Gay's *The Beggar's Opera* in 1728.

It is possible that Doyle based the notion of Moriarty as arch-criminal and mastermind on Wild, but Moriarty and Wild have almost nothing else in common. Wild was a low-minded criminal, who consorted with prostitutes, and also co-operated with the law when it suited him. Curiously, he worked with another criminal named Charles Hitchen whose followers were known as his 'Mathematicians' and this may have given Doyle the notion of making Moriarty a mathematician also. But Wild was poorly educated and his criminality was based on animal cunning rather than intelligence.

OTHER POSSIBLE MODELS FOR MORIARTY

Mathematicians that have been suggested as models for Moriarty include the great German Carl Friedrich Gauss (1777–1855) who did indeed write a famous paper on the dynamics of an asteroid, and the Indian genius

Srinivasa Ramanujan (1887–1920) who wrote about generalisations of the binomial theorem, but in these cases no analysis of 'how' or 'why' has been put forward, and these suggestions would appear to be far-fetched.

It has also been suggested that Moriarty's appearance and build may have been inspired by those of Father Thomas Kay, prefect of discipline at Stonyhurst, whom Doyle may have disliked when presumably punished for his behaviour and lack of attention to his studies. For completeness, we also mention the names of James Payn, Robert Christison, and even Nietzsche; Christison has been proposed as a model for both Holmes and Moriarty! On investigation, we did not feel that a serious case could be made for any of these candidates.

Other ingenious theories have been put forward over the years which suggest that either Moriarty did not exist at all or was simply Holmes himself, who tired of the ease with which he solved all the crimes he was presented with and desired a worthy criminal opponent. With regard to the first of these theories A.G. Macdonnell in *Baker Street Studies* (1934) wrote:

> Moriarty did not exist. He was invented by Holmes. Or rather Holmes selected a perfectly ordinary ex-professor and fastened on to the unfortunate man the fearful reputation which has dogged him ever since.[887]

He goes on to state that Holmes, after a series of partial failures and less than satisfactory outcomes, excused himself by claiming that criminals were becoming more ingenious, culminating in the imaginary Moriarty. This theory is certainly consistent with some extracts from the Sherlock Holmes stories. For example:

> My mind rebels at stagnation. Give me problems, give me work, give me the most abstruse cryptogram, or the most intricate analysis, and I am in my own proper atmosphere! I can dispense then with artificial stimulants. But I abhor the dull routine of existence. That is why I have chosen my own particular profession – or rather created it, for I am the only one in the world.[888]

> You know my powers, dear Watson and yet at the end of three months I was forced to confess that I had at last met an antagonist who was my intellectual equal.[889]

The second theory that Moriarty was actually Holmes himself is both ingenious and frightening, if a little unlikely. It is akin to suggesting to a believer that God and Satan are one, equating pure goodness with pure evil. Admittedly, nobody ever saw Holmes and Moriarty together even at the Reichenbach Falls, and we have only the word of Holmes that the two of them did actually meet. It is plausible that Moriarty did represent the evil side of Holmes' character and how he imagined he would behave if he were a super-intelligent arch-criminal. The theme has of course been well explored by Doyle's friend Robert Louis Stevenson in his masterpiece *The Strange Case of Dr Jekyll and Mr Hyde* (1886), the classic novel of the ongoing fight between the good and evil natures in the heart of every human being.[890]

Doyle and Stevenson had a great deal in common; both were authors, natives of Edinburgh, graduates of Edinburgh University, cricketers and intensely interested in spiritualism. Doyle studied medicine at Edinburgh just after Stevenson graduated in law there and there is no evidence the two men ever met there or elsewhere, but they certainly corresponded by letter. Doyle planned a trip to Samoa to visit Stevenson but it never took place, probably because of Stevenson's final illness. Since Doyle had already 'borrowed' part of the backdrop of 'A Study in Scarlet' from *The Dynamiter* written by Stevenson and his wife Fanny in 1903,[891] it is not implausible to suggest that in creating Moriarty, Doyle may have been influenced, consciously or unconsciously, by Dr Jekyll and Mr Hyde.

Finally, we mention in passing a mysterious but significant paragraph written by Mary Everest Boole in her biographical essay on her husband, 'Home Side of a Scientific Mind', published in 1878 but written a number of years earlier, probably shortly soon after his death:

> It is a curious thing that all my husband's early friends speak of him as if he had been a saint from his cradle, and as if evil had been naturally further from him, and goodness easier to him than other men. I think, on the contrary, that I never saw anyone in whom the possibilities of evil seemed more rife.[892]

It is possible that Doyle read this paragraph, published in an Irish periodical, and that it planted the idea in his mind to demonise Boole.

We are now at the stage in this book described by Holmes himself in the story 'The Crooked Man':

Having gathered these facts, Watson, I smoked several pipes over them, trying to separate those which were crucial from those which were merely incidental.[893]

To summarise and conclude, we contend that the concept of Moriarty as a master criminal may have been inspired by both Wild and Worth, who were actual historical figures of some disrepute. There the resemblance ends. The titles of Moriarty's mathematical works may have been based on those of Newcomb. But all the other characteristics of Moriarty – an intellectual giant, a mathematical genius, a university professor, a logician to match Holmes, a probability and statistics theorist – correspond closely to those of Boole. Add to these Moriarty's appearance and dress in the Paget drawings and the Cork origins of the Moriarty brothers. The weight of this evidence makes a very strong case for the claim that Doyle based the character of Professor James Moriarty primarily on that of Professor George Boole.

NOTES AND REFERENCES

All references in the format BP/1/... *refer to the Boole Papers in the Boole Archive of University College Cork.*

1. Susannah Chaloner (1772–1825) was the sister of George Boole's father, John Boole.

2. Thomas Cooper was a Chartist leader. He married George Boole's first cousin, Susanna Chaloner.

3. George Boole, 'On a General Method in Analysis', *Philosophical Transactions of the Royal Society*, vol. 134, 1844, pp. 225–82.

4. Mary Everest Boole, 'Home Side of a Scientific Mind', *Mary Everest Boole Collected Works*, edited by E.M. Cobham (Essex: C.W. Daniel, 1931), p. 1341.

5. Ibid.

6. Abraham Cowley (1618–67) was a popular English poet of the seventeenth century.

7. The daughter of George Boole's paternal aunt Susannah Chaloner, Susanna, married the Chartist Thomas Cooper. See Chapter Nine.

8. George Quilter, Vicar of Canwick, near Lincoln. *The Clergy List for 1841* (London: C. Cox, 1841), p. 163.

9. MaryAnn is most likely referring to the Latin text book *Latin Delectus with a Copious Vocabulary for the Use of the Edinburgh Academy* (Edinburgh: Oliver & Boyd and Simpkin & Marshall, 1832).

10. Richard Andrew, MA, was the curate of St Michael's Lincoln. *The Clergy List for 1841* (London: C. Cox, 1841), p. 5.

11. For a full account of the controversy surrounding the translation of *Ode to the Spring*, see Desmond MacHale, *The Life and Work of George Boole: a prelude to the digital age* (Cork: Cork University Press, 2014), pp. 8–17.

12. George Boole to Joseph Hill, 26 December 1832, BP/1/221/1.

13. Mary Davis was a friend of George Boole, the niece of Robert Hall of Waddington. For details on her correspondence with Boole, see Chapter Ten.

14. Philip Cipriani Hambly Potter (1792–1871) was a British composer, pianist and educator.

15. George Boole, 'Researches on the Theory of Analytical Transactions, with a Special Application to the Reduction of the General Equation of the Second Order' (1841), *Cambridge Mathematical Journal*, vol. 2, pp. 64–73.

16. Robert Grosseteste (1175–1253) was an English statesman, scholastic philosopher, theologian, scientist and Bishop of Lincoln.

17. George Boole, 'On a General Method in Analysis', *Philosophical Transactions of the Royal Society*, vol. 134, 1844, pp. 225–82.

18. Samuel Hunter Christie (1784–1865) was a British scientist and mathematician. He served as Secretary of the Royal Society between 1837 and 1853.

19. Marshall Hall FRS (1790–1857) was an English physician and physiologist.

20. Philip Kelland (1808–79) was an English mathematician. He was appointed Professor of Mathematics at the University of Edinburgh in 1838.

21. Felicia Hemans (nee Browne) (1793–1835) was a popular English Romantic poet. She published nineteen volumes of poetry. Her best-known works included 'Casabianca' (The boy stood on the burning deck) and 'The Homes of England' (The stately homes of England).

22. George Boole, *The Mathematical Analysis of Logic, being an Essay towards a Calculus of Deductive Reasoning* (Cambridge: Macmillan, Barclay & Macmillan, 1847).

23. George Boole, *An Investigation of the Laws of Thought, on which are Founded the Mathematical Theories of Logic and Probabilities* (London: Walton & Maberly, 1854).

24. John Hannah, DD (1792–1867) was an English Wesleyan Methodist minister.

25. The Ranters were one of a number of nonconformist dissenting groups that emerged around the time of the English Commonwealth (1649–60). Ranters were regarded as heretical by the established Church and seem to have been regarded by the government as a threat to social order. They denied the authority of churches, of scripture, of the current ministry and of services, instead calling on men to listen to the divine within them. Ranters were often associated with nudity, which they may have used as a manner of social protest as well as religious expression as a symbol of abandoning earthly goods.

26. Dinah Morris was a Methodist lay preacher in George Eliot's novel *Adam Bede* (1859).

27. William Henry Channing (1810–84) was an American Unitarian clergyman, writer and philosopher. James Martineau (1805–1900) was an English religious philosopher influential in the history of Unitarianism. For forty-five years he was professor of mental and moral philosophy and political economy in Manchester New College, the principal training college for British Unitarianism. See Chapter Seven.

28. MaryAnn is referring to their paternal uncle, William Boole. See Chapter Three.

29. Charles Seely (1803–87) was a nineteenth-century industrialist and British Liberal Party politician, who served as an MP for Lincoln.

30. The Reform Act of 1832 introduced wide-ranging electoral change to the electoral system in England and Wales, including the creation of new seats and the extension of the franchise.

31. Charles de Laet Waldo Sibthorp (1783–1855), popularly known as Colonel Sibthorp, was a widely caricatured British Ultra-Tory politician in the early nineteenth century. He sat as an MP for Lincoln.

32. Charles James Fox (1749–1806) was a prominent British Whig statesman whose parliamentary career spanned 38 years of the late eighteenth and early nineteenth centuries and who was the arch-rival of William Pitt the Younger.

33. Sir Francis Burdett, 5th Baronet (1770–1844) was an English reformist politician. He became an MP and an opponent of William Pitt the Younger. He was an advocate of parliamentary reform and denounced corporal punishment. In 1817 he proposed universal suffrage and rights for Roman Catholics. In the final years of his life he sided with the Conservatives.

34. Letter to Mary Boole, 9 January 1850, BP/1/147.

35. Letter to MaryAnn Boole, 25 October 1849, BP/1/6.

36. Letter to Mary Boole, 30 October 1849, BP/1/141.

37. *Irish Historic Towns Atlas Cork*, Royal Irish Academy, July 2012.

38. Letter to MaryAnn Boole, 11 November 1849, BP/1/9.

39. A coenobite or cenobite is a member of a religious order living in a convent or community.

40. Letter to Charles Boole, 25 November 1849, BP/1/155.

41. Letter to MaryAnn Boole, 25 November 1849, BP/1/11.

42. Letter to Mary Boole, 29 November 1849, BP/1/144.

43. Letter to MaryAnn Boole, 12 December 1849, BP/1/16.

44. Letter to Mary Boole, 23 October 1849, BP/1/140.

45. Letter to Mary Boole, 30 October 1849, January, BP/1/141.

46. Letter to Mary Boole, 1 November 1849, BP/1/142.

47. Letter to Augustus De Morgan, 8 November 1849. Quoted in G.C. Smith, *The Boole–De Morgan Correspondence 1842–1864* (Oxford: Oxford University Press, 1982), p. 37.

48. Letter to Charles Boole, 25 November 1849, BP/1/155.

49. Letter to MaryAnn Boole, 3 December 1849, BP/1/13.

50. Letter to MaryAnn Boole, 12 December 1849, BP/1/16.

51. Letter to MaryAnn Boole, 11 December 1849, BP/1/15.

52. Letter to MaryAnn Boole, 3 November 1849, BP/1/8.

53. Letter to MaryAnn Boole, 10 January 1850, BP/1/17.

54. Letter to MaryAnn Boole, 26 February 1850, BP/1/24.

55. Letter to MaryAnn Boole, 1 February 1850, BP/1/21.

56. Letter to MaryAnn Boole, 10 January 1850, BP/1/17.

57. Letter to MaryAnn Boole, 1 February 1850, BP/1/21.

58. Letter to MaryAnn Boole, 30 March 1850, BP/1/28.

59. Letter to MaryAnn Boole, 2 December 1850, BP/1/49.

60. Letter to Mary Boole, 7 March 1850, BP/1/149. The 1851 Census contains a record for the Atkinson family in a village called Lutton outside Lincoln. The head of the family is recorded as Susan Atkinson, a widow with five children aged between two and fourteen years, who was 'in receipt of parish relief'. Her husband Edward had died at some time since the 1841 census. This may have been the family that Boole was trying to assist.

61. Letter to MaryAnn Boole, 8 March 1850, BP/1/25.

62. Letter to MaryAnn Boole, 16 March 1850, BP/1/26.

63. Letter to MaryAnn Boole, 14 April 1850, BP/1/30.

64. Letter to MaryAnn Boole, 30 January 1850, BP/1/20.

65. Letter to MaryAnn Boole, 1 February 1850, BP/1/21.

66. Letter to MaryAnn Boole, 26 February 1850, BP/1/24.

67. Letter to MaryAnn Boole, 16 March 1850, BP/1/26.

68. Letter to MaryAnn Boole, 4 April 1850, BP/1/29.

69. Letter to MaryAnn Boole, 28 March 1850, BP/1/27.

70. Letter to MaryAnn Boole, 3 May 1850, BP/1/32.

71. Letter to MaryAnn Boole, 19 February 1850, BP/1/23.

72. Letter to Mary Boole, 20 March 1850, BP/1/150.

73. Letter to MaryAnn Boole, 16 March 1850, BP/1/26.

74. Letter to MaryAnn Boole, 4 April 1850, BP/1/29.

75. Letter to MaryAnn Boole, 3 May 1850, BP/1/32.

76. Letter to MaryAnn Boole, 1 July 1850, BP/1/36.

77. Letter to MaryAnn Boole, 3 May 1850, BP/1/32.

78. Letter to MaryAnn Boole, 14 August 1850, BP/1/39.

79. Letter to MaryAnn Boole, 17 March 1851, BP/1/61.

80. Letter to MaryAnn Boole, 14 August 1850, BP/1/39.

81. J.C. Beckett, *The Making of Modern Ireland 1603–1923* (London: Faber & Faber Limited, 1981), p. 331.

82. Letter to MaryAnn Boole, 3 November 1850, BP/1/44.

83. Seán F. Pettit, 'The Queen's College Cork: its origins and early history 1803–1858', unpublished PhD thesis, UCC, 1973.

84. Letter to MaryAnn Boole, 10 November 1850, BP/1/47.

85. Letter to MaryAnn Boole, 18 November 1850, BP/1/46.

86. Letter to MaryAnn Boole, 21 November 1850, BP/1/48.

87. Letter to MaryAnn Boole, 9 November 1850, BP/1/45.

88. Letter to MaryAnn Boole, 2 December 1850, BP/1/49.

89. This Latin proverb, 'No day without a line', is attributed to the Roman philosopher Pliny the Elder.

90. Letter to MaryAnn Boole, 3 November 1850, BP/1/44.

91. Letter to MaryAnn Boole, 18 December 1850, BP/1/51.

92. Letter to MaryAnn Boole, 9 December 1850, BP/1/50.

93. Letter to Mary Boole, 9 February 1850, BP/1/148.

94. Letter to MaryAnn Boole, April 1851, BP/1/63.

95. Letter to MaryAnn Boole, 9 May 1851, BP/1/67. Boole was referring to friends in Lincoln.

96. Letter to Mary Boole, 27 February 1851, BP/1/152.

97. Letter to MaryAnn Boole, 21 November 1850, BP/1/48.

98. Letter to MaryAnn Boole, 18 December 1850, BP/1/51.

99. Letter to MaryAnn Boole, 31 December 1850, BP/1/52.

100. Ibid.

101. Letter to MaryAnn Boole, 27 February 1851, BP/1/152. Joseph Martin was a lay vicar of Lincoln Cathedral. The Census of March 1851 shows him as the father of three children, including a son called George aged two months.

102. Letter to MaryAnn Boole, 23 January 1851, BP/1/56.

103. Letter to MaryAnn Boole, 27 January 1851, BP/1/57.

104. A number of papers by Boole were published in 1851 in the *Cambridge and Dublin Mathematical Journal*:

'On the Theory of Linear Transformations', *Cambridge and Dublin Mathematical Journal*, vol. 6, 1851, pp. 87–106

'On the Reduction of the General Equation of the nth Degree' (Sequel to a Memoir on the Theory of Linear Transformations), *Cambridge and Dublin Mathematical Journal*, vol. 6, 1851, pp. 106–113

'Letter to the Editor', *Cambridge and Dublin Mathematical Journal*, vol. 6, 1851, pp. 284–5

'Proposed Question in the Theory of Probabilities', *Cambridge and Dublin Mathematical Journal*, vol. 6, 1851, p. 286

105. Boole is referring to James Wilson, the Church of Ireland Bishop of Cork. Wilson was elected a fellow of the Royal Irish Academy in 1822.

106. Letter to MaryAnn Boole, 27 January 1851, BP/1/57.

107. Letter to MaryAnn Boole, 13 January 1851, BP/1/55.

108. Letter to Mary Ann Boole, 6 February 1851, BP/1/58.

109. Ibid.

110. Letter to MaryAnn Boole, 9 February 1851, BP/1/59.

111. Letter to Mary Boole, 27 February 1851, BP/1/152.

112. Ibid.

113. Letter to MaryAnn Boole, March 1851, BP/1/60.

114. Letter to MaryAnn Boole, 17 March 1851, BP/1/61.

115. Letter to MaryAnn Boole, March 1851, BP/1/60.

116. Desmond MacHale, *The Life and Work of George Boole: a prelude to the digital age*, (Cork: Cork University Press, 2014), pp. 109–111.

117. Letters to MaryAnn Boole, 17 March 1851, BP/1/61 & BP/1/62.

118. Letter to MaryAnn Boole, April 1851, BP/1/63.

119. See details of the trip to Killarney in Chapter Four.

120. Letter to MaryAnn Boole, 23 May 1851, BP/1/125.

121. J.C. Beckett, *The Making of Modern Ireland 1603-1923*, (London: Faber & Faber Limited, 1981), p. 331.

122. Letter to MaryAnn Boole, 30 May 1852, BP/1/80.

123. Letter to MaryAnn Boole, 25 January 1852, BP/1/72.

124. Letter to MaryAnn Boole, 27 February 1852, BP/1/75.

125. Ibid.

126. *The Cork Examiner*, 12 May 1852.

127. Letter to MaryAnn Boole, 12 May 1852, BP/1/77.

128. Letter to MaryAnn Boole, 14 May 1852, BP/1/78.

129. Letter to MaryAnn Boole, 30 May 1852, BP/1/80.

130. Letter to MaryAnn Boole, 25 May 1852, BP/1/79. Sir William Hamilton was the professor of logic and metaphysics at the University of Edinburgh. He referred to Boole's 1847 book *The Mathematical Analysis of Logic* in his work *Discussions on Philosophy and Literature* which was published in 1853.

131. Letter to MaryAnn Boole, 25 May 1852, BP/1/79.

132. Letter to Mary Boole, 20 July 1852, BP/1/153.

133. Letter to MaryAnn Boole, 31 July 1852, BP/1/83.

134. Letter to MaryAnn Boole, 29 September 1852, BP/1/85. *The Laws of Thought* was published in 1854 by Walton & Maberly in London and by Macmillan in Cambridge.

135. Letter to MaryAnn Boole, 7 January 1853, BP/1/87.

136. Letter to MaryAnn Boole, 20 February 1853, BP/1/92.

137. Letter to MaryAnn Boole, 2 February 1853, BP/1/90.

138. Letter to MaryAnn Boole, 10 February 1853, BP/1/91.

139. Letter to MaryAnn Boole, 8 March 1853, BP/1/94.

140. Letter to MaryAnn Boole, 20 March 1853, BP/1/96.

141. *The Cork Examiner*, March 1853.

142. Letter to MaryAnn Boole, April 1853, BP/1/97.

143. *The Cork Examiner*, 1 April 1853.

144. Letter to MaryAnn Boole, 19 April 1853, BP/1/98.

145. Ibid.

146. *The City of Cork Directory with which is incorporated The Commercial Directory of Queenstown 1871*, published by R.E. Fulton & Co, May 1871.

147. Letter to MaryAnn Boole, 4 May 1853, BP/1/99. Income tax was first introduced in England in 1798 by William Pitt as a means of raising finance in the wars against France. It ceased in 1816 but was imposed again by Robert Peel in 1842 and extended until 1852. In 1853 William Gladstone, then Chancellor of the Exchequer, extended income tax for another seven years and imposed income tax on Ireland for the first time.

148. Boole was referring to the oratorio 'Daniel', written by George Lake.

149. Letter to MaryAnn Boole, 4 May 1853, BP/1/99.

150. Letter to MaryAnn Boole, 5 June 1853, BP/1/102.

151. Letter to MaryAnn Boole, 19 May 1853, BP/1/100.

152. Letter to MaryAnn Boole, 31 May 1853, BP/1/101.

153. Letter to MaryAnn Boole, 19 October 1853, BP/1/104.

154. Ibid.

155. Letter to MaryAnn Boole, 27 October 1853, BP/1/105.

156. Letter to MaryAnn Boole, 15 November 1853, BP/1/106.

157. Vincenzo Gioberti was an Italian cleric, politician and philosopher.

158. Letter to MaryAnn Boole, 15 November 1853, BP/1/106.

159. Letter to MaryAnn Boole, 11 December 1853, BP/1/109.

160. Letter to MaryAnn Boole, 26 November 1853, BP/1/108.

161. Letter to MaryAnn Boole, 3 January 1854, BP/1/111.

162. Letter to MaryAnn Boole, 2 January 1854, BP/1/110.

163. Brocklesby is a village in Lincolnshire. We do not know what engagement Boole is referring to.

164. Letter to MaryAnn Boole, 29 January 1854, BP/1/112.

165. Ibid.

166. Ibid.

167. Ibid.

168. Letter to MaryAnn Boole, 10 February 1854, BP/1/114.

169. Ibid.

170. Letter to MaryAnn Boole, 16 February 1854, BP/1/115.

171. Ibid.

172. Letter to MaryAnn Boole, 2 April 1854, BP/1/118.

173. Letter to MaryAnn Boole, 14 April 1854, BP/1/119.

174. Letter to MaryAnn Boole, undated 1854, BP/1/130.

175. Letter to MaryAnn Boole, 4 March 1854, BP/1/116.

176. Letter to MaryAnn Boole, April 1854, BP/1/120.

177. Letter to MaryAnn Boole, 4 March 1854, BP/1/116.

178. Letter to MaryAnn Boole, 2 April 1854, BP/1/118.

179. Letter to MaryAnn Boole, 14 April 1854, BP/1/119.

180. William Boole was married to Elizabeth Pacey in 1799, so it is likely that John Pacey was a relation of hers.

181. Letter to MaryAnn Boole, 14 April 1854, BP/1/119.

182. Letter to MaryAnn Boole, 30 May 1854, BP/1/122.

183. Letter to MaryAnn Boole, 6 June 1854, BP/1/123.

184. Ibid.

185. Ibid.

186. J.C. Beckett, *The Making of Modern Ireland 1603–1923* (London: Faber & Faber Limited, 1981), p. 350.

187. Ibid, p. 344.

188. Joseph Lee, *The Modernisation of Irish Society 1848–1918* (Dublin: Gill & Macmillan, 2008), Chapter One.

189. Letter to MaryAnn Boole, 25 October 1849, BP/1/6.

190. Letter to MaryAnn Boole, 29 October 1849, BP/1/7.

191. Letter to MaryAnn Boole, 7 December 1849, BP/1/14.

192. Lecture to the Mechanics' Institute partially reproduced in the *Lincolnshire Chronicle*, 31 January 1868. Also, reproduced in Desmond MacHale, *The Life and Work of George Boole: a prelude to the digital age* (Cork: Cork University Press, 2014), p. 185.

193. Letter to Mary Boole, 20 March 1850, BP/1/150.

194. Letter to Mary Boole, 27 February 1851, BP/1/152.

195. Letter to MaryAnn Boole, 9 May 1851, BP/1/67.

196. Letter to Mary Boole, 1 November 1849, BP/1/142.

197. Letter to Mary Boole, 7 March 1850, BP/1/149.

198. Letter to Mary Boole, 20 March 1850, BP/1/150.

199. Letter to MaryAnn Boole, 26 February 1850, BP/1/24.

200. Letter to MaryAnn Boole, 12 December 1853, BP/1/109. The *Journal of the Royal Irish Academy* contains a paper from Francis Jennings discussing the similarities he noticed on a trip to Morocco in April 1856 between brooches worn by Bedouin women and ancient brooches excavated in Ireland.

201. Letter to MaryAnn Boole, 28 March 1850, BP/1/27.

202. Letter to MaryAnn Boole, undated, BP/1/131.

203. Letter to Mary Boole, 29 November 1849, BP/1/144.

204. Letter to Mary Boole, 9 December 1849, BP/1/146.

205. Letter to MaryAnn Boole, 30 January 1850, BP/1/20.

206. Letter to MaryAnn Boole, 18 October 1850, BP/1/42.

207. Slater's *National Commercial Directory of Ireland* (1856). See http://www.corkpastandpresent.ie/places/streetandtradedirectories/slatersdirectory1856.pdf [accessed 11 April 2018].

208. Louise Fletcher Chesney and Jane Chesney O'Donnell, *The Life of the Late General F.R. Chesney, Colonel Commandant Royal Artillery D.C.L., F.R.S., F.R.G.F.S. etc.* (London: W.H. Allen & Co. 1885), p. 392.

209. Letter to MaryAnn Boole, 9 November 1850, BP/1/45.

210. Letter to MaryAnn Boole, 3 November 1850, BP/1/44.

211. Letter to MaryAnn Boole, 9 November 1850, BP/1/45.

212. Letter to MaryAnn Boole, 27 October 1853, BP/1/105.

213. Letter to MaryAnn Boole, 15 November 1853, BP/1/106; Letter to MaryAnn Boole, 18 May 1854, BP/1/121.

214. Letter to MaryAnn Boole, early 1852, BP/1/76.

215. Peter Murray, *The Cooper Penrose Collection*, Irish Arts Review Summer 2008. See http://www.crawfordartgallery.ie/images/Exhibitions/CooperPenroseCollectionbook.pdf [accessed 11 April 2018].

216. Letter to MaryAnn Boole, 19 April 1853, BP/1/98.

217. Exeter Hall was on the north side of London and was used for public meetings and concerts. Its large auditorium could seat up to four thousand.

218. Letter to MaryAnn Boole, 28 June 1851, BP/1/70.

219. Letter to Charles Boole, 25 November 1849, BP/1/155.

220. Letter to MaryAnn Boole, 12 December 1849, BP/1/16.

221. For further information on Boole's religious beliefs, see: Desmond MacHale, *The Life and Work of George Boole: a prelude to the digital age* (Cork: Cork University Press, 2014), pp. 220–38.

222. Letter to MaryAnn Boole, 18 October 1850, BP/1/42.

223. Letter to MaryAnn Boole, 9 November 1850, BP/1/45.

224. Letter to Mary Boole, 21 November 1849, BP/1/143.

225. Ibid.

226. Letter to MaryAnn Boole, BP/1/134. Undated – possibly written in March 1850.

227. Letter to MaryAnn Boole, 3 November 1850, BP/1/44.

228. Letter to MaryAnn Boole, 9 November 1850, BP/1/45.

229. Letter to MaryAnn Boole, 12 May 1852, BP/1/77.

230. Letter to MaryAnn Boole, 27 October 1853, BP/1/105.

231. Desmond MacHale, *The Life and Work of George Boole*, pp. 232–5.

232. Paul Waterhouse, *Penrose, Francis Cranmer*, Dictionary of National Biography, 1912 supplement.

233. Ibid.

234. Letter to MaryAnn Boole, 26 November 1853, BP/1/108.

235. Boole is referring to the Great Flood of Cork that occurred in November 1853.

236. Letter to MaryAnn Boole, 11 December 1853, BP/1/109.

237. Jim Blaney, 'Alexander Mitchell (1780–1868): Belfast's blind engineer', *History Ireland*, vol. 14, no. 3, May/Jun 2006.

238. The lighthouse is one of only three remaining surviving examples of Mitchell's design and underwent an extensive renovation project in 2013.

239. *National Inventory of Architectural Heritage*, Building of the Month – November 2009, Spit Bank Lighthouse, Cobh, County Cork.

240. Letter to MaryAnn Boole, 29 October 1849, BP/1/7.

241. Letter to MaryAnn Boole, 25 May 1852, BP/1/79.

242. Letter to MaryAnn Boole, 9 February 1851, BP/1/59.

243. Letter to MaryAnn Boole, 18 May 1850, BP/1/33.

244. Letter to MaryAnn Boole, 26 October 1850, BP/1/43.

245. http://www.corkharbourmarina.ie/places-to-visit.html

246. Letter to MaryAnn Boole, 18 November 1850, BP/1/46.

247. Letter to MaryAnn Boole, 31 December 1850, BP/1/52.

248. Letter to MaryAnn Boole, 7 April 1851, BP/1/63.

249. Letter to MaryAnn Boole, 3 May 1851, BP/1/66.

250. Letter to MaryAnn Boole, March 1851, BP/1/60.

251. *Illustrated London News*, vol. IX, 1846, pp. 327–8.

252. Letter to MaryAnn Boole, 17 March 1851, BP/1/61. Boole was quoting from a popular folk song written by Henry Bennett in the 1820s.

253. Letter to MaryAnn Boole, 20 March 1853, BP/1/96.

254. Letter to MaryAnn Boole, 23 April 1850, BP/1/31.

255. Helen E. Hatton, *The Largest Amount of Good: Quaker Relief in Ireland 1654–1921* (Ontario: The McGill-Queen's University Press, 1993), p. 210.

256. Andrew Roberts, *Waterloo: Napoleon's last gamble* (London: Harper Perennial, 2005), p. 57.

257. C. Davies, 'Prince of Wales unveils Waterloo memorial', *The Guardian*, 17 June 2015.

258. Letter to MaryAnn Boole, 23 April 1850, BP/1/31.

259. Letter to MaryAnn Boole, 2 January 1854, BP/1/110; Letter to MaryAnn Boole, 30 May 1854, BP/1/122.

260. Letter to MaryAnn Boole, 11 June 1850, BP/1/35.

261. Letter to MaryAnn Boole, 2 January 1854, BP/1/110.

262. Letter to MaryAnn Boole, April 1854, BP/1/120.

263. Ibid.

264. http://www.birdwatchireland.ie/IrelandsBirds/Raptors/WhitetailedEagle/tabid/1153/default.aspx [accessed 11 April 2018].

265. Letter to MaryAnn Boole, undated, BP/1/133.

266. Letter to MaryAnn Boole, 14 June 1852, BP/1/82.

267. In 1847 the British adventurer Austen Henry Lanyard explored the ruins of Nineveh, the capital of the Assyrian Empire and rediscovered the lost palace of Sennacherib across the Tigris River from modern Mosul in northern Iraq. Sennacherib was the Assyrian king who held Jerusalem under siege in 701 BC. Representatives of European governments descended on the palaces of Mesopotamia in the nineteenth century and sacked them to fill the halls of the British Museum, the Louvre, and the Berlin Museum. See John Malcolm Russell, 'Stolen Stones: the modern sack of Nineveh', *Archaeology Archive*, 30 December 1996. See http://archive.archaeology.org/online/features/nineveh/ [accessed 11 April 2018].

268. Letter to MaryAnn Boole, 1 July 1850, BP/1/36.

269. Henry Scherrin, *The Zoological Society of London: a sketch of its foundation and development and the story of its Farm, Museum, Gardens, Menagerie and Library* (London: Cassell, 1905), p. 91.

270. Ibid, p. 102.

271. Letter to MaryAnn Boole, 6 August 1850, BP/1/38.

272. Letter to MaryAnn Boole, 11 June 1851, BP/1/69.

273. R. Beasland, 'London Companion during the Great Exhibition' (London: R. Donaldson, 1851) reproduced in http://www.vam.ac.uk/content/articles/t/the-great-exhibition-visitor-experience/ [accessed 11 April 2018].

274. Letter to MaryAnn Boole, 28 June 1851, BP/1/70.

275. 'Architecture of Cork City: Lost Buildings of Ireland' http://archiseek.com/2011/1852 -national-exhibition-cork/ [accessed 11 April 2018].

276. John Francis Maguire, *The Industrial Movement in Ireland as illustrated by the National Exhibition 1852* (Cork: John O'Brien, 1853), p. 457.

277. Letter to MaryAnn Boole, 30 May 1852, BP/1/80.

278. Letter to MaryAnn Boole, 9 June 1852, BP/1/81.

279. Letter to MaryAnn Boole, 14 June 1852, BP/1/82.

280. Maguire, *The Industrial Movement in Ireland*, p. 468.

281. Letter to MaryAnn Boole, 2 April 1854, BP/1/118.

282. Letter to MaryAnn Boole, 19 May 1853, BP/1/100.

283. Letter to MaryAnn Boole, 25 February 1852, BP/1/74. The Right Rev. John Gregg MA, DD was the Rector of Holy Trinity Dublin and was appointed Bishop of Cork in 1862. 'The Pretender' referred to the Stuart King James II, whose son was recognised by the Holy See in Rome as being the legitimate King of England and Ireland until his death in 1766. The Oath of Abjuration had to be taken to obtain a degree from TCD. This measure had been passed as part of the Penal Laws in 1703 to prevent 'the further growth of Popery'.

284. Allman was a medical graduate and a fellow of the Royal College of Surgeons. In 1856 he left Trinity to take up the professorship of natural history at the University of Edinburgh, a post he held from 1856 until his retirement in 1870. In 1876 he was appointed a commissioner to inquire into the working of the Queen's Colleges in Ireland.

285. Ibid.

286. Letter to MaryAnn Boole, 27 February 1852, BP/1/75.

287. Letter to MaryAnn Boole, 9 June 1853, BP/1/103.

288. Edmund Spenser, 'The Faerie Queene', 11th Canto, Book IV, 1596.

289. Letter to MaryAnn Boole, 30 March 1850, BP/1/28.

290. *Illustrated London News*, vol. XXIII, 1853, p. 407.

291. Letter to Mary Boole, 5 November 1853, BP/1/154.

292. Letter to MaryAnn Boole, 15 November 1853, BP/1/106.

293. Tal P. Shaffner, *Shaffner's Telegraphic Companion Devoted to the Science and Art of the Morse American Telegraph*, 1854.

294. Letter to MaryAnn Boole, April 1854, BP/1/120.

295. Ibid.

296. Letter to MaryAnn Boole, 5 July 1849, BP/1/5.

297. Ibid.

298. Letter to MaryAnn Boole, 3 December 1849, BP/1/13.

299. Letter to MaryAnn Boole, 1 July 1850. BP/1/36.

300. Letter to Mary Boole, 27 February 1851, BP/1/152.

301. Letter to MaryAnn Boole, 3 May 1851, BP/1/66.

302. Letter to MaryAnn Boole, 20 February 1853, BP/1/92.

303. Letter to MaryAnn Boole, 20 March 1853, BP/1/96.

304. 'The Late Dr Bury', *Chester Chronicle*, 20 April 1867.

305. George Boole to John Bury, 11 February 1850, BP/1/162.

306. Ibid. Boole is referring to Dr A. Fleming, Professor of Materia Medica at QCC, who was the author of a treatise on the *Aconitum Napellus*.

307. George Boole to John Bury, 5 June 1850, BP/1/164.

308. George Boole to John Bury, 2 December 1850, BP/1/196.

309. George Boole to John Bury, 19 December 1850, BP/1/166.

310. George Boole to John Bury, 11 October 1854, BP/1/193.

311. George Boole to John Bury, 15 October 1860, BP/1/201.

312. George Boole to John Bury, 18 March 1856, BP/1/194.

313. George Boole to John Bury, 29 March 1856, Boole Archives UCC.

314. For commentary on Boole's and Victorian attitudes to pregnancy and breastfeeding, see C. Anthony Ryan, Desmond MacHale and Yvonne Cohen, 'A Letter from George Boole and Victorian Attitudes towards Pregnancy, Childbirth and Breastfeeding', *Hektoen International*, Spring 2017, Volume 9, Issue 2.

315. George Boole to John Bury, 21 June 1856, Boole Archives, UCC.

316. George Boole to John Bury, 6 August 1862, BP/1/211.

317. For more detail on the context of the vaccination of Alice Boole, see C. Anthony Ryan, D. MacHale and Y. Cohen, 'George Boole, Saucy Little Alice and an Uneventful Smallpox Vaccination: one of the greatest stories never told', *Archives of Disease in Childhood*, Published Online First: 24 February 2017. doi: 10.1136/archdischild-2016-311939.

318. George Boole to John Bury, 21 January 1863, BP/1/197.

319. George Boole to John Bury, 18 August 1863, BP/1/213.

320. George Boole to John Bury, 21 June 1861, BP/1/202.

321. George Boole to William Brooke, 15 September 1861, Box 1, Rollett Collection, Lincolnshire Archives.

322. George Boole to John Bury, 18 September 1861, BP/1/203.

323. George Boole to John Bury, 11 February 1850, BP/1/162.

324. George Boole to John Bury, 5 June 1850, BP/1/164.

325. George Boole to John Bury, 24 March 1851, BP/1/169.

326. George Boole to John Bury, 11 February 1850, BP/1/162.

327. George Boole to John Bury, 24 March 1851, BP/1/169.

328. George Boole to John Bury, 26 August 1850, BP/1/167.

329. George Boole to John Bury, 2 December 1850, BP/1/196.

330. George Boole to John Bury, 23 March 1852, BP/1/174.

331. George Boole to John Bury, 11 July 1853, BP/1/181.

332. George Boole to John Bury, 24 October 1853, BP/1/187.

333. George Boole to John Bury, 2 April 1854, BP/1/188.

334. George Boole to John Bury, 7 April 1854, BP/1/189.

335. E.T. Bell, *Men of Mathematics 2* (Harmondsworth: Pelican Books, 1965), p. 493.

336. George Boole to John Bury, 4 January 1853, BP/1/176.

337. George Boole to John Bury, 30 May 1853, BP/1/178.

338. George Boole to John Bury, 13 July 1862, BP/1/209.

339. George Boole to John Bury, 4 January 1853, BP/1/176.

340. See http://pigott-gorrie.blogspot.ie/2013/07/william-giles-senior-peripatetic.html for information on the Giles family. [Accessed 11 April 2018].

341. George Boole to John Bury, 28 March 1864, BP/1/215.

342. John Bury to Mary Boole, 18 November 1865, BP/1/335.

343. James Gregory, *Conspectus Medicinae Theoreticae* (1836).

344. The Senior Wrangler was the candidate who was placed first in the Mathematical Tripos examination for BA in Mathematics at the University of Cambridge. The next candidates were called Second Wrangler, Third Wrangler, etc.

345. Arabella Goddard was a famous nineteenth-century English pianist.

346. George Boole to Mary Ellen Boole, 13 September 1863, BP/1/328.

347. It is not clear what 'Bill' Boole was referring to. It may have been the 1832 Representation of the People Act, which introduced wide-ranging electoral reforms in England and Wales. Alternatively, he may have been referring to the Slavery Abolition Act of 1833 which abolished slavery throughout the British Empire.

348. George Boole to Joseph Hill, 23 December 1833, BP/1/221/2.

349. George Boole to Joseph Hill, 22 February 1834, BP/1/221/3.

350. Joe Albree and Scott H. Brown, '"A valuable monument of mathematical genius": The Ladies' Diary (1704–1840)', *Historia Mathematica*, vol. 36, no. 1, pp. 10–47.

351. The *Epistolæ Obscurorum Virorum (Letters of Obscure Men)* was a celebrated collection of satirical Latin letters which appeared from 1515–19 in Germany. The letters were published anonymously but Erasmus was said to have contributed to the second volume.

352. George Boole to Joseph Hill, 11 February 1837, BP/1/221/5.

353. Ibid.

354. Ibid.

355. George Boole to Joseph Hill, 30 May 1837, BP/1/221/6.

356. Ibid.

357. George Boole to Joseph Hill, 30 November 1840, BP/1/221/25.

358. Boole was referring to James Gall of Edinburgh, the author of *End and Essence of Sabbath School Teaching* (1831) and *A Practical Enquiry into the Philosophy of Education* (Edinburgh: James Gall & Son, 1840).

359. Boole is referring to Erasmus, *Eximii Doctoris Hieronymi vita* (Basel: Johann Froben, 1519).

360. George Boole to Joseph Hill, 30 November 1840, BP/1/221/25.

361. Ibid.

362. George Boole to Joseph Hill, 5 May 1840, BP/1/221/7.

363. Ibid.

364. Ibid.

365. Ibid.

366. George Boole to Joseph Hill, 9 May 1840, BP/1/221/8.

367. Jeremy Taylor (1613–67) was an English cleric and writer who became Bishop of Down, Connor and Dromore. Reginald Heber (1783–1826) was an English bishop, traveller and hymn writer whose edition of the works of Taylor was published in 1822.

368. J. Everett, *The Polemic Divine: or memoirs of the life, writings, and opinions of the Rev. Daniel Isaac,* (London: Hamilton & Co. 1839).

369. Elizabeth Rowe (1674–1737) was a widely read English author and poet. She wrote mainly religious poetry and her most popular work was *Friendship in Death* (1728).

370. James Boswell, *The Life of Samuel Johnson, LL.D* (London: Henry Baldwin for Charles Dilly, 1791).

371. Samuel Johnson, *The Lives of the Most Eminent English Poets; with critical observations on their works, in four volumes* (London: 1781).

372. George Boole to Joseph Hill, 27 May 1840, BP/1/221/9.

373. Ibid.

374. George Boole to Joseph Hill, 19 January 1841, BP/1/221/10.

375. Ibid.

376. George Boole to Joseph Hill, 22 February 1841, BP/1/221/11.

377. Daniel Neal (1678–1743) was an English historian. His *History of the Puritans* was published in four volumes between 1732 and 1738. Boole may have been referring to Edward Parsons, *History of the Puritans; or the Rise, Principles and Sufferings of the Protestant Dissenters, to the Glorious Era of the Revolution; Abridged in Two Volumes* (London: Longman, 1811).

378. George Boole to Joseph Hill, 22 February 1841, BP/1/221/11.

379. George Boole to Joseph Hill, 29 December 1841, BP/1/221/12.

380. Translated as 'staying awake in the gentle nights' (Lucretius).

381. George Boole to Joseph Hill, 17 February 1844, BP/1/221/13.

382. W.F. Lloyd, *A Catechism on the Principal Parables of the New Testament* (Philadelphia: Committee of Publication of American Sunday School Union, 1827).

383. George Boole to Joseph Hill, 13 July 1844, BP/1/221/14.

384. George Boole to Joseph Hill, 4 June 1846, BP/1/221/29.

385. Sir James Mackintosh (1765–1832) was a Scottish lawyer, politician and historian. See James Mackintosh, *A Discourse on the Study of the Law of Nature and Nations* (London: 1799).

386. William Whewell, *The Elements of Morality, including Polity* (London: J.W. Parker, 1845).

387. George Boole to Joseph Hill, 16 July 1846, BP/1/221/15.

388. Rev. Ralph Wardlaw (1779–1853) was a Scottish Presbyterian minister and writer. His writings included *Christian Ethics, or Moral Philosophy on the Principles of Divine Revelation* (London: Jackson & Walford, 1833).

389. Boole may have been referring to Mackintosh's *Dissertation on the Progress of Ethical Philosophy* (1830).

390. George Boole to Joseph Hill, 2 February 1847, BP/1/221/16.

391. George Boole to Joseph Hill, 15 February 1847, BP/1/221/17.

392. Richard Whately, *Essays (third series) on the Errors of Romanism, having their Origin in Human Nature* (London: B. Fellowes, 1837).

393. Richard Whately, *The Kingdom of Christ: delineated, in two essays on Our Lord's own account of His person and of the nature of His kingdom, and on the constitution, powers, and ministry of a Christian Church, as appointed by Himself* (London: B. Fellowes, 1842).

394. George Boole to Joseph Hill, 14 July 1847, BP/1/221/18.

395. George Boole to Joseph Hill, 15 July 1847, BP/1/221/19.

396. George Boole to Joseph Hill, 19 June 1848, BP/1/221/20; George Boole to Joseph Hill, 21 June 1849, BP/1/221/27.

397. George Boole to Joseph Hill, 13 August 1849, BP/1/221/21.

398. George Boole to Joseph Hill, 30 July 1850, BP/1/221/22.

399. Ibid.

400. See also Desmond MacHale, *The Life and Work of George Boole*, pp. 105–7.

401. Ibid, p. 260.

402. George Boole to Joseph Hill, 11 December 1850, BP/1/221/23.

403. George Boole to Joseph Hill, 9 February 1852, BP/1/221/24.

404. Joseph Hill to MaryAnn Boole, 1 December 1865, BP/1/258.

405. William Paley, *The Principles of Moral and Political Philosophy* (London: Longman, 1829)

406. William Paley, *Horae Paulinae or The truth of the scripture evinced by a comparison of the Epistles which bear his name, with the Acts of the Apostles* (Dublin: McKenzie, Moore, Grueber, Jones, Milliken & White, 1801).

407. Joseph Hill to MaryAnn Boole, 20 March 1866, BP/1/259.

408. For more detail on this translation by Boole, see MacHale, pp. 8–16.

409. Richard Watson, *A Biblical and Theological Dictionary: explanatory of the history, manners, and customs of the Jews, and neighbouring nations* (New York: B. Waugh & T. Mason, 1833).

410. George Whittaker, *Florilegium Poeticum: A selection of elegiac extracts from the works of Ovid, Tibullus, Propertius, Martial & Ausonius* (London: Whittaker & Co., 1835).

411. Joseph Hill to MaryAnn Boole, 24 May 1866, BP/1/260.

412. Ignace Gaston Pardies, SJ (1636–73) was a French scientist and mathematician who corresponded with Newton.

413. Ada Lovelace (1815–52) was the daughter of the poet Lord Byron. She was a mathematician and writer. In 1833 she met Charles Babbage, the Cambridge Professor of Mathematics, and developed a lifelong friendship and working relationship with him. In 1843 she published a translation of the Italian engineer Luigi Menabrea's work 'Sketch of the Analytical Engine', and added notes of her own. She saw the capability of the calculating machines or early computers to go beyond mathematics and for this reason has been regarded as the first computer programmer and referred to as the 'prophet of the computer age'. See http://www.computerhistory.org/babbage/adalovelace/ [accessed 11 April 2018]. We wonder if the lady at the exhibition could have been Harriet Martineau (1802–76)?

414. The Beverley Minster in East Yorkshire is one of the largest parish churches in England. It is regarded as a gothic masterpiece.

415. Joseph Hill to MaryAnn Boole, 12 July 1866, BP/1/261.

416. Elihu Burritt (1810–79), the 'Learned Blacksmith', was an American pacifist, self-taught in many languages, who visited England in 1847 where he organised the League of Universal Brotherhood. He advocated many causes including the abolition of slavery, temperance and world peace. He refused a place at Harvard on the grounds that his place was with the common people. Burritt was appointed United States consul in Birmingham by Abraham Lincoln in 1864. Clearly Boole met him and admired his ideals.

417. Joseph Hill to MaryAnn Boole, 12 July 1866, BP/1/261.

418. Joseph Hill to MaryAnn Boole, 23 May 1867, BP/1/262.

419. Joseph Hill to MaryAnn Boole, 25 June 1868, BP/1/263.

420. George Boole to Mary Boole, 9 December 1849, BP/1/146.

421. Letter from Edmund Larken to his mother, 13 April 1851, Larken Papers 5-1-9, Lincolnshire Archives.

422. George Boole to E.R. Larken, 31 May 1847, BP/1/223/8.

423. Ibid.

424. George Boole to E.R. Larken, 13 September 1847, BP/1/223/10.

425. Ibid.

426. Ibid.

427. George Boole, *The Mathematical Analysis of Logic, being an Essay towards a Calculus of Deductive Reasoning,* (Cambridge: Macmillan, Barclay & Macmillan, 1847).

428. George Boole to E.R. Larken, 15 December 1847, BP/1/223/12.

429. George Boole to E.R. Larken, 14 January 1848, BP/1/223/13.

430. For details of Boole's application, see: MacHale, *The Life and Work of George Boole,* Chapter Five.

431. George Boole to E.R. Larken, 29 September 1846, BP/1/223/2.

432. George Boole to E.R. Larken, 6 January 1847, BP/1/223/3.

433. MacHale, *The Life and Work of George Boole,* pp 94–5.

434. George Boole to E.R. Larken, 15 December 1847, BP/1/223/12.

435. Ibid.

436. 9 October 1846, quoted in Noel Kissane, *The Irish Famine: a documentary history* (Dublin: National Library of Ireland, 1995), p. 51. See Chapter Four for Boole's experiences of the Famine after his arrival in Ireland in 1849.

437. George Boole to E.R. Larken, 24 September 1849, BP/1/223/15.

438. George Boole to E.R. Larken, 29 April 1847, B.P./1/223/7. Rev. James Simkiss is listed in *The Catholic Directory and Annual Register for the year 1840* (London: Simpkin, Marshall & Co. Stationers Court, 1840*)*, p. 18 in the parish of Hainton, Lincolnshire.

439. George Boole to E.R. Larken, 7 October 1847, BP/1/223/11.

440. George Boole to M.C. Taylor, April 1840, BP/1/226.

441. Ibid.

442. Ibid.

443. See handwritten note of Mary Ellen Hinton at the end of the letter from George Boole to M.C. Taylor, April 1840, BP/1/226.

444. George Boole to E.R. Larken, January 1847, BP/1/223/4.

445. Letter from E.R. Larken to Mary Boole, 14 February 1866, Box 12, Rollett Collection, Lincolnshire Archives.

446. Obituary of William Brooke, *Stamford Mercury*, 27 December 1872.

447. Letter to Mary Ellen Boole from George Boole, 13 September 1863, BP/1/328.

448. Richard Valpy (1754–1836) was a British school teacher whose Greek and Latin grammar books enjoyed a wide circulation.

449. Letter to MaryAnn Boole from William Brooke, 2 January 1865, BP/1/244.

450. 'Lindum Colonia' was the Latin name for Lincoln.

451. Letter to George Boole from William Brooke, undated, BP/1/160.

452. Footnote to a transcript of a letter from William Brooke to George Boole, undated, BP/1/160.

453. Letter to MaryAnn Boole, 31 December 1850, BP/1/52.

454. Letter to MaryAnn Boole, 16 February 1854, BP/1/115.

455. Letter to William Brooke from George Boole, 4 February 1854, Box 1, Rollett Collection, Lincolnshire Archives.

456. Greetwell is an area in Lincoln.

457. Letter to William Brooke from George Boole, 24 October 1854, Box 1, Rollett Collection, Lincolnshire Archives.

458. Skellingthorpe Wood is an ancient woodland that is close to the village of Skellingthorpe, Lincoln.

459. Letter to William Brooke from George Boole, 18 June 1855, Box 1, Rollett Collection, Lincolnshire Archives. Boole quoted verses from the popular poem *The Bells of Shandon* written by Francis Sylvester Mahony (1804–66), also known by the pen name Father Prout, who was an Irish humorist and journalist.

460. Letter to William Brooke from George Boole, 18 June 1855, Box 1, Rollett Collection, Lincolnshire Archives.

461. MacHale, *The Life and Work of George Boole*, Chapter Seven.

462. Boole's possible motivation for marrying Mary Everest has been discussed at length in MacHale, *The Life and Work of George Boole*, Chapter Seven.

463. Letter to MaryAnn Boole from William Brooke, December 1864, BP/1/243.

464. Letter to William Brooke from George Boole, 3 October 1855, Box 1, Rollett Collection, Lincolnshire Archives.

465. Letter to William Brooke from George Boole, 12 June 1856, Box 1, Rollett Collection, Lincolnshire Archives. Boole is referring to a dinner organised by Professor Jack, Professor of Engineering, in December 1855. See MacHale, *The Life and Work of George Boole*, Chapter Ten.

466. Letter to William Brooke from George Boole, 12 June 1856, Box 1, Rollett Collection, Lincolnshire Archives.

467. Ibid.

468. Letter to William Brooke from George Boole, 18 June 1855, Box 1, Rollett Collection, Lincolnshire Archives.

469. Letter to William Brooke from George Boole, 10 August 1858, Box 1, Rollett Collection, Lincolnshire Archives.

470. Letter to William Brooke from George Boole, 1 December 1859, Box 1, Rollett Collection, Lincolnshire Archives.

471. Letter to Benjamin Brooke from George Boole, 5 May 1857, Box 1, Rollett Collection, Lincolnshire Archives.

472. Letter to William Brooke from George Boole, 12 June 1856, Box 1, Rollett Collection, Lincolnshire Archives. Esaias Tegnér (1782–1846) was a Swedish writer, professor of Greek language, and bishop. He was during the nineteenth century regarded as the father of modern poetry in Sweden due to his epic poem *Frithjof's Saga*.

473. Ibid.

474. Boole is referring to William Boole, his father's brother, who was a school teacher at Bassingham.

475. Letter to William Brooke from George Boole, 22 June 1856, Box 1, Rollett Collection, Lincolnshire Archives.

476. Letter to William Brooke, 8 July 1856, Box 1, Rollett Collection, Lincolnshire Archives.

477. Letter to Benjamin Brooke, 5 May 1857, Box 1, Rollett Collection, Lincolnshire Archives.

478. Letter to William Brooke, 10 August 1858, Box 1, Rollett Collection, Lincolnshire Archives.

479. Ibid.

480. Boole is referring to Lincoln Cathedral.

481. Ibid.

482. Letter to William Brooke from George Boole, 26 August 1858, Box 1, Rollett Collection, Lincolnshire Archives.

483. Letter to William Brooke from George Boole, 3 September 1858, Box 1, Rollett Collection, Lincolnshire Archives.

484. Letter to William Brooke from George Boole, 11 December 1859, Box 1, Rollett Collection, Lincolnshire Archives.

485. Letter to William Brooke from George Boole, 3 July 1860, Box 1, Rollett Collection, Lincolnshire Archives.

486. Ibid.

487. Letter from Harriet Martineau to Dr John Ryall, 27 September 1852, BP/1/369.

488. Joseph Priestley was an eighteenth-century English theologian, chemist, educator and dissenting clergyman. He is considered the founder of Unitarianism in England.

489. Letter to William Brooke from George Boole, 11 December 1859, Box 1, Rollett Collection, Lincolnshire Archives. Boole's religious thinking was most strongly influenced by Frederick Denison Maurice. See MacHale, *The Life and Work of George Boole*, Chapter Fourteen.

490. Boole was referring to the establishment of Dr Barter in Blarney where MaryAnn had convalesced in 1852 and again in 1860. Boole had also taken some hydropathic therapies there in 1853. See Chapter Twelve.

491. The uvula is a fleshy extension at the back of the soft palate which hangs above the throat.

492. Letter to William Brooke from George Boole, 25 March 1861, Box 1, Rollett Collection, Lincolnshire Archives.

493. Letter to Dr John Bury from George Boole, 21 June 1861, BP/1/202.

494. Letter to William Brooke from George Boole, 15 September 1861, Box 1, Rollett Collection, Lincolnshire Archives.

495. Ibid.

496. Ibid. Boole is referring to Benjamin Jowett (1817–93) a theologian, translator and Master of Balliol College, Oxford

497. http://www.colognecathedral.net/Cologne-Cathedral-Facts.html [accessed 11 April 2018].

498. A triforium is a gallery or arcade above the arches of the nave, choir and transepts of a church.

499. The clerestory is the upper part of the nave, choir and transepts of a large church, containing a series of windows.

500. Bacharach is a town in the Rhine Gorge.

501. Letter to William Brooke from George Boole, 15 September 1861, Box 1, Rollett Collection, Lincolnshire Archives.

502. Ibid.

503. Ibid.

504. Ibid.

505. Letter to W.A.J. Turner from George Boole, 26 January 1860, BP/1/232.

506. Letter to William Brooke from George Boole, 15 September 1861, Box 1, Rollett Collection, Lincolnshire Archives.

507. Letter to William Brooke from George Boole, 3 April 1864, Box 1, Rollett Collection, Lincolnshire Archives.

508. Letter to William Brooke from George Boole, 13 May 1864, Box 1, Rollett Collection, Lincolnshire Archives.

509. Letter to William Brooke from George Boole, 28 July 1864, Box 1, Rollett Collection, Lincolnshire Archives.

510. Letter to William Brooke from George Boole, 24 October 1864, Box 1, Rollett Collection, Lincolnshire Archives.

511. Penrose had visited Cork in the 1850s and met Boole there. He was the son of John Penrose, a Church of England clergyman and theological writer, and was the designer of the tomb of the Duke of Wellington in St Paul's Cathedral. See Chapter Four.

512. Sir James Shaw Willes (1814–72) was a Judge of the English Court of Common Pleas. He was born in Cork and was educated at Trinity College Dublin. In 1856 Willes married Helen Jennings, daughter of Thomas Jennings of Cork. From 1865 Willes' home became Otterspool, a house near Aldenham outside Watford in Hertfordshire. He took his own life in 1872. See A.W.B. Simpson, 'Willes, Sir James Shaw (1814–1872)', *Oxford Dictionary of National Biography* (Oxford: Oxford University Press, 2004). Boole was very friendly with the Jennings family in Cork, and this was probably how he had made the acquaintance of Sir James. See Chapter Three.

513. Letter to William Brooke from George Boole, 8 August 1864, Box 1, Rollett Collection, Lincolnshire Archives.

514. The consul referred to was R.A. Jamieson, who was a student of the Faculty of Arts in QCC. (See Chapter Ten).

515. Letter to William Brooke from George Boole, 8 August 1864, Box 1, Rollett Collection, Lincolnshire Archives.

516. Letter to William Brooke from George Boole, 18 June 1855, Box 1, Rollett Collection, Lincolnshire Archives.

517. Letter to W.A.J. Turner from George Boole, 26 January 1860, BP/1/232.

518. Letter to William Brooke from George Boole, 5 October 1864, Box 1, Rollett Collection, Lincolnshire Archives.

519. Letter to William Brooke from George Boole, 11 December 1859, Box 1, Rollett Collection, Lincolnshire Archives.

520. Letter to William Brooke from George Boole, 5 October 1864, Box 1, Rollett Collection, Lincolnshire Archives.

521. Letter to William Brooke from George Boole, 28 August 1864, Box 1, Rollett Collection, Lincolnshire Archives.

522. Richard Chenevix Trench (1807–86) was an Anglican archbishop and poet. He was the Archbishop of Dublin from 1864 to 1884.

523. Between 1860 and 1865 St Patrick's Cathedral was closed for massive restoration and repair. Benjamin Lee Guinness funded the renovations. Overall Guinness spent approximately £150,000 on the restoration of the building.

524. Letter to William Brooke from George Boole, 5 October 1864, Box 1, Rollett Collection, Lincolnshire Archives.

525. Letter to William Brooke from George Boole, 20 October 1864, Box 1, Rollett Collection, Lincolnshire Archives.

526. Letter to William Brooke from George Boole, 20 July 1864, Box 1, Rollett Collection, Lincolnshire Archives.

527. Letter to William Brooke from George Boole, 28 July 1864, Box 1, Rollett Collection, Lincolnshire Archives.

528. Letter to William Brooke from George Boole, 28 August 1864, Box 1, Rollett Collection, Lincolnshire Archives.

529. Letter to MaryAnn Boole from William Brooke, undated but probably December 1864, BP/1/243.

530. Ibid.

531. Ibid.

532. Charles Clarke, *Sixty Years in Upper Canada with Autobiographical Recollections* (Toronto: William Briggs, 1908), Chapter Two.

533. Thomas Cooper, *The Life of Thomas Cooper written by Himself* (London: Hodder & Stoughton, 1872), p. 59.

534. Ibid., p. 94.

535. Ibid., p. 117.

536. For further details of Boole's early teaching career, see MacHale, *The Life and Work of George Boole*, Chapter One.

537. MacHale, *The Life and Work of George Boole*, p. 38.

538. Cooper, *The Life of Thomas Cooper*, p.117.

539. Ibid., pp. 116–17.

540. See Chapter Two.

541. Stephen Roberts, 'Thomas Cooper in Leicester, 1840–1843', *Transactions of the Leicestershire Archaeological and Historical Society*, vol. 61, 1987, pp. 62–76.

542. Letter to MaryAnn Boole, 15 July 1850, BP/1/37.

543. Boole was referring to the first Persian-Arabic-English dictionary edited by John Richardson of Oxford. John Richardson, *A Dictionary, Persian, Arabic, and English* (Oxford: Clarendon Press, 1777).

544. Cooper, *The Life of Thomas Cooper*, p. 119.

545. Ibid., p. 118.

546. Letter to Mary Boole, 27 February 1851, BP/1/152.

547. Roberts, 'Thomas Cooper in Leicester, 1840–1843', *Transactions of the Leicestershire Archaeological and Historical Society*, vol. 61, 1987, pp. 62–76.

548. Cooper, *The Life of Thomas Cooper*, p. 139.

549. Queen Victoria to Sir Robert Peel, 17 August 1842, MS 40, 434, Peel Papers, CCLIV, fos. 318–19. Quoted in Roberts, 'Thomas Cooper in Leicester, 1840–1843', *Transactions of the Leicestershire Archaeological and Historical Society*, vol. 61, 1987, pp. 62–76.

550. The Seditious Meeting Acts were a series of acts passed between 1795 and 1819 which made it illegal to convene a meeting of fifty or more people without the permission of a magistrate or sheriff if it was concerned with matters of church or state.

551. Letter to E.R. Larken, January 1847, Box 1, Rollett Collection, Lincolnshire Archives.

552. Letter to E.R. Larken, 15 January 1847, Box 1, Rollett Collection, Lincolnshire Archives.

553. Letter to Mary Boole, 25 June 1849, BP/1/139.

554. Stephen Roberts, *The Chartist Prisoners: the radical lives of Thomas Cooper (1805–1892) and Arthur O'Neill (1819–1896)* (Bern: Peter Lang, 2008), p. 51.

555. Letter to MaryAnn Boole, 18 December 1850, BP/1/51.

556. Letter from Thomas Cooper to Thomas Chambers, 20 December 1864, Bishopsgate Institute, Howell 17/1/3.

557. Ibid.

558. *The Times*, 30 April 1892, http://gerald-massey.org.uk/cooper/ [accessed 11 April 2018].

559. For more details of Boole's work in the Lincoln Mechanics' Institute, see MacHale, *The Life and Work of George Boole*, Chapter Three.

560. Boole's friend the Rev. E.R. Larken was the first chairman of the society. See Sir Francis Hill, *Victorian Lincoln* (London: Cambridge University Press, 1971), p. 130.

561. See MacHale, *The Life and Work of George Boole*, Chapter Three.

562. See Chapter Two.

563. Sir Francis Burdett, 5th Baronet (1770–1844) was an English reformist politician. He became an MP and an opponent of William Pitt the Younger. He was an advocate of parliamentary reform and denounced corporal punishment. In 1817 he proposed universal suffrage and rights for Roman Catholics. He raised Feargus O'Connor, the Chartist leader. In the final years of his life he sided with the Conservatives.

564. Letter from Charles Clarke to MaryAnn Boole, 17 December 1865, BP/1/254.

565. Kenneth C. Dewar, *Charles Clarke, Pen and Ink Warrior* (Montreal: McGill-Queen's University Press, 2002), pp. 31–2.

566. Letter from Charles Clarke to MaryAnn Boole, 17 December 1865, BP/1/254.

567. Clarke, *Sixty Years in Upper Canada*, pp. 19–20.

568. Letter from Charles Clarke to MaryAnn Boole, 17 December 1865, BP/1/254.

569. Clarke, *Sixty Years in Upper Canada*, p. 17.

570. Letter from Charles Clarke to MaryAnn Boole, 17 December 1865, BP/1/254.

571. Clarke, *Sixty Years in Upper Canada*, p. 18.

572. Ibid, p18.

573. Letter from Charles Clarke to MaryAnn Boole, 17 December 1865, BP/1/254.

574. Ibid.

575. Clarke, *Sixty Years in Upper Canada*, p. 17.

576. Letter from Charles Clarke to MaryAnn Boole, 17 December 1865, BP/1/254.

577. Clarke, *Sixty Years in Upper Canada*, pp. 20–1.

578. Letter from Charles Clarke to MaryAnn Boole, 17 December 1865, BP/1/254.

579. Ibid.

580. Ibid.

581. Ibid.

582. Ibid.

583. Ibid.

584. Dewar, *Charles Clarke*, p.179.

585. Letter from Charles Clarke to MaryAnn Boole, 17 December 1865, BP/1/254.

586. Presumably a reference to Helen of Troy in Virgil's *Aeneid*.

587. Charles Boole was the youngest brother of George Boole.

588. Letter from Charles Clarke to MaryAnn Boole, 17 December 1865, BP/1/254.

589. See Chapter Two.

590. Prosy is an adjective meaning commonplace or dull.

591. Letter from Charles Clarke to MaryAnn Boole, 17 December 1865, BP/1/254.

592. Ibid.

593. Dewar, *Charles Clarke*, p.41.

594. MPP: Member of the Provincial Parliament of the Legislative Assembly of the Province of Ontario.

595. Kenneth C. Dewar, *Dictionary of Canadian Biography*, vol. XIII (1901–1910).

596. Dewar, *Charles Clarke*, p. 257.

597. Letter from MaryAnn Boole to Charles Clarke, 14 June 1867, Clarke Collection, Wellington County Museum and Archives.

598. Letter from George Boole to Charles Clarke, 29 August 1848, Charles Clarke Papers, Archives of Ontario.

599. R. Valpy, *The Elements of Greek Grammar* (New York: Collins & Co., 1829).

600. Letter to MaryAnn Boole from Thomas Bainbridge, 2 December 1852, BP/1/241.

601. Letter to MaryAnn Boole from William Brooke, 2 January 1864, BP/1/244.

602. Letter to MaryAnn Boole from Thomas Dyson, 18 March 1853, BP/1/267.

603. William Paley, *Natural Theology or Evidences of the Existence and Attributes of the Deity*, (London: R. Foulder, 1802).

604. Letter to MaryAnn Boole from Thomas Dyson, 18 March 1853, BP/1/267.

605. Ibid.

606. Letter to Maryann Boole from Thomas Dyson, undated BP/1/256.

607. For more detail on this translation by Boole, MacHale, *The Life and Work of George Boole*, pp. 8–16.

608. Letter to MaryAnn Boole from Thomas Dyson, 18 March 1853, BP/1/267.

609. Letter to MaryAnn Boole from Thomas Dyson, undated, BP/1/256.

610. Joseph Louis Lagrange, *Leçons sur le Calcul des Fonctions* (Paris: Chez Courcier, 1806).

611. Letter to MaryAnn Boole from Thomas Dyson, 20 November 1865, Box 5, Rollett Collection, Lincolnshire Archives.

612. Letter to MaryAnn Boole from George Boole, 18 December 1850, BP/1/22.

613. Letter to MaryAnn Boole from George Boole, 26 November 1853, BP/1/108.

614. Letter to MaryAnn Boole from Thomas Dyson, 20 November 1865, Box 5, Rollett Collection, Lincolnshire Archives.

615. A typescript of the notice is contained in Box 5, Rollett Collection, Lincolnshire Archives.

616. Letter to MaryAnn Boole from Thomas Dyson, 20 November 1865, Box 5, Rollett Collection, Lincolnshire Archives.

617. Ibid.

618. Letter to Mary Boole from Thomas Dyson, 29 August 1884, Box 5, Rollett Collection, Lincolnshire Archives.

619. Richard Whately, *Elements of Logic* (London: J. Mawman, 1826).

620. Letter to MaryAnn Boole from Thomas Dyson, 27 August 1884, Box 5, Rollett Collection, Lincolnshire Archives.

621. Letter from George Boole to Mary Davis, 13 August 1849, BP/1/218.

622. Letter from George Boole to Mary Davis, 2 October 1849, BP/1/217.

623. Letter from George Boole to Mary Davis, 21 August 1854, BP/1/219.

624. Letter from Mary Davis to MaryAnn Boole, 29 March 1865, BP/1/255.

625. Ibid.

626. Felicia Hemans (nee Browne) (1793–1835) was a popular English Romantic poet. She published nineteen volumes of poetry. Her best-known works included 'Casabianca' (The boy stood on the burning deck) and 'The Homes of England' (The stately homes of England).

627. Thomas Campbell (1777–1844) was a Scottish poet. His poem *The Wounded Hussar* was a popular poem which became the lyrics of a popular folksong. This poem was published in the first edition of Campbell's *Pleasures of Hope* (1799).

628. Letter from William Atkin to MaryAnn Boole, 13 January 1865, BP/1/268.

629. Letter from William Atkin to MaryAnn Boole, 28 January 1866, BP/1/240.

630. Letter from William Atkin to MaryAnn Boole, 13 January 1865, BP/1/268

631. Ibid.

632. Francesco Francia, *Mourning over the Dead Christ* (circa 1514).

633. Letter from William Atkin to MaryAnn Boole, 13 January 1865, BP/1/268.

634. Ibid.

635. Ibid.

636. See MacHale, *The Life and Work of George Boole*, pp. 87–92.

637. Letter from George Boole to Charles Kirk, 10 August 1846, BP/1/222/2.

638. Letter from George Boole to Charles Kirk, 30 April 1847, BP/1/222/3. J.B. Cherriman (1823–1908) was born in Doncaster. He entered St John's College Cambridge in 1841 and graduated as sixth wrangler in the mathematical tripos in 1845 and was awarded an MA in 1848. In 1850 he was appointed assistant professor of mathematics at the University of Toronto in Canada, and in 1853 was appointed to the chair of mathematics and natural philosophy there. His publications reflect his training in mathematics and his interest in their practical application to the social sciences. See http://www.biographi.ca/en/bio/cherriman_john_bradford_13E.html [accessed 11 April 2018]. Antoine Augustin Cournot (1801–77) was a French philosopher and mathematician who contributed to the development of economics theory.

639. Letter from George Boole to Charles Kirk, 30 April 1847, BP/1/222/3.

640. Letter from George Boole to Charles Kirk, 9 August 1847, BP/1/222/4.

641. Letter from George Boole to Charles Kirk, 15 November 1847, BP/1/222/5.

642. Letter from George Boole to Charles Kirk, 3 January 1848, BP/1/222/6.

643. Letter from George Boole to Charles Kirk, 21 March 1848, BP/1/222/7.

644. Ibid.

645. Letter from George Boole to Charles Kirk, 24 April 1848, BP/1/222/8.

646. Letter from George Boole to Charles Kirk, 24 January 1849, BP/1/222/10.

647. For general information on T.W. Moffett, see Chapter Fourteen by Tadhg Foley and Fiona Batemen in T. Foley (ed.), *From Queen's College to National University: essays on the academic history of QCG/UCG/NUIG* (Dublin: Four Courts Press, 1999), pp. 390–5.

648. Letter from T.W. Moffett to George Boole, 6 September 1864, Box 12, Rollett Collection, Lincolnshire Archives.

649. Letter from T.W. Moffett to George Boole, undated, Box 12, Rollett Collection, Lincolnshire Archives.

650. George Stoney (1826–1911) was born in Birr, Co. Offaly. He studied physics and mathematics in Trinity College Dublin and was awarded a BA in 1848 and MA in 1852. From 1848 to 1852 he worked as an astronomy assistant to William Parson, the 3rd Earl of Rosse at Birr Castle. Between 1852 and 1857 he was Professor of Physics at Queen's College Galway. In 1857 he became the secretary of the Queen's University of Ireland, an administrative post which he held until 1882. In 1891 he proposed the term 'electron' to describe the fundamental unit of electrical charge. His contributions influenced J.J. Thomson who discovered the electron in 1887.

651. John Mulcahy, *Principles of Modern Geometry with Numerous Applications to Plane and Spherical Figures* (Dublin: Hodges Smith & Co., 1862).

652. Letter from T.W. Moffett to John Ryall, 16 December 1864, Box 12, Rollett Collection, Lincolnshire Archives.

653. Ibid. Lord Palmerston was the Liberal Prime Minster between 1859 and 1865. Edward Cardwell held the position of Chief Secretary of Ireland between 1859 and 1861 and was succeeded by Sir Robert Peel who held the post until 1865.

654. See MacHale, *The Life and Work of George Boole*, p. 286.

655. Letter from T.W. Moffett to Mary Boole, December 1865, Box 1, Rollett Collection, Lincolnshire Archives.

656. Ibid.

657. Mary Everest Boole (1878), 'Home side of a Scientific Mind', *University Magazine*, vol 1, which is reprinted in full in *Mary Everest Boole: collected works*, edited by E.M. Cobham, CESSek; C.W. Daniel, 1931).

658. See letters from R.A. Jamieson to George Boole, Box 1, Rollett Collection, Lincolnshire Archives.

659. Letter from R.A. Jamieson to Mary Boole, 13 April 1866, Box 12, Rollett Collection, Lincolnshire Archives.

660. *The Freeman's Journal*, 8 June 1860.

661. John Francis Popham, 'My Recollections of Dr Boole in his Capacity of Mathematical Lecturer of Queen's College Cork', undated, Box 12, Rollett Collection, Lincolnshire Archives.

662. Letter from E.J. Warmington to Mary Boole, 2 December 1865, Box 12, Rollett Collection, Lincolnshire Archives.

663. Letter from H.S. Ridings to Mary Boole, 10 November 1865, Box 12, Rollett Collection, Lincolnshire Archives.

664. Letter from H.S. Ridings to Mary Boole, 27 November 1865, Box 12, Rollett Collection, Lincolnshire Archives.

665. George Peacock, *A Treatise on Algebra* (London and Cambridge: J. & J.J. Deighton, 1830).

666. Duncan Gregory, 'On the Real Nature of Symbolical Algebra', *Transactions of the Royal Society of Edinburgh*, vol. XIV, 1838, pp. 268–81.

667. D.F. Gregory, *Examples of the Processes of the Differential and Integral Calculus* (Cambridge: J. & J.J. Deighton and John W. Parker, 1841).

668. George Boole, 'On a General Method in Analysis', *Philosophical Transactions of the Royal Society*, vol. 134, 1841, pp. 225–282.

669. George Boole, *The Mathematical Analysis of Logic*. (Cambridge: Macmillan, Barclay and Macmillan, 1847).

670. Letter to George Boole from D.F. Gregory, 4 November 1839, Box 1, Rollett Collection, Lincolnshire Archives.

671. Ibid.

672. Letter to George Boole from D.F. Gregory, 15 December 1839, Box 1, Rollett Collection, Lincolnshire Archives.

673. Letter to George Boole from D.F. Gregory, 5 February 1840, Box 1, Rollett Collection, Lincolnshire Archives.

674. Letter to George Boole from D.F. Gregory, 16 February 1840, Box 1, Rollett Collection, Lincolnshire Archives.

675. Ibid.

676. Gregory's letter to Boole of 29 March 1840 is quoted in full in MacHale, *The Life and Work of George Boole*, pp. 60–1.

677. Letter to George Boole from D.F. Gregory, May 1840, Box 1, Rollett Collection, Lincolnshire Archives.

678. Ibid.

679. Letter to George Boole from D.F. Gregory, 24 May 1840, Box 1, Rollett Collection, Lincolnshire Archives.

680. Letter to George Boole from D.F. Gregory, 11 February 1841, Box 1, Rollett Collection, Lincolnshire Archives.

681. George Boole, 'Exposition of a General Theory of Linear Transformations. Part I', *Cambridge Mathematical Journal*, vol. 3, 1842, pp. 1–20 and George Boole, 'Exposition of a General Theory of Linear Transformations. Part II', *Cambridge Mathematical Journal*, vol. 3, 1842, pp. 106–19.

682. Letter to George Boole from D.F. Gregory, 21 October 1841, Box 1, Rollett Collection, Lincolnshire Archives.

683. Letter to George Boole from D.F. Gregory, 28 December 1841, Box 1, Rollett Collection, Lincolnshire Archives.

684. Letter to George Boole from D.F. Gregory, 7 March 1843, Box 1, Rollett Collection, Lincolnshire Archives. The reference is to Robert Murphy, *Elementary Principles of the Theories of Electricity, Heat and Molecular Actions* (Cambridge: J. & J.J. Deighton, 1833).

685. Letter to George Boole from D.F. Gregory, 19 June 1843, Box 1, Rollett Collection, Lincolnshire Archives.

686. Ibid.

687. Ibid.

688. *The Works of Francis Bacon*, edited and collected by James Spedding, Robert Leslie Ellis and Douglas Denon Heath (London: Longman & Co., 1857–74).

689. Robert Leslie Ellis, 'On the Foundations of the Theory of Probabilities' (read to the Cambridge Philosophical Society on 14 February 1842); published in *Proceedings of the Cambridge Philosophical Society*, vol. IV, 1844.

690. Letter to George Boole from R.L. Ellis, January 1844, Box 1, Rollett Collection, Lincolnshire Archives.

691. George Boole, 'On the Inverse Calculus of Definite Integrals', *Cambridge Mathematical Journal*, vol. 4, 1845, pp. 82–7.

692. Letter to George Boole from R.L. Ellis, 2 February 1844, Box 1, Rollett Collection, Lincolnshire Archives.

693. George Boole, 'On a General Method in Analysis'.

694. Letter to George Boole from R.L. Ellis, 13 June 1844, Box 1, Rollett Collection, Lincolnshire Archives.

695. George Boole, 'Exposition of a General Theory of Linear Transformations. Part I'. Cambridge Mathematical Journal, vol. 3, 1842, pp. 1–20

696. Letter to George Boole from R.L. Ellis, 13 June 1844, Box 1, Rollett Collection, Lincolnshire Archives.

697. As quoted by Harvey Goodwin in 'A Biographical Memoir', in William Walton (ed.), *The Mathematical and Other Writings of Robert Leslie Ellis* (Cambridge: Deighton Bell & Co., 1863).

698. MacHale, *The Life and Work of George Boole*, pp. 89–90.

699. Ibid.

700. Quoted in V. Peckhaus, 'Was George Boole Really the "Father" of Modern Logic?' in James Gasser (ed.), *A Boole Anthology* (Berlin: Springer Science & Business Media, 2000), p. 277.

701. For extracts from Thomas Hirst's Diary, see http://www-groups.dcs.st-and.ac.uk/ history/HistTopics/Hirst_comments.html# [accessed 11 April 2018].

702. Barnaba Tortolini (1808–74) was an Italian priest and mathematician. He is mainly remembered for his role in founding and publishing the first Italian international scientific journal, *Annali di Scienze Matematiche e Fisiche*, from 1850 to 1857. Placido Tardy (1816–1914) was an Italian mathematician and physicist. With Betti and Brioschi he designed the publication of an Italian mathematical journal that would later become known as *The Annals of Pure and Applied Mathematics*.

703. George Boole, 'On a General Method in Analysis', *Philosophical Transactions of the Royal Society*, vol. 134, 1841, pp. 225–282

704. Letter to T.A. Hirst from George Boole, 11 October 1859, Box 14, Rollett Collection, Lincolnshire Archives.

705. Letter to George Boole from T.A. Hirst, 5 December 1862, Box 1, Rollett Collection, Lincolnshire Archives.

706. Letter to T.A. Hirst from George Boole, 1 July 1863, Box 14, Rollett Collection, Lincolnshire Archives.

707. Letter to T.A. Hirst from George Boole, 9 July 1863, Box 14, Rollett Collection, Lincolnshire Archives.

708. Letter from George Salmon to T.A. Hirst, 2 January 1865, Box 1, Rollett Collection, Lincolnshire Archives.

709. Smith's Prizeman was a mathematical award in the University of Cambridge.

710. Letter to George Boole from Isaac Todhunter, 8 July 1861, Box 1, Rollett Collection, Lincolnshire Archives.

711. Ibid.

712. George Boole, *A Treatise on Differential Equations* (Cambridge: Macmillan, 1859).

713. Letter to Mary Everest Boole from Isaac Todhunter, 29 December 1864, Box 12, Rollett Collection, Lincolnshire Archives.

714. Letter to George Boole from Isaac Todhunter, 26 June 1862, Box 1, Rollett Collection, Lincolnshire Archives.

715. Letter to George Boole from Isaac Todhunter, 2 October 1862, Box 1, Rollett Collection, Lincolnshire Archives.

716. Letter to George Boole from Isaac Todhunter, 18 October 1862, Box 1, Rollett Collection, Lincolnshire Archives.

717. John Grote (1813–66) was an English moral philosopher and Anglican clergyman. He was Vicar of Trumpington from 1847 to 1866 and was a friend and neighbour of Robert Leslie Ellis.

718. Letter to George Boole from Isaac Todhunter, 9 January 1863, Box 1, Rollett Collection, Lincolnshire Archives.

719. Letter to George Boole from Isaac Todhunter, 23 May 1863, Box 1, Rollett Collection, Lincolnshire Archives.

720. Letter to George Boole from Isaac Todhunter, 10 June 1863, Box 1, Rollett Collection, Lincolnshire Archives.

721. Letter to George Boole from Isaac Todhunter, 7 December 1863, Box 1, Rollett Collection, Lincolnshire Archives.

722. Isaac Todhunter, *A History of the Mathematical Theory of Probability from the Time of Pascal to that of Laplace* (Cambridge: Macmillan, 1865).

723. Letter to George Boole from Isaac Todhunter, 29 December 1863, Box 1, Rollett Collection, Lincolnshire Archives.

724. Letter to George Boole from Isaac Todhunter, 9 January 1864, Box 1, Rollett Collection, Lincolnshire Archives.

725. Letter to George Boole from Isaac Todhunter, 25 June 1864, Box 1, Rollett Collection, Lincolnshire Archives. Joseph Louis François Bertrand (1822–1900)

was a French mathematician who worked in the fields of number theory, differential geometry, probability theory, economics and thermodynamics.

726. Moses Mendelssohn (1729–86) was a German Jewish philosopher. He was an ancestor of the great composer Mendelssohn, whose music Boole greatly admired.

727. Letter to George Boole from Isaac Todhunter, 2 August 1864, Box 1, Rollett Collection, Lincolnshire Archives.

728. Thomas Bayes (1701–64) was an English statistician, philosopher and Presbyterian minister. Bayes' Theorem bears his name.

729. Letter to George Boole from Isaac Todhunter, 2 August 1864, Box 1, Rollett Collection, Lincolnshire Archives.

730. Ibid.

731. Letter to Mary Everest Boole from Isaac Todhunter, 15 December 1864, Box 12, Rollett Collection, Lincolnshire Archives.

732. Letter to Mary Everest Boole from Isaac Todhunter, 10 January 1865, Box 12, Rollett Collection, Lincolnshire Archives.

733. Ibid.

734. Ibid.

735. Letter to Mary Everest Boole from Isaac Todhunter, 3 February 1865, BP/1/334.

736. Francis W. Newman, *Theism, Doctrinal and Practical; or, didactic religious utterances* (London: Chapman, 1858).

737. Letter to George Boole from Francis W. Newman, 11 January 1860, Box 1, Rollett Collection, Lincolnshire Archives.

738. George Boole, 'On Simultaneous Differential Equations of the first order in which the number of variables exceeds by more than one the number of the equations', *Philosophical Transactions of the Royal Society*, vol. 152, 1862, pp. 437–54.

739. Letter to George Boole from Francis W. Newman, 17 January 1863, Box 1, Rollett Collection, Lincolnshire Archives.

740. James Wood, *The Elements of Algebra* (Cambridge: Cambridge University Press, first published 1795).

741. Letter to George Boole from Francis W. Newman, undated, Box 1, Rollett Collection, Lincolnshire Archives.

742. Francis W. Newman, *The Difficulties of Elementary Geometry, especially those which concern the straight line, the plane, and the theory of parallels* (London: W. Ball & Co., 1841).

743. Letter to George Boole from Francis W. Newman, 9 November 1864, Box 1, Rollett Collection, Lincolnshire Archives.

744. Mary Everest Boole, 'Home Side of a scientific mind', *Mary Everest Boole Collected Works*, edited by E.M. Cobham (Essex; C. W. Daniel, 1931), p. 40.

745. Letter to Mary Everest Boole from Francis W. Newman, 30 November 1864, BP/1/333.

746. Francis Newman was a supporter of temperance legislation. In 1865 he published *The Permissive Bill*, which related to liquor laws.

747. Letter to George Boole from Francis W. Newman, 21 March 1865, Box 1, Rollett Collection, Lincolnshire Archives.

748. Letter to Mary Everest Boole from Francis W. Newman, 27 April 1865, Box 1, Rollett Collection, Lincolnshire Archives.

749. George Boole, *An Address on the Genius and Discoveries of Sir Isaac Newton* (1835), Gazette Office, Lincoln.

750. https://en.wikipedia.org/wiki/George_Boole [accessed 11 April 2018].

751. *The Freeman's Journal*, 12 December 1864.

752. Franz Mesmer (1734–1815) was a Viennese physician. His theories on animal magnetism are considered formative in the development of modern hypnosis.

753. Samuel Hahnemann (1755–1843) was a German physician and founder of homeopathy.

754. James Hinton (1822–75) was an ear surgeon who had been introduced to homeopathy by Mary Everest's father, Thomas Roupell Everest. Mary became his secretary after George's death. For further details on James Hinton, see MacHale, *The Life and Work of George Boole*, pp. 288–90 and Gerry Kennedy, *The Booles & The Hintons* (Cork: Atrium, 2016), pp. 89–103.

755. Ethel was referring to Rabbi David Woolf Marks (1811–1909), the first leader of the West London synagogue.

756. Letter to Geoffrey Taylor from Ethel Voynich, 30 April 1954, Box 12, Rollett Collection, Lincolnshire Archives.

757. Letter to MaryAnn Boole, 6 April 1851, BP/1/64.

758. James Currie, *Medical Reports, on the Effects of Water, Cold and Warm, as a remedy in Fever and Other Diseases, Whether applied to the Surface of the Body, or used Internally* (London: T. Cadell & W. Davies, 1805).

759. Robin Price 'Hydropathy in England 1840–70', *Journal of Medical History*, vol. 25, no. 4, October 1981.

760. Ibid.

761. Ita Marguet, 'Doctor Richard Barter: hydropathy in Ireland', *Diva International*, February 2012. See http://divainternational.ch/spip.php?article671 [accessed 11 April 2018].

762. David Urquhart, *The Pillars of Hercules, Or, A Narrative of Travels in Spain and Morocco in 1848* (London: R. Bentley, 1850).

763. Letter to MaryAnn Boole, 25 January 1852, BP/1/72.

764. Letter to MaryAnn Boole, Undated, BP/1/76.

765. Letter to MaryAnn Boole, 19 April 1853, BP/1/98.

766. Letter to MaryAnn Boole, 20 November 1853, BP/1/107.

767. Letter to MaryAnn Boole, 11 December 1853, BP/1/109.

768. Letter to MaryAnn Boole, 29 January 1854, BP/1/112.

769. Letter to William Brooke from George Boole, 25 March 1861, Box 1, Rollett Collection, Lincolnshire Archives.

770. Letter to William Brooke from George Boole, 20 July 1864, Box 1, Rollett Collection, Lincolnshire Archives.

771. Letter to William Brooke from George Boole, 28 July 1864, Box 1, Rollett Collection, Lincolnshire Archives.

772. Mary Everest Boole, 'Home Side of a scientific mind', *Mary Everest Boole Collected Works*, edited by E.M. Cobham, (Essex; C. W. Daniel, 1931), p. 23.

773. *Henry & Coughlan's General Directory of Cork for 1867* (Cork: Henry & Coughlan, London: Longmans, Green, Reader & Dyer, 1867).

774. *Francis Guy's County and City of Cork Directory for the Years 1875–1876* (Cork: Francis Guy, 1875), p. 541.

775. Mary Everest Boole, 'Home Side of a scientific mind', *Mary Everest Boole Collected Works*, edited by E.M. Cobham, (Essex; C. W. Daniel, 1931), p. 5.

776. Joseph Blanco White (1775–1841) was a Spanish theologian and poet. His most famous work was the sonnet 'Night and Death' (1828), which Annie Gibson is referring to.

777. Letter to MaryAnn Boole from Annie Gibson, 22 January 1865, BP/1/257.

778. William Allingham, 'The Fairies', in *Poems* (London: Chapman & Hall, 1850).

779. This correspondence was mentioned by Professor Ryan of QCC in a letter to *The Nation* newspaper on 12 June 1889.

780. George Harding, *My Stolen City: a collection of poems* (Limerick: Revival Press, 2011).

781. George Harding, *Last Bus to Pewterhole Cross: a collection of poems* (Limerick: Revival Press, 2015).

782. The Library of Congress has kindly made an excellent digitised version of its copy of *Other Notes* freely available via the Internet Archive at: https://archive.org/stream/ othernotes00hint?ref=ol#page/n0/mode/2up [accessed 11 April 2018].

783. *Washington Times*, 28 May 1908.

784. For further details see Chapter Thirteen 'Boole and Hamilton: some unanswered questions' in MacHale, *The Life and Work of George Boole*, pp 206–219.

785. George Boole, 'Notes on Quaternions', *Philosophical Magazine*, vol. 30, No. 3, 1848, pp. 278–80.

786. William Rowan Hamilton, *Lectures on Quaternions* (Dublin: Hodges & Smith, 1853).

787. *The Mathematical Analysis of Logic, being an Essay towards a Calculus of Deductive Reasoning* (Cambridge: Macmillan, Barclay & Macmillan, 1847) and 'The Calculus of Logic', *Cambridge and Dublin Mathematical Journal*, 1848, vol. 3, pp.183–98.

788. George Boole, 'Notes on Quaternions', *Philosophical Magazine*, vol. 30, No. 3, 1848, pp. 278–80.

789. George Boole to William Thomson, 6 August 1845. Cambridge University Library, Add Ms 7342.B145.

790. *Stamford Mercury*, 20 May 1836.

791. Box 5, Rollett Collection, Lincolnshire Archives.

792. Letter to Herbert McLeod from George Boole, 21 July 1864, Box 1, Rollett Collection, Lincolnshire Archives.

793. Address by Professor J. Clerk Maxwell, President of the Section, Mathematics and Physics, *Report of the Fortieth Meeting of the British Association for the Advancement of Science*, Liverpool, September 1870.

794. https://www.bonhams.com/press_release/20025/ [accessed 11 April 2018].

795. Michael Parsons, 'A Matter of Faith for Charles Darwin', *The Irish Times*, 19 September 2015.

796. Mary Everest Boole, edited by E.M. Cobham, *Mary Everest Boole Collected Works* (London: The C.W. Daniel Company, 1931).

797. Darwin Correspondence Database, http://darwinproject.ac.uk/entry-5303 [accessed 11 April 2018].

798. Darwin Correspondence Database, http://darwinproject.ac.uk/entry-5307 [accessed 11 April 2018].

799. Darwin Correspondence Database, http://darwinproject.ac.uk/entry-5310 [accessed 11 April 2018].

800. Mary Boole, *The Message of Psychic Science to Mothers and Nurses* (London: Trübner & Co., 1883), p. 43.

801. Ibid., p. 25.

802. Ibid., p. 264.

803. Typed copy of 'Rules and Instructions addressed to his pupils and more particularly to those who are under his immediate care as members of his household' by George Boole, also copybook entitled 'School Rules and Arrangements', BP/1/275.

804. Box 1, Rollett Collection, Lincolnshire Archives.

805. Letter to MaryAnn Boole, 26 October 1849, BP/1/135.

806. Letter to MaryAnn Boole, 12 December 1849, BP/1/16.

807. Letter to MaryAnn Boole, 16 March 1850, BP/1/26.

808. Ibid.

809. Letter to MaryAnn Boole, May 30 1852, BP/1/80.

810. http://www.buildingsofireland.ie/ [accessed 11 April 2018], website of the National Inventory of Architectural Heritage.

811. Benjamin Bousfield (1784–1846) was the High Sherriff of Cork in 1771, the representative of the sovereign in County Cork, a role with ceremonial and administrative duties. In 1799, Bousfield published an open letter to the citizens of Cork which supported the continued existence of the Irish parliament and opposed the proposed Act of Union; B. Bousfield, *A Letter from Ben. B. Bousfield, Esq. to the Citizens of Cork* (Cork: James Haly, 1799).

812. Letter to MaryAnn Boole, 19 October 1853, BP/1/104.

813. Letter to Mary Boole, 4 March 1854, BP/1/116.

814. Letter to Mary Boole, April 1854, BP/1/120. See details of the dispute in Chapter Three.

815. Letter to John Larkin, 27 February 1861, BP/1/223/17.

816. Letter to John Larkin, 13 April 1861, BP/1/223/18.

817. Letter to John Bury, undated, BP/1/216.

818. Letter to William Brooke, August 1858, Box 1, Rollett Collection, Lincolnshire Archives.

819. Letter to William Brooke, 15 September 1861, Box 1, Rollett Collection, Lincolnshire Archives.

820. Tommy Barker, 'Have a look inside the home of UCC maths professor George Boole', *Irish Examiner*, 13 June 2015.

821. https://stairnaheireann.net/2016/11/29/1895-death-of-denny-lane-young-irelander-author-and-poet-2/ [accessed 11 April 2018].

822. John Henry Sugrue was chairman of the Cork, Blackrock and Passage Railway Company in the late nineteenth century. It is likely that this is the Mr Sugrue referred to.

823. E.M. Cobham (Ed.) *Mary Everest Boole Collected Works* (Essex: C.W. Daniel, 1931).

824. MacHale, *The Life and Work of George Boole*, pp. 286–314.

825. Gerry Kennedy, *The Booles & The Hintons*. (Cork: Atrium, 2016).

826. Ibid., p. 236.

827. MacHale, *The Life and Work of George Boole*, pp. 305–6 and Gerry Kennedy, *The Booles & The Hintons*, pp. 374–97.

828. See obituary of Julian Taylor in the *British Medical Journal*, vol. 1, no. 5234, 29 April 1961, pp. 1255–6.

829. For further details of the window, reference MacHale, *The Life and Work of George Boole*, pp. 278–9 and M.J. O'Kelly, 'The Boole Memorial Window in the Aula Maxima, University College, Cork', in Patrick D. Barry (ed.), *George Boole: a miscellany* (Cork: Cork University Press, 1969).

830. Harry Lande, 'Boole Window Designer Identified', *The College Courier*, staff magazine of UCC, Spring 2002, pp. 20–1.

831. Letter from John Ryall to Messrs Hardman, 1 February, 1866, The Hardman Archive, by kind permission of The Library of Birmingham, MS 175a/4/3/22/361.

832. Letter from F.C. Penrose to John Ryall, 2 November, 1865, The Hardman Archive, by kind permission of the Library of Birmingham, MS 175.

833. Olivia Kelleher, 'UN Marks Impact of George Boole', *Irish Examiner*, 6 June 2015.

834. https://www.youtube.com/watch?v=nccTW_29IFo [accessed 11 April 2018].

835. John Bowers, 'James Moriarty: a forgotten mathematician', *New Scientist Magazine*, December 1989, pp. 17–19.

836. Isabel Healy, 'Elementary My Dear Boole', *Cork Examiner*, 9 January 1990.

837. Arthur Conan Doyle, *Memories and Adventures* (Cambridge: Cambridge University Press, 1924).

838. The general reference for the Sherlock Holmes stories referenced in this chapter is Arthur Conan Doyle, *Original Illustrated Strand Sherlock Holmes: the complete facsimile edition* (Hertfordshire: Wordsworth Editions, 1989).

839. 'A Study in Scarlet', in ibid.

840. 'The Sign of the Four', in ibid.

841. 'The Sign of the Four', in ibid.

842. 'The Sign of the Four', in ibid.

843. 'The Sign of the Four', in ibid.

844. 'A Scandal in Bohemia', in ibid.

845. 'The Adventure of the Speckled Band', in ibid.

846. 'The Adventure of the Copper Beeches', in ibid.

847. 'The Adventure of the Copper Beeches', in ibid.

848. 'The Adventure of the Speckled Band', in ibid.

849. Anthony Berkeley, *Jumping Jenny* (London: Penguin Books, 1923).

850. Arthur Conan Doyle, 'The Adventure of the Final Problem', in *Original Illustrated Strand Sherlock Holmes*.

851. Ibid.

852. Hugh Leonard, *The Mask of Moriarty* (Dublin: Canavaun Publications, 1987).

853. George Boole, 'On a General Method in Analysis', *Philosophical Transactions of the Royal Society*, vol. 134, 1844, pp. 225–282.

854. George Boole, *Are the Planets Inhabited?* BP/1/272.

855. MacHale, *The Life and Work of George Boole*, p. 317.

856. Notes of Mother Rosemary Boole, Box 1, Rollett Collection, Lincolnshire Archives.

857. H.G. Wells, *The New Machiavelli*, 2nd edition (London: Penguin Classics, 2005). Originally published by Duffield & Co., New York, 1917.

858. H.G. Wells, *The War in the Air* (London: George Bell & Sons, 1907).

859. H.G. Wells, *World Brain* (London: Methuen, 1937).

860. *A Life in Letters – Arthur Conan Doyle,* edited by Jon Lellenberg, Daniel Stashower and Charles Foley (London: The Penguin Press, 2007).

861. Ibid.

862. Andrew Lycett, *The Man who Created Sherlock Holmes: the life and times of Sir Arthur Conan Doyle* (London: Free Press, 2007).

863. Arthur Conan Doyle, *Memories and Adventures.* (Cambridge: Cambridge University Press, 1924)

864. Lycett, *The Man who created Sherlock Holmes.*

865. Jane Stanford, *Moriarty Unmasked* (Dublin: Carrowmore Publishing, 2017).

866. Licentiate of the Royal College of Surgeons of Edinburgh.

867. Letter from William Cummins to George Boole, undated, BP/1/237.

868. Mary Everest Boole, *Symbolical Methods of Study* (Essex: C.W. Daniels & Co., 1884).

869. Geraldine Cummins, *The Scripts of Cleophas* (London: Rider & Co., 1928).

870. Geraldine Cummins, *Paul in Athens* (London: Rider & Co., 1930).

871. Geraldine Cummins, *The Great Days of Ephesus* (London: Rider & Co., 1933).

872. Letter from Edmund Larken to George Boole, 4 October 1860, Notebook 1, Rollett Notebooks, Rollett Collection, Lincolnshire Archives. Broach, now known as Bharuch, is a city in western India.

873. Anthony Horowitz, *Moriarty* (London: Orion Books, 2014).874. Arthur Conan Doyle, 'The Valley of Fear', in *Original Illustrated Strand Sherlock Holmes*.

875. Ibid.

876. Arthur Conan Doyle, 'The Hound of the Baskervilles', in ibid.

877. Arthur Conan Doyle, 'A Scandal in Bohemia', in ibid.

878. Bradley E. Schaefer, 'Sherlock Holmes and Some Astronomical Connections', *Journal of the British Astronomical Association*, vol. 103, no. 1, 1993, pp. 30–4.

879. Simon Newcomb, *Reminiscences of An Astronomer* (Boston: Houghton, Mifflin & Co.,1903).

880. Vincent Starrett, 'Books Alive', *Chicago Sunday Tribune*, 26 December 1943. Vincent Starrett was an American writer who wrote extensively on Sherlock Holmes, including a biography of Holmes: *The Private Life of Sherlock Holmes* (New York: The Macmillan Company, 1933). Dr Gray C. Briggs was a St Louis physician who was a member of 'The Baker Street Irregulars', a group of Sherlock Holmes enthusiasts. Briggs met Conan Doyle on a trip to London in 1921.

881. Arthur Conan Doyle, 'The Adventure of the Final Problem', in *Original Illustrated Strand Sherlock Holmes*

882. Arthur Conan Doyle, 'The Valley of Fear', in ibid.

883. Arthur Conan Doyle, 'The Red Headed League', in ibid.

884. Ben Macintyre, *The Napoleon of Crime: the life and times of Adam Worth, the real Moriarty* (London: Harper Press, 1997).

885. T.S. Eliot, 'Macavity: the mystery cat', *Old Possum's Book of Practical Cats* (London: Faber & Faber, 1939).

886. Arthur Conan Doyle, 'The Valley of Fear', in *Original Illustrated Strand Sherlock Holmes*.

887. A.G. Macdonnell, *Baker Street Studies*, 1934.

888. Arthur Conan Doyle, 'The Sign of the Four', in *Original Illustrated Strand Sherlock Holmes*.

889. 'The Adventure of the Final Problem', in ibid.

890. R.L. Stevenson, *The Strange Case of Dr Jekyll and Mr. Hyde* (London: Longmans, Green & Co., 1886).

891. R.L. Stevenson in collaboration with Fanny Van de Grift Stevenson, *The Dynamiter* (London: Longmans, Green & Co., 1903).

892. Mary Everest Boole, 'Home Side of a Scientific Mind', *University Magazine*, vol. 1, 1878.

893. Arthur Conan Doyle, 'The Crooked Man', in *Original Illustrated Strand Sherlock Holmes*.

INDEX

In this index, George Boole is referred to by the abbreviation GB. Married women are listed under their married names with the maiden name in parentheses. Illustrations are indicated by page numbers in **bold**.